# Assessment and Evaluation in Bilingual Education

Margarita Machado-Casas and
Yolanda Medina
*General Editors*

Vol. 28

The Critical Studies of Latinxs in the Americas series
is part of the Peter Lang Trade Academic and Textbook list.
Every volume is peer reviewed and meets
the highest quality standards for content and production.

PETER LANG
New York • Bern • Berlin
Brussels • Vienna • Oxford • Warsaw

# Assessment and Evaluation in Bilingual Education

Margarita Machado-Casas,
Saúl Isaac Maldonado
and Belinda Bustos Flores, Editors

PETER LANG
New York • Bern • Berlin
Brussels • Vienna • Oxford • Warsaw

Library of Congress Cataloging-in-Publication Data

Names: Machado-Casas, Margarita, editor. | Maldonado, Saúl Isaac, editor. | Flores, Belinda Bustos, editor.
Title: Assessment and evaluation in bilingual education / Margarita Machado-Casas, Saúl Isaac Maldonado and Belinda Bustos Flores, editors.
Description: New York: Peter Lang, 2022.
Series: Critical studies of Latinxs in the Americas; vol. 28
ISSN 2372-6822 (print) | ISSN 2372-6830 (online)
Includes bibliographical references and index.
Identifiers: LCCN 2021038299 (print) | LCCN 2021038300 (ebook)
ISBN 978-1-4331-8701-8 (hardback) | ISBN 978-1-4331-8702-5 (paperback)
ISBN 978-1-4331-8698-1 (ebook pdf) | ISBN 978-1-4331-8699-8 (epub)
Subjects: LCSH: Education, Bilingual—United States—Evaluation. | Educational tests and measurements—United States. | Education and state—United States. | Education, Bilingual—Study and teaching—United States.
Classification: LCC LC3731 .A828 2022 (print) | LCC LC3731 (ebook) |
DDC 370.117/50973—dc23
LC record available at https://lccn.loc.gov/2021038299
LC ebook record available at https://lccn.loc.gov/2021038300
DOI 10.3726/b18236

Bibliographic information published by **Die Deutsche Nationalbibliothek**.
**Die Deutsche Nationalbibliothek** lists this publication in the "Deutsche Nationalbibliografie"; detailed bibliographic data are available on the Internet at http://dnb.d-nb.de/.

© 2022 Peter Lang Publishing, Inc., New York
80 Broad Street, 5th floor, New York, NY 10004
www.peterlang.com

All rights reserved.
Reprint or reproduction, even partially, in all forms such as microfilm, xerography, microfiche, microcard, and offset strictly prohibited.

# Table of Contents

| | |
|---|---|
| List of Figures | ix |
| List of Tables | xi |
| Foreword<br>José Medina | xv |
| Preface | xix |

Introduction
*Bilingual Education/Dual Language Assessment and Evaluation Principles: A Decolonial Approach for Practitioners and Policymakers*    1
Margarita Machado-Casas, Belinda Bustos Flores and Saúl I. Maldonado

## Evaluation Processes for Bilingual Education

*1. Prioritizing Sociocultural Competence as Indicator of Quality in Dual-language Programs: Cultural, Historical, Identity, Socio-emotional, Pedagogy, Action and Sustainability (CHISPAS)*    23
Veronica Johnson, Janet Gabriela Cariño Ramsay and Saúl I. Maldonado

*2. Advancing the Achievement of Dual Language Learners through Program Evaluation: A Framework for Assessing the Effectiveness and Impact of Dual Language Programs*    45
Alexandra S. Guilamo

## Equitable and Fair Assessment Systems for Bilingual Education/Dual Language Learners

3. *The Assessment of Mathematical Knowledge in Elementary Level Dual Language Programs*    69
KIP TÉLLEZ

4. *Assessment of Bilingual Students: Best Practices and Recommendations for Members of the Multidisciplinary IEP Committee*    87
FELICIA CASTRO-VILLARREAL, VICTOR VILLARREAL AND ILEANA UMAÑA

5. *Assessing Bicultural-Bilinguals' Language Development: Difference or Disorder?*    105
JANELLE BETH FLORES, KARLA C. GARZA, T. BREANNE ROCHESTER, YVONNE VERA AND BELINDA BUSTOS FLORES

## Developing Bilingual/Dual Language Educators' Assessment Practices

6. *Understanding Assessment and Evaluation When Preparing Bilingual Teacher Candidates*    129
MARGARITA MACHADO-CASAS AND KATHERINE ESPINOZA

7. *Uncovering Surprises: Teacher Candidates Learning to Assess Biliteracy in Argumentative Writing*    147
LESLIE C. BANES

8. *A Classroom Observation Tool for Assessing Mathematics in Two Languages*    167
MARCO A. BRAVO, EDUARDO MOSQUEDA AND JORGE L. SOLÍS

9. *Evaluating Teacher Attitudes towards Bilingualism and Best Science Teaching Practices for Bilingual Learners*    189
TIBERIO GARZA, MARGARITA HUERTA AND JULIE K. JACKSON

10. *How Institutions of Higher Education Prepare Bilingual Teachers' Understanding, Developing and Use of Diversity-Differentiated Assessments*    207
XOCHITL ARCHEY

# Table of Contents

## Measuring Bilingualism, Biliteracy and Sociocultural Competence

11. Assessing Emergent Bilingual Learners' Mathematical Biliteracy: Authentic Mathematics Writing Assessment System — 223
EDUARDO MOSQUEDA, MARCO A. BRAVO, JORGE L. SOLÍS AND SAÚL I. MALDONADO

12. Learning about My Students: Examination of Cultural Asset-Based Assessments in Dual Language Education — 245
ANA M. HERNÁNDEZ AND ANNETTE M. DAOUD

*Appendices* — 267

*List of California's State Standards and Frameworks for Sociocultural Competence Considerations* — 269
VERONICA JOHNSON, JANET GABRIELA CARIÑO RAMSAY AND SAÚL I. MALDONADO

*Activities for Evaluating Mathematics Learning in Dual Language Programs* — 271
KIP TÉLLEZ

*Considerations Before Special Education Recommendations for Bilingual Students* — 275
FELICIA CASTRO-VILLARREAL, VICTOR VILLARREAL AND ILEANA UMAÑA

*Training Sequence for IEP Committee Professional Development* — 279
FELICIA CASTRO-VILLARREAL, VICTOR VILLARREAL AND ILEANA UMAÑA

*Critical Points for Collaboration in the Multidisciplinary IEP Committee* — 281
FELICIA CASTRO-VILLARREAL, VICTOR VILLARREAL AND ILEANA UMAÑA

*Receptive and Expressive Language Pre-Referral Protocol for Bilingual Learners (RELPP-BL)* — 283
JANELLE BETH FLORES, KARLA C. GARZA, T. BREANNE ROCHESTER, YVONNE VERA AND BELINDA BUSTOS FLORES

*Process for Engaging Teachers in Collaborative Rubric Design for Biliterate Writing* — 293
LESLIE C. BANES

*MALLI Classroom Observation Protocol*   301
MARCO A. BRAVO, EDUARDO MOSQUEDA AND JORGE L. SOLÍS

*Attitudes Towards Teaching Science to Bilingual Learners Instrument (ATTS-BL) Instrument*   305
TIBERIO GARZA, MARGARITA HUERTA AND JULIE K. JACKSON

*Diversity-Differentiated Assessments Template*
XOCHITL ARCHEY   313

*AMWAS Administration Guidelines/Guía de administración de la evaluación AMWAS*   315
EDUARDO MOSQUEDA, MARCO A. BRAVO, JORGE L. SOLÍS AND SAÚL I. MALDONADO

List of Contributors   319

Index   327

# List of Figures

| | | |
|---|---|---|
| Figure 0.1 | A Decolonial Assessment and Evaluation Approach for Bilingual Education | 9 |
| Figure 2-1 | Strand 1 \| Principle 1 \| Key Point A—Rubric Sample ($GP^3$, 2018) | 52 |
| Figure 2-2 | Three Pillars of DL Education Data-Metric Sources | 52 |
| Figure 2-3 | Sample Annual Cycle of DL Improvement | 55 |
| Figure 2-4 | Theory of Action Process | 57 |
| Figure 2-5 | Theory of Action Macro-Questions | 58 |
| Figure 2-6 | The Hexagon Tool for Systems Planning | 59 |
| Figure 2–7 | Decision-making Protocol with a DLE Lens | 60 |
| Figure 2–8 | DLLT Continuous Improvement Action Planning Template | 61 |
| Figure 2-9 | Sample DL Data Dashboard | 62 |
| Figure 6-1 | Bilingual Teacher Candidate Reflections on Biliteracy and Assessment | 138 |
| Figure 6-2 | Bilingual Teacher Candidate Reflections on Languages and Assessment | 139 |
| Figure 6-3 | Bilingual Teacher Candidate Reflections on Sociocultural Competence and Assessment | 141 |
| Figure 7-1 | PSTs' Reflections on Students' Bilingual Argumentative Writing before and after Rubric Development/Analysis | 155 |
| Figure 8-1 | MALLI Theory of Change | 169 |

| | | |
|---|---|---|
| Figure 8-2 | Sample Narrative Notes | 172 |
| Figure 8-3 | Writing Math | 178 |
| Figure 10-1 | Course Syllabi Assignments that Integrated Diversity-Differentiated Processes | 214 |
| Figure 11-1 | Paco's Response to Second Formative Assessment | 238 |
| Figure 11-2 | Josi's Response to Third Formative Assessment | 240 |
| Figure 12-1 | Dual Language Educator Equity Lens, IPAE Framework (Alfaro & Hernández, 2016) | 250 |

# List of Tables

| | | |
|---|---|---|
| Table 1-1 | Guiding Principles for Dual Language Education, Curriculum Strand, Principle 2, Key Point D | 28 |
| Table 1-2 | CHISPAS Tool for Assessing Sociocultural Competence in California's Dual Language Schools | 31 |
| Table 2-1 | Possible Quantitative Data & Metric Sources | 51 |
| Table 2-2 | Dual Language Continuous Improvement Cycle (DLCIP) Data Analysis Template | 56 |
| Table 2-3 | Implications for Stakeholders | 63 |
| Table 3-1 | List of Assessments Suitable for Evaluating Mathematics Learning in DLP, Including Descriptions, Benefits and Disadvantages of Each | 77 |
| Table 5-1 | Some Initial Considerations for Suspected Language Disorder | 114 |
| Table 7-1 | PSTs' Reflections on Students' Bilingual Argumentative Writing Before and After Rubric Development/Analysis | 156 |
| Table 8-1 | Math Instruction | 174 |
| Table 8-2 | Vocabulary | 175 |
| Table 8-3 | Literacy | 176 |
| Table 8-4 | Math Discourse | 179 |
| Table 9-1 | Sample Characteristics | 197 |

| | | |
|---|---|---|
| Table 9-2 | Standardized Beta Coefficients for Predictors of Attitudes towards Best Science Teaching Practices for Bilingual Learners among a Sample of Science Educators, According to Two Regression Models | 199 |
| Table 11-1 | Rúbrica de Escritura Matemática (REM) | 231 |
| Table 11-2 | Mean Pre- and Post-Scores by Domain | 235 |
| Table 12-1 | Asset-Based Assessments Used in Project ACCEPT PD | 251 |
| Table 12-2 | Asset-based Writing Analysis for Spanish Writing | 253 |
| Table 12-3 | Asset-based Grade Level Summary of Writing Analysis, Rubrics and Strategies | 254 |
| Table 12-4 | Common Core Español Estándar 4.2: Textos informativos y explicativos para examinar un tema y transmitir ideas e información con claridad | 255 |
| Table 12-5 | Asset-based Lesson Study Feedback Form–Spanish Language Development | 257 |
| Table 12-6 | Teacher Comments on Lesson Study Feedback Form: Reconstructing Sentences in Spanish by Condensing or Expanding | 257 |
| Table 12-7 | Asset-based Grade Level Summary Lesson Study Feedback | 259 |
| Table 12-8 | Structuring Cohesive Texts: Academic Word Misuse (Inspired by Cons, 2012) | 261 |
| Table 12-9 | Asset-based Lesson Study Feedback Form—English Language Development | 262 |

# *Acknowledgments*

Margarita Machado-Casas: I acknowledge my family: husband, Lauro Casas, my wonderful daughters, Natassia, Lina, and Paola. Girls, you are my everything! My amazing parents, Lina and Jose Machado, for their support and love. *¡Familia no tengo como agradecerles todo su amor y apoyo!* This has been a labor of love and I feel honored I had the great privilege to work and learn from Dr. Belinda Bustos Flores and Dr. Saúl Isaac Maldonado. *¡Gracias colegas!* To all our co-authors, thank you for your contributions to this book and the field of bilingual assessment and evaluation. Let's continue to work together to fight colonial assessment policies and practices currently hindering our students, teachers, teacher preparation programs, and our future! *¡Si se puede!*

Saúl I. Maldonado: I express my gratitude to God, my familia, my fellow editors, Drs. Margarita Machado-Casas and Belinda Bustos Flores, and my doctoral student-colleague, Mariano Lozano-Soto, for working with me on this volume from conceptualization to publication. I also want to express my respect and appreciation to each and every author that contributed their perspectives to collectively improve assessment and evaluation policies and practices in bilingual education. Finally, this volume would not be possible without all of the support, guidance and patience from Dr. Dani Green, Megan Madden, Ashita Shah, Jacqueline Pavlovic and the Peter Lang community - gracias por su colaboración.—*Proverbs 11:1*

Belinda Bustos Flores: I want to acknowledge my familia, especially my querido esposo, Mario Enrique Flores, and my hija de oro, Janelle Beth Flores, as well as my parents, Arturo Silvano Bustos and Frances Salazar Bustos, for their constant support and love. I also want to thank my colegas, Margarita Machado-Casas and Saúl Isaac Maldonado for inviting me to join them in this critical work. Mil gracias to all our authors who provided chapters that will move the assessment and evaluation of dual language and bilingual education programs forward, provide guidance to dual language/bilingual educators, and ensure the fair and authentic assessment of dual language/bilingual learners.

# *Foreword*

Dr. José Medina, Chief Educational Advocate
*Dr. José Medina Educational Solutions*

Mi nombre es José, but when I was six years old, my first-grade teacher changed it to Joe. She wanted me to more quickly become Americanized and forget el español that was a part of my home and corazón. Even as I begin to write this Foreword focused on assessments and evaluation in dual language bilingual education (DLBE) programs, I carry the childhood scars resulting from a sistema de educación that viewed my inability to language en inglés, via assessments that were never designed to embrace my linguistic dexterity, as something that required immediate intervención.

A quick note. Please understand that like many of the bilingual learners described in *Assessment and Evaluation in Bilingual Education*, I am able to leverage my entire linguistic repertoire and solely mobilize English as I write. También puedo escribir completamente en español porque tengo la destreza de lectoescritura en ambos idiomas. But, today, I choose to disrupt this space and write en inglés y español because I can. This is what linguistic liberation looks like—desmadre, good trouble, in the name of equidad and social justice. One might say this is fitting, considering that this book, in many ways, also challenges the status quo and provides conexiones to a more culturally sustaining perspective of evaluation, assessment, and support for students representing culturally and linguistically diverse communities.

Dual language bilingual education is reparation for the opresión lingüística that has been historically inflicted upon comunidades estudiantiles that do not fit a U.S. monolingual and monocultural perspective of teaching and learning. Evaluación that is culturally sustaining and that embraces all that students bring into the educational space, continues to be an area of need in our field. Margarita Machado-Casas, Saúl Isaac Maldonado, and Belinda Bustos Flores move this conversación forward without apology, by providing a comprehensive framework that is supported by the chapters included in the resource and representing the work of experts and practitioners in the field. Este texto focuses on evaluation processes, equitable assessment systems, supporting practitioner assessment understanding, and ultimately, grounding all assessment conversations as they intersect with la competencia sociocultural y conciencia crítica.

For too long, as U.S. educators, we have used assessment tools that were conceptualized para promover an English-centric perspective. That is, if schooling en este país was designed to promote a White, middle-income ideology of education, entonces, assessments utilized served to identificar if estudiantes, specifically Brown, Indigenous, Students of Color (BISoC) were White-adjacent enough. When evaluation results identify gaps in learning, it is many times, done so by ignoring the gifts that diverse student comunidades bring into the school building. The editors here, take the reins y organizan the chapters in this book as a way to cause desmadre to an existing system via an assessment and evaluation asset-based lens.

As co-author of the *Guiding Principles for Dual Language Education: Third Edition* (GP3), I appreciate the alignment to, and the expansion of the work y recomendaciones en el GP3, as related to assessment and evaluation in DLBE programs. *Assessment and Evaluation in Bilingual Education*, in its overt call to acción, underlines la importancia of sociocultural competence and critical consciousness as the foundation of any bilingual dual language program. Without this targeted focus, we cannot effectively ensure that los estudiantes engage in ongoing work towards el bilingüismo, biliteracy, and grade level academic achievement in dos idiomas. Ultimately, the editors underscore the fact that evaluaciones that don't fully leverage bilingual learners' cultural and linguistic repertoires are in fact, oppressive.

Practitioners will be grateful for the many assessment and evaluation resources that are shared en el texto. Whether leveraging the CHISPAS tool as a way to support a sociocultural and critical consciousness journey, embracing protocolos de liderazgo to empower educators who facilitate instruction in DLBE programs, utilizando a checklist that guía conversations focused on la intersección de special education and language learning, delineating ways to promover continued biliteracy assessment professional learning for DLBE teachers, or leveraging frameworks that continúan to guide our life-long work around bias, prejuicio, y privilegio, all are present in the chapters included herein.

The editors and contributing authors are to be commended por introducir this valuable recurso to the world of assessment in DLBE. No podemos continuar to advocate for culturally sustaining biliteracy instructional practices sin también demandar that the assessment and evaluation tools we leverage reflect this mindset. In calling the reader to action, nos obligan to be critically self-reflective about our own understanding of assessments en la clase dual y bilingüe. How have we—or not, fully empowered our bilingual learners, via instrucción y evaluación, to love their entire self as they enter the space? How have we—or not, oppressed las comunidades de estudiantes that we are charged to serve?

As a child entering la escuela, so many years ago, I understood that whatever I was and el español that I spoke, was not what was wanted or needed in that educational environment. It took me a lifetime para comenzar to love myself, to embrace el idioma of my home, and to reclaim mi nombre, José, that was stolen from me. Unfortunately, for many BISoC this is still the case. I am eternally grateful for this new assessment resource porque estoy seguro that it will surely cause desmadre in our field. Liberación lingüística, today and always!

# Preface

> Tenemos mucho orgullo presentarles este trabajo que representa nuestra obligación a la población bilingüe. Dedicamos nuestro trabajo a nuestro pueblo y esperamos que siga la conversación en el área de evaluación.

We are proud to present our book that fills a void in the assessment of bilingual/dual language learners and the evaluation of bilingual/dual language programs. For too long, we have relied on the assessment and evaluation approaches that are situated in a monolingual, majoritarian perspective. Further, assessment has been used to categorize and subjugate *nuestra gente* using this monolithic lens. Grosjean's foundational research clearly countered various myths about bilingual learners, specifically that a bilingual learner was not two monolingual learners in one. Hence, we cannot use measures or assessment tools developed for and with monolingual populations; otherwise we are violating linguistic justice.

We grounded our work within a social justice lens, that considers the linguistic and cultural prowess of the bilingual population. Given that labels often delimit, define, and often subjugate our bilingual population, we use an asset-based lens which recognizes learning, the uniqueness of bilinguals' language and knowledge acquisition, as well as the knowledge, *conocimientos*, and *sabiduría* of the community beyond the sanctioned official, Western knowledge that is promulgated within the school walls. Thereby, we used the term bilingual/dual language learners throughout the book to convey that they are not simply learning English, but rather are continuously learning their heritage or native language whether it be in the home, community, or the school.

We acknowledge the work of others who have continued to provide us with the theoretical underpinnings, policy, and resources in the area of assessment and evaluation for bilingual/dual language populations. In developing this book, we examined various national standards to develop an assessment and evaluation approach that centers bilingual education/dual language programs and learners. As a result of exploring the research and examining these different standards, we proposed a comprehensive assessment and evaluation approach to Bilingual/Dual Language Education:

1. Evaluation Processes for Bilingual Education/Dual Language Programs
2. Equitable and Fair Assessment Systems for Bilingual Education/Dual Language Learners
3. Developing Bilingual/Dual Language Educators' Assessment Practices
4. Measuring Bilingualism, Biliteracy, and Sociocultural Competence

The purpose of this book is to communicate how bilingual/dual language education programs in the United States measure bilingual/dual language learners' learning in language, literacy and culture and to provide examples of institutional policies and instructional practices that promote high-quality assessment and evaluation in bilingual/dual language teaching and learning.

Hence, our book extends the bilingual/dual language assessment and evaluation conversation, in that experts from across the United States have written chapters with examples and tools to approach assessment and evaluation for bilingual students. In order to ensure that fair and equitable assessment occurs within the classroom, we provide chapters that speak to the preparation of bilingual/dual language teacher candidates as well as chapters that address the need for professional learning opportunities for our practicing and dedicated bilingual/dual language educators.

The intended primary audience for this book are educators interested in practical tools for assessing bilingual students' learning and evaluating the quality of bilingual education programs; we also intended this book for policymakers and researchers. We hope that our collective work encourages others to explore assessment and evaluation from this approach and that we, collectively as researchers, extend the conversation to move us forward in ensuring that bilingual/dual language learners are assessed fairly and evaluated equitably.

¡Adelante!

## References

Grosjean, F. (1989). Neurolinguists, beware! The bilingual is not two monolinguals in one person. *Brain and Language*, 36, 3–15.

# Introduction
# Bilingual Education/Dual Language Assessment and Evaluation Principles: A Decolonial Approach for Practitioners and Policymakers

MARGARITA MACHADO-CASAS
San Diego State University

BELINDA BUSTOS FLORES
University of Texas, San Antonio

SAÚL I. MALDONADO
San Diego State University

Assessment practices and evaluative processes influence curricular and instructional choices as well as policymaking decisions for PK-12 schools and districts implementing bilingual education programs in the United States. Bilingual education programs use two languages as medium of instruction and assessment, and vary in design, implementation goals, practices and evidence of effectiveness. García and Woodley (2015) remind us that bilingual education is inextricable from power dynamics across majoritarian and minoritized identities as well as ideologies. Bilingual education programs that intentionally address power dynamics by integrating minoritized and majoritarian students to develop bilingualism, biliteracy and sociocultural competence are referred to as dual language (DeMatthews & Izquierdo, 2018; Howard et al., 2018; Lindholm-Leary, 2001).

Practitioners and policymakers in U.S. schools and districts have access to a limitless flow of books, tools, and learning platforms marketed to address the assessment and evaluation needs of bilingual learners (BLs); however, few resources specifically attend to culturally and linguistically diverse populations—and, relatively less are exclusively designed to meet the assessment and evaluation needs of BLs in dual language programs (Gottlieb, 2016; Gottlieb & Nguyen, 2007; Lindholm-Leary & Hargett, 2006). As dual language programs increase in the U.S., educators continue to struggle with acquiring appropriate bilingual assessment materials and administrators grapple with appropriate evaluative evidence of effectiveness for bilingual education programs. Critical issues include equitable representation of assessment practices and evaluation processes in at least two languages, bilingual assessment exams and calibration tools for bilingual/dual language classrooms, critical and culturally responsive pedagogies that integrate assessment, the teaching of assessment and evaluation in the preparation of future bilingual and dual language teachers, as well as professional development opportunities for bilingual/dual language assessment and evaluation communities. Regrettably, many assessment practices and evaluation processes ignore equity, and linguistic as well as social justice as it pertains to BLs. This book brings to light many unique considerations required when assessing bilingual learners and evaluating bilingual/dual language programs.

Taking a decolonial approach, we move away from assessment and evaluation as being decontextualized and situated within a U.S., White, monolingual, majoritarian perspective. A majoritarian perspective often disregards minoritized bilingual students, making this neglect one of the most important inequitable and discriminatory issues facing students and educators working with bilingual learners (Cervantes-Soon et al., 2017; Flores, 2016; Heiman & Yanes, 2018). Assessment practices and evaluative processes used to measure BLs in bilingual/dual language classrooms are often reflective of an assimilative stance in which the "official" majoritarian knowledge and skills are disproportionately valued and measured. This book prioritizes equity, linguistic, and social perspectives of assessment and evaluation of BLs in dual language programs from a sociopolitical perspective (Maldonado & Machado-Casas, 2019). Addressing assessment and evaluation from a decolonial approach guides us from the "what" of inadequate access to appropriate curricular materials to the "how" of addressing disparities and equity issues via content and resources for both bilingual students in PK-12 contexts, as well as bilingual teacher candidates in Institutions of Higher Education (IHEs). It is imperative to prepare future bilingual teachers and provide practicing bilingual/dual language educators tools for the assessment and evaluation of bilingual/dual language learners.

Assessment practices and evaluation processes are distinctive as well as complementary. Assessment practices in bilingual education are designed to collect formative information *for* students' learning or designed to collect summative information *of* students' learning; and practices are often implemented without explicit considerations for alignment and consistency between formative and summative data collection (Maldonado & Andrade, 2018). Evaluation processes in bilingual education are intended to collect information for the purpose of providing judgments about programs' quality and effectiveness (Maldonado et al., 2018). The relationship between assessment practices and evaluation processes is bidirectional. Information collected by educators to measure BLs' bilingualism, biliteracy, sociocultural competence, and content-area achievement is used to evaluate appropriateness of dual language implementation as well as degree of students' preparation (Georges et al., 2019). Information collected by evaluators is used to provide program stakeholders with suggestive guidance for improvement.

*A Decolonial Approach for Assessment Practices and Evaluative Processes in Bilingual Education.*

A decolonial approach encourages bilingual educators and dual language program evaluators to analyze if existing measures of achievement and accountability are aligned with the "why" as well as the "how" of *"la lucha" (the collective struggle)* (Flores & García, 2017). Informed by sociopolitical dimensions of power and purpose, culturally responsive evaluation methodological processes are essential to bilingual education programs (Guajardo et al., 2020; Gutiérrez, 2013). Situated within a continuum of power, evaluation processes are either reinforcing or dismantling structural barriers for BLs. Which stakeholders determine what evidence is considered appropriate for evaluating program effectiveness? What are the purposes and intended, as well as unintended, consequences of making program quality judgments?

When dual language programs are informed by culturally responsive evaluation processes, practitioners and policymakers are able to communicate how their accountability infrastructure integrates formative program improvement measures *and* summative program achievement measures to influence policymaking decisions. Essential to assessment systems are analyses of cultural, linguistic and consequential validity (Abedi, 2004; Basterra et al., 2011; Shaw, 1997; Solano-Flores & Nelson-Barber, 2001). Is the data collection and assessment system fair and equitable across BLs, educators and policymakers, or are compliance indicators disproportionately prioritized at the expense of other relevant and actionable information (e.g., biliteracy policies)? Is the progress monitoring system regularly refined for appropriateness across persons, programs and policies, or is the system exclusively in the interests of maintaining the hierarchical continuum of power where policymakers use assessment data to evaluate programs and educators use assessment data to evaluate BLs?

In considering a decolonial approach for BLs in PK-12 contexts, addressing the pedagogical assessment knowledge, dispositions and skills of bilingual teacher candidates is essential (Alfaro, Cadiero-Kaplan & Ochoa, 2018; Bunch, 2013). How IHEs design, deliver and assess bilingual teacher candidates' knowledge, dispositions and skills of assessment practices requires a developmental process of critical consciousness (Bartolomé & Balderrama, 2001; Darder, 2012; Flores, Sheets, & Clark, 2011). What sociopolitical stances influence why bilingual candidates pursue teacher preparation programs and how do IHEs intentionally integrate ideological development of critical consciousness (Valenzuela, 2016)? How are bilingual teacher candidates' assessment practices developed across: (a) knowledge and use of bilingual assessment tools, instruments and systems, (b) dispositions toward linguistic justice for BLs, and (c) culturally responsive and sustainable pedagogical skills across curriculum, instruction and assessment in two or more languages as well as during translanguaging practices (Musanti & Rodríguez, 2017)?

When critical consciousness guides bilingual teacher education programs, how practitioners and policymakers design and implement assessment practices and evaluative processes is inextricable from learning indicators of both equity as well as expertise. A linguistic justice perspective calls into question if and to what extent the measurement of BLs' bilingualism, biliteracy and sociocultural competence is necessary (and for what purposes), whether (or not) existing measures are appropriate, and whether all program goals are connected to assessment practices and evaluative processes. Are dual language program measures used for establishing and maintaining information systems across languages and all content areas or is BLs' biliteracy monitored for assimilationist, majoritarian purposes?

*Addressing Assessment in Bilingual Education/Dual Language Teacher Preparation*

It is critical that educators be well informed to ensure that assessment and evaluation is approached from an educational, linguistic, and social justice stance in which bilingual learners' cultures and languages are considered and implemented into daily practices. Much research addresses the need to increase the number of bilingual/dual language educators who are biliterate, possess knowledge and skills, as well as demonstrate political and ideological clarity to engage in transformative practices and to effectively implement bilingual and dual language programs (Bartolomé, & Balderrama, 2001; Clark & Flores, 2001; Flores, Sheets, & Clark, 2011). Recently, scholars have begun to delve into specific arenas within the field of bilingual teacher preparation. Collins et al. (2019) suggests that bilingual teacher preparation programs dedicate efforts to sustain teacher candidates' bilingualism in approaches such as assessments that are inclusive of their diverse linguistic experiences. Similarly, Garza et al. (2020) reveal that bilingual teacher preparation programs must be dedicated to pedagogical, curricular, and evaluative alignment. Nevertheless, there is a gap in the literature in regards to assessment within bilingual education teacher preparation programs.

Maldonado and Machado-Casas (2019) proposed the need for developing assessment practices and evaluative policies that sustain "the sociopolitical spirit of bilingual education." These new approaches must be considered collectively when designing bilingual teacher preparation programs to ensure that bilingual/dual language teacher candidates readily see the connection between practice and assessment. Opportunities for bilingual teacher candidates to make connections to what they are witnessing in their classroom practices must reinforce what they have learned in their coursework.

As aforementioned, there is a need for bilingual teacher education research that addresses the multidimensional and dynamic intersectionality of bilingual/dual language instruction, teaching, and evaluative practices. Teacher candidates must have opportunities where they learn how to use assessment results in a myriad of ways including: (1) to plan instruction for their students, (2) to promote the use of self-monitoring and self-assessment practices, and (3) the ability to use multiple types of assessment across content areas. Ultimately, expanding this area of research will grow the field of bilingual/dual language teacher preparation and yield bilingual teacher candidates who can effectively implement curriculum, instruction and assessment in English and partner languages across all content areas, while considering the language proficiency and the sociopolitical context of their bilingual learners.

In sum, to move our conversation forward, it is critical to offer an approach in which we situate assessment and evaluation from a decolonial framework that considers these aforementioned factors. To ensure equity, bilingual education/dual language teachers must be well prepared to attend to these factors. Solano-Flores and Soltero-González (2011) poignantly stated:

> Challenges stemming from increased testing and accountability policies add to the formidable challenges inherent in teaching heterogeneous linguistic groups who typically attend low-income schools with high teacher turnover rates. Due to increased pressure on teachers and schools, probably never before in history have teachers, especially those who teach BLs, need to be more knowledgeable on testing issues as they do in these times. (p. 146)

Moreover, as we develop assessment and evaluation approaches for BLs framed from a decolonial framework, we must consider Anzaldúa's (2009) consejo: *"Caminante, no hay puentes, se hace puentes al andar"* (Voyager, there are no bridges, one builds them as one walks; p. 73). In building assessment and evaluation approaches for bilingual/dual language learners, we first consider the role of assessment within bilingual education/dual language programs and the principles that guide such practices. Next, we consider the role of evaluation processes on bilingual education/dual language programs. Finally, we consider the interdependent relationship between assessment practices and evaluation process in bilingual/dual language education.

Evaluating bilingual education programs requires assessing educators' and students' bilingualism, biliteracy, and sociocultural competence. This book documents how bilingual education/dual language classrooms and programs in the United States implement institutional policies and instructional practices for evaluating program quality and measuring student achievement. Literature consistently identifies seven guiding principles, with associated criteria, for implementing quality dual language programs, and we suggest the same criteria should be used in bilingual education programs in general: (a) program structure, (b) curriculum, (c) instruction, (d) assessment and accountability, (e) staff quality and professional development, (f) family and community, and (g) support and resources. Emphasizing the assessment and accountability strand of quality bilingual education/dual language programs, this book provides policymakers, practitioners, as well as family and community members, explicit guidance regarding:

1. How to develop and maintain an infrastructure that supports continuous assessment and accountability processes as well as communication of program outcomes to all stakeholders;
2. How to align bilingual learner assessment and program goals with state/national standards; and
3. How to systematically collect, analyze and use bilingual progress monitoring measures.

## *Bilingual Education/Dual Language: Role of Assessment*

Over the years, researchers have used assessment to gauge the impact of bilingual education/dual language instruction on learners, the evaluation of programs, and to create educational and language policy. Moreover, assessment has played a key role in assisting teachers to critically think about their instructional approaches, determining their students' progress, and in examining the fidelity of their bilingual education/dual language programs.

Nevertheless, it is important to recognize that assessment has its limitations, especially the standardized testing that has been validated with non-bilingual populations or with distinct non-U.S. linguistic-cultural groups. Given our unique circumstances, rather than following traditional assessment practices which were developed for monolingual groups, we contend that we must create our own approach situated in bilingual education/dual language theory and assessment principles. We considered various documents in constructing our approach:

1. Guidelines for the Assessment of English Language Learners (Educational Testing Service, 2009);
2. Guiding Principles for Dual Language Education (Howard et al., 2018),
3. The National Association Bilingual Education's ([NABE], 2018) Bilingual Education Standards for the preparation of bilingual teachers, specifically Standard #3: Bilingual Assessment, currently under consideration by the Council for the Accreditation of Educator Program (CAEP), and
4. The National Dual Language Education Teacher Preparation Standards ([NDLETPS], 2018), specifically Standard #4: Authentic Assessment in Dual Language also under consideration by CAEP.

We first examined the Guidelines for the Assessment of English Language Learners (Educational Testing Services [ETS], 2009). Given the high-stakes nature of assessment, to assist educators in making educational decisions for English Language Learners (ELs), these ETS macro-level guidelines:

> offer recommendations on many important assessment issues regarding ELLs, including the development of assessment specifications and items, reviewing and field-testing items, scoring of constructed responses, test administration, testing accommodations, and the use of statistics to evaluate the assessment and scoring. (p. 27)

These guidelines also address the importance of equity and fairness in the assessment process by considering the bilingual/English learner's language proficiency; education background factors such as formal schooling in their home country, type of instruction (e.g., bilingual immersion, dual language, English as second language), experience with formal testing processes; and cultural factors influenced by acculturation and socioeconomic levels.

In surveying the Guiding Principles for Dual Language Education (Howard et al., 2018), Strand 4: Assessment and Accountability lists the following macro-level assessment principles:

1. The program creates and maintains an infrastructure that supports an accountability process.
2. Student assessment is aligned with program goals and with state content and language standards, and the results are used to guide and inform instruction.
3. Using multiple measures in both languages of instruction, the program collects and analyzes a variety of data that are used for program accountability, program evaluation, and program improvement.
4. The program communicates with appropriate stakeholders about program outcomes. (pp.139–141).

We also posit that bilingual/dual language teachers and teacher candidates must have a strong understanding of bilingual language theory and assessment principles. Further, bilingual/dual language teachers and teacher candidates must be prepared to use these principles in planning and assessing their practices. At present, there are two concerted efforts in establishing bilingual/dual language educator standards. The NABE (2018) has proposed to become a CAEP Specialized Professional Association and has identified five standards for the accreditation of bilingual teacher preparation programs. Specifically, the Bilingual Assessment Standard #3 encompasses three components: *Assessment Decision Making and Policy, Content of Assessment, and Process of Assessment*. The committee stance in the area of bilingual assessment is that "the candidate is expected to understand the different purposes of assessment, make assessment an integral part of the teaching and learning process, and demonstrate expertise in the processes of implementing bilingual assessment effectively" (NABE, 2018, p. 13).

Similarly, the National Dual Language Education Teacher Preparation Standards ([NDLETPS], 2018) were prepared to ensure the quality of dual language education programs and consistency in preparing dual language bilingual educators. Using the framework of critical consciousness and aligning with the Guiding Principles for Dual Language Education (Howard et al., 2018), six standards were proposed and, of these, *Authentic Assessment in Dual Language* was proposed as the fourth standard. The Authentic Assessment domain encompasses four components: *Assessment and Biliteracy, Assessment and Equity, Assessment and Variation, and Assessment, Evaluation, and Accountability*. According to the NDLETPS:

> The premise for Standard Four is that teacher candidates must be prepared to authentically and holistically assess dual language learners for specific purposes, including program evaluation, using multiple, intricate measures with

*Bilingual Education/Dual Language Principles* 9

multilingualism in mind. Authentic assessment in dual language is fundamentally informed by principles of additive biliteracy development, pedagogy and instrument design, as well as holistic, formative and summative multilingual assessments inclusive of learners with special needs. (p. 54)

In developing a comprehensive assessment and evaluation approach for Bilingual/Dual Language Education, we identified four overarching principles for assessment and evaluation in bilingual education:

1. Evaluation Processes for Bilingual Education/Dual Language Programs,
2. Equitable and Fair Assessment Systems for Bilingual Education/Dual Language Learners,
3. Developing Bilingual/Dual Language Educators' Assessment Practices, and
4. Measuring Bilingualism, Biliteracy, and Sociocultural Competence.

These principles reflect a comprehensive approach to assessment and evaluation that is guided by research in the field of bilingual education/dual language (Figure 0.1). We consider it important to ensure that these principles are enacted from a decolonial lens, and that bilingual/dual language educators be prepared with a deep understanding of equity and fairness as vital knowledge in order to implement assessment and evaluation.

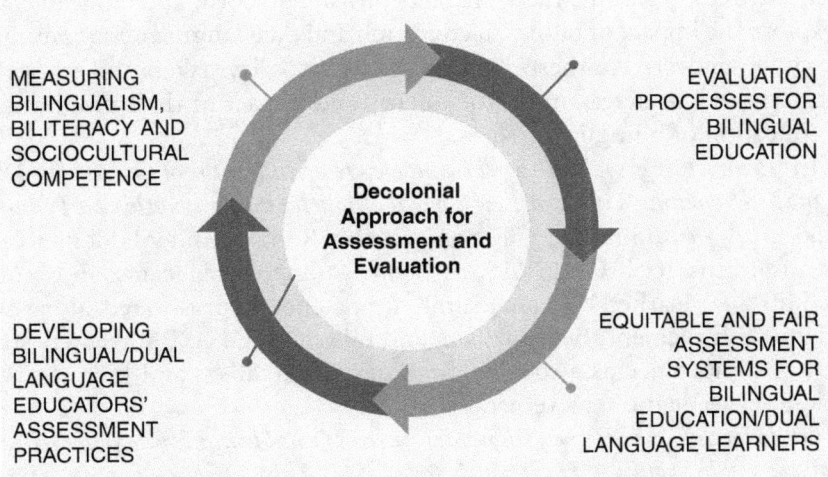

*Figure 0.1.* A Decolonial Assessment and Evaluation Approach for Bilingual Education

## Overview and Organization

This book contributes chapters from emerging and established U.S. scholars in the field of bilingual/dual language education. Chapters in this volume report on the following: (a) how bilingual education/dual language programs create, maintain and improve culturally valid assessment systems, (b) how bilingual education/dual language programs negotiate multiple development timelines of student achievement measures, and (c) how to evaluate bilingual education/dual language programs with cultural competency. An additional feature of this volume is the inclusion of appendices, where chapter authors provide evaluation and assessment process tools and instruments.

We have organized this book to reflect a comprehensive approach of assessment and evaluation for bilingual education/dual language into four sections: (a) Evaluation Processes for Bilingual Education/Dual Language Programs, (b) Equitable and Fair Assessment Systems for Bilingual Education/Dual Language Learners, (c) Developing Bilingual/Dual Language Educators' Assessment Practices, and (d) Measuring Bilingualism, Biliteracy, and Sociocultural Competence. An overview of each of the chapters associated with these four sections is presented in the subsequent section.

### *Evaluation Processes for Bilingual/Dual Language Education*

Within this section, there are two critical chapters that extend the conversation beyond the Guiding Principles for Dual Language Education (Howard et al., 2018). Specifically, these chapters provide practical and replicable tools to explore the impact of bilingual education and dual language programming. The content covered in these chapters can assist policymakers and school district personnel in determining the fidelity and impact of their programs on the education of bilingual learners.

In *Prioritizing Sociocultural Competence as Indicator of Quality in Dual-language Programs: Cultural, Historical, Identity, Socio-emotional, Pedagogy, Action and Sustainability,* Johnson, Cariño Ramsay and Maldonado provide a reflective tool, CHISPAS, to support bilingual educators in ensuring that bilingual learners' sociocultural competence is prioritized along with academic achievement, bilingualism, and biliteracy. CHISPAS centers sociocultural competence as a tool for bridging bilingualism and biliteracy with grade-level academic achievement.

Guilamo, in *Advancing the achievement of dual language learners through program evaluation: A framework for assessing the effectiveness and impact of dual language programs,* provides guidance, tools, and sample templates for evaluating the effectiveness of the dual-language and bilingual programs, decision-making protocols, and for developing an aligned, data-based continuous improvement process. Guilamo offers pertinent improvement science theory and accessible leadership strategies sourced directly from firsthand experiences in bilingual education and evidence-based approaches.

## *Equitable and Fair Assessment Systems for Bilingual Education/Dual Language Learners*

The four chapters in this section provide specific recommendations for assessing dual language learners. The recommendations also extend the conversation in assessing bilingual learners with special needs. To ensure that bilingual learners are assessed fairly and to reduce their misidentification, this section addresses the need to use multiple tools, multidisciplinary teams and/or a transdisciplinary lens.

In *The assessment of mathematical knowledge in elementary level dual language programs*, Téllez discusses the importance of assessing mathematical knowledge and describes and provides a comprehensive list of several assessment tools as well as other strategies to measure mathematical learning in both English and Spanish. Téllez includes examples of school level program evaluations, several insights for assessing mathematical knowledge, as well as suggestions for interpreting and using data-driven decision-making.

Castro-Villarreal, Villarreal, and Umaña, in *Assessment of bilingual students: Best practices and recommendations for members of the multidisciplinary IEP committee,* present an overview of the Individualized Education Program (IEP) committees' role in developing education plans to meet the unique needs of second language learners with disabilities. To ensure appropriate placement decisions and to reduce the misidentification of English Language Learners (ELLs), the authors describe best practices and important considerations in the special education evaluation of ELLs, as well as critical practices for ensuring that IEP committees are working collaboratively. To assist with this process, the authors provide a checklist of unique factors to consider in the evaluation section, as well as additional tools and recommendations for effective education and training for IEP committee members.

In *Assessing bicultural-bilinguals' language development: Difference or disorder?*, Flores, Garza, Rochester, Vera and Flores use a transdisciplinary lens to develop a shared understanding of language development among educators who serve bilingual learners. They provide an overview of prototypical language development and proficiency theories as well as common characteristics of bicultural-bilingual learners (BBLs) as compared to learners who present with language disorders. Further, to assist bilingual educators in their referral decision-making, they identify the characteristics that must be present in order to qualify for speech-language services as well as the tools used for identification. They posit that bilingual educators must display language awareness in which they attend to language acquisition processes in their daily practices to ensure that enriching language development opportunities are provided to BBLs to assist their language and communication development.

## *Developing Bilingual/Dual Language Educators' Assessment Practices*

In order to ensure that the aforementioned guidelines and recommendations are followed, we recognize the importance of ensuring that teachers are well prepared to engage in assessment practices that value bilingual learners' biculturalism and bilingualism from an asset perspective. Bilingual teacher candidates must critically understand assessment to advocate for their learners. There are five chapters that provide asset-based assessment practices for preparing bilingual teacher candidates. Of these five chapters, three chapters attend to bilingual learners' biliteracy when assessing content knowledge in writing, mathematics, and science.

Machado-Casas and Espinoza, in *Understanding assessment and evaluation when preparing bilingual teacher candidates*, present findings on the importance of implementing a course dedicated to developing and preparing bilingual teacher candidates to tackle issues related to the assessment of bilingual students through the use of a cultural validity framework. Findings reflect the need for examining: (a) The role of biliteracy in understanding the implications of assessment in bilingual settings, and (b) assessing language and the language of assessment in bilingual classrooms. Machado-Casas and Espinoza expand notions of language and the need to recognize language variations as opportunities for expanding academic linguistic repertoire and knowledge. The implications discuss the importance of bilingual teacher candidates' voices in the field of assessment for the development of courses to meet these particular needs in teacher preparation programs.

In *Uncovering surprises: Teacher candidates learning to assess biliteracy in argumentative writing*, Banes addresses common core standards that require students to write effective arguments in all content areas, increasing the overlap between content and language learning. Banes argues that teachers cannot assume students' writing in one language represents their knowledge and skills across languages. Banes' chapter documents the learning of 19 bilingual teacher candidates (12 multiple subject and 7 single subject) in a university classroom-based inquiry course as they develop formative assessment tools and practices for assessing the argumentative writing of their bilingual students. Findings suggest the benefits of engaging in a collaborative design process that includes: (a) looking through a holistic biliteracy lens, (b) exploring content-specific writing genres, and (c) analyzing students' writing. Results include teacher candidates' reflections demonstrating greater understanding of students' strengths and their developing bilingualism, ideas for discipline-specific literacy instruction, and shifts toward a more positive view of bilingual writing strategies. Banes also offers implications for classroom assessment and teacher education.

Bravo, Mosqueda and Solís in *A classroom observation tool for assessing mathematics in two languages,* outline the development of the Mathematics Classroom Observation Protocol (M-COP), which was used to capture instruction that integrates language and literacy with mathematics instruction in bilingual classroom settings. The teacher candidates in their study received professional learning opportunities in their mathematics methods courses through their teacher education program to address mathematics vocabulary, literacy and discourse across languages of instruction. The professional learning opportunities reported were conducted in Spanish and the instruction teacher candidates provided in their practicum placement was delivered in Spanish, English, and in some instances with translanguaging approaches (García & Wei, 2014), where the teachers leveraged the students' linguistic repertoire across languages.

In *Evaluating teacher attitudes towards bilingualism and best science teaching practices for bilingual learners,* Garza, Huerta and Jackson present an overview of research related to science education and teacher attitudes with respect to bilingual learners in science learning contexts. The purpose of this chapter is to provide educators and policymakers with an instrument, the *Attitudes Towards Teaching Science to Bilingual Learners* (ATTS-BL), for evaluating science-focused bilingual professional development impact on: (a) teacher attitudes towards bilingualism and (b) best science teaching practices for bilingual learners. The chapter describes the instrument, illustrates how it has been used with a sample of teachers attending science professional development workshops, and provides instructions for educators and policymakers on how to use the ATTS-BL.

In *How institutions of higher education prepare bilingual teachers' understanding, developing, and use of diversity-differentiated assessments,* Archey contextualizes diversity-differentiated assessments by exploring how some institutions of higher education (IHE) prepare teachers' understanding, development, and use of diversity-differentiated assessments in Bilingual

Authorization (BILA) Programs. The purpose of this chapter is to enhance IHE's preparation of bilingual teachers as they engage in this process of assessment. The Understanding, Developing, Use (UDU) Framework for learning and assessment is used as the theoretical underpinning for this chapter. The UDU framework is a three-tiered model that aims to provide deeper approaches to learning by operating within interchanges of ideas, connections, and extensions (Fostaty Young, 2005). Using this framework and data from the top five BILA-recommending California State Universities, the chapter provides a strategic sequencing template (matrix) for teacher preparation to address assessment in diverse classrooms. Archey suggests that this chapter may be of interest to teachers, as they are the most important contributors to student success and to IHEs that prepare bilingual teachers and are committed to continuous improvement.

## *Measuring Bilingualism, Biliteracy, and Sociocultural Competence*

In this last section, there are two substantive chapters that specifically hone into assessing bilingual learners' biliteracy from an asset-based perspective. These chapters are critical in ensuring that we go beyond simply measuring content knowledge, but also consider the bilingual learners' bilingualism and biculturalism. These chapters recognize the intersectionality of language and content and contribute assessment recommendations that ensure linguistic justice.

In *Assessing emergent bilingual learners' mathematical biliteracy: Authentic mathematics writing assessment system*, Mosqueda, Bravo, Solís and Maldonado contend that Emergent Bilingual Learners (EBLs) in English-dominant mathematics classrooms have the dual responsibility of understanding mathematics content while simultaneously acquiring mathematical language in English. They describe the implementation of the Authentic Mathematics Writing Assessment System (AMWAS), a bilingual formative assessment tool developed to offer middle school mathematics teachers' instructional guidance to help EBLs further expand their mathematical language and reasoning across English and Spanish. Mixed methods analysis of student writing samples focused on mathematical content and revealed possibilities for informing teachers about practices that address both language and content learning goals. Specifically, their findings demonstrated that allowing EBLs to respond to the assessment writing prompt in the language of their choice revealed insights into students' mathematical understanding and reasoning that would not have otherwise been observed if students had been directed to respond in their non-dominant language, which was English for most secondary school EBLs in their study.

Hernández and Daoud, in *Learning about my students: Examination of cultural asset-based assessments in dual language education,* provide a critical lens to consider when assessing bilingual learners. They designed a professional development series to help teachers focus on the counter constructs, strengths, resources and capacities of their students using asset-based assessments, collaborative conversations, and an online platform for dialogue. They share the experiences of PreK-8th grade teachers in which they examined their own critical consciousness about the students they serve through activities grounded in the Ideology, Pedagogy, Access and Equity (IPAE) Framework (Alfaro & Hernández, 2016). Teachers analyzed writing samples from their students through a strength-based approach, rather than a deficit mindset towards language development in Spanish and English. Their goal was to help teachers foster a critical lens on diversity and equity by understanding the importance of building relationships with their students, collaborating with colleagues, and reflecting on their ideology and pedagogy as critically conscious educators.

## Conclusion

This book attempts to examine the critical issues of assessment practices and evaluation processes centered on the complexities of bilingual learners and bilingual/dual language classrooms and programs. Informed by a decolonial approach, the contributions of this volume attend to linguistic justice and cultural validity. Research has been critical of assessment and evaluation that too often uses measurement tools to marginalize and subjugate BL populations, and reproduce educational inequities (Valenzuela, 2005). Insidious educational inequities ensure that power and positionality is maintained by the status quo. As practitioners and policymakers, we must dispel colonial assimilationist notions that use assessment and evaluation as means to define and regulate bilingual learners and programs without fully considering their purpose, potential, and power. While we recognize the limitations of assessment both for evaluative and every-day practice, throughout this book, we offer a comprehensive approach which presents a myriad of assessment and evaluation guiding principles as well as research-based practices and tools. Several of the chapters presented within the book focus on formative or performance assessment as well as tools that consider BLs' bilingualism and biculturalism. As Solano-Flores and Soltero-González (2011) recommend, educators must consider assessment as a tool for making data-driven decisions in improving instruction. As educators, if bilingual learners are having difficulty in acquiring a concept, it behooves us to examine our practices in terms of language of delivery, measures used, and opportunity to learn via differentiated instruction or modalities. If we are truly employing critical and culturally responsive pedagogy, bilingual/dual language teachers must use an iterative approach in which we plan for instructional and assessment activities concurrently, and then critically evaluate the impact of such plans in terms of lesson delivery and modality as well as the assessment modality and the BLs' feedback (Solano-Flores & Soltero-González, 2011). Such practices and processes will ensure that BLs have access to an equitable, linguistically and socially just, bilingual/dual language education.

## *References*

Abedi, J. (2004). The no child left behind act and English language learners: Assessment and accountability issues. *American Educational Research Association, 33*, 4–14.

Alfaro, C., Cadiero-Kaplan, K., & Ochoa, A. M. (2018). Teacher education and Latino emergent bilinguals: Knowledge, dispositions and skills for critically conscious pedagogy. In P. C. Ramírez, C. J. Faltis, & E. J. de Jong (Eds.), *Learning from emergent bilingual Latinx learners in K-12*. Routledge.

Alfaro, C., & Hernández, A. M. (2016). Ideology, pedagogy, access, and equity: A critical examination for dual language educators. In *Multilingual educator* (pp. 8–11). California Association for Bilingual Education. https://www.gocabe.org/index.php/communications-2/multilingual-educator/

Anzaldua, G. (2009). In A. Keating (Ed.), *The Gloria Anzaldúa reader (Latin America otherwise)*. Duke University Press.

Bartolomé, L. I., & Balderrama, M. V. (2001). The need for educators with political and ideological clarity: Providing our children with "the best." In *The best for our children: Critical perspectives on literacy for Latino students* (pp. 48–64).

Basterra, M. A., Trumbull, E., & Solano-Flores, G. (2011). *Cultural validity in assessment: Addressing linguistic and cultural diversity (language, culture, and teaching series)*. (1st ed.). Routledge.

Bunch, G. C. (2013). Pedagogical content knowledge: Preparing mainstream teachers for English learners in the new standards era. *Review of Research in Education, 37*, 298–341.

Cervantes-Soon, C. G., Dorner, L., Palmer, D., Heiman, D., Schwerdtfeger, R., & Choi, J. (2017). Combating inequalities in two-way language immersion programs: Toward critical consciousness in bilingual education spaces. *Review of Research in Education, 41*, 403–427. https://doi.org/10.3102/0091732X17690120

Clark, E. R., & Flores, B. B. (2001). Is Spanish proficiency simply enough? An examination of normalistas attitudes towards Spanish, bilingualism, and bilingual teacher pedagogy. *MexTesol Journal, 25*(3), 13–27.

Collins, B. A., Sánchez, M. T., & España, C. (2019). Sustaining and developing teachers' dynamic bilingualism in a re-designed bilingual teacher preparation program. *International Journal of Bilingual Education and Bilingualism*. https://doi.org/10.1080/13670050.2019.1610354

Darder, A. (2012). *Culture and power in the classroom: Educational foundations for the schooling of bicultural students* (Rev. ed.). New York, NY: Bergin and Garvey.

DeMatthews, D., & Izquierdo, E. (2018). The importance of principals supporting dual language education: A social justice leadership framework. *Journal of Latinos and Education, 17*(1), 53–70. https://doi.org/10.1080/15348431.2017.1282365

Educational Testing Service. (2009). *Guidelines for the assessment of english language learners*. Retrieved from https://www.ets.org/s/about/pdf/ell_guidelines.pdf

Flores, N. (2016). A tale of two visions: Hegemonic whiteness and bilingual education. *Educational Policy, 30*(1), 13–38. https://doi.org/10.1177/0895904815616482

Flores, N., & García, O. (2017). A Critical Review of Bilingual Education in the United States: From Basements and Pride to Boutiques and Profit. *Annual Review of Applied Linguistics, 37*, 14–29. https://doi.org/10.1017/S0267190517000162

Flores, B. B., Sheets, R. H., & Clark, E. R. (2011). *Teacher preparation for bilingual student populations: Educar para transformar*. New York, NY: Routledge.

Fostaty Young, S. (2005). Teaching, learning, and assessment in higher education: Using ideas, connections, and extensions to improve student learning. *Improving Student Learning Symposium. London, UK, Imperial College, 13*, 105–115.

García, O., & Wei, L. (2014). Translanguaging and education. In *Translanguaging: Language, bilingualism and education* (pp. 63–77). London: Palgrave Macmillan.

Garcia, O., & Woodley, H. (2015). Bilingual education. In M. Bigelow & J. Ennser-Kananen (Eds.), *The Routledge handbook of educational linguistics* (pp. 132–144). Routledge.

Garza, E., Talati, K., Machado-Casas, M., Schouten, B., & Jimena Guerra, M. (2020). Highly effective practices of three bilingual teacher preparation programs in US Hispanic Serving Institutions (HSIs). *Ehquidad International Welfare Policies and Social Work Journal, 14*, 95–128. doi: 10.15257/ehquidad.2020.0014

Georges, A., Maldonado, S. I., & Uppal, H. K. (2019). Learning content, language and culture: The academic achievement, aspirations, and social experiences of eighth grade dual immersion students. *NABE Journal of Research and Practice, 9*(3–4), 166–180.

Gottlieb, M. (2016). *Assessing English language learners: Bridges to educational equity: Connecting academic language proficiency to student achievement* (2nd ed.). Thousand Oaks, CA: Corwin.

Gottlieb, M., & Nguyen, D. (2007). *Assessment and accountability in language education programs*. Philadelphia, PA: Caslon Publishing.

Guajardo, A. D., Robles-Schrader, G. M., Aponte-Soto, L., & Neubauer, L. C. (2020). LatCrit theory as a framework for social justice evaluation: Considerations for evaluation and evaluators. In L. C. Neubauer, D. McBride, A. D. Guajardo, W. D. Casillas, & M. E. Hall (Eds.), *Examining issues facing communities of color today: The role of evaluation to incite change*. New Directions for Evaluation, 166, 65–75.

Gutiérrez, R. (2013). The sociopolitical turn in mathematics education research. *Journal for Research in Mathematics Education, 44*(1), 37–68. https://doi.org/10.5951/jresematheduc.44.1.0037

Heiman, D., & Yanes, M. (2018). Centering the fourth pillar in times of TWBE gentrification: "Spanish, love, content, not in that order." *International Multilingual Research Journal, 12*(3), 173–187. https://doi.org/10.1080/19313152.2018.1474064

Howard, E. R., Lindholm-Leary, D., Rogers, D., Olague, N., Medina, J., Kennedy, B., Sugarman, J., & Christian, D. (2018). *Guiding principles for dual language education* (3rd ed.). Washington, DC: Center for Applied Linguistics.

Lindholm-Leary, K. J. (2001). *Dual language education*. Avon, England: Multilingual Matters.

Lindholm-Leary, K., & Hargett, G. (2006). *Evaluator's toolkit for dual language programs*. Washington, DC: Center for Applied Linguistics. Retrieved from http://www.cal.org/twi/EvalToolkit/

Maldonado, S. I., & Andrade, R. J. (2018). After the press release on mathematics achievement: The alignment of formative assessments and summative standardized tests for students from minoritized language backgrounds. *Revista de Sociología de la Educación, 11*(3), 421–432.

Maldonado, S. I., Georges, A., Puglisi, J., & Hernandez, M. M. (2018). Partnership pathways in a two-way bilingual immersion program: From evaluation to constructing capacity. *NABE Perspectives, 41*(2), 13–19.

Maldonado, S. I., & Machado-Casas, M. (2019). Sustaining the sociopolitical spirit of bilingual education: Assessment practices and evaluative policies for students minoritized by national background and English-language proficiency. In S. Keengwe & G. Onchwari (Eds.) *Handbook of research on assessment practices and pedagogical models for immigrant students* (pp. 1–17). Hershey, PA: IGI Global.

Musanti, & Rodríguez, (2017). Translanguaging in bilingual teacher preparation: Exploring pre-service bilingual teachers' academic writing. *The Journal of the National Association for Bilingual Education, 40*(1), 38–54. DOI: 10.1080/15235882.2016.1276028

National Association for Bilingual Education. (2018). *Bilingual education teacher standards*. Retrieved from: https://www.multibriefs.com/briefs/nabe/SPAStandards.pdf

National Dual Language Education Teacher Preparation Standards (2018). Retrieved from https://atdle.org/wp-content/uploads/2018/07/ndletps_publicvetting.pdf

Shaw, J. M. (1997). Threats to the validity of science performance assessments for English language learners. *Journal of Research in Science Teaching, 34*(7), 721–743.

Solano-Flores, G., & Nelson-Barber, S. (2001). On the cultural validity of science assessments. *Journal of Research in Science Teaching, 38*(5), 553–573.

Solano-Flores, G., & Soltero-González, L. (2011). Meaningful assessment in linguistically diverse classrooms. In B. B. Flores, R. H. Sheets, & E. R. Clark, *Teacher preparation for bilingual student populations: Educar para transformar* (pp. 146–173). New York: Routledge: Taylor & Francis Group.

Valenzuela, A. (Ed.). (2005). *Leaving children behind: How "Texas-style" accountability fails Latino youth.* SUNY Press.

Valenzuela, A. (Ed.). (2016). *Growing critically conscious teachers: A social justice curriculum for educators of Latino/a youth.* Teachers College Press.

# *Evaluation Processes for Bilingual Education*

# 1. Prioritizing Sociocultural Competence as Indicator of Quality in Dual-language Programs: Cultural, Historical, Identity, Socio-emotional, Pedagogy, Action and Sustainability (CHISPAS)

VERONICA JOHNSON
*San Diego State University*

JANET GABRIELA CARIÑO RAMSAY
*San Diego State University*

SAÚL I. MALDONADO
*San Diego State University*

## *Ideological Clarity and Culturally Responsive Pedagogy*

Bilingual education programs in the United States exist to support students that are developing their English-language fluency and literacy (Flores & García, 2017). Although numerous bilingual education programs are available, our study focuses on dual language programs that promote students' grade-level academic achievement, bilingualism and biliteracy, and sociocultural competence. Recent legislative mandates in California (i.e., Proposition 58) have created the social conditions for school districts and communities to consider developing or increasing dual language programs. Guadalupe Valdés (1997) analyzed the relationship of language and power in dual language programs and proposed intergroup relations as indicative of quality programming. In our experiences as teachers implementing dual language programs at elementary schools and at a university bilingual teacher preparation program, we have found that prioritizing students' sociocultural competence is often neglected in curriculum, instruction and assessment.

We are bilingual education teachers of color with social justice values that design and implement learning experiences that disrupt dominant, hegemonic and status quo power dynamics in schools (Darder, 2018). We teach for social change to transform the racial-ethnic neutrality, heteronormativity, and meritocracy our students experience in schools and therefore value sociocultural competence as a learning goal in bilingual education programs. Although there is an abundance of research literature regarding the importance of teaching for social justice, we have found it challenging to identify specific social justice frameworks, tools and instruments for bilingual education programs, particularly in elementary schools, where cognitive and cultural sophistication is required to introduce and support students in developing critical interpretations of cultural and historical processes such as civil rights, gender studies and language equity.

We have developed a reflective process tool for teachers that prioritize students' sociocultural development in dual language schools. We designed this tool for current and future teachers and administrators of dual language programs as well as bilingual teacher educators and administrators at universities that are committed to designing and implementing learning experiences that support children in understanding the complexities of power differentials in society and disrupting manifestations of bias, microaggressions, prejudice and discrimination in schools. Our purpose in designing this tool was to provide our colleagues with suggestive practical guidance regarding how to analyze the relationship between curriculum, instruction and assessment in dual language schools and students' sociocultural competence.

The development of our reflective process tool was informed by our co-developed framework of ideological clarity and culturally responsive pedagogy in dual language programs (Alfaro & Hernández, 2016; Ladson-Billings, 1995; Thomas & Collier, 2014). We selected students' sociocultural competence as the most appropriate learning goal for bridging students' familial pride and culture, heritage and identity as well as compassion and empathy for all community members. We are hopeful that a deeper understanding of how to design and implement learning experiences that develop students' sociocultural competence in dual language programs will improve upon superficial notions of tolerance and promote cultural understanding as a sustainable solution to fear, division, and hatred in schools and society. Although not specific to students' sociocultural competence in dual language schools, the design of our tool was informed by existing frameworks, tools and instruments for curricular materials and instructional practices in California Schools.

## California State Standards and Frameworks

Teachers in California schools use standards and frameworks to design and implement learning experiences to over 6 million students. Standards define the knowledge, concepts, and skills for each grade and frameworks are curricular guidelines for implementing the standards. The *History-Social Science Framework for Public Schools (HSSF)* features evaluative criteria for teachers and administrators to evaluate the role of instructional materials in "furthering the collective goal of creating, active, engaged, and civic-minded students" (California Department of Education, 2017, p. v). Specifically, *HSSF* requires instructional materials portray the experiences, roles and contributions of "lesbian, gay, bisexual, and transgender Americans; persons with disabilities; and members of other ethnic and cultural groups to the total development of California and the United States," including immigrants, Natives, African Americans, Mexican Americans, Asian Americans, Pacific Islanders and Filipino Americans (*Education Code*, § 60040). Using *HSSF* criteria as guidance, we analyzed the content of the *K-12 History-Social Science Content Standards* and found none of the grade-specific knowledge, concepts and skill goals were explicitly written to develop students' understanding of LGBTQ experiences, persons with disabilities, or socio-economic classification (California Department of Education, 2000). Additionally, K-6 standards superficially reference Natives, immigrants, and Mexicans as cultural groups of importance only in relation to prior periods of history and completely ignore the social, cultural and political contributions of African Americans, Asian Americans and Pacific Islanders. The omission and limited representation of such learning goals in the K-6 state standards communicates that developing students' knowledge, concepts and skills in history-social science is learning about past eras, persons and events, such as colonization and immigration, without making connections to the present, such as crimmigration. First grade is the only K-6 grade where standards require teachers prepare students to know and understand how beliefs, customs, traditions and social practices provide continuity and community to persons of diverse backgrounds in the United States. Teachers in dual language schools are responsible for developing students' sociocultural competence in all grades and therefore require additional standards and frameworks beyond the *K-12 History-Social Science Content Standards* to design and implement appropriate learning experiences.

With the primary goal of developing students' global competency and literacy, the *California World Languages Standards (CWLS)* are organized into three strands: (a) communication, (b) cultures and (c) connections (California Department of Education, 2019). Additionally, *CWLS* are connected to students' development instead of grade levels and are designed for heterogeneity in language learners and communities, including recent immigrants, and importantly, describe learning languages and learning cultures as a concurrent process. Moreover, *CWLS* explicitly aligns to state policies (e.g., Proposition 58, Global California 2030) promoting students' linguistic, global and intercultural competency in dual language schools and offers valuable guidance to teachers developing students' sociocultural competence. *CWLS* is comprised of four cultures standards: (a) culturally appropriate interaction, (b) cultural products, practices and perspectives, (c) cultural comparisons, and (d) intercultural influences. Each standard is associated with a learning goal and students' learning is evaluated on a range that includes four categories: novice, intermediate, advanced and superior. One example of a learning goal of the cultures strand of the *CWLS* includes students' investigating the relationship between cultural products, practices and perspectives. Our analysis of the *CWLS* concluded that the knowledge, concepts and skills featured in the cultures strand are an appropriate reference framework for designing process tools to develop students' sociocultural competence in dual language programs. Specifically, assessment tools and evaluation processes could include measures of students' development of emotional literacy via self-awareness, community building and understanding as well as empathetic interactions (California Department of Education, 2019, p. 1).

### *Guiding Principles for Dual Language Education and Cultural Proficiency*

Unlike the *K-12 History-Social Science Content Standards* and the *California World Languages Standards*, the *Guiding Principles for Dual Language Education (GPDLE)* are specifically designed to support dual language programs' learning goals of developing students' bilingualism, biliteracy, grade-level academic achievement, and sociocultural competence, which includes "identity development, cross-cultural competence, and multicultural appreciation" (Howard, Lindholm-Leary, Rogers, Olague, Medina, Kennedy, Sugarman, & Christian, 2018, p. 3). *GPDLE* is a comprehensive resource for teachers and administrators of K-12 dual language programs that includes process tools for planning, assessing and improving dual language programs. The *GPDLE* framework is organized into seven strands: (a) program structure, (b) curriculum, (c) instruction, (d) assessment and accountability, (e) staff quality and professional development, (f) family and community, and (g) support and resources. Each strand includes guiding principles and key points with progress indicators on a range of four categorical levels of alignment: minimal, partial, full, and exemplary. We identified which of the framework's strands, guiding principles and key points would inform the design of assessment tools and evaluation processes for developing students' sociocultural competence (Table 1-1) and identified specific criteria for evaluating if and to what extent curriculum in dual language programs: (a) "promotes appreciation of multiculturalism and linguistic diversity" and is (b) culturally responsive and representative of the cultural and linguistic backgrounds of all students (Howard et al., 2018 p. 42). Considering the diversity in communities and school contexts of dual language programs, our review of the *GPDLE* resource reinforced our commitment to equity and access in both ideological stances and pedagogical practices as a prerequisite condition for developing dual-language students' sociocultural competence (Alfaro & Hernández, 2016).

Although *GPDLE, California World Languages Standards,* and *K-12 History-Social Science Content Standards* are informative to all dual language stakeholders, we identified the *Guiding Principles of Cultural Proficiency (GPCP) framework* and the *Cultural Proficiency Continuum (CPC)* as complementary reference tools for bilingual teacher educators and administrators at universities preparing teachers to design and implement learning experiences for K-12 students' sociocultural competence (Lindsay, Nuri-Robins, Terrell, & Lindsey, 2019). The *GPCP* framework is comprised of nine statements that articulate how cultural knowledge, concepts and skills could be introduced, performed and assessed at institutions of higher education, such as, "School systems must recognize that marginalized populations have to be at least bicultural and that this status creates a distinct set of issues to which the system must be equipped to respond" (Lindsay et al., 2019, p. 119). The *CPC* is a tool that includes six points for assessing the sociocultural competence of both individuals and institutions: (a) destructiveness, (b) incapacity, (c) blindness, (d) pre-competence, (e) competence and (f) proficiency. Our analysis of the *GPCP* and the *CPC* concluded that such frameworks were important resources to inform the design of assessment tools and evaluation processes for teacher educators and administrators developing teacher candidates' sociocultural competence at colleges and universities. Additionally, we considered the classification system of *either* reactive tolerance for mandated equality *or* proactive transformation for desired equity a useful process tool for evaluating the curriculum, instruction and assessment of bilingual teacher

*Table 1-1. Guiding Principles for Dual Language Education,* Curriculum Strand, Principle 2, Key Point D

| Key Point D<br>*The curriculum promotes appreciation of multiculturalism and linguistic diversity* | | | |
|---|---|---|---|
| **Minimal Alignment** | **Partial Alignment** | **Full Alignment** | **Exemplary Practice** |
| The curriculum provides minimal opportunities for students to develop positive attitudes about themselves and others in a non-stereotyped fashion. Multicultural resources are scarce in both languages and may not be authentic. Only standard language varieties are used in curricular materials. | The curriculum provides some opportunities for students to develop positive attitudes about themselves and others in a non-stereotyped fashion. Multicultural resources are used to some extent (e.g., in one language or content area only) and may not be authentic. Multiple language varieties and registers are sometimes used in curricular materials. | The curriculum provides multiple opportunities for students to develop positive attitudes about themselves and others in a non-stereotyped fashion. Authentic multicultural resources are used for instruction in both languages. Multiple language varieties and registers are regularly used in curricular materials. | The curriculum provides multiple opportunities for students to develop positive attitudes about themselves and others in a non-stereotyped fashion. Authentic multicultural resources are used for instruction in both languages. Multiple language varieties and registers are regularly used in curricular materials. Collaborations with external partners (e.g., community members, international organizations) are created to extend the appreciation of multiculturalism and linguistic diversity to real-world contexts. |

preparation programs as *either* exemplifying cultural differences as problematic and deficit-based and perpetuating systemic and institutional oppression *or* exemplifying proactive transformation views of cultural diversity as assets for organizational practices and personal behaviors with institutional structures that regularly disrupt manifestations of bias, microaggressions, prejudice and discrimination.

## *Social Justice Standards and Curriculum Design Elements*

As bilingual education teachers, we have found it useful to reference the *Social Justice Standards (SJS)*, a framework inspired by early education research that is comprised of four domains, twenty standards, and eighty grade-specific outcomes and scenarios (Derman-Sparks, 1989; Southern Poverty Law Center, 2016). Available in both Spanish and English, the framework domains of *SJS* are: identidad, diversidad, justicia y accíon. Although *SJS* is not specific for teachers and administrators of K-12 dual language programs, our analysis concluded that the outcomes and scenarios are appropriate references to inform the design of assessment tools and evaluations processes for developing students' sociocultural competence at elementary, middle and high schools. Specifically, *SJS* is informative to designing and implementing curriculum to explicitly address anti-bias, multicultural and social justice as well as for meeting learning goals of prejudice reduction and collective action advocacy. Additionally, the *SJS* framework is associated with a digital repository of classroom resources that includes a learning plan feature where educators can connect sociocultural competence goals to ready-to-implement classroom lessons with associated performance assessment tasks on topics such as race-ethnicity, class, ability, immigration and activism.

Another framework that we found informative to designing and implementing learning experiences that support students' sociocultural competence is the *Elements of Social Justice Curriculum Design (ESJCD)*. Although not designed specifically for dual language educators, *ESJCD* provides six curriculum design elements for educators with social justice values to consider when designing and implementing classroom learning experiences. The *ESJSCD* design elements are: (a) self-love and knowledge, (b) respect for others, (c) issues of social injustice, (d) social movements and social change, (e) awareness raising, and (f) social action. Picower (2012) highlights specific student outcomes associated with curriculum informed by the *ESJCD* framework: recognition of individual and community strengths, respect for the history and characteristics of persons different from themselves, examination of the relationship between identities and oppression as well as learning about and practicing social action activities. Combined, our analysis of *SJS* and *ESJCD* frameworks, tools and instruments concluded that the development of students' sociocultural competence in dual language programs will require the explicit integration of learning experiences that are associated with action-oriented outcomes that disrupt heteronormativity, xenophobia and gentrification as well as a range of social action activities, from role-playing cultural and historical representations of past and present social movements to conducting interviews, creating public announcements and participating in public meetings, campaigns and protests.

Our ideological clarity and our commitment to students' development of sociocultural competence in dual language schools (Alfaro & Hernández,

2016; Howard et al., 2018), informed our review and analysis of existing frameworks, tools and instruments for evaluating the appropriateness of curricular materials and instructional practices in California Schools. Our review and analysis revealed the need to contribute a reflective process tool for current and future teachers and administrators of dual language programs as well as bilingual teacher educators and administrators at universities that are committed to designing and implementing learning experiences that develop students' sociocultural competence. We designed this tool with the purpose of providing our colleagues with suggestive practical guidance regarding how to analyze the relationship between curriculum, instruction and assessment in dual language schools and students' sociocultural competence. Specifically, we designed a tool for teachers to assess if and to what extent curriculum design elements as well as instructional practices promote students' sociocultural competence with active learning participation opportunities to understand and refute Eurocentric values, white supremacy, racial-ethnic neutrality and meritocracy from individual, interpersonal and institutional perspectives.

## *Method*

Informed by our co-developed framework of ideological clarity and culturally responsive pedagogy we developed Cultural, historical, identity, socio-emotional, pedagogy, action and sustainability (CHISPAS), a reflective process tool for current and future teachers and administrators of dual language programs as well as bilingual teacher educators and administrators at universities (Table 1-2). We used our review of standards and frameworks to co-design a reflective process tool for bilingual educators to analyze the relationship between curriculum, instruction and assessment in dual language schools and students' sociocultural competence. CHISPAS is comprised of four categories: (a) domains, (b) teacher reflections, (c) considerations for students, and (d) measures to analyze curriculum, instruction and assessment. Domains of sociocultural competence include: cultural, historical, identity, socio-emotional, pedagogy, action and sustainability. We designed the teacher reflections category as prompts for educators to reflect on their experiences and current instructional practices; and the category, considerations for students, as prompts to consider for creating sociocultural competence learning goals. We created the last category, curriculum, instruction and assessment (CIA), as a tool to evaluate if learning materials and instructional practices develop students' sociocultural competence. We piloted the tool in our analysis of literature and imagery from World-Book (2019), a pseudonym for a K-6 Spanish and English literacy curriculum from an educational publishing company.

Table 1-2. *CHISPAS Tool for Assessing Sociocultural Competence in California's Dual Language Schools*

| Domains | Teacher Reflections | Considerations for Students | Curriculum, Instruction & Assessment (CIA) |
|---|---|---|---|
| Cultural | –How do I define culture?<br>–What are my multiple cultural groups?<br>–How do I learn and teach about other cultural groups?<br>–How do I promote diversity as an asset and implement culturally responsive education? | –How do students define culture?<br>–What are students' cultural groups and language backgrounds?<br>–How do students learn about: (a) race-ethnicity, (b) social class and (c) gender spectrum?<br>–How do students learn about beliefs, customs, traditions and cultural practices? | –Is CIA aligned to cultural standards and objectives?<br>–Does CIA promote appreciation of multiculturalism and linguistic diversity?<br>–Is CIA representative of students' cultural and linguistic backgrounds?<br>–Does CIA develop students' understanding of LGBT experiences, persons with disabilities, or socio-economic classification? |
| Historical | –How did my social, cultural, and political experiences influence my decision to become an educator?<br>–What is the historical context of our school, district and community?<br>–What persons and events influenced our school's vision, district goals, and community participation objectives? | –How do students learn the social, cultural and political contributions about past eras, persons and events and make meaningful connections to the present (e.g., colonization and immigration)?<br>–How do students learn about power dynamics in school and community? | –Is CIA aligned to history standards and objectives?<br>–Does CIA develop students' understanding of historical processes such as civil rights, gender studies and language equity?<br>–Does CIA make meaningful connections between past eras and contemporary events?<br>–Does CIA provide students an opportunity to role-play and analyze historical representations of past and present social movements? |

*Continued*

Table 1-2. Continued

| Domains | Teacher Reflections | Considerations for Students | Curriculum, Instruction & Assessment (CIA) |
|---|---|---|---|
| Identity | –How do I define my identity?<br>–What is the relationship between my identity and my cultural groups?<br>–How do I develop students' self-awareness, community pride, and positive social identity?<br>–How do I develop students' compassion and empathy for all community members? | –How do students define identity?<br>–How do students learn about the visible and invisible characteristics that co-construct their personal and social identity?<br>–How do students learn that identity is unique, complex and dynamic?<br>–How do students negotiate the relationship between identity characteristics and dominant cultures in school and community? | –Does CIA develop the visible and invisible characteristics of students' identity?<br>–Does CIA include measures of emotional literacy, such as self-awareness and self-love?<br>–Does CIA provide opportunities for students to describe and analyze their personal and social identity characteristics?<br>–Does CIA provide opportunities for students to examine the relationship between identities and oppression? |
| Socio-emotional | –How do I define bias, stereotypes, educational equity and social justice?<br>–What microaggressions have I experienced?<br>–How do I develop a safe and inclusive learning environment?<br>–How do I contribute to improving the health and wellness of students, families and communities? | –How do students define community?<br>–How do students learn about the relationship between bias, stereotypes, individuals, community and society?<br>–How do students develop awareness of issues of social injustice and social change?<br>–How do students learn about neurodiversity and diverse physical abilities?<br>–How do students learn to express empathy and concern for others? | –Is CIA aligned to social science standards and objectives?<br>–Is CIA aligned to social and emotional learning guiding principles?<br>–Does CIA explicitly disrupt bias, stereotypes, microaggressions, prejudice and discrimination?<br>–Does CIA provide opportunities for students to describe and analyze social movements?<br>–Does CIA develop students' global competency, community building, empathy and compassion toward others? |

Table 1-2. Continued

| Domains | Teacher Reflections | Considerations for Students | Curriculum, Instruction & Assessment (CIA) |
|---|---|---|---|
| Pedagogy | –How do I teach and asses sociocultural competence?<br>–What resources do I use to develop students' sociocultural competence?<br>–What is my social and political ideology as an educator?<br>–What values and theories influence my lessons and units?<br>–How do I create universal access for all students?<br>–How do I honor students' assets and funds of knowledge? | –How do students define sociocultural competence?<br>–How do students co-create and participate in dialogical learning?<br>–How do students contribute to validating instructional practices and assessments?<br>–How do students analyze and recommend modifications to curriculum, instruction and assessment? | –Is CIA aligned to dual language principles of sociocultural competence?<br>–Is sociocultural competence represented in CIA from both languages of instruction?<br>–Is sociocultural competence represented in all content areas?<br>–Does CIA provide opportunities for students to compare and critique curriculum, instruction and assessment materials? |
| Action | –How do I define collective action advocacy?<br>–How do I advocate for collective action at our school, district and community?<br>–How do I develop students' social activism? | –How do students define collective action advocacy?<br>–How do students learn about the positive and challenging attributes of participating in social action activities?<br>–How do students learn about and practice disrupting heteronormativity, xenophobia and gentrification?<br>–How do students learn about and practice planning and implementing local and global collective action against bias and injustice? | –Does CIA provide opportunities for students to become active, engaged, and civic-minded students?<br>–Does CIA make meaningful connections bilingual education programs, civil rights and language equity?<br>–Does CIA provide opportunities for students to conduct interviews, create public announcements and participate in public meetings, campaigns or protests? |

*Continued*

*Table 1-2. Continued*

| Domains | Teacher Reflections | Considerations for Students | Curriculum, Instruction & Assessment (CIA) |
|---|---|---|---|
| *Sustainability* | –How do I define sustainability at our school, district and community?<br>–How do I implement CHISPAS to evaluate curriculum, instruction and assessment?<br>–How do I communicate findings from CHISPAS evaluations to students, families, community members and colleagues? | –How do students define sustainability at our school, district and community?<br>–What resources and tools do students use to measure sociocultural competence?<br>–What resources and tools do students use to address fear, division and hatred in schools and society? | –Does CIA primarily promote Eurocentric values, white supremacy, racial-ethnic neutrality and meritocracy?<br>–Does CIA contribute to sustaining and perpetuating students' sociocultural competence consistently throughout a preK-12 pathway?<br>–Is developing students' sociocultural competence a priority across all strands of dual language guiding principles? |

World-Book in English was designed to address California's English-language arts as well as Integrated and Designated English-language development standards. World-Book in Spanish was designed to address Spanish-language arts as well as Spanish-language development standards, using authentic literature from Spanish-speaking authors. World-Book has been adopted by many school districts in California for both English-only as well as dual immersion programs. World-Book is structured as a series of three-week units that prioritizes five thematic objectives: (a) building content knowledge, (b) meaning making, (c) effective expression, (d) foundational skills, and (e) language development. World-Book suggests twenty instructional days to establish classroom routines followed by 10 3-week units that purposefully integrate both science and social science content standards. Unit cycles are structured around "short reads" in week one and around "extended reads" in weeks two and three. The content knowledge strand of the 10 units are vertically aligned across all K-6 grades by unit topics and essential questions. Each unit includes literature for read-alouds, shared readings and guided readings as well as writing fluency and language development exercises.

*Literature.* We referenced CHISPAS to evaluate if and to what extent World-Book literature developed students' sociocultural competence in language immersion programs. We analyzed the "extended reads" literature selections in three kindergarten units that integrated social science standards: (a) Rules at Home and School, (b) Every Story has Characters, and (c) Writer's Tell Many Stories. We referenced the CHISPAS cultural, identity and action domains to asses if and to what extent the selected World-Book literature (a) developed students' self-awareness, community pride and positive social identity, (b) made meaningful connections to language equity, and (c) promoted multiculturalism and linguistic diversity.

First, we reviewed the learning objectives of the three units and concluded that literature selections did not develop students' sociocultural competence. Learning objectives prioritized literacy knowledge and skills such as reading fluency, genre-recognition and comparison, as well as identification of main ideas and details without explicit alignment to cultural standards and learning objectives. We also analyzed the degree of authenticity of the extended reads literature selections and found that most World-Book in Spanish extended readings were direct translations from World-Book in English materials, with the exception of the Writer's Tell Many Stories unit. For example, the World-Book in Spanish unit, Every Story has Characters, translated Eurocentric folk tales instead of presenting fables from authentic Spanish-speaking cultural contexts. This finding revealed a missed opportunity to develop students' self-awareness, community pride and positive social identity. Finally, we also cross-referenced *The Guiding Principles of Dual Language Education* and concluded that World-Book "extended reads" minimally promote the appreciation of multiculturalism and linguistic diversity. Although learning materials are available in both Spanish and English, the literature is: (a) not authentic, (b) does not represent dialect variations, (c) does not develop students' understanding of LGBTQ experiences, persons with disabilities, or socio-economic classification, (d) does not provide opportunities for students to describe and analyze their personal and social identity characteristics, and (e) does not make meaningful connections to bilingual education programs, civil rights and language equity.

*Curricular Modifications.* After identifying World-Book literature minimally developed students' sociocultural competence, we reviewed the CHISPAS categories, teacher reflections and considerations for students, to identify potential curricular modifications. First, we accessed the trade books listed in the World-Book repository, classified as supplemental resources, and we identified titles that were more likely to be authentic and include content that: (a) promoted diversity, as well as (b) was representative of students' cultural and linguistic backgrounds. We also identified cultural standards and learning objectives from the *California World Languages Standards (CWLS)* and the *Social Justice Standards (SJS)* that appropriately complemented the literacy knowledge and skills prioritized by World-Book.

We selected the World-Book unit, Writer's Tell Many Stories to make curricular modifications. First, we modified the learning goal, "In this unit, students read and compare stories to understand the purpose of storytelling," to "In this unit, students will read and compare stories to understand the purpose of storytelling as well as learn about themselves and others." We also included diversity standards from *SJS* to identify complementary student learning objectives: (a) I like being around people who are like me and different from me, and I can be friendly to everyone, and (b) I can describe some ways that I am similar to and different from people who share my identities and those who have other identities. Finally, we identified World-Book supplemental literature resources that were authentic and representative of students' cultural backgrounds.

We designed and implemented a three-week curricular unit focused on differences and similarities of persons' visible characteristics of identity. First, students read *Somos diferentes* by Maribel Suárez, a World-Book supplemental literature resource, to understand and develop vocabulary to describe visible characteristics of identity. The students were able to develop a writing piece with the following sentence frame: *Yo soy especial porque* . . . We purposefully selected the qualifier, special, to develop students' self-awareness and positive social identity.

Next, students developed a self-portrait using sentence frames for writing and collaborative conversation discussion prompts, such as: *Mi pelo es* . . ., and *Mis ojos son* . . . to compare and contrast (*Soy igual que* . . . *Soy diferente porque* . . .) self-portraits with classmates. Lastly, students referenced *Somos diferentes* and their self-portraits to co-develop a definition for culture. Using a graphic organizer with a definition and a sentence with culture as a vocabulary word, framed how students learned about the contribution of invisible characteristics (*Mi familia es* . . ., and *Mis lenguajes son* . . .) to constructing personal and social identity. Importantly, students' comprehension of the visible and invisible characteristics of identity was complementary to the literacy goals of contrasting stories to understand the purpose of storytelling.

*Images.* We also used CHISPAS to evaluate if and to what extent World-Book images contributed to developing students' sociocultural competence in language immersion programs. Particularly in dual language programs, images are critical text features for making content comprehensible in the process of acquiring bilingualism and biliteracy. We analyzed the images in student workbooks for the first unit, "Government and Citizenship," in kindergarten, third and fourth grades: (a) Rules at Home and School, (b) Government for the People, and (c) Government in Action, respectively. We referenced the CHISPAS cultural and identity domains, and *The Guiding Principles of Dual*

*Language Education,* to asses if and to what extent the selected World-Book images (a) developed students' self-awareness, community pride and positive social identity, and (b) promoted multiculturalism and linguistic diversity.

First, we analyzed the three images of the kindergarten workbook, Rules at Home and School, that featured photographs of persons (we excluded drawings and pictures from our analysis), and concluded that two images minimally promoted the appreciation of multiculturalism and linguistic diversity and one image fully promoted the appreciation of multiculturalism and linguistic diversity. One image featured four children in a classroom, in a single-file line; another image featured two children playing soccer; and the last image featured an adult and child in close proximity. The image of the four children in a classroom only features white students, with normative gender attire and embedded text is in English (although the workbook is in Spanish). The image of the two children playing soccer only features white boys and is also prominently featured by World-Book on the cover of the workbook as well as on the table of contents. The image of the adult and child feature a man and child of color.

Next, we analyzed the twenty images of the third-grade workbook, Government for the People, and concluded that five images minimally promoted the appreciation of multiculturalism and linguistic diversity; 14 images partially promoted the appreciation of multiculturalism and linguistic diversity; and one image fully promoted the appreciation of multiculturalism and linguistic diversity. An example of minimal promotion of multiculturalism and linguistic diversity is the cover of the workbook, an image that features six children's hands raised in front of a chalkboard. Only one of the six hands belong to a child of color. An example of partial promotion of multiculturalism and linguistic diversity is the photograph of the Women's Suffrage March, which provides opportunities for students to develop a positive social identity of white women—without referencing linguistic diversity. Another example of partial promotion of multiculturalism and linguistic diversity is the photograph of Thurgood Marshall, which provides opportunities for students to develop a positive social identity of Black men—without referencing linguistic diversity. An example of full promotion of multiculturalism and linguistic diversity is the photograph of the March on Washington, an image that features persons of diverse racial-ethnic and gender backgrounds participating in a public protest for collective social action: school integration, employment opportunities and fair housing demands. Although this image provides students an opportunity to analyze historical representations of past social movements and make meaningful connections to civil rights, none of the print in the photograph promotes linguistic diversity.

Finally, we analyzed the 10 images of the fourth-grade workbook, Government for the Action, and concluded that six images minimally promoted the appreciation of multiculturalism and linguistic diversity; two images partially promoted the appreciation of multiculturalism and linguistic diversity; and two images fully promoted the appreciation of multiculturalism and linguistic diversity. An example of minimal promotion of multiculturalism and linguistic diversity is an image that features two rescue workers and two rescue dogs at a playground with a child and two adults. All persons featured in the image are white, with normative gender attire and embedded text in English (although the workbook is in Spanish). Moreover, the print materials include references to the U.S. Department of Homeland Security and the Federal Emergency Management Agency, government organizations that are not always associated with the positive social identity of children of color. An example of partial promotion of multiculturalism and linguistic diversity is the photograph of President Barack Obama presiding over a legislative meeting in the U.S. government. Although the image of the president and others in the photograph provide students opportunities to develop a positive social identity of Black men, and persons of color, the overwhelming numerical majority of the hundreds of persons in the photograph are white. An example of full promotion of multiculturalism and linguistic diversity is the image of six persons at a ribbon-cutting ceremony and the accompanying Spanish-language caption reads, "Los gobernadores participan en ceremonias especiales." Additionally, only two of the six persons are white and three of the six persons are women. Although this photograph provides students an opportunity to view an example of active, engaged and civic-minded women and men of color, the image does not promote linguistic diversity.

*Curricular Modifications.* After identifying World-Book images tended to minimally develop students' sociocultural competence, we reviewed the CHISPAS categories, teacher reflections and considerations for students, to identify potential curricular modifications. We participated in collaborative conversations to articulate recommendations regarding how images could be purposefully selected to communicate our commitment to prioritizing students' sociocultural competence. We recommend substituting the image of the two children playing soccer in the kindergarten workbook with a photograph that includes girls of color, perhaps in an international competition or variance in physical ability. We recommend substituting the image that features six children's hands raised in front of a chalkboard to a photograph that includes at least four of the six hands belonging to children of color, and perhaps representative of diverse physical appearances, such as Vitiligo. We recommend substituting the photograph of President Barack Obama presiding over a legislative meeting with an image of a woman, perhaps Michelle Lynn Lujan Grisham, or a similar legislative meeting with more representation of politicians of color.

## *Developing Pedagogical Responsibility*

Informed by our co-developed framework of ideological clarity and culturally responsive pedagogy we developed CHISPAS as a tool for current and future educators and administrators and bilingual teacher educators and administrators at universities. We piloted CHISPAS to analyze World-Book literature as well as images and found that our existing curriculum, instruction and assessment did not appropriately develop our students' sociocultural competence. Moreover, CHISPAS provided us with reflective questions to examine the relationship between our personal, professional and political experiences and perspectives as well as the instructional practices we prioritize. Interacting with content from the teacher reflections and considerations for students categories of CHISPAS deepened our understanding of how to design and implement learning experiences that support students in developing sociocultural competence.

Teacher reflections required us to bolster our ideological and pedagogical clarity as bilingual education teachers with social justice values. Implementing CHISPAS provided us an opportunity to analyze our pathways and purposes as educators (Alfaro & Hernández, 2016) as well as make explicit the sophisticated demands of teaching and learning in dual language programs (Maldonado, Georges, Puglisi, & Hernández, 2018). Considerations for students guided our creation of sociocultural competence learning objectives. Before creating learning objectives of sociocultural competence for our lessons and units, we needed to learn lessons of definitional consensus and vulnerability. First, we learned that we needed to develop consensus regarding our definitions of culture, identity, community, collective action advocacy and sustainability with each other as well as with our students. We also learned how to be vulnerable with each other and with our students in relation to our experiences with bias, stereotypes, microaggressions, prejudice, discrimination, empathy, and concern for others. The mutually respectful climate of our collective conversations allowed us to examine how our biases perpetuated dominant cultures in school and community via the curriculum we select, the instructional practices we implement, and the assessments we use to measure student learning. Unchallenged policies and practices in schools make educators complicit in the problem of minoritizing students and community members. The curriculum we select either supports or refutes dominant cultures' ideas and values that silence stories from traditionally marginalized groups. We accepted responsibility for our students' minimal opportunities to develop self-awareness, community pride and positive social identity, and we hope CHISPAS contributes to a meaningful contribution. Our suggested curricular modifications to World-Book images were designed to promote multiculturalism and linguistic diversity as well as make meaningful connections to civil rights and language equity.

Although CHISPAS is a tool designed for all teachers, we believe other school level and district level personnel and administration can use the tool to support system transformation at all levels. Specifically, we believe all educators require tools to examine their pathways and purposes as well as how their policies and practices produce and perpetuate Eurocentric values, white supremacy, racial-ethnic neutrality, meritocracy and other hegemonic ideologies that support social class formation and gender inequities (Alfaro & Bartolome, 2017). We believe assessing the relationship between sociocultural competence, curriculum, instruction and assessment provides practical insights regarding high-quality bilingual education programs.

## *Prioritizing Sociocultural Competence*

Our purpose in authoring this chapter was to contribute a tool that assists in the development and implementation of curriculum and instruction that prioritizes sociocultural development for students in the United States. Prioritizing sociocultural competence in bilingual education programs requires attentiveness to students' individual factors, interpersonal factors between students and teachers, and institutional factors of program policies and practices. Prior research demonstrates that socioemotional learning has a significant impact on students' success at all grade levels in behavior, attitudinal and academic development (Howard et al., 2018 Kosciw, Greytak, Giga, Villenas, & Danischewski, 2016). We consider socioemotional learning as one dimension of sociocultural competence that is observable when students express empathy and concern for others different than themselves, outside of their communities, or social groups. When students develop sociocultural competence they value the health and wellness of others and personify a stance that exemplifies that differences are not deficits. A safe and inclusive learning environment where socioemotional learning is valued also develops students' self-awareness, community pride and positive social identity. When students learn about the visible and invisible identity characteristics and analyze their relationship with dominant cultures, community pride is cultivated. Cultivating students' positive social identities provides an opportunity to learn about the social, cultural and political contributions from past eras, persons and events as well participate in courageous conversations about race-ethnicity, social class, the gender spectrum, diverse physical abilities and non-standard language use. Courageous conversations provide students the opportunity to learn about others' identities, as well as their own.

We consider pedagogy, action and sustainable dimensions of sociocultural competence as observable when teachers honor students' assets and funds of knowledge as co-creators of learning experiences. When teachers invite students as participants in dialogical learning, teachers have the opportunity to develop consensus with students regarding definitions of culture, identity, community, collective action advocacy and sustainability. All students have opinions, feelings, motivations and circumstances (Robinson & Aronica, 2015) and they have valuable insights regarding teachers' instructional practices and assessments. Interpersonal factors influence if and how students become active, engaged and civic-minded. Students' motivation to learn about and practice planning and implementing local and global collective action against bias and injustice is only possible when students feel respected by teachers. Teachers that redistribute power dynamics in schools and develop students' social activism create the conditions for self-directed and proactive learning. And, together, in solidarity, students and teachers may co-determine if and to what extent instructional practices and assessments are valid and how to appropriately modify curriculum, instruction and assessment.

Questioning the validity and appropriateness of instructional practices is observable of students' critical thinking and creativity (a pre-condition is a safe and inclusive learning environment). Students and teachers that collectively define sociocultural competence and develop consensus regarding which resources and tools are most appropriate to teach and assess sociocultural competence contribute a sustainable solution to fear, division, and hatred in schools and society. Although we designed CHISPAS for teachers, we hope that colleagues will create the learning conditions necessary to co-analyze curriculum, instruction and assessment with students using the tool. We recommend teachers and students refer to our analyses of literature and images in the World-Book literacy curriculum as a reference point. Teachers may even encourage students' analyses of literature and images in curriculum as measures of students' development of sociocultural competence. For example, when students analyze curricular materials, do they: (a) identify biases and stereotypes, (b) demonstrate positive social identity and (c) exemplify compassion and empathy for community members of diverse cultural groups (particularly from minoritized communities)?

A particular instructional emphasis of dual language programs is to develop students' bilingualism, biliteracy, content-area achievement, as well as connect different persons via cultural practices such as traditions, food, music, and visual and performing arts. Most curricula, and corresponding assessments, are not designed for dual language programs. Howard and colleagues (2018) have identified numerous policy and practice adaptations that may be necessary to create and sustain successful dual language schools and programs. Specifically, the *Guiding Principles for Dual Language Education* call for curricula and assessment that are aligned with meaningful standards related to the three pillars of dual language education: bilingualism, biliteracy, grade-level academic achievement, and sociocultural competence. Our design and implementation of the CHISPAS tool call for a re-imagining of social competence not as one of three pillars but rather as the central pillar that bridges bilingualism and biliteracy with grade-level academic achievement. Dual language educators that prioritize students' sociocultural competence create a bridge between culture, biliteracy and academic achievement where learning becomes student-centered, personalized and meaningful. Another metaphor that is substantiated by our results is framing sociocultural competence as the source of bilingual education programming from which grade-level academic achievement as well as bilingualism and biliteracy flows. We conclude this chapter with potential benefits for teachers, administrators and family members of dual language programs using CHISPAS to evaluate the sociocultural competence of curriculum, instruction and assessment:

1. Educators and administrators will have the opportunity to develop students' sociocultural competence while they promote visual and performing arts, oral language and literacy;
2. Educators and administrators will have the opportunity to use a framework for assessing if and to what extent curriculum, instruction and assessment is culturally-responsive;
3. Educators and administrators may reference the research-based tool (e.g., *Guiding Principles for Dual Language Education, Cultural Proficiency Continuum*) of sociocultural competence to advocate for curricular modifications to ensure fidelity to the model of dual language programs;
4. Educators and administrators may reference the tool to substantiate why curricular modifications are necessary in bilingual education programs;
5. Educators and administrators from both K-12 and higher education bilingual education will have the opportunity to assess the relationship

between their social and political ideology, their pedagogical practices and students' development of sociocultural competence.

# References

Alfaro, C., & Bartolome, L. (2017). Preparing ideologically clear bilingual teachers: Honoring working-class non-standard language use in the bilingual education classroom. *Issues in Teacher Education, 26*(2), 11–34.

Alfaro, C., & Hernández, A. M. (2016). Ideology, pedagogy, access, and equity [IPAE]: A critical examination for dual language educators. *Multilingual Educator, March*, 8–11. https://www.gocabe.org/index.php/communications-2/multilingual-educator/

California Department of Education (2019). *World languages standards for California public schools Kindergarten through grade twelve.* Retrieved from: https://www.cde.ca.gov/be/st/ss/worldlanguage.asp

California Department of Education (2017). *History social science framework for California public schools: Kindergarten through grade twelve.* Retrieved from: https://www.cde.ca.gov/ci/hs/cf/documents/hssframeworkwhole.pdf

California Department of Education (2000). *History-social science content standards for California public schools Kindergarten through grade twelve.* Retrieved from: https://www.cde.ca.gov/be/st/ss/documents/histsocscistnd.pdf

Collier, V. P., & Thomas, W. P. (2014). *Creating dual language schools for a transformed world: Administrators speak.* Albuquerque, NM: Dual Language Education of New Mexico Fuente Press.

Darder, A. (2018). *The student's guide to Freire's 'Pedagogy of the Oppressed.'* Bloomsbury Academic.

Derman-Sparks, L. (1989). *Anti-bias curriculum: Tools for empowering young children.* National Association for the Education of Young Children, Washington, DC. Education Code, 2 California Legislative Information. §1–60040 (2012).

Flores, N., & García, O. (2017). A critical review of bilingual education in the United States: From basements and pride to boutiques and profit. *Annual Review of Applied Linguistics, 37*, 14–29.

Howard, E. R., Lindholm-Leary, K. J., Rogers, D., Olague, N., Medina, J., Kennedy, D., Sugarman, J., & Christian, D. (2018). *Guiding principles for dual language education* (3rd ed.). Washington, DC: Center for Applied Linguistics.

Kosciw, J. G., Greytak, E. A., Giga, N. M., Villenas, C., & Danischewski, D. J. (2016). The 2015 National School Climate Survey: The experiences of lesbian, gay, bisexual, transgender, and queer youth in our nation's schools. *Report from GLSEN.* Retrieved from: www.glsen.org

Ladson-Billings, G. (1995). But that's just good teaching! The case for culturally relevant pedagogy. *Theory Into Practice, 34*(3), 159–165.

Lindsey, R. B., Nuri-Robins, K., Terrrel, R. D., & Lindsey, D. B. (2019). *Cultural proficiency a manual for school leaders* (4th ed.). Thousand Oaks, CA: Corwin Sage Publications.

Maldonado, S. I., Georges, A., Puglisi, J., & Hernandez, M. M. (2018). Partnership pathways in a two-way bilingual immersion program: From evaluation to constructing capacity. *NABE Perspectives, 41*(2), 13–19.

Picower, B. (2012) Using their words: Six elements of social justice curriculum design for the elementary classroom. *International Journal of Multicultural Education, 14*(1), 1–17.

Robinson, K., & Aronica, L. (2015). *Creative schools: The grassroots revolution that's transforming education.* New York: Viking Penguin.

Southern Poverty Law Center (2016). *Social justice standards: The teaching tolerance anti-bias framework.* Retrieved from: https://www.tolerance.org/magazine/publications/social-justice-standards

Valdés, G. (1997). Dual-language immersion programs: A cautionary note concerning the education of language-minority students. *Harvard Educational Review, 67*(3), 391–429.

World-Book (a pseudonym) (2019). Retrieved from: http://california.benchmarkeducation.com/

## 2. Advancing the Achievement of Dual Language Learners through Program Evaluation: A Framework for Assessing the Effectiveness and Impact of Dual Language Programs

ALEXANDRA S. GUILAMO
TaJu Educational Solutions

There is no doubt that the students educated in U.S. classrooms have undergone massive changes with each generation. And since 2014, U.S. classrooms have reflected a new majority demographic of students that were once considered minorities (Maxwell, 2014). In fact, as of 2017, "the young Dual Language Learner (DLL) population in the United States has grown by 24 percent," (Park, O'Toole, & Katsiaficas, p. 1). This shift has serious implications for schools all across the country. When more than one third of all U.S. students in grades Pre-K—3$^{rd}$ grade are emergent bilinguals (Park, Zong, & Batalova, p. 33), the educational imperative shifts for us all: "improve the quality and impact of instruction for this growing number of students or face the consequence of a nation's majority without the expertise and training necessary to be our future workforce" (Guilamo, 2020, p. 4).

In an effort to rise to the occasion, many school communities have shifted both policy and program offerings to include dual language (DL) programs. With its promise of bilingualism/biliteracy, academic achievement, and socio-cultural competence (Howard et al., 2018), many K-12 schools have been quick to make the change. So much so, that in the year 2000, the US only had about 260 DL programs documented across the nation. However, even though the federal education department has been unable to provide an exact number of current DL programs, the Harvard Graduate School of

Education (2011) reported that this number had grown to around 2,000 in 2011, and has more than doubled that figure as of 2019.

This growth and expansion are exciting—one that honors the content, language, and cultural competencies needed to truly prepare our students for a changing world. However, the budding programs and the educators that serve them are in varying stages of expertise, understanding of critical program components, capacity to identify strategic priorities and agency over a continuous improvement process that is not designed with a "one size fits all" approach. If Dual Language (DL) programs are to change the narrative of low achievement and increasing drop-out rates for DLL's, they will need support in understanding the impact of their DL programs thus far and in creating a clear path for improving outcomes for all. This requires a clear framework to improve outcomes, capacity building and alignment of resources.

The benefits of dual language education (Berman et al., 1995; Collier & Thomas, 2007; de Jong, 2011; Genesee et al., 2006; Lindholm-Leary, 2001; Lindholm-Leary & Genesee, 2010; Montecel & Cortez, 2002), and the need for well-prepared and supported DL educators leverages additive bilingual education and second language acquisition theories (Collier, 1992; García, 2009; Guerrero, 1997) along with exemplary practices that serve dual language learners has long been documented. The effectiveness of these programs depends on the success of the implementation efforts themselves, and the decisions-making process needed to support the changes being made at multiple levels. A range of decision making models (Keefer, Kirkwood & Comer, 2004; Skinner, 2009) serve as the basis for the framework outlined, along with teacher agency, and the ability for educators to implement change through phases (Fullan, 2007). All change, like implementing or improving a DL program, is a process with both individual and organizational factors impacting its success (Fullan, 2007).

## *Five Essential Pre-requisites to the Framework's Success*

*Dual Language Leadership Teams (DLLTs).* Dual language leadership teams (DLLTs) are the first prerequisite to building a comprehensive framework and DL programs must first understand who that team represents. There is no exact formula for who should be on the DLLT—it is a reflection of (and different for) each school community. In general, though, DLLTs are comprised of 5–10 committed people that represent the school's diverse perspectives and share a commitment and earnest care for the success of the students served by the program.

More than the size of the group, the diverse ways of seeing or understanding issues and their commitment to the DL program's success are critical factors in the success of this team. Because of the range of connection to the program's success, these diverse lenses could include: parent, support staff, site-based leaders, the program principal, district leaders and (at the secondary levels where appropriate) student-leaders. Having this diversity of perspectives helps to uncover the range of shifts and implications across all layers of the schools' community—from the implications of homework, grading policies, assessment systems and data infrastructures, communication tools, effective instructional practices, resources and much more. In short, implementing effective and sustainable DL programs without a DLLT is quite challenging. In the long run, they will play a vital role in DL programs' ability and effectiveness in assessing the effectiveness and impact of their programs. Then based on the assessment findings, the DLLT will be instrumental in sharing their passion, advocacy efforts, and knowledge of those foundational bodies of research and principles that informed the improvement plan that will follow.

*Shared Mission & Vision.* This group's dedication and will to understand the 'ins and outs' of how their DL program impacts dual language students, and emergent bilinguals especially, stems from earnest care and value for a mission that is bigger than any one person in the system. In order to realize the 'dream' of DL education, there must be a clear mission, vision, and set of goals that guides the many steps that will need to be taken to ensure program success. And this is complex work, regardless of whether or not the DLLT and broader school community spent the necessary time to develop a shared mission and vision for their new school reality. All DLLT's and DL programs will regularly need to reflect on how close their programs are to that mission and vision, as well as what the program model was designed to be. For many, it is only through this reflection on the gaps that exist between the current reality and the original mission and vision, that the opportunities for change and improvement become clear to the broader school community.

One critical benefit of a well-developed mission and vision is that it will serve as a reminder of the core values, beliefs and grass-root beginnings of bilingual and dual language education. However, this anchoring can only happen for those DLLTs that have developed the requisite knowledge and understanding of the program they have chosen to implement before implementation. There are many schools, districts, and regional offices of education that have chosen to implement DL programs without a full understanding of the shifts that are necessary to ensure their success and so will never see the positive effects and outcomes that were promised. That is why it is important to note pillar three (socio-cultural competency), in particular, as we discuss the necessity of a shared mission and vision. DL programs were born from a grave need to move beyond programmatic resources and quick fixes that leverage little of what we know about how language is acquired and leveraged, which continue to result in the under-education of the students served by those programs.

Any mission and vision that does not include socio-cultural competency as a core component will likely continue the pattern of under-education/underachievement and lack the deep-felt urgency to change the deficit perspective that seems to dominate the conversation about language learners and decisions made on their behalf, in exchange for efforts to increase equity and access to effective educational models for emergent bilinguals. The promise of DL education was never intended to be a means of enriching the educational experience of all, including those who were already finding considerable success in schools. It was meant to shift how inaccessible the other educational models are for some students. DLLTs that miss the importance of this third pillar will find substantial challenges in taking strategic steps that move their programs closer to their vision and to the promise that so many have envisioned. That is why ensuring this pillar in the mission and vision, along with close analysis of the program's impact on the success of emergent bilinguals, must be a matter of social justice and a shared imperative for the broader educational community.

*Comprehensive Training & PD for DL Teachers & Leaders.* There is no universal and precise sequence of steps that guarantees increased educational access, outcomes and alignment to a DL program's mission and/or goals for every school community. Schools are unique and diverse micro-societies with individual needs, strengths, resources, and dynamics. This context will have an impact on the number of opportunities and barriers that emerge as they work to develop a coherent program design. For this reason, as is the case with all new programs and initiatives, it is essential that programs take the time to receive comprehensive training and technical support during the implementation process. While national conferences, DL program visits, and learning from colleagues who are already engaged in the work helps, it is not sufficient to navigate the complex network of school-based decisions and district-level cross-departmental changes that will be necessary to ensure the program is effective.

*Coherent Program Design.* New DL programs, as well as well-established programs that offered robust training and professional development early on, must continually refer back to the Guiding Principles of Dual Language Education (GP[3]) (2018), as it provides clear guidance of the seven strands and the proper sequence of implementation decisions taken by the most successful programs implemented across the country. While often overlooked in the frenzy of curriculum decisions and event-planning to build interest and enrollment, the GP³ emphasizes the significance to fully plan the program's design which should span no less than 6 years. Six years is a commitment that educators must be prepared to honor when adopting a DL program. However, this is merely one of the many design components that must be understood for a well-articulated and sound program design to exist. That is why 'Program Structure' is the first strand, a shift from the previous strand sequence from the GP². With the information, references and rubrics found in just this first strand, budding DL programs can become more knowledgeable about other pre-requisites and a range of considerations that schools must understand and decide upon such as: the program duration, language allocation, literacy instruction and more.

*A Pre-Established Commitment to & Structures for the Continuous Improvement Process Prior to Program Implementation.* It is reasonable to expect achievement and have accountability metrics for DL programs that have been thoughtfully implemented. However, determining the effectiveness and impact of DL programs requires a collective commitment to working with a range of stakeholders, to using a range of valid and reliable data sources to identify program strengths and opportunities, and to strategically planning for greater progress towards the immediate goals and the long-term shared mission and vision of the DL program.

DL programs, much like all schools seeking to improve, require those processes and structures needed to engage in a continuous improvement process that includes planning, supporting, aligning resources, evaluating or monitoring progress towards goals, and adjusting and following up in order to implement adjustments that lead to real outcomes that can be measured. This is a data-based and systematic process that allows people to work together to increase students' attainment of all three goals of dual language.

The GP³ states that, "the program engages in regular self- evaluation and internal review every 1–3 years and has defined processes for soliciting input from stakeholders about changes that may be needed. The program also seeks out and engages in external review at regular intervals and uses the results to guide program change. The program addresses needed changes through a data cycle process that includes the identification of issues, the implementation of potential solutions, and evaluation of the effectiveness of those solutions. Program evaluation processes and ensuing program changes are fully supported at the district level" (Howard et al., 2018, p. 29). This final pre-requisite brings together the previous four while positioning DLLTs and DL programs within the context of a learning organization designed to strategically coordinate policy, processes, monitoring systems that provide responsive actions and evidence-based practices as the basis for continuous improvement. It is the last and final key to ensuring fully-proficient bilingualism/biliteracy, academic achievement across two languages, and improved attitudes, behaviors towards, and interactions with a range of diverse people and the perspectives that they bring.

## *Assessing the Impact of DL Programs with Effective Data Sources*

First, if DLLTs truly want to measure impact and effect, they will also need to know the extent to which their school implemented the DL model as it was intended to be implemented—or program fidelity. This fidelity plays a substantial role in the impact of that program on student achievement. As I tell schools often, every concession DL programs make that change the program structure's intended design and take it further away from program alignment, should be considered one step back from the achievement and growth results that can be expected.

Also, each DL program will need varied data sources in order to determine how successful their programs are in meeting the needs of the students served. However, educators will need to take pause before reaching out to the same sources of information that is typically used in the improvement process. There are a number of considerations that DLLTs must keep in mind in order to know the most likely sources for accurate data. Most important, is that DLLTs will need both quantitative and qualitative data.

At its most foundational level, qualitative data expresses the qualities pertaining to and/or related to a given area. As such, it can be susceptible to more subjectivity and is dependent on the knowledgeability of the person collecting data from qualitative sources. Typical sources for qualitative data include a range of surveys, observations, inventories, lesson plan reviews, school and district-level documentation, and interviews. Including this qualitative data in the program evaluation allows DLLTs to reflect on the context and 'inputs' that created the achievement and growth outcomes.

Quantitative data, on the other hand, represents information that is expressed in numerical form. Typical sources for quantitative data include a range of local, district, and state assessments and should represent data across both program languages in your DL program (Table 2-1).

*Table 2-1. Possible Quantitative Data & Metric Sources*

| Possible Language Data | Possible Learner Profile Data | Possible Achievement Data | Possible Equity & Access Data |
|---|---|---|---|
| Listening proficiency Speaking proficiency Reading proficiency Writing proficiency Proficiency growth | Native language Date first enrolled in U.S. school Length of time in the DL/ELL program % of Long-term ELs | Spanish Literacy and SLA performance level English Literacy and ELA performance level SLA & ELA growth Math performance Math growth | Attendance Drop-out rates Graduation rates IP identification Enrollment in AP, Honors, IB, etc. |

Finally, DL programs must reject the urge to determine the effectiveness of implementation using any general, district, and/or state level school effectiveness framework. While many School Performance Scores (SPS) are calculated using formulas embedded in SPS tools, they are insufficient to determine these complex DL environments. Instead, DLLTs must use the rubrics provided at the end of each strand contained in the GP$^3$ (Figure 2-1). These rubrics allow DLLTs to be more objective in determining the effectiveness of their own implementation against a set of best practices that position them on a path to mastery of each of those principles needed for student and program success (GP$^3$, 2018).

In addition, DLLTs will need to consider their data sources to ensure that these sources are reliable, valid and align to the three pillars of their DL program. Developing bilingualism/biliteracy, academic achievement in two languages, and socio-cultural competency cannot simply be tag-lines worthy of a bumper sticker. They must be the source of strength for all stakeholders. As such, schools should ensure that they have access to metrics and data that provide insight into each pillar (Figure 2-2). Finally, checking the content and language plan to ensure that the language of quantitative data source aligns to the particular model being implemented is critical. For example, for schools implementing a 90:10 model where Spanish and English are leveraged need to prioritize the analysis of early Spanish literacy data in light of proportion of Spanish literacy instruction. While English literacy data might be available in the building to serve as a baseline, it should not be used to determine the effectiveness of any program and/or teacher as students do not receive what is typically considered early English literacy instruction.

STRAND

# 1 Program Structure

**Principle 1**
All aspects of the program work together to achieve the three core goals of dual language education: grade-level academic achievement, bilingualism and biliteracy, and sociocultural competence.

**Key Point A**
The program design is aligned with program mission and goals.

| Minimal alignment | Partial alignment | Full alignment | Exemplary practice |
|---|---|---|---|
| It is not clear that the program design is aligned with the mission (e.g., through length of program, language allocation, language of initial literacy instruction, recruitment of students) or will enable students to attain the goals of the program. | The program design is somewhat aligned with the mission (e.g., through length of program, language allocation, language of initial literacy instruction, recruitment of students) and will enable students to attain some but not all goals of the program. | The program design is fully aligned with the program mission (e.g., through length of program, language allocation, language of initial literacy instruction, recruitment of students) and will enable students to attain all program goals. | The program design is fully aligned with the program mission (e.g., through length of program, language allocation, language of initial literacy instruction, recruitment of students) and will enable students to attain all program goals. The mission and goals are supported by district leadership and community members in addition to program personnel, and there are systems in place to ensure that alignment continues as the program mission or goals evolve. |

*Figure 2-1. Strand 1 | Principle 1 | Key Point A—Rubric Sample (GP³, 2018)*

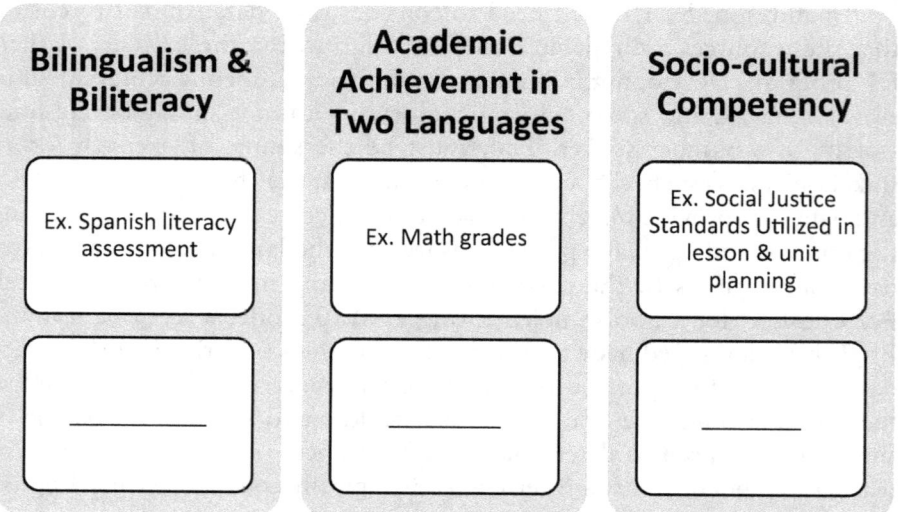

*Figure 2-2. Three Pillars of DL Education Data-Metric Sources*

## Systems and Processes Needed for Effective Continuous Improvement Efforts

DL programs who have paid close attention to the prerequisites and data sources discussed, will be well-positioned to tackle the systems and processes inherent in strategic planning and the continuous improvement of DL programs process. Why do DLLTs need these systems (or set of methods and procedures)? After all, many school systems who rely only on general education programming lack systems for the continuous data analysis and improvement cycle. While this is true, the fact that others don't use effect systems and processes is not a trustworthy reason.

Many DLLTs need the clarity offered by well-defined systems or practices in order to yield an honest evaluation and safely navigate this much new data with limited time. Well-designed systems will help DLLTs put aside personal beliefs about students' abilities and personal language learning opinions so that they can more accurately see and understand the web of complex interactions that take place in DL classrooms and programs. While personal beliefs matter, they can often interfere with a DLLTs end goal in the evaluation process, which is to effectively identify high leverage next steps and supports that will improve student outcomes.

Not only that, but effective systems are necessary for teams to understand how many successes and challenges within DL classrooms and programs may reflect the support or limitations of the broader and even more complex educational system itself. No DL program exists in isolation. Rather, it is one part of a broader educational community. The decisions, practices and supports offered to DL programs reflect its relationship between DL educators and their building administrators, district policies, assessment mandates, funding allocations, and many other factors. Without the right structures and protocols, DLLTs often struggle to understand the short and long term consequences of small changes that they think are simple.

Seeing how, when and why there are successes and failures of emergent bilinguals without falling back on the same deficit thinking is challenging. It is not challenging to do with in and of themselves, especially when well-defined protocols have been leveraged. However, they force DLLTs to resist the temptation to draw quick and easy conclusions, in order to find the intended and unintended consequences of a range of factors that created the results being analyzed. In considering the data fully, DLLT members will need to be a bit vulnerable as they explore and hear a range of perspectives of various DLLT members in order to better understanding these relationships. Four protocols and structures, in particular, have been instrumental in creating the conditions needed by our fast-paced K-12 DL programs and district partners. The four structures and protocols, described below, include: the codification of an annual cycle of improvement that are integrated into the broader school improvement process, a transparent timeline of the continuous improvement process with the goal and data source needed for each event, a protocol for developing a shared theory of action, and creating internal monitoring structures that offer clear checkpoints and assurances of progress acknowledgement.

*Codifying and Integrating an Annual Cycle of Improvement.* When the success of the DL program is a priority and stakeholders are committed to advancing the program, it shows. More than any other place, it is observed in the time, consideration and integration with other tools the district provides to continually monitor student learning. There is a message that is communicated when the district's strategic plan includes the DL program, its goals, and the range of supports that the district is willing to provide. Equally so, there is a message that is communicated when DLLTs understand how all this will be managed against their other assignments and responsibilities.

The annual continuous improvement cycle for dual language programs should follow a parallel cycle to their monolingual counterparts. This cycle should include time for gathering the data previously described, analyzing the data and setting goals and priorities that address the needs reflected in the data. It also must include a transparent language that speaks to how budgets, new initiatives, staffing and PD will be responsive and supportive to the goals and priorities identified. This transparency is not about DL educators wanting to be at the table and heard while improvement plans are being developed. More importantly, they'll need to know that additional changes to budgets, initiatives, PD, etc., will be fair, supported and acknowledged when it finds success. DL program improvement cycles do not need to be elaborate. Rather a simple model, shared with all stakeholders, included as part of the strategic plan, and included in board updates is more than sufficient, and still a far cry from the current reality (Figure 2-3).

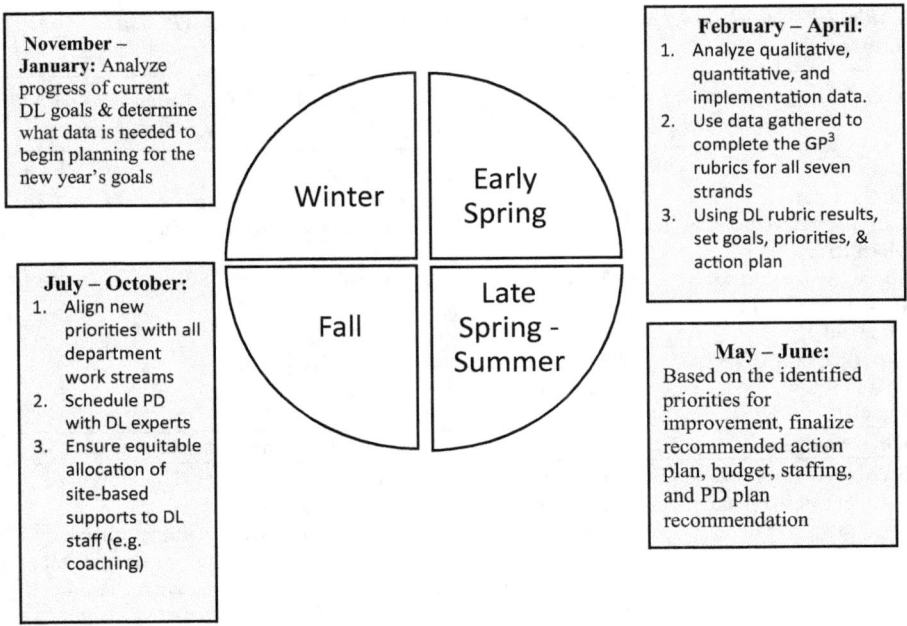

*Figure 2-3. Sample Annual Cycle of DL Improvement*

*Sharing a Timeline of Events, Goals and Data Sources.* The above cycle helps DL educators build trust in that they can see how their efforts, experiences, knowledge, and interest in the DL programs' success is reflected in a forward path for the DL program. It provides the balance of support and accountability that will help every stakeholder reach their goals. However, the transparency of this visual gives only a glance at the work that needs to be done and leaves many of the details to chance. A strong support to the annual cycle for DL improvement includes a range of templates and tools that support the analysis as in the example shown below (Table 2-2).

*Table 2-2. Dual Language Continuous Improvement Cycle (DLCIP) Data Analysis Template*

| | | |
|---|---|---|
| **Goal**: *Analyze data to identify successes & opportunities, determine level of alignment with the Guiding Principles of Dual Language Education, and set goals* | | |

| | |
|---|---|
| **Data Sets**: | **Participants**: |
| Literacy data | DLLT members, including: |
| Language development data | where appropriate, student-leaders, |
| Math data | parents, |
| Social justice and social action data | support staff, |
| Implementation data | teachers, |
| **Materials**: | site-based leaders, |
| Chart paper, markers and sticky notes | the program principal, |
| Shared folder/file for recording analysis and goals | district leaders |

| Data Analysis: | Procedure: | Guiding Questions: |
|---|---|---|
| **Step 1**: Identify DL student performance | DLLT members have been listed in a particular sequence in order to change the power dynamics of this analysis. The guiding questions are only effective at understanding each data set when power and oppression that typically plays out in schools, districts, organizations, etc. are neutralized. | What evidence do you have of success? What evidence do you have of opportunities for improvement? Is there a time when there were prior successes that are no longer seen? Are these assessments that align to the program structure and standards that are being implemented? |
| **Step 2**: Review the goals (across ALL 3 pillars) and gaps between the current performance and the goal | Ensure that any conclusion from data analysis is based on the truth as it is seen by data, 'decision-givers' (e.g. superintendent), and 'decision-receivers (e.g. teachers and students). From what perspective am I seeing this? What other perspectives would help me understand this? | How might these successes and improvement opportunities be connected to other things? Where were the places that DL programs got stuck? Why did that happen? Is there any relationship between any of the gaps discovered and the qualitative data below? |
| **Step 3**: Review the qualitative and implementation data | To ensure everyone feels safe sharing their truth, we consider the following questions: Who's at this data analysis meeting? Who has power & what power do they have? | Is there evidence of clearly understanding how to implement DL? Did everyone involved in the implementation have the skills and knowledge needed to meet the DL program goals? |
| **Step 4**: Identify the earliest GP³ strand that most supports the goal | For those with less power, how will we elevate their ability to be heard and their perspective on the data be included in the plan forward? | What is the earliest strand that reflects a level of alignment that compromises our program? |

*Theory of Action Protocols.* DL programs require us to look critically at how each piece fits together, what patterns or threads define how and why some DL students or programs are more successful, and which trends or high leverage actions created better or worse outcomes for all DLLs. While test scores can narrow the focus, DLLTs will typically find these patterns of 'why' things happened lingering just below the surface of qualitative data sources—places like the amount of student discourse, student-teacher interactions, effectiveness of language and content goals, student engagement, assessment practices, who's received professional developments, etc.

Often, DLLTs will see more than one trend or pattern emerge as they analyze the data. This is both normal and to be expected. This is where resisting the urge to state opinions and reach for easy solutions is critical to better understand whether student performance reflects a connection to other things like: assessments that don't align to standards or are not designed for DL students, quality of the DL implementation, the impact of interactions across cultures or the cultural responsiveness of a school environment, or potential capacity building and support gaps. Emerging trends or patterns must reflect evidence gathered and all DLLT members should go back to the guiding questions offered in Table 2-2 if members fall back on talk of opinions or previous deficit narratives.

In the end, DLLTs will need to hypothesize which actions and opportunities have the greatest likelihood of improving DL student performance and program sustainability in the years to come. This is the essence of developing theories of action. A simplified version of this process is outlined in Figure 2-4. The best theories of action begin by prioritizing the highest leverage actions and improvements that will be made (rather than resources or things to be acquired), which are commonly the earliest GP³ strand challenge identified during analysis—a challenge that might have been seen across performance, implementation, knowledge, etc.

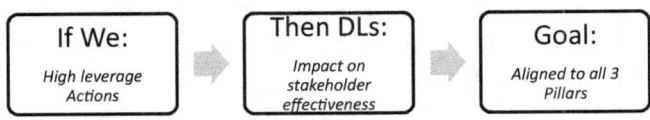

*Figure 2-4. Theory of Action Process*

DLLTs should also openly discuss why this theory of action has the potential to improve student success. For new DLLTs, theories of actions are easiest to develop when the team thinks about these "if – then" statements through a series of questions at the macro-level. When teams can see the bigger picture, first, they are better able to identify more powerful action and should offer DLLTs confidence in identifying high leverage actions. The macro-questions found in Figure 2-5 can also help DLLTs narrow which source may be needed to "drill down" the data. These four essential questions also align to the essential questions used to observe and provide feedback in DL classrooms (Guilamo, 2020).

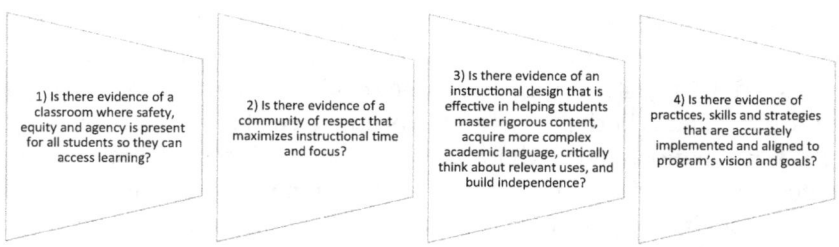

*Figure 2-5. Theory of Action Macro-Questions*

Finally, DLLTs should remember that theories of action are rarely perfect. Instead they are fluid, living and evidence-based hypothesis of actions that will likely help. Cross-checking those theories using the questions found below is one way to increase the accuracy and effectiveness of the theory of improvement. These questions help DLLTs reflect on the full theory of action process in order to be more strategic in their ability to use data findings to accelerate the success of all DL classrooms.

## *Guiding Questions to Increase the Theory of Improvement Effect Size*

1. What happened? What information, tools, and time did each school have access to that led to this outcome? Was that information used?
2. Why did we get this outcome? What extra practices, resources, training was present but not used?
3. Is building, supporting, and focusing on this the best starting point when building a series of improvements? Have needs across both language been explored, how do you know?
4. What do you predict will be the outcome of changing this practice long-term?

Finally, the improvement plan selected will have to be one that is feasible. By that I mean every school has a continuum of actions they could take to improve.

*Advancing the Achievement of Dual Language Learners*  59

Even the earliest improvement action or change from the GP³ will need to have a level of readiness if the change is going to work. It is like asking someone to prepare a 'paleo' meal before the person even understands what a paleo diet even is—we must put the cart before the horse. A tool that I have often used with DL partners is *The Hexagon Tool for Systems Planning*, found in Figure 2-6, below. Planning action that account for the DL program's need, fit, resource availability, evidence, readiness, and capacity, will position the change for success, or allow space for the development of those systems that are needed but don't yet exist.

The Hexagon Tool for Systems Planning:

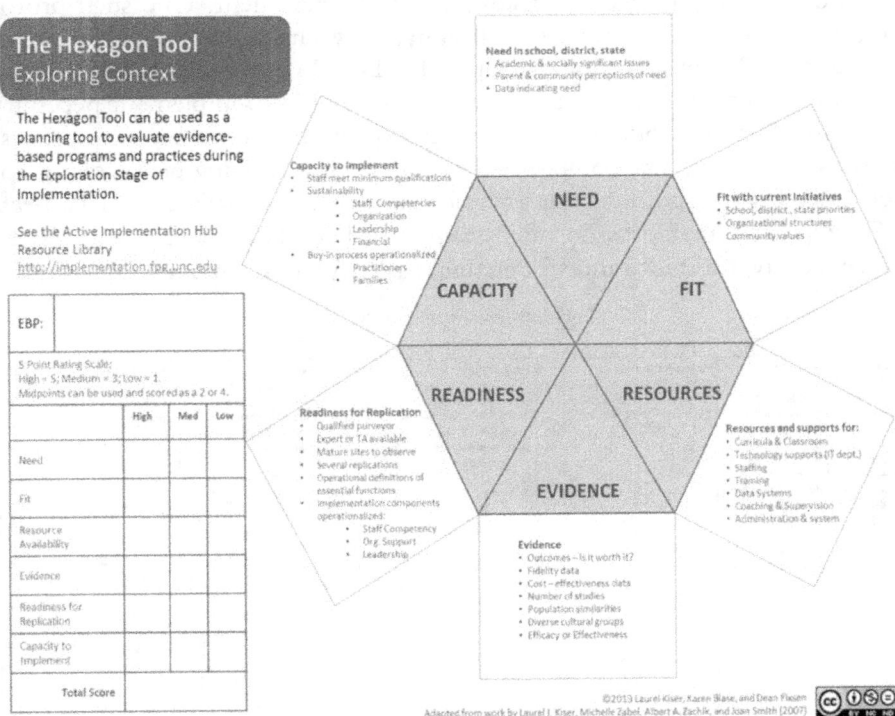

*Figure 2-6.* The Hexagon Tool for Systems Planning

*Monitoring Structures with Checkpoints & Assurances.* Once the school year begins, schools move at the speed of light. Some colleagues and I used to joke that schools, DL school especially, live in dog years—for every day served in a school, it was the equivalent to 7 days worked in another field. That is why even the most strategic and effective improvement plans require user-friendly monitoring systems and checkpoints that are not overly-cumbersome. Monitoring systems and periodic checkpoints provide a system of assurances that guarantee follow through to the continuous improvement process even when the school year gets busy.

DL programs do this in a number of ways. First, DLLT meeting dates and times should be scheduled before the start of the school year in order to ensure the time needed for monitoring and timely adjustments do not have to be squeezed in amongst competing meetings already scheduled. Second, protocols for data-based decision making should be in place to ensure that the proper lens is being utilized as the improvement plan is being implemented, monitored, and adjusted to ensure student achievement. One such protocol, designed by DL coach and colleague, Amy Finsmith, is included below in Figure 2-7. This protocol is helpful for DLLTs and their stakeholders as they make decisions that impact the school's ability to implement necessary program shifts with fidelity and integrity and during the monitoring process of those decisions. The components of the decision-making protocol are not sequenced in any specific order. Instead, they serve as equally-essential aspects of the process that provide offer teams checkpoints for alignment, shared voice, equity, feasibility and sustainability as they make a range of decisions.

Decision-making with a DLE Lens

| Guiding Principles and Program Mission | Collaboration | Equity Check | Resources | Sustainability |
|---|---|---|---|---|
| To what extent does each option align with the Guiding Principles? What would the program need to do modify each option so that it does align with the Principles? To what extent does each option align with the mission and vision of the program? | Which stakeholders should be part of the decision? What have other programs done? | Who does each option help the most? Who does each option hurt the most? Switch the place of English and Spanish in each option- does it still feel right? | What instructional and assessment resources are already in place for each option? What will be needed? What training have staff already had to make each option work? What will be needed? | What budget and time investments will need to be made to support each option? |
|  |  |  |  |  |

©2019 Amy Finsmith

*Figure 2-7. Decision-making Protocol with a DLE Lens*

One additional consideration for DL programs during the monitoring process is to ensure that prior to the start of the year, an effective and ongoing data collection system has been designed and is supported with the technology infrastructure needed to avoid any undue burden to dual language teachers. The ease and accessibility of this data will be a critical resource throughout the year as a number of DLLT meetings will be identified specifically to monitor and track the progress of the each of the priority actions identified. When we work with DL programs, we find it helpful to put these progress monitoring meetings into a shared calendar with preset alarms so that it can serve as a reminder to everyone on the team. One such progress monitoring tool can be found below in Figure 2-8.

| | Theory of Action: Priority Level: | | | | | |
|---|---|---|---|---|---|---|
| Action Steps: | Timeline: | Resources: | Owner: | Status: | Next Steps: |
| | | | | | |

*Figure 2-8. DLLT Continuous Improvement Action Planning Template*

With each progress monitoring meeting, the status of the action steps determined should be updated to reflect whether the step has been completed, cancelled, on-track for completion, or behind schedule. With each update that veers from the plan, critical dialogue will be needed in order to ensure that real barriers are resolved, unanticipated challenges are addressed, and/or that each member of the DL and broader school team is accountable to improving. In the end, even those critical dialogues and postponed milestones will require the team to think through and plan the steps that will be taken to continue progress towards the ultimate goal.

In addition, user-friendly tools and easily-understood dashboards that communicate student progress, strategic actions, and how effective each investment or change action is working is critical. User-friendly dashboards can be especially powerful in garnering continued support and leveraging forward momentum. TaJu Educational Solutions has worked with several districts who now use one such district level DL dashboard which can be found below in Figure 2-9.

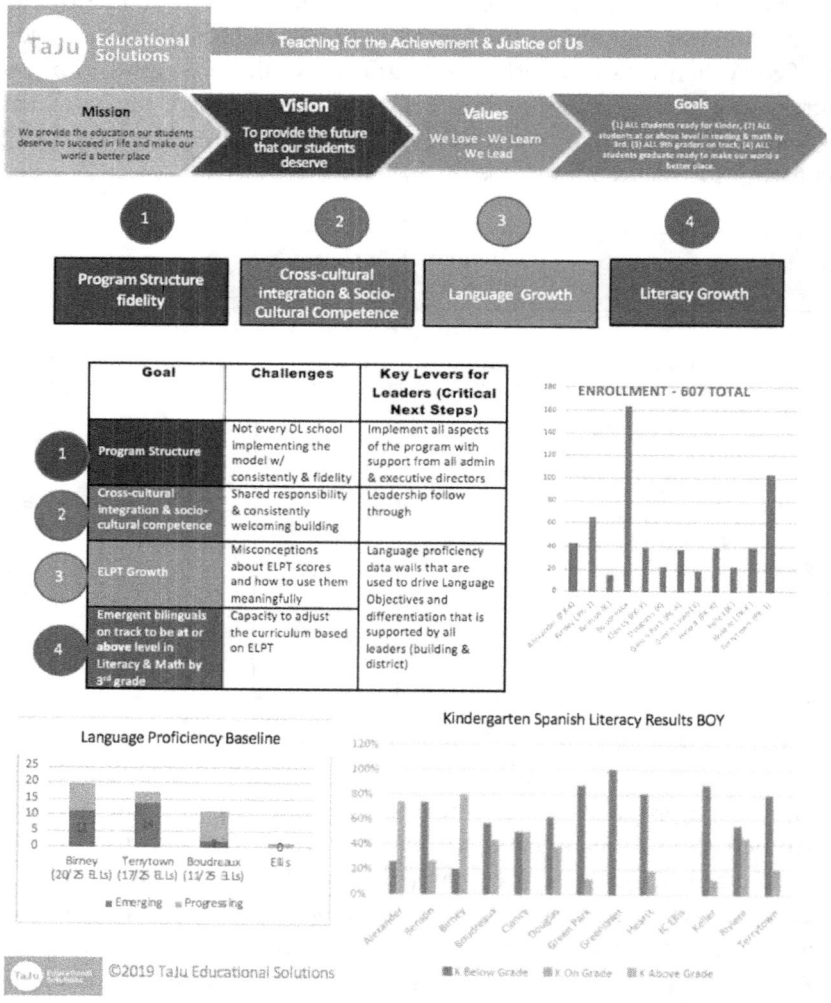

Figure 2-9. Sample DL Data Dashboard

## Broader Implications for K-12 Schools, Districts, and other LEA Agencies:

What does all this mean for dual language educators, schools, districts, regional offices and state departments of education? In truth, it all points to what—for the most part—we already knew. We cannot approach the evaluation of impact and effectiveness using the same methods used for other schools and general education programming. Dual language programs and schools are not like other schools and general education programs. They require different curriculum, best practices and instructional planning, professional development supports, assessments and more. There are a number of practices and policies that help programs increase the effectiveness of the assessment and continuous improvement cycles (Table 2-3). These practices and policies are not meant to be an exhaustive list of strategies within the framework for assessing the effectiveness and impact of DL programs. However, the codified and communicated practice along with the district-level policies that follow provide DL programs with the transparency, problem-solving protocols and systems alignment needed for any continuous improvement efforts to be successful.

*Table 2-3. Implications for Stakeholders*

| Effective Practice | Effective Policies |
|---|---|
| 1. Just as any new initiative would receive robust training and support, new DL programs will have a clearly articulated training and support plan. | 1. Teacher effectiveness metrics such as Student Learning Targets (SLTs) or Student Learning Outcomes (SLOs) for DL educators are outlined, clearly communicated to DL educators, based on most effective assessments that provide the best information needed by teachers in order to positively impact the student learning that align to the program goals. |
| 2. DLLTs come together on a quarterly basis to determine whether building level focus initiatives do not interfere with content and language allocation structures. | |
| 3. Teachers have an opportunity to review the vertical literacy, content and language allocation plan in order to consider the alignment of the current assessment calendar with the (1) amount of time allotted for literacy instruction in each language and (2) alignment to the standards assigned to each teacher within their assignment. | 2. Grading policies and grade reporting structures reflect the standards and content areas that align to the program model that has been adopted and approved. |
| 4. Include members of the DLLT to inform, review, and be a part of the approval process for any multi-tiered system of supports designed to support dual language learners. Processes must include (at a minimum) literacy and language data across both program languages. | 3. As a matter of district policy, board policy and/or procedures relating to the funding of essential and equitable resources that would otherwise be provided to any monolingual classroom. |
| | 4. Include DL student academic and linguistic growth metrics as a subgroup metric to ELL subgroup district monitoring systems. |

In the end, if DL programs are not provided a framework for improvement, they will never improve enough to realize the promise of DL that lured schools to it. Without this framework for data-based improvement, schools can expect the same narrative of underachievement as seen before—not because DL programs cannot deliver results, but because they were denied the opportunity to continuously improve.

## *References*

Berman, P., Minicucci, C., McLaughlin, B., Nelson, B., & Woodworth, K. (1995). *School reform and student diversity: Case studies of exemplary practices for English language learner students.* Santa Cruz, CA, and Berkeley, CA: National Center for Research on Cultural Diversity and Second Language Learning, and B.W. Associates.

Collier, V. P. (1992). A synthesis of studies examining long-term language minority student data on academic achievement. *Bilingual Research Journal, 16*: 1–2, 187–212. DOI: 10.1080/15235882.1992.10162633

Collier, V. P., & Thomas, W. P. (2007). Predicting second language academic success in English using the Prism Model. In J. Cummins & C. Davison (Eds.), *International handbook of English language teaching, Part 1* (pp. 333–348). New York: Springer.

de Jong, E. J. (2011). *Foundations for multilingualism in education: From principles to practice.* Philadelphia, PA: Caslon.

Fullan, M. (2007). *The new meaning of educational change.* New York: Teachers College Press.

Genesee, F., Lindholm-Leary, K. J., Saunders, W., & Christian, D. (2006). *Educating English language learners.* New York, NY: Cambridge University Press.

García, O. (2009). Education, Multilingualism and Translanguaging in the 21st Century (Chapter 8). In T. Skutnabb-Kangas, R. Phillipson, A. Mohanty & M. Panda (Ed.), *Social Justice through Multilingual Education* (pp. 140-158). Bristol, Blue Ridge Summit: Multilingual Matters. https://doi.org/10.21832/9781847691910-011

Guilamo, A. (2020). *Coaching teachers in bilingual and dual language classrooms: A responsive cycle for observation and feedback.* Bloomington, IN: Solution Tree Press.

Guerrero, M. D. (1997) Spanish Academic Language Proficiency: The Case of Bilingual Education Teachers in the US, *Bilingual Research Journal, 21*:1, 65–84, DOI: 10.1080/15235882.1997.10815602

Howard, E., Sugarman, J., Christian, D., Lindholm-Leary, K., & Rogers, D. (2018). *Guiding principles for dual language education.* Washington, DC: Center for Applied Linguistics. Retrieved from: http://www.cal.org/resource-center/publications-products/guiding-principles-3rd-edition-pdf-download

Keefer, D. L., Kirkwood, C. W., & Corner, J. L. (2004). Perspective on decision analysis applications, 1990–2001. *Decision Analysis, 1*(4), 4–22.

Lindholm-Leary, K. J. (2001). *Dual language education.* Clevedon, UK: Multilingual Matters.

Lindholm-Leary, K. (2012). Success and challenges in dual language education. *Theory Into Practice, 51*(4), 256–262. https://doi.org/10.1080/00405841.2012.726053

Lindholm-Leary, K., & Genesee, F. (2010). Alternative educational programs for English language learners. In California Department of Education (Eds.), *Improving education for English learners: Research-based approaches* (pp. 323–382). Sacramento: CDE Press.

Maxwell, Lesli A. (April 2014). U.S. Schools Become 'Majority Minority'. *Education Week. (34)-01* pages 1, 12, 14–15.

Montecel, M. R., & Cortez, J. D. (2002). Successful bilingual education programs: Development and the dissemination of criteria to identify promising and exemplary practices in bilingual education at the national level. *Bilingual Research Journal, 26*(1), 1–21.

Park, M., O'Toole, A., & Katsiaficas, C. (2017, October). *Dual language learners: A demographic and policy profile for California.* Washington, DC: Migration Policy Institute.

Park, M., Zong, J., & Batalova, J. (2018). *Growing superdiversity among young U.S. dual language learners and its implications.* Washington, DC: Migration Policy Institute.

Skinner, D. (2002, 2009). *Decision analysis.* Gainesville, FL: Probablistic Publishing.

*Equitable and Fair Assessment Systems for Bilingual Education/ Dual Language Learners*

# 3. The Assessment of Mathematical Knowledge in Elementary Level Dual Language Programs

KIP TÉLLEZ
*University of California, Santa Cruz*

## Chapter Introduction and Overview

For all their promise, Dual Language Programs (DLP)[1] are a leap of faith for the educators, parents and students who participate in this pedagogical and social experiment. Of course, all education is experimental—or perhaps should be—but DLP programs push the boundaries of typical school practices. First, routine elementary schools do not attempt to teach an entirely new language to all the students; second, most elementary schools do not explicitly seek out two different groups of students, who often differ by culture and economic background, and put them into the same classroom, regardless of their existing academic knowledge. Third, most schools are not required to convince parents, administrators, and the local community of their mission and methods; DLP programs are largely optional and must recruit families who willingly and enthusiastically participate.

These additional tasks, regardless of the value of DLPs, take time and energy, both from the general curricula and the educators themselves. I would also add that the stakes are higher for DLP: Poor academic programming may result in students who fail to gain grade level literacy skills in either English or the Language Other Than English (LOTE).[2]

Given the challenges of implementing an effective DLP, effective program evaluation is paramount. Data must inform instructional and curricular decisions regarding literacy growth in both languages (and the relation between the two), progress in oral language development and student learning in other academic areas. The existing literature on the evaluation of language development in DLPs is established, although we could make the case that better tools and additional evaluation is needed. However, few DLP program evaluations include a deliberate assessment of mathematics instruction in both languages, although several excellent evaluations (e.g., de Jong, 2002) of DLP include mathematics scores and analyses.

With the expansion of DLPs nationwide and the shift to the Common Core State Standards (CCSS), which regards mathematics as a form of literacy, I believe it is time to reassess how mathematics achievement in both languages in DLPs is assessed, analyzed and used for program improvement.

My goal in this chapter is to share with interested educators my own experiences evaluating DLPs, with a specific focus on using mathematics assessments to guide programming. I intend to be practical in my advice, thus avoiding much discussion on the wider issues in the evaluation of language programs. Those interested might wish to read an earlier work in this area (Téllez, Flinspach, & Waxman, 2005). Neither do I have the space to explain many of the technical tools needed by evaluators to test, for instance, statistical significance or effect sizes. Other resources and texts of interest (e.g., Creighton, 2006) offer educators the opportunity to develop their own skills.

My argument for including mathematics assessment in DLP evaluations is three-fold. First, mathematics is language and language is mathematics, and with the new CCSS, the literacy skills needed to understand mathematics has increased. Educators are still orienting themselves to this new way of conceiving mathematics instruction, but the concept of "academic language" is certainly part of these new understandings. Indeed, the definition of academic language itself and how to teach it are still inchoate, but the general view is that learners must develop a discourse of the discipline. For instance, the CCSS suggest that 4$^{th}$ grade students be able to "Construct viable arguments and critique the reasoning of others" (CDE, 2013, p. 29). Students cannot achieve this goal without the capacity to "speak like a mathematician." DLP educators must therefore consider carefully if mathematics will be taught in English or the LOTE. Regardless of the language of instruction, how will program leaders know if the students are meeting grade level standards? I explore the meaning of academic language more fully in the next section.

Second, because DLP programs have typically been highly focused on literacy development in both languages, mathematics achievement may be lost in the wider language goals. This lack of focus is unacceptable. Whether or not educators agree with the role mathematics achievement plays in educational achievement, students who do not master mathematical content, especially algebra, find their options for postsecondary education curtailed. Some have even called mathematics achievement the new civil rights cause (Moses & Cobb, 2002). Furthermore, Latina/o/x students, who represent the majority of students enrolled in DLP, tend to score lower in mathematics than their white or Asian counterparts (Téllez, Moschkovich, & Civil, 2011). Without careful tracking of their mathematics achievement progress in DLP, these students could fall further behind.

Third, collecting data on mathematics achievement offers teachers another point of data to discuss and learn from. Teachers tend to misunderstand the role, purposes, and analyses of assessments outside of their teacher-created tests, but standardized tests offer much information to consider. And it has been argued that teachers who understand assessment are better able to instruct language learners (Téllez & Mosqueda, 2015). I recognize that additional testing takes time away from instruction, but assessments can be used to thoughtfully inform instruction.

Program evaluation methods have not typically been taught in programs preparing teachers or school administrators, which I suppose is good news for evaluation specialists like me, who are paid to assist schools collect and analyze program data. But the truth is that I would prefer to have school personnel grow their own skills. To this end, I hope the chapter will help DLP educators address the following questions regarding mathematics achievement in DLP:

1. How are our DLP students performing in mathematics, in both English and the LOTE?
2. Does their achievement compare to similar students who are not in a DLP?
3. Are our DLP students making sufficient gains in mathematics?
4. If our DLP teaches mathematics in the LOTE, how can we use mathematics achievement data to inform the decision about when to switch to teaching mathematics in English?
5. What are the advantages and disadvantages of various mathematics assessments (e.g., state mandated, commercially available, district created, teacher-made)?
6. If our DLP teaches mathematics in the LOTE, how much does it help students' literacy development?

In the remainder of this chapter, I hope to convince DLP educators to use thoughtful program evaluation strategies to improve the educative experiences of their learners. As John Dewey pointed out in his groundbreaking work, *Logic: The Theory of Inquiry* (1938), the tools of the scientific methods can be used to judge the value of programs for the betterment of the human condition. As a program designed, at least partially, to lower the social and economic barriers that monoglossic societies routinely erect (del Valle, 2000) and thus improve the overall human experience, as well as enhancing the life chances of the students, the oversight of DLP programs must be informed by careful evaluation and reflection on quality data.

## *Assessing Growth in Mathematics in Two Languages Informs Growth in Bilingualism and Biliteracy*

The link between mathematical knowledge and linguistic knowledge is strong and growing stronger as a result of contemporary mathematics curricula, in which language is considered an important resource for learning mathematics (Moschkovich, 2012). My intent in this section to offer additional evidence that the assessment of DLP students' mathematical knowledge informs literacy knowledge, recognizing that language development (reading, writing, speaking, listening) tends to be the primary focus of most DLPs.

We can begin with a brief overview of the relation between mathematics and language growth by recognizing that mathematics *is* language; not *a* language, but language itself. Scholars such as Pimm (1987) and others (e.g., Spanos, Rhodes, Dale & Crandall, 1988) have dispelled the view that mathematics is a "language free" discipline. Research by MacGregor and Price (1999) found that a general knowledge of syntax in language is associated with mastering the syntax of algebra. Furthermore, Danesi (2003) has shown that knowledge of metaphor and figurative language is key to understanding and solving "story problems."

The relationship between language and the various disciplines is generally referred to as "academic language" (AL) or the academic "register." Definitions of AL are varied, but a general consensus is emerging, as Snow (2010) suggests. In her view, AL refers "to the form of language expected in contexts such as the exposition of topics in the school curriculum, making arguments, defending propositions, and synthesizing information" (p. 450). AL exists in all academic disciplines, and some intersect through genres and registers. Mastery of the words, symbols, and forms used in a particular specialization (Halliday, 1993), such as the mathematics register, are considered a key element of school success in mathematics competence (Celedón-Pattichis, Musanti & Marshall, 2010).

Teachers and researchers now realize that ordinary words and symbols have significantly added or altered meaning in different contexts of math.

For instance, the terms "of" in English and "de" in Spanish are transformed from their common definitions to entirely different meanings in mathematics (e.g. "what is 3/4 *of* 12? / *que es* 3/4 *de* 12?"). This simple example offers evidence that mathematics is a language in and of itself, complete with a syntax, punctuation and symbols that serve as "nouns" and "verbs." Nominalizations are also very common in the mathematics register (e.g., subtract to subtraction). Mathematics AL plays a role in providing students with access to a rigorous mathematics curriculum, but it also may help DLP students become aware of meta-linguistic aspects of mathematical language and thereby enhance literacy skills. The larger point is that mathematics AL must be explicitly taught.

Research has made clear the link between mathematics and literacy achievement (Chen & Chalhoub-Deville, 2016; U.S. Department of Education, 2008). Indeed, in their comprehensive study of the relationship between mathematics and literacy, Abedi and Lord (2001) argue "that the interaction between language and mathematics achievement is real. This interaction must be a critical consideration in future mathematics assessment research and practice" (p. 232). These studies are, however, correlational and therefore do not necessarily imply that improved mathematics achievement will boost literacy achievement or vice versa, but understanding the exact causal connection would require knowing much more about the brain than our current knowledge allows. Nevertheless, I am convinced that learning mathematics "bootstraps" language learning, especially in the upper grades (Cheng, Li, Kirby, Qiang, & Wade-Woolley, 2010). Mathematics learning adds to a learner's ability to make logical connections between symbols and other abstractions, which is, more or less, what all AL requires learners to do.

DLP educators are well aware of the claim of cross-linguistic transfer; that is, the literacy skills gained from learning to read in one language transfer to reading in a second language. This simple claim needs specificity, and Cummins (2008) has suggested several categories of linguistic transfer: (a) conceptual elements (e.g., understanding the concept of photosynthesis across languages); (b) metacognitive and metalinguistic strategies (e.g., strategies of visualizing, use of graphic organizers); (c) pragmatic aspects of language use (willingness to take risks in communication through L2); (d) specific linguistic elements (knowledge of the meaning of "photo" in photosynthesis); (e) phonological awareness—the knowledge that words are composed of distinct sounds. I suggest that cross-linguistic transfer relates to literacy development *and* mathematics education. For example, young DLP students must have a deep conceptual understanding of mathematics operations in order for linguistic elements to transfer from one language to the other.

Most of these cross-linguistic transference effects also apply to cross-*content* transfer; that is, content learned in literacy will transfer to learning in mathematics and vice versa. In fact, metacognitive transfer might be more pronounced in cross-content transfer. For instance, students who can use a graphic organizer to show cause and effect, for example, in a story, will also gain the metacognitive skill to show cause and effect in mathematics (e.g., "if I change the exponent in a function like y=x^2, what happens to the line?"). In the main, if DLP students are not learning deep, conceptual knowledge in mathematics, they are losing ground in their literacy growth, especially as they move up in grade level, when the emphasis on understanding logical inferences in a text increase. Assessing cross-linguistic and cross-content transfer is why DLP programs teaching mathematics in a LOTE must assess mathematics achievement in the language of instruction.

## *Practical Aspects of Assessing Mathematics in DLP*

I hope that the former section has pointed out the potential for mathematics learning to assist in literacy learning, regardless of the language of instruction. Cross-linguistic and cross-content transfer both play an important role. The proper assessment of mathematics achievement in DLP, if nothing else, will likely increase the attention paid to mathematics instruction. A truism in education is that what gets assessed is what gets taught. Leaving aside the negative connotation of the statement, it has been my experience that many DLP educators tend to give too much attention to literacy growth in the language of instruction—especially English—while obsessing over various models (e.g., 90/10, 70/30) when the more important concerns are what is being taught in which language and how.

I will move on now to several important points to consider if DLP leaders wish to better assess their students' mathematical knowledge and how the data might be used to improve their program. I will address four general topics in the remainder of the chapter: (a) the general assessment of mathematics learning, (b) existing resources for evaluating DLP, (c) specific mathematics assessments and their advantages and disadvantages and (d) examples of three DLP evaluations in mathematics taken from different contexts. I end the chapter with some general advice for DLP evaluations.

*The general assessment of mathematics learning.* Although a full review of the evaluation of mathematical achievement is beyond our scope in this chapter, a brief overview is shared to provide readers with some context before we begin exploring the assessment of mathematical knowledge in DLP programs. Like other content areas, the assessment of mathematical knowledge has been beset with arguments about our capacity or interest in measuring procedural vs. conceptual knowledge (Crooks & Alibali, 2014). As might be predicted, educators are generally more interested in assessing students' conceptual knowledge, but as with most dualisms, this one is fuzzy. As a shorthand example, the following will suffice: Assessing procedural knowledge using addition might be represented by the following problem: 3+4+5 = __, while the assessment of conceptual knowledge using addition can be expressed as an equivalence problem (e.g., 3+4+5 = 3+__). Putting aside the instructional approaches for teaching simple addition vs. equivalence, it is generally easier to measure procedural knowledge, so this is what tends to get measured. Without venturing too deep into psychometric theory, the assessment of procedural knowledge yields greater reliability while measuring conceptual knowledge yields better information about how students will perform as they move up in grade and thus mathematics complexity. Therefore, DLP educators should always choose to measure as much conceptual knowledge as possible, regardless of the language of instruction.

*Existing resources for evaluating DLP.* The good news is that we already have a few explicit guidelines for assessing DLP. The most extensive resource, by far, for evaluating DLP was developed by Lindholm-Leary and Hargett (2006). The document was sponsored by the California Department of Education and is available at the Center for Applied Linguistics web site (see URL in References). The authors must be recognized for creating an extraordinarily thorough guide to evaluating DLP, which I have to assume was motivated by the many schools required to provide an evaluation of their DLP to their funding agencies. The requirements for a formal evaluation of a funded project are greater than those for an "internal" evaluation of a DLP for a local audience and Lindholm-Leary and Hargett do an excellent job of providing the sample documents and templates needed to document the achievement of DLP students. They also provide sample surveys for parents, students, and teachers. Although they do not specifically address the assessment of mathematics in a DLP, the general guidelines they provide would work for mathematics evaluation.

The strength of this toolkit is its comprehensiveness and the "step-by-step" guidance. However, I do not think the data analysis advice is practical. For instance, Chapter 9 of the document is a 100-page guide to analyzing data utilizing spreadsheets and specialized statistical software, which most districts do not purchase. If DLP educators were to read this chapter and decide it was worth embarking on such an analysis, I would recommend they enroll in a graduate degree program in quantitative research in education, an endeavor which I endorse without reservation, but which I think would take more time than many DLP educators have to spare. A better option, in my view, is to (a) work with the school district's research and evaluation staff (if such a staff exist), (b) reach out to researchers from local universities who might be able to assign a graduate student to the project, or (c) hire a professional evaluator (The American Evaluation Association has a searchable list of professional evaluators https://my.eval.org/find-an-evaluator). I will have a few more comments to share on this topic at the end of the chapter. Nevertheless, the toolkit is free and clearly worth an examination.

Another good resource, also available from the Center for Applied Linguistics website, is the Spanish-Language Assessments for Dual Language Programs (Sugarman et al., 2007). This useful guide lists approximately 25 assessments (all available in Spanish) suitable for DLP evaluations. For our purposes, they list two mathematics assessments in Spanish: the Spanish Assessment of Basic Education Version 2 (now out of print) and SUPERA, which I have included in the list of mathematics assessments below.

Finally, DLP educators can rely on other, more general guides for evaluating educational programs. There are several excellent resources in this category, but I recommend Morrison and Harms (2018). This text offers excellent advice on how to present the results of a program evaluation and is especially helpful if teacher professional development is part of a funded DLP project. I also recommend Creighton's (2006) book which shares techniques for analyzing data that clearly explain the concepts behind comparing scores between two groups. However, as mentioned previously, it is often easier to find an expert to assist with data analyses than to learn these techniques from scratch.

*Specific mathematics assessments and their advantages and disadvantages.* I imagine this section will be of great interest to DLP educators, but I must first offer several caveats before describing specific assessments. First, the publishers of assessments are constantly changing and often tests are discontinued as publishers try to keep only the revenue generating products in their catalog. Next, assessments go out of print on occasion. As I noted, the Spanish Assessment of Basic Education (SABE/2), which was included in an earlier guide for DLP assessment, is no longer in print, even though the guide was published in 2007. In addition, the names of tests seem to change every few years. Therefore, I make no guarantees that this list will be accurate even one year after the publication of this book (Table 3-1). Second, some of these assessments are expensive and require specific qualifications to purchase them, although it likely that at least one professional in the school district, a psychologist with a doctoral degree for instance, can purchase them. Third, some of the assessments are individually administered (i.e., a staff member has to give each student the assessment individually), which makes the assessment very time consuming.

*Table 3-1.* List of Assessments Suitable for Evaluating Mathematics Learning in DLP, Including Descriptions, Benefits and Disadvantages of Each

| Assessment Title or Series / Publisher | Description | Advantages and Disadvantages |
|---|---|---|
| *State-mandated assessments /* Various Publishers | The Every Student Succeeds Act requires each state to assess reading and mathematics at grades 3–8 and 11, so all have developed a valid and reliable assessment. In California, for instance, which is part of the Smarter Balanced Assessment Consortium, the mathematics test in closely aligned to state standards. | Free to schools. Linked to state standards. Offered only in English in some states. Smarter Balanced Assessments are computer adaptive so results should be more reliable than "fixed form" paper and pencil. |
| *Logramos®* / Houghton Mifflin Harcourt | Parallels the scope and sequence of the *Iowa Assessments, also published by* Houghton Mifflin Harcourt. | In addition to mathematics, it also assesses social studies and science. National norms are provided, so schools can make comparisons to populations. |
| *Aprenda®: La Prueba de Logros en Español Tercera* / Pearson | Stanford 10 edition (Pearson) offers a parallel English version. | Very commonly used tests of achievement across a wide range of subjects. |
| *STAR Mathematics* / Renaissance | Equated Spanish and English versions. | May not be aligned to state standards. A literacy test in Spanish and English is also available. |
| *Batería III Ior IV NU Pruebas de aprovechamiento* / Riverside | Parallel to Woodcock Johnson III. While both the Batería and Woodcock Johnson III are achievement tests, they are more commonly used to assess students for placement in specialized programs. | Spanish test equated to English versions, which allows direct comparisons between languages and content. Tends to be used for diagnostic purposes, which can provide very detailed information on student performance. |

*Continued*

*Table 3-1. Continued*

| Assessment Title or Series / Publisher | Description | Advantages and Disadvantages |
|---|---|---|
| SUPERA PLUS/ CTB McGraw-Hill | McGraw-Hill (CAT/6) parallels the TerraNova in English English. | Requires purchasing the "PLUS" version to assess mathematics computation. "Open-ended" responses used in some of the mathematics items, which allows for some literacy assessment in mathematics. |
| Locally developed assessments | DLP leaders often decide to create their own test to use for an evaluation, but this task is more difficult than it appears. If this is the chosen strategy, it would be very helpful to partner with a measurement expert who can provide advice to the team. | Because it is locally developed, the test is aligned to both state and local standards. No national or state norms, so DLP student performance cannot be compared to populations. |
| Locally developed translations of mathematics assessments | The measurement community generally believes that test translation is inferior to assessments development in the language from "the ground up", but this might be a viable option for some DLP programs if resources are limited. | Might be an infringement of copyright. Check with the test publisher. Translating an existing test is not a simple task. Can serve as a good professional development opportunity for teachers. No national or state norms. |

*Case studies of three school DLP evaluations.* I have conducted dozens of evaluations of DLP programs, sometimes mathematics was part of the evaluation, sometimes not. The three described below all assessed mathematics knowledge, but for different reasons.

## *Case Study #1: Mann Elementary (All Names are Pseudonyms)*

Mann Elementary is a neighborhood attendance-based school located in a middle to upper middle-class neighborhood in a large urban area. About half the school's students, at the time of the evaluation, were native Spanish speakers (NSS). Most of the NSS lived in a large apartment complex near the school; their families were mostly working-class and many worked in semi-skilled jobs at a massive hospital and medical enterprise near the school.

# The Assessment of Mathematical Knowledge

The other half of the students were native English speakers (NES) and lived in single-family homes surrounding the school. Many of the NES parents worked as skilled, medical professionals. Several of the NES parents were bilingual, and in a few cases, they had raised their children bilingually. The DLP program (Spanish/English) was optional and filled one class per grade level (of three to four total at the school).

This evaluation was driven partly by the need to report its success and challenges to a funding agency and thus required an "external" evaluation, which I conducted. The funding agency did not require an assessment of mathematics, but in order to convince the NES parents to participate in the DLP, they wanted to have their children's mathematics knowledge assessed in both English and Spanish (mathematics was taught in Spanish from grades K-2). The NES parents were mostly concerned that their children's achievement might not keep up with other students not in the DLP. The NSS parents had similar concerns but were not as vocal. I administered the *Logramos*® literacy and mathematics tests, and the parallel ITBS tests in English. The results demonstrated that the NES students were performing slightly below their non-DLP counterparts on Spanish mathematics in the early grades, but that by the time the DLP students were in 4$^{th}$ grade, they were performing at or above the non-DLP students in mathematics in English. In fact, the NES (middle class students) were outperforming NSS (working class students) in mathematics, even when the test was given *in Spanish*.

## Case Study #2: Wheatley Elementary School

Wheatley is located in a town of approximately 50,000. The population is largely working class. The neighborhood surrounding the school is largely older single-family homes, many built in the 1920s, now rentals and many in need of repair. The compelling aspect of the DLP was that the NES students in the DLP were nearly all African-American, most of whom spoke a local version of African-American Vernacular English Dialect. The purpose of the evaluation was two-fold. First, it was grant funded and therefore required an evaluation. Second, the school leaders wanted to know if the DLP students would outperform students enrolled in the traditional early-exit bilingual program, also offered at the school. The evaluation found that the DLP NSS students learned Spanish literacy skills at rates that matched, and at times, exceed those in the traditional bilingual program. Also of interest was the Spanish achievement of NES students, in both mathematics and literacy. For this evaluation, I selected a random sample of students to take the *Batería III* and the *Woodcock-Johnson III*. A random sample of students was necessary because both these assessments require an individual administration, but also provide much more information than any of the group administered tests. DLP educators should know that effective evaluations can be done without assessing all the students, and in some cases, this is the preferred strategy. In any event, the evaluation found that the NES students needed more time (i.e., grade levels) to meet the mathematics achievement of their peers in an English only program. However, by 5th grade, the NES students were performing as well as their English only program peers, and, of course, they had strong Spanish language skills by this time.

### *Case Study #3: Rivera Elementary School*

This evaluation at Rivera was motivated by a desire to learn which language learning program in a single district was most effective. I was asked to compare (a) an SEI program, (b) a "late-exit" program where students transitioned to all English instruction at about 3rd–4th grade and (c) a DLP program. Readers of this volume and those familiar with language program evaluation will recognize the assessment of these three programs as common to many studies in language education (e.g., The Ramirez Report [Ramirez, Yuen & Ramey (1991)]). The school district wanted to know which program was most effective in teaching English, but I convinced them to also assess the late-exit and DLP students in Spanish mathematics as well, hoping to find the cross-content transfer I mentioned earlier. I should point out that the DLP program did not reflect the desired mix of students' native languages (e.g., half NES and half NSS) in the same classroom. In this case, the DLP students were over 90% NSS, thus they did benefit from NES models. Of course, the SEI students were not tested in Spanish mathematics, but the results indicated that the late-exit students and the DLP students performed equally in mathematics, in both languages, until the later grades when the DLP students moved well ahead of their late-exit counterparts in Spanish mathematics. Although it was not a strict research study, I believe these findings are evidence that the DLP students benefitted from cross-content transfer. These findings were sufficient to convince the district that the DLP was effective and merited continued support and resources.

### *General Suggestions for Evaluating Mathematics in DLP Programs*

1. **If you do not intend to analyze it, do not collect it.** Far too many educators believe that assessing students indicates that they are "data

driven" and care deeply about student achievement. The burden for this over-assessment falls on teachers (and the students), who are apt to grow cynical of all the testing when no one uses the results for any meaningful decisions. Do not assess students unless you (a) have a genuine purpose in mind and can justify that purpose to teachers and other stakeholders (including the students), (b) are willing to analyze the results, (c) share the findings with your stakeholders in an open forum and (d) invite everyone to consider how the results can be used to make important decisions about the curriculum, instruction, or programming.

2. **Be prepared to find class differences, regardless of native language.** I have found in my evaluations of DLP programs that native language is a poor predictor of mathematics achievement. Students from middle and upper-class backgrounds—whose parents typically have more education—begin to outperform working class students in *both* languages beginning at about 3$^{rd}$ or 4$^{th}$ grade, in both literacy and mathematics, but mathematics in particular. As I noted in Sample Evaluation #1, many of the NES students began to outperform their NSS peers in Spanish version tests of mathematics as early as 3$^{rd}$ grade. By 5$^{th}$ grade, the difference was even more pronounced. At first, the DLP leaders thought I had incorrectly analyzed the data. They asked, "How could NES students do better than NSS on a test of mathematics *in Spanish*?" After making sure I had not made any mistakes, I explained that part of the reason is that they had done their jobs well. The NES students learned Spanish with great success. Accounting for all the reasons they outperformed the NSS would suggest I have a theory to explain why we find myriad class differences in educational achievement, especially on tests of achievement. I do not, but do not be surprised if you find them in your DLP evaluation.

3. **Present your findings at professional meetings and engage teachers to the extent possible.** As Naqvi, Schmidt and Krickhan (2014) point out, the best route to teachers who understand linguistic transfer and other DLP features is the development of professional learning networks where teachers can participate and collaborate in research and evaluation.

4. **Consider using more participatory evaluation methods to evaluate DLP.** Because it is grounded in the experience of administrators, teachers, parents, and students, participatory evaluation is more likely to provide information that is useful to program administrators and policy makers (Brisolara, 1998). Participatory evaluation often results

in positive changes within an organization or project, including increased communication between staff members, beneficial effects on program development, and higher quality evaluations (Upshur, & Barreto-Cortez, 1995). But do not hesitate to enlist the help of professionals.[3] Program evaluation is a specific discipline that requires training.

5. **Use caution in interpreting achievement scores for students under the age of 9.** Young children are notorious for providing unreliable data. It is fine to assess students at these ages (most tests offer versions for students as young as Kindergarten age), but use the results with caution.

6. **Use the right units when comparing groups.** Often, the benchmarks used in school accountability are not useful in a program evaluation. For example, in a published evaluation which admittedly addressed many more variables than mathematics student achievement alone, the researchers found that the students at an established DLP had a higher *percentage* of students passing a standardized examination in mathematics (tested in English) than the state average or other students in the same district. Good evidence, but in order to make a valid claim, they should have used *scaled scores* rather than percent passing. Those mean (average) scores should have then been compared to other students in the district and matched by class (e.g., free and reduced-price lunch).

7. **Mathematics instruction in the LOTE will end, and DLP educators must plan for the transition.** There is no school system in the US that allows students to take all their mathematics courses required for graduation in a LOTE. We may claim that this is a flawed plan, but it is unlikely to change. Therefore, mathematics instruction in the LOTE, which is typically a wise idea (recall our discussion of cross-linguistic and cross-content transfer), must be assessed carefully so that DLP educators can plan for the inevitable move to instruction in English.

In conclusion, I hope that DLP educators will consider mathematics, both its instruction (not just the language of instruction) and assessment, more carefully. I further hope that this chapter has promoted a new understanding of the importance of assessing mathematical knowledge in two languages, as well as provided some tools and advice. Conducting a rigorous and valid program evaluation of a DLP program is no "mean" feat, but done well it is a worthwhile endeavor that can inform the work of administrators, teachers, parents, and other school personnel. DLP are a leap of faith, but with a strong evaluation component, the leap can be made with confidence.

## Notes

1 The editors of the volume have chosen to use the term Dual Language Programs, instead of others (e.g., two-way immersion, two-way bilingual education). I find the term useful and have followed suit.
2 The majority of DLPs offer instruction in English and Spanish, but I prefer to use the more general term LOTE in this case to recognize the many programs teaching English and a language other than Spanish (e.g., Mandarin). However, the assessment examples provided are in Spanish and the programs I highlight are all Spanish/English DLP. However, most of the other information should be relevant for any DLP, regardless of which languages are taught. The chapter is clearly designed to inform DLP programs in the US, but the foundational suggestions will apply to international contexts.
3 A strong evaluation can come only from the result from collaboration of an entire DLP team, which might include the use of an expert program evaluator.

## References

Abedi, J., & Lord, C. (2001). The language factor in mathematics tests. *Applied Measurement in Education, 14*(3), 219–234.
Brisolara, S. (1998). The history of participatory evaluation and current debates in the field. In E. Whitmore (Ed.), *Understanding and practicing participatory evaluation* (pp. 25–41). San Francisco: Jossey-Bass.
Celedón-Pattichis, S., Musanti, S. I., & Marshall, M. E. (2010). Bilingual elementary teachers' reflections on using students' native language and culture to teach mathematics. In *Mathematics Teaching and Learning in K-12* (pp. 7–24). Palgrave Macmillan US.
Chen, F., & Chalhoub-Deville, M. (2016). Differential and long-term language impact on math. *Language Testing, 33*(4), 577–605.
Cheng, L., Li, M., Kirby, J. R., Qiang, H., & Wade-Woolley, L. (2010). English language immersion and students' academic achievement in English, Chinese and mathematics. *Evaluation & Research in Education, 23*(3), 151–169.
California Department of Education [CDE] (2013). The California Common Core State Standards: Mathematics. Sacramento: Author. Retrieved from https://www.cde.ca.gov/be/st/ss/documents/ccssmathstandardaug2013.pdf, October 31, 2019
Creighton, T. B. (2006). *Schools and data: The educator's guide for using data to improve decision making*: Thousands Oaks, CA: Corwin Press.
Crooks, N. M., & Alibali, M. W. (2014). Defining and measuring conceptual knowledge in mathematics. *Developmental Review, 34*(4), 344–377.

Cummins, J. (2008). Teaching for transfer: Challenging the two solitudes assumption in bilingual education. In *Encyclopedia of language and education* (pp. 1528–1538). New York: Springer.

Danesi, M. (2003). Conceptual metaphor theory and the teaching of mathematics: Findings of a pilot project. *Semiotica, 145*, 71–83.

de Jong, E. J. (2002). Effective bilingual education: From theory to academic achievement in a two-way bilingual program. *Bilingual Research Journal, 26*(1), 65–84.

del Valle, J. (2000). Monoglossic policies for a heteroglossic culture: Misinterpreted multilingualism in modern Galicia. *Language and Communication, 20*(2), 105–132.

Dewey, J. (1938.) *Logic: The theory of inquiry.* Published as Volume 12 of *The Later Works (1925–1953)*, J. A. Boydston (Ed.). Carbondale, IL: Southern Illinois Press.

Halliday, M. A. (1993). Towards a language-based theory of learning. *Linguistics and Education, 5*(2), 93–116.

Lindholm-Leary, K., & Hargett, (2006). *Evaluator's toolkit for dual language programs.* Washington, DC: Center for Applied Linguistics. Retrieved 3/23/2019 http://www.cal.org/twi/EvalToolkit/downloads.htm#evaluator

MacGregor, M., & Price, E. (1999). An exploration of aspects of language proficiency and algebra learning. *Journal for Research in Mathematics Education, 30*, 449–467.

Morrison, J. Q., & Harms, A. L. (2018). *Advancing evidence-based practice through program evaluation: A practical guide for school-based professionals*: Oxford University Press.

Moschkovich, J. (2012). Mathematics, the Common Core, and language: Recommendations for mathematics instruction for ELs aligned with the Common Core. *Commissioned papers on language and literacy issues in the Common Core State Standards and Next Generation Science Standards, 94*, 17.

Moses, R., & Cobb, C. E. (2002). *Radical equations: Civil rights from Mississippi to the Algebra Project.* Beacon Press.

Naqvi, R., Schmidt, E., & Krickhan, M. (2014). Evolving 50%–50% bilingual pedagogy in Alberta: What does the research say? *Frontiers in Psychology, 5*, 413.

Pimm, D. (1987). *Speaking mathematically: Communication in mathematics classrooms.* New York: Routledge.

Ramirez, J. D., Yuen, S. D., & Ramey, D. R. (1991). *Longitudinal study of structured English immersion strategy, early-exit, and late-exit transitional bilingual education programs for language-minority children.* San Mateo, CA: Aguirre International.

Snow, C. E. (2010). Academic language and the challenge of reading for learning. *Science, 328*(5977), 450–452.

Spanos, G., Rhodes, N. C., Dale, T. C., & Crandall, J. (1988). Linguistic features of mathematical problem solving: Insights and applications. In R. Cocking & J. Mestre (Eds.), *Linguistic and cultural influences on learning mathematics* (pp. 221–240). Hillsdale, NJ: Lawrence Erlbaum.

Sugarman, J., Arteagoitia, I., Coburn, C., Gallagher, C., Montee, M., & Schissel, J. (2007). Spanish-language assessments for dual language programs. *Center for Applied Linguistics*. Retrieved http://www.cal.org/twi/pdfs/assessments.pdf

Téllez, K., Flinspach, S., & Waxman, H. (2005). Resistance to scientific evidence: Program evaluation and its lack of influence on policies related to language education programs (pp. 57–76). In R. Hoosain & F. Salili (Eds.), *Language in multicultural education*. Charlotte, NC: Information Age Publishing.

Téllez, K., Moschkovich, J. N., & Civil, M. (2011). *Latinos/as and mathematics education: Research on learning and teaching in classrooms and communities*. Charlotte, NC: Information Age Pub Incorporated.

Téllez, K., & Mosqueda, E. (2015). Developing teachers' knowledge and skills at the intersection of English language learners and language assessment. *Review of Research in Education, 39*(1), 87–121. https://doi.org/10.3102/0091732X14554552

Upshur, C. C., & Barreto-Cortez, E. (1995). What is participatory evaluation (PE) and what are its roots. *The Evaluation Exchange: Emerging Strategies in Evaluating Child and Family Services, 1*(3/4). Retrieved March 10, 1998 from the World Wide Web: http://gseweb.harvard.edu/~hfrp

# 4. Assessment of Bilingual Students: Best Practices and Recommendations for Members of the Multidisciplinary IEP Committee

FELICIA CASTRO-VILLARREAL
*The University of Texas at San Antonio*

VICTOR VILLARREAL
*The University of Texas at San Antonio*

ILEANA UMAÑA
*Texas A&M University College Station*

The National Center for Education Statistics (McFarland et al., 2018) reported an increase of approximately 1,000,000 English Language Learner (ELL) students from 2000 to 2015, with ELL students now representing 9.5% of all public-school students in the United States (US). This represents a significant increase in the number of ELL students and an increased need for appropriate educational programming. Though we know ELL students are most effectively served in bilingual general education programs (Goldenberg, 2008), a sizeable proportion of ELLs—approximately 14.5%—are identified as having disabilities under the Individuals with Disabilities Education Improvement Act (IDEA, 2004), making them eligible to receive special education and related services. Briefly, IDEA requires schools to make available a free and appropriate public education (including special education) via individualized education programs (IEPs) to all eligible students with disabilities (IDEA, 2004; 34 CFR § 300.8[a]). Moreover, federal law requires that student IEPs be developed by IEP committees that are multidisciplinary (thus often referred to as multidisciplinary teams [MDTs]) and include parents (and/or students if they have reached the age of majority), general and special education teachers, other school representatives that will be responsible for the provision of services and specialists who can interpret evaluation results (Jacob, Decker, & Lugg, 2016). In these situations, IEP committees come together to gather and review student data in order to formally plan and implement services.

The major roles of IEP committees are well defined (e.g., Maanum, 2009); however, several studies have identified challenges for IEP committees when it comes to serving ELLs. These include a lack of knowledge of policy and best practice regarding IEP committee decision making for ELLs, overlooking key information in the special education evaluation of ELLs, and missing and/or excluding important Multidisciplinary personnel (e.g., Klinger & Harry, 2006; Sadowski, O'Neil, & Bermingham, 2014; Wilkinson, Ortiz, Robertson, & Kushner, 2006). Thus, the purpose of this chapter is to discuss key information to consider in IEP committee decision making when evaluating ELLs for special education eligibility and services. The chapter is based, in part, on the training and experiences of the authors, which include extensive training and professional development in issues related to evaluation for special education, legal issues in education, and school-based consultation models, as well as each author having provided direct services to culturally and linguistically diverse students in K-12 settings across Texas, Oklahoma, and Missouri. The chapter authors are licensed School Psychologists with research interests in improving education and equity for culturally and linguistically diverse populations. In this chapter, we first describe best practices and important considerations in the special education evaluation of ELLs. We then discuss critical practices for ensuring that IEP committees are working collaboratively in order to best serve ELLs. A checklist, professional development series, and timeline document that highlight these key considerations are included as appendices.

## *Evaluating ELL Students*

IDEA requires schools to complete a full and individual evaluation of each student who may qualify as having a disability. This represents a key responsibility of IEP committees, as the evaluation must be completed prior to the initial provision of special education and related services (Jacob et al., 2016). Notably, IDEA states that assessment methods—used to identify whether or not a student has a disability and whether or not a student needs services—must be validated for the purpose for which they are used and appropriate for the population being assessed. They are also required to be fair and must be "selected and administered so as not to be discriminatory on a racial or cultural basis" (IDEA, 2004; 34 CFR § 300.304[c][1][i]). These standards have led to important implications and specific recommendations for IEP committees working with ELLs. For example, the U.S. Departments of Education and Justice (2015) have issued a joint statement regarding schools' obligation to ensure that ELLs participate meaningfully and fairly in the evaluation process. In this section, we focus on these and other issues to consider when evaluating ELLs. In the appendix titled *Considerations before special education recommendations for bilingual students*, we provide a checklist of factors to consider when evaluating ELL students for special eligibility; it is recommended that personnel use this checklist, in addition to other tools and information from this chapter, in decision-making for ELL students.

## Assessment of Language Proficiency

Language proficiency assessment refers to the evaluation of one's competence in the use of a language (Duarte, Greybeck, & Simpson, 2013). The results of language proficiency assessment are crucial when evaluating ELLs. In fact, the U.S. Departments of Education and Justice (2015) have specifically noted that a student cannot be determined to have a disability if the determinant factor is limited English proficiency and if the student does not otherwise meet the definition of a student with a disability. Furthermore, to avoid inappropriately identifying ELL students as students with disabilities because of their limited English proficiency, ELL students must be evaluated in their dominant language based on multiple sources of data. Appropriate language proficiency assessment helps IEP teams meet these standards by helping them select the least biased assessment measures and methods (Liu & Anderson, 2008). This process can be aided by ensuring that IEP committees include team members versed in second language development and acquisition and that actively advocate for the use of appropriate language proficiency evaluation practices (Cummins, 1984; Guajardo Alvarado, 2011; Ochoa & Rhodes, 2005).

Formal measures of language proficiency include standardized assessments that examine language ability and performance as compared to other same-age students. Some formal measures are available in two or more languages, which allows for a comparative assessment of proficiency in multiple languages (typically the student's native language and English) (e.g., Muñoz-Sandoval, Cummins, Alvarado, & Ruef, 2005; Woodcock, Alvarado, Ruef, & Schrank, 2005). Formal measures of language proficiency also typically provide Cognitive Academic Language Proficiency (CALP) scores, which indicate academic language competency (Cummins, 1984; Villar Cole, 2014), as well as comparative language scores. CALP scores indicate the degree of ease (or difficulty) a student will have when presented with language based tasks in various domains (e.g., reading, oral expression) (Cummins, 1984; Duarte et al., 2013). CALP scores can assist in determining a student's degree of proficiency in a given language and whether additional language support is recommended. Comparative language scores compare language proficiency results from tests administered in multiple languages. These scores are particularly helpful when determining whether a student displays language dominance. Together, CALP and comparative language scores can assist IEP teams in determining the most appropriate test language for evaluation in all other domains.

In the event that standardized measures are not available, or if students happen to speak a low incidence language, the IEP committee should consider the use of informal measures with a trained assessor with proficiency in the student's native language. Even if formal language proficiency measures are available, informal methods may yield additional, essential information about ELLs. Informal measures include home language surveys, which are typically completed by parents at the time of enrollment in schools. These surveys ask about language use at home and may ask about educational and instructional language history (Villar Cole, 2014). Parent interviews about language use can also be completed by the IEP committee. In these cases, it is important to ask how the native language and second language (i.e., English) have developed. Some students learn both languages simultaneously, while others learn them sequentially, which can lead to different language proficiency outcomes. Information about translanguaging (i.e., how students merge languages) should also be asked (García, 2009). Classroom observations can also serve as informal measure of language proficiency and can provide unique information about language use in social settings. Teacher-made tests, assignments and activities can also provide important language proficiency information. Information such as language use patterns, language history and concerns with language can be solicited through these means.

## *Assessment of Cognitive Ability*

Although evaluations of cognitive ability are not required as part of the IEP process, they are typically conducted and are specifically used to determine whether a child has an intellectual disability or specific learning disability, among others. They may also be helpful for determining appropriate interventions and supports, particularly for students that have significant developmental problems. The process of evaluating a student's cognitive ability becomes complicated when assessing ELL students. This is because language proficiency can have a significant effect on the validity of scores derived from standardized tests of cognitive ability.

If a student is clearly fluent and language dominant in a language other than English, it is recommended that the IEP committee solely use tests of cognitive ability in the student's native language (often referred to as *native-language assessment*). This practice may diminish problems associated with limited English proficiency (Gonzalez, 2012), such as reduced overall cognitive ability scores. Cognitive ability tests are readily available for use in native-language assessments in Spanish (e.g., Muñoz-Sandoval, Woodcock, McGrew, & Mather, 2005b) and, in such cases, would require test administration by a specialist who is a fluent Spanish-speaker. However, problems with this approach include the lack of tests available in languages other than Spanish. In addition, even though tests of cognitive ability may be available in other languages, they do not typically account for differences in dialects or culture within the same language, and they can lead to different results (Solano-Flores & Li, 2008). Native-language assessment is also not recommended if the student does not demonstrate adequate language skills in their native language. For example, a student may be more proficient in their native language than they are in their acquired language (i.e., English) but may nonetheless lack the native language proficiency needed to yield valid results on native-language assessments.

In such cases, an alternative method is to administer language-diminished or nonverbal tests of cognitive ability. This practice is based on findings that students with lower English language proficiency tend to perform significantly below average on verbal tests of cognitive ability; thus, language-reduced and nonverbal methods are used as a substitute (Sotelo-Dynega, Ortiz, Flanagain, & Chaplin, 2013). There is some evidence that results of nonverbal cognitive ability tests yield non-significant differences when assessing ELL and non-ELL students (Naglieri, Booth, & Winsler, 2004). However, it is important to consider that nonverbal tests of cognitive abilities are not typically normed on bilingual students and still may include verbal components, particularly in test instructions (Carvalho, Dennison, & Estrella, 2014; Lohman & Gambrell, 2012). Nonverbal tests may also suffer from unexplored cultural bias, as they may reflect mainstream cultural standards and experiences instead of those typical for ELLs (Blatchley & Lau, 2010). In addition, nonverbal tests are narrower in scope; they do not provide as comprehensive an evaluation as cognitive tests that include verbal abilities.

Alternative models have been conceptualized to allow practitioners to differentiate whether cognitive assessment results are due to (a) student differences in cultural and linguistic background or (b) valid differences in underlying cognitive ability (Cormier, McGrew, & Ysseldyke, 2014). For example, the Culture-Language Interpretive Matrix (C-LIM) attempts to categorize cognitive tests (and subsequent results) on linguistic demand and cultural loading (Flanagan & Ortiz, 2001). Linguistic demand refers to the complexity and length/verbosity of test directions and requirements (Cormier, McGrew, & Evans, 2011). Cultural loading is related to acculturation and the extent to which cultural knowledge influences performances on tests (Cormier et al., 2014). In applying models such as the C-LIM, practitioners consider a student's English language proficiency and the amount of time they have resided in the United States in order to aid in interpreting test performance. This method emphasizes that performance should be evaluated in light of the cultural and linguistic demands of cognitive ability tests and a student's unique background (Sotel-Dynega et al., 2013). Regardless of the methods chosen, the IEP committee must ensure that it includes members that are trained to consider the unique situations of ELLs and that can administer and interpret various types of cognitive ability measures.

## *Assessment of Academic Achievement*

Assessing academic achievement is a critical part of the evaluation process and is important for developing subsequent goals to be addressed in a student's IEP, but assessing the academic achievement of ELLs is complex. Practitioners often struggle to distinguish between (a) ELLs who are otherwise developing typically with academic weaknesses associated primarily with limited language proficiency and (b) ELLs who are experiencing significant academic failure, beyond what would be expected based on their language abilities (Artiles & Klingner, 2006; Keller-Allen, 2006). For example, ELLs who are exposed to a second language may demonstrate lower second language reading abilities because they are still in the process of learning the new language but do not have a reading disability (Pollard-Durodola, Cardenas-Hagan, & Tong, 2014). On the other hand, ELLs may experiences reading difficulties in their primary language and similar difficulties when learning to read in a second language (Gorman, 2009), suggesting universal reading problems.

Thus, a crucial first step in academic achievement evaluation is assessing a student's language proficiency. If a student has demonstrated fluent proficiency in their native language language, a student's academic achievement may be evaluated using standardized tests in their native language. By using native language tests in this method, IEP committees can account for language factors that, if unaccounted for by using non-native language tests, can reduce the validity and reliability of inferences drawn about a student's level of academic achievement (Abedi, 2002). There are some standardized, Spanish-language tests of academic achievement that can serve this purpose (e.g., Muñoz-Sandoval, Woodcock, McGrew, & Mather, 2005a), but options for tests in other languages are limited.

Conversely, in some cases students may exhibit difficulties with limited language proficiency in both their native language and acquired language (i.e., English) (Klinger, Artiles, & Barletta, 2006). In these cases, it is inappropriate to base evaluations of a student's academic achievement on testing administered in a single language. Rather, it is suggested that the IEP committee use an integrated assessment approach. In such models, students are administered a comprehensive test across all academic areas of interest in their native language; in those areas in which they performed poorly, they are administered parallel tests in their acquired language. The purpose of completing parallel tests is to identify academic problems that are similar across both languages, which represents a better predictor of true learning difficulty than simply identifying difficulties in one language. For example, having reading problems in both English and Spanish represents a greater indicator of a true learning difficulty than if the student is assessed in both languages but only demonstrates reading problems in one language. This type of integrated approach can be particularly useful for determining if a student would benefit most from supports that focus on improving their language abilities only or from supports focused on both their language and reading abilities.

Notably, there are several concerns when using standardized achievement tests, including non-English standardized tests, as part of the process of identifying a student's level of academic achievement. These include a mismatch with norm groups used in test standardization, inattention to the language demands of the tests, and differing results for different groups of speakers even in the same language (Pollard-Durodola et al., 2014; Sandberg & Reschly, 2011; Solano-Flores & Li, 2008). Because of these and other issues, it has been suggested that curriculum-based measurement (CBM) should be used when evaluating ELLs (Sandberg & Reschly, 2011). CBM relies on assessments that are closely aligned to the curriculum, and it generates information about skills students have yet to acquire in order to aid with instructional decisions (Shapiro, 2011). CBM tools are available in Spanish (e.g., Good, Bank, & Watson, 2003). Research indicates that methods that use CBM may be particularly beneficial for ELLs (Castro-Villarreal, Villarreal, & Sullivan, 2016; Sandberg & Reschly, 2011) and may be useful for monitoring their academic progress, monitoring their response to intervention, and predicting their standardized assessment performance (Yeo & Park, 2014).

## Assessment of Social-Emotional and Behavioral Functioning

IEP committees may also be tasked with evaluating a student's social-emotional functioning, particularly in cases in which a student's behavior is interfering with their academic achievement and ability to establish appropriate relationships with others in school. There are multiple methods for assessing this type of functioning, but for ELLs, special attention must placed on the effects of language proficiency and the influence of acculturation. Briefly, acculturation refers to the process of adapting one's behaviors and beliefs with those of a new culture (Rhodes, Ochoa, & Ortiz, 2005; Olvera & Gomez-Cerillo, 2011; O'Bryon & Rogers, 2010). The most commonly reported informal measures of acculturation used in schools are interviews, questionnaires, observations and record reviews (O'Bryon & Rogers, 2010). Although difficult, Rhodes and colleagues (2005) also recommend home-based observations to detail acculturation across settings and to determine the most appropriate methods for meaningful parent involvement in the IEP process. Regardless of the assessment method, it is critical for the IEP committee to understand the influence of acculturation and utilize that knowledge to enhance understanding of students' behavior (O'Byron & Rogers, 2010).

Methods for assessing social-emotional and behavioral functioning include the use of norm-based behavior and emotional rating scales, observations, and interviews. Rating scales in this domain can provide data about a wide variety of student strengths and weaknesses (e.g., externalizing problems, internalizing problems, social skills, adaptive behavior). If IEP committees will be using rating scales to assess ELLs, it is important to identify scales that are available in multiple languages (e.g., Reynolds & Kamphaus, 2015) and that can completed by multiple informants across multiple settings. Notably, although rating scales may be available in multiple languages, the score interpretation is nonetheless based on behaviors that are considered to be typical for the mainstream United States culture. As this may represent a mismatch for many ELLs, IEP committees should interpret global results with caution and should consider item-level analysis and follow-up interviews to determine the validity of results (Hass & Kennedy, 2014).

Observations are also useful (and required) when evaluating students, including when assessing a student's social-emotional and behavioral functioning. When conducting observations, it is recommended that ecology-based, classroom observations take place to better understand the contexts in which students are expected to learn and participate (Klinger & Harry, 2006). This is critical for ELLs because it shifts focus from students' individual characteristics and, instead, highlights the role that the environment plays on student functioning. Things to consider for ELLs that can be gained from observations include whether behavior supports include components of ELL students' culture, whether motivators for prosocial behavior reflect the preference of ELLs, and whether lesson plans consider the unique needs of ELLs, including necessary language supports (Neely, Gann, Castro-Villarreal, & Villarreal, 2019). A mismatch between ELL students' needs and availability supports in the classroom environment could contribute to difficulties. Interviews represent another key method for assessing a student's social-emotional and behavioral functioning. IEP committees can attain comprehensive information when they interview teachers, students, and parents. For ELL students, it is important to ask teachers to identify any classroom ecological factors that may be influencing their functioning; this can include a discussion of how the teacher is meeting the unique needs of ELLs. When interviewing ELL students and their parents, it is important to consider cultural differences and that interviews about social-emotional and behavioral functioning can be highly personal and sensitive (Hass & Kennedy, 2014). Individuals from different cultural backgrounds may have different beliefs about these issues, and it important that IEP committees ensure that they establish rapport with ELL families to ensure that valid data is collected. In addition, IEP committees should be prepared to ensure that trained language interpreters are available to ensure meaningful participation of ELL families in this process (U.S. Department of Education & U.S. Department of Justice, 2015).

## IEP Committee Challenges and Collaborative Solutions for ELLs

As indicated in the previous section, the complexity involved in assessing ELL students for special education and related services is unequivocal. The IEP process may be further complicated when IEP committees experience knowledge and training gaps for evidenced based decision making for ELLs, lack culturally and linguistically diverse of team membership, and lack clear guidelines for how to collaborate when managing complex ELL cases. Such problems have resulted in IEP committee members working and making decisions in isolation, a lack of standardized processes, and the underutilization of best practices for working with ELLs (Roach, Shore Gouleta, & Obaldia Butkevich, 2003). These poor practices have been linked to inappropriate placement and eligibility decisions for ELLs. In this section, we discuss general methods for addressing these and other issues in order to improve the collaborative functioning of IEP committees when working with ELL students.

## Training of Multidisciplinary IEP Committee Members

Methods for improving the functioning and decision making of IEP committees for ELLs include improved training, diversification of team membership, and enhanced collaboration among all IEP members. In terms of improved training, systematic, research-based training in best practices for all potential IEP members is in order (Kretlow & Bartholomew, 2010). Recent research particularly highlights the importance of training format for learning and skill acquisition (Kretlow & Bartholomew, 2010). Research on professional development and training suggests support for short, well sequenced, and well-distributed training on carefully planned topics (DiGennaro, Martens, & Kleinmann, 2007). In the case of effective practices for working with ELLs, training should begin with current demographic statistics and trends on the ELL student population. This would serve to set the context for anticipated work with this population. Next, training should focus on the unique and complex challenges when evaluating and determining eligibility for this population, as indicated in the previous section. Of critical importance, sufficient time should be devoted to language development, effective instruction and differentiation, and intervention for struggling learners (Ortiz et al., 2011). Some research shows that educators who have had professional development training in working with ELLs and who work with ELLs on a regular basis are more likely to rely on multiple methods of assessment in eligibility decision making (Sadowski et al., 2014). Professionals who have taken two or more classes in the assessment of ELLs report increased confidence in working with ELLs (Sadowski et al., 2014). This highlights the importance of training and experience working with ELLs for IEP members. In the appendix titled *Training Sequence for IEP Committee Professional Development* we outline data, demographics and knowledge basis critical for work with ELL students.

In terms of diversifying the IEP committee, efforts should be made to include culturally and linguistically diverse IEP members with a special effort to recruit members who match the demographic makeup of the ELLs most frequently being evaluated in the area. IEP members with shared socio-cultural and linguistic backgrounds would be able to better assist in understanding the context and origins of students' difficulties. It is recommended that team membership include bilingual and migrant student educators for enhanced perspective and understanding of language acquisition processes and acculturation impacts. As research indicates, it would also behoove the IEP committee if educator members were trained in bilingual assessment and evidence-based instructional practices for ELLs. This knowledge base would foster collective and collaborative ELL assessment planning and decision-making. Research has shown that professionals who speak a second language are more likely to use recommended and best practices assessment strategies with ELLs (Ortiz et al., 2011). Thus, bilingual education teachers can play an integral role in preventing student academic underachievement and supporting struggling and diverse learners in the classroom (Ortiz et al., 2011). It is important to note, however, that best practice and culturally informed decision making involves more than speaking the same language; IEP committees must include members who understand the unique characteristics and social cultural histories of ELLs (Ortiz et al., 2011) in order to make fair and valid decisions making.

In terms of distinctive or adapted IEP processes for evaluation and eligibility determination of ELLs, little guidance has been offered to IEP teams. Some researchers have offered tools to aid in the process of developing assessment plans and making eligibility decisions for ELLs (Salend & Salinas, 2003). Critical areas to be explored in the assessment of ELLs, as previously discussed, include comparison of performance in the native and second language. Another area to include in assessment planning is identifying and exploring diverse socio-cultural life experiences that may have an adverse effect on achievement. Within this section, IEP members would explore the student's schooling history and record, language of instruction, migrant status, household makeup, family separation, acculturation, trauma, economic hardships and lack of adequate and appropriate instruction. Finally, in a collaborative and interdisciplinary partnership, IEP assessment planning should conclude with IEP committee data analysis and educational planning. Damico (1991) provided some questions that can guide the data analysis and decision-making process. In the checklist, the author stressed the importance of identifying all factors that may explain learning and language difficulties. Second, the author asks IEP members to consider the degree to which the learning and language problems occur in social versus the school settings. With advanced knowledge and training of second language acquisition processes, IEP members are encouraged to question the degree to which language difficulties are seen in community and social settings as compared to the school setting. IEP members are also asked to question the degree to which language difficulties are due to normal second language acquisition processes. Another inquiry would examine for bias and/or unfair testing procedures and/or interpretation in the assessment process such as, "to what extent were student's cultural background and experiences considered in data interpretation?" Asking and thinking about these types of questions can help IEP committee members differentiate between two types of second language learners. One type of second language learners shows proficiency in the native language and difficulties and errors in the second language typical of similar peers and of the second language acquisition process and the other type of second language learners show language, academic, and social behavior difficulties in the native and second language that are significantly different and below expectations for those of similar age and ethnic and linguistic background (Ortiz et al., 2011; Salend & Salinas, 2003).

## *Collaborative Practices for Multidisciplinary IEP Committee Members*

Collaboration among team members for best practices based in culturally and linguistically sensitive evaluation is not an easy task. However, the goal of the IEP is for all members to work together to make a collaborative decision regarding the student's eligibility. Every team member constitutes an important role in the team as diverse training and backgrounds can result in more equitable services and supports for students (Roach et al., 2003). Still, a common practice is that assessment staff (e.g., school psychologists) perform the assessment and makes the eligibility determination. In this case, the meeting convenes not to collaborate on the decision nor problem solve, but to share a previously made decision (Klinger & Harry, 2006; Schoorman et al., 2011). This lack of collaboration may stem from professionals' unwillingness to share territory and trust each other, making collaboration difficult. Other impediments to effective collaboration include not knowing others' roles and functions and inadequate training in collaboration processes and practices (Roach et al., 2003). Lack of training and direction in collaboration practices has also been found to link with poorly coordinated services that ultimately contribute to inequitable services and supports (Roach et al., 2003).

Poor collaboration extends to parents as well, as research shows that parents do not always participate meaningfully in IEP meetings and processes (Garcia, 2009; Klinger & Harry, 2006; Schoorman et al., 2011). Research suggests that parents often lack the knowledge of IEP function and process, often feel left out of the process, have few positive and collaborative interactions with MDT members, feel intimidated, and disproportionately experience logistical challenges (Klinger & Harry, 2006). Ways to circumvent the challenges involving parents include better communication with families and more inclusion and transparency in the IEP process. As a team member, parents should be informed of processes beyond parent handbooks and state and LEA guide books. As such, establishing equal status relationships among all members is key to effective collaboration. All parents could benefit from attending a workshop on IEP processes, procedures, roles and functions.

One way to encourage parent participation and input is to schedule meetings around parent work hours and arranging for transportation and child care. Efforts such as these are important as parents' unique understanding of students' home and past school histories is crucial to assessment, eligibility and instructional planning purposes. Another important way to improve collaboration is to show parents they are valued members of the team by inviting them to trainings, being available for support along the process, and providing parents with the opportunity to share their voice and opinion through the use of home language surveys, questionnaires, interviews and the simple asking for their input and perspective on the child's social and academic functioning.

Processes integral to effective collaboration include keeping all IEP members on the same page across the teaming process. To that end, some type of pre-determined informed process with checkpoints along the way is recommended. Regular team meetings to develop and refine IEP agendas is also recommended in route to developing improved processes and procedures. IEP meeting agendas should outline a problem-solving approach that structures content and fosters effective interpersonal communication skills. Communication is also critical especially if increased collaboration is going to occur. Thus, regular email and shared drive communication and updates are strongly recommended. At the very least one or two staffings or "pre" IEP meetings should occur prior to the official IEP meeting. This checkpoint meeting designed to enhance collaboration and communication would ensure that all are on the same page, all questions have been asked, processes have been checked and assessment and interpretation decisions are *multidisciplinary* and *team-based*. Advance meetings and check-ins would also provide for the opportunity to ask additional questions, complete additional assessments, or collect additional data that may be recommended by multidisciplinary team members. Last, frequent pre-determined check-ins would minimize the occurrence of the "listening" phenomenon noted in IEP meetings and would encourage more active participation based on well informed and knowledgeable team members (Klinger & Harry, 2006; Schoorman et al., 2011). In the appendix titled *Critical Points For Collaboration in the IEP Committee* we provide checkpoints for collaboration among IEP members and recommendations for discussion and decision-making.

## *Implications for Educators and Policymakers*

Students with disabilities have unique needs and ELLs who have been disproportionately represented among this larger population have additional needs associated with being both an ELL and a student with a disability.

Problems in the ways we evaluate, identify, and serve our ELLs have long been documented, but one way to move toward more fair and equitable practice is to ensure that those who make decisions and compose IEP committees recognize these problems and then become educated in the linguistic, social-cultural, learning and academic needs of this population. The most critical challenge for IEP members is to be able to differentiate between language difference and disability characteristics. In this chapter, we have highlighted key considerations in the process and have provided tools for IEP committees to use in decision-making when evaluating ELLs for Special Education services. The checklist (appendix), *Considerations Before Special Education Recommendations for Bilingual Students*, in particular highlights factors to consider that will assist the IEP committee in determining appropriate education planning, whether that includes additional intervention in typical bilingual education programs or additional, intensive services via special education in order to meet the unique needs of children with disabilities. The collaboration timeline highlights important junctures for coming together and sharing, deliberating, and collaborating in the best interest of the bilingual student and to help bridge regular, special and bilingual education programs. Last, the professional development sequence makes recommendations for a best practice training sequence that educates professionals on the unique background, experiences and needs of the bilingual student to foster informed decision-making by emphasizing the need to understand the bilingual student's unique bilingual programming history and how it may impact behavior and performance.

State and district policy should then build from this research-based foundation whereby policies are developed to safeguard this vulnerable population and progress toward more fair and equitable practices and decision-making. Once best practice information and the most recent research on linguistic and social development is shared among decision makers and IEP members, policy and practices to include effective collaboration and fair and equitable assessment should follow. Enhanced knowledge of evaluation best practices, second language acquisition processes and effective collaboration among IEP members is necessary if we are to meet the diverse needs of ELLs and is critical if we are to address the disproportionate representation of ELLs in special education.

## *References*

Abedi, J. (2002). Standardized achievement tests and English language learners: Psychometrics issues. *Educational Assessment, 8,* 231–257. https://doi.org/10.1207/S15326977EA0803_02

Artiles, A. J., & Klingner, J. K. (2006). Forging a knowledge base on English language learners with special needs: Theoretical, population, and technical issues. *Teachers College Record, 108*, 2187–2194.

Blatchley, L. A., & Lau, M. Y. (2010). Culturally competent assessment of English language learners for special education services. *National Association of School Psychologists Communiqué, 38*, 27–29.

Carvalho, C., Dennison, A., & Estrella, I. (2014). Best practices in the assessment of English Language Learners. In J. P. L. Harrison & A. Thomas (Eds.), *Best practices in school psychology: Foundations* (pp. 75–88). Bethesda, MD: National Association of School Psychologists.

Castro-Villarreal, F., Villarreal, V., & Sullivan, J. (2016). Special education policy and response to intervention: Identifying promises and pitfalls to advance social justice for diverse students. *Contemporary School Psychology, 20*, 10–20. https://doi.org/10.1007/s40688-015-0077-3

Cormier, D. C., McGrew, K. S., & Evans, J. J. (2011). Quantifying the "degree of linguistic demand" in spoken intelligence test directions. *Journal of Psychoeducational Assessment, 29*, 515–533. https://doi.org/10.1177/0734282911405962

Cormier, D. C., McGrew, K. S., & Ysseldyke, J. E. (2014). The influences of linguistic demand and cultural loading on cognitive test scores. *Journal of Psychoeducational Assessment, 32*, 610–623. https://doi.org/ 10.1177/0734282914536012

Cummins, J. C. (1984). *Bilingual and special education: Issues in assessment and pedagogy*. Austin, TX: PRO-ED.

Damico, J. S. (1991). Descriptive assessment of communicative ability in Limited English Proficient students. In E. Hamayan & J. S. Damico (Eds.), *Limiting bias in the assessment of bilingual students* (pp.157–218). Austin, TX: PRO-ED.

DiGennaro, F. D., Martens, B. K., & Kleinmann, A. E. (2007). A comparison of performance feedback procedures on teachers' treatment implementation integrity and students' inappropriate behavior in special education classrooms. *Journal of Applied Behavior Analysis, 40*, 447–461.

Duarte, B. A., Greybeck, B., & Simpson, C. G. (2013). Evaluating bilingual students for learning disabilities. *Advances in Special Education, 24*, 129–139.

Flanagan, D. P., & Ortiz, S. O. (2001). *Essentials of cross-battery assessment*. New York: NY. John Wiley.

García, O. (2009). *Bilingual education in the 21st century. A global perspective*. London: Wiley/Basil Blackwell.

Goldenberg, C. (2008). Teaching English language learners: What the research does—and does not—say. *American Educator, 32*, 8–44.

Gonzalez, V. (2012). Assessment of bilingual/multilingual pre-K–grade 12 students: A critical discussion of past, present, and future issues. *Theory Into Practice, 51*, 290–296. https://doi.org/10.1080/00405841.2012.726058

Good, R. H., Bank, N., & Watson, J. M. (Eds.). (2003). *Indicadores Dinamicos del Exito en la Lectura (Dynamic indicators of reading success)*. Eugene, OR: Institute for the Development of Educational Achievement.

Gorman, B. (2009). Cross-linguistic universals in reading acquisition with applications to English-language learners with reading disabilities. *Seminars in Speech and Language, 30*, 246–260. https://doi.org/10.1055/s-0029-1241723

Guajardo Alvarado, G., (2011) *Best practices in the special education evaluation of culturally and linguistically diverse students*. Pearland, TX: Education & Evaluation Consultants.

Hass, M. R., & Kennedy, K. S. (2014). Integrated social-emotional assessment of the bilingual child (pp. 163–187). In A. B. Clinton (Ed.) *Assessing bilingual children in context: An integrative approach*. Baltimore, MD: American Psychological Association. Individuals with Disabilities Education Act, 20 U.S.C. § 1400 (2004).

Individuals with Disabilities Education Improvement Act [IDEA] of 2004, 20 U.S.C.§ 614 et seq.

Jacob, S., Decker, D. M., & Lugg, E. T. (2016). *Ethics and law for school psychologists* (7th ed.). Hoboken, NJ: Wiley.

Keller-Allen, C. (2006). *English language learners with disabilities: Identification and other state policies and issues*. Alexandria, VA: Project Forum.

Klingner, J. K., Artiles, A. J., & Barletta, L. M. (2006). English language learners who struggle with reading. *Journal of Learning Disabilities, 39*, 108–128. https://doi.org/10.1177/00222194060390020101

Klingner, J. K., & Harry, B. (2006). The special education referral and decision-making process for English language learners: Child study team meetings and placement conferences. *Teachers College Record, 108*, 2247–2281. https://doi.org/10.1111/j.1467-9620.2006.00781.x

Kretlow, A. G., & Bartholomew, C. C. (2010). Using coaching to improve the fidelity of evidence-based practices: A review of studies. *Teacher Education and Special Education, 33*(4), 279–299.

Liu, K. K., & Anderson, M. (2008). Universal design considerations for improving student achievement on English language proficiency tests. *Assessment for Effective Intervention, 33*, 167–176. https://doi.org/10.1177/1534508407313242

Lohman, D. F., & Gambrell, J. L. (2012). Using nonverbal tests to help identify academically talented children. *Journal of Psychoeducational Assessment, 30*, 25–44. https://doi.org/10.1177/0734282911428194

Maanum, J. L. (2009). *The general educator's guide to special education* (3rd ed.). Thousand Oaks, CA: Corwin.

McFarland, J., Hussar, B., Wang, X., Zhang, J., Wang, K., Rathbun, A., Barmer, A., Forrest Cataldi, E., & Bullock Mann, F. (2018). *The Condition of Education 2018* (NCES 2018-144). U.S. Department of Education. Washington, DC: National Center for Education Statistics. Retrieved 11/12/18 from https://nces.ed.gov/pubs2018/2018144.pdf

Muñoz-Sandoval, A. F., Cummins, J., Alvarado, C. G., & Ruef, M. L. (2005). *Bilingual verbal ability tests*. Rolling Meadows, IL: Riverside Publishers.

Muñoz-Sandoval, A. F., Woodcock, R. W., McGrew, K. S., & Mather, N. (2005a). *Batería III Woodcock-Muñoz: Pruebas de aprovechamiento*. Itasca, IL: Riverside Publishing.

Muñoz-Sandoval, A. F., Woodcock, R. W., McGrew, K. S., & Mather, N. (2005b). *Batería III Woodcock-Muñoz: Pruebas de habilidades cognitivas*. Itasca, IL: Riverside Publishing.

Naglieri, J. A., Booth, A. L., & Winsler, A. (2004). Comparison of Hispanic children with and without limited English proficiency on the Naglieri Nonverbal Ability Test. *Psychological Assessment, 16*, 81–84. https://doi.org/10.1037/1040-3590.16.1.81

Neely, L., Gann, C., Castro-Villarreal, F., & Villarreal, V. (2019). *A behavior analytic case example of culturally responsive consultation in schools.* Manuscript submitted for publication.

O'Bryon, E. C., & Rogers, M. R. (2010). Bilingual school psychologists' assessment practices with English language learners. *Psychology in the Schools, 47*, 1018–1034. https://doi.org/ 10/1002/pits.20521

Ochoa, S. H., & Rhodes, R. L. (2005). Assisting parents of bilingual students to achieve equity in public schools. *Journal of Educational and Psychological Consultation, 16*, 75–94. https://doi.org/ 10.1080/10474412.2005.9669528

Olvera, P., & Gomez-Cerrillo, L. (2011). A bilingual (English and Spanish) psychoeducational assessment MODEL grounded in Cattell-Horn Carroll (CHC) theory: A cross battery approach. *Contemporary School Psychology, 15*, 117–127.

Ortiz, A., Robertson, P.M., Wilkinson, C. Y., Liu, Y., McGhee, D., & Kushner, M. (2011). The role of bilingual education teachers in preventing inappropriate referrals of ELLs to special education: Implications for response to intervention. *Bilingual Research Journal, 34*, 316–333.

Pollard-Durodola, S. D., Cardenas-Hagan, E., & Tong, F. (2014). Implications of bilingualism for reading assessment (pp. 214–264). In A. B. Clinton (Ed.), *Assessing Bilingual Children in Context: An Integrative Approach*. Baltimore, MD: American Psychological Association.

Reynolds, C. R., & Kamphaus, R. W. (2015). *Behavior assessment system for children* (3rd ed.). Bloomington: NCS Pearson, Inc.

Rhodes, R. L., Ochoa, S. H., & Ortiz, S. O. (2005). *Assessing culturally and linguistically diverse students: A practical guide*. New York: Guilford Press.

Roach, M., Shore, J., Gouleta, E., & Obaldia Butkevich, E. (2003). An investigation of collaboration among school professionals in serving culturally and linguistically diverse students with exceptionalities. *Bilingual Research Journal, 27*, 117–136.

Sadowski, G., O'Neill, R., & Bermingham, D. (2014). Assessment practices of multi-disciplinary school team members in determining special education services for English language learners. *Multicultural Learning and Teaching, 9*, 121–141. https://doi.org/10.1515/mlt-2012-0010

Salend, S. J., & Salinas, A. (2003). Language differences or learning difficulties: The work of the multidisciplinary team. *TEACHING Exceptional Children, 35,* 36–43.

Sandberg, K. L., & Reschly, A. L. (2011). English Learners: Challenges in assessment and the promise of curriculum-based measurement. *Remedial and Special Education, 32,* 144–154. https://doi.org/10.1177/0741932510361260

Schoorman, D., Zainuddin, H., & Sena, S. R. (2011). The politics of a child study team: Advocating for immigrant families. *Multicultural Education, 18,* 31–38.

Shapiro, E. S. (2011). *Academic skills problems: Direct assessment and intervention* (4th ed.). New York, NY: Guilford Press.

Solano-Flores, G., & Li, M. (2008). Examining the dependability of academic achievement measures for English language learners. *Assessment for Effective Intervention, 33,* 135–144. https://doi.org/10.1177/1534508407313238

Sotelo-Dynega, M., Ortiz, S. O., Flanagan, D. P., & Chaplin, W. F. (2013). English language proficiency and test performance: An evaluation of bilingual students with the Woodcock-Johnson III Tests of Cognitive Abilities. *Psychology in the Schools, 50,* 781–797. https://doi.org/10.1002/pits.21706

U.S. Department of Education, & U.S. Department of Justice (2015). *Ensuring English learner students can participate meaningfully and equally in educational programs.* Retrieved from the U.S. Department of Education website at: https://www2.ed.gov/about/offices/list/ocr/docs/dcl-factsheet-el-students-201501.pdf

Villar Cole, C. (2014). Special education evaluation of English language learners (ELLs): The importance of language proficiency determination. *Dialog: Journal of the Texas Educational Diagnosticians Association, 43*(1), 7–11.

Wilkinson, C. Y., Ortiz, A. A., Robertson, P. M., & Kushner, M. I. (2006). English language learners with reading-related LD: Linking data from multiple sources to make eligibility determinations. *Journal of Learning Disabilities, 39,* 129–141. https://doi.org/10.1177/00222194060390020201

Woodcock, R., Alvarado, C. G., Ruef, M. L., & Schrank, F. A. (2005). *Woodcock-Muñoz Language Survey III.* Itasca, IL: Riverside Publishers.

Yeo, S., & Park, S. (2014). Developmental differences in curriculum-based measurement (CBM) reading aloud growth rates between English-speaking students and English Language Learners in grade 8. *Exceptionality, 22,* 91–110. https://doi.org/10.1080/09362835.2013.865528

# 5. Assessing Bicultural-Bilinguals' Language Development: Difference or Disorder?

JANELLE BETH FLORES
*Independent Researcher*

KARLA C. GARZA
*University of Texas at San Antonio*

T. BREANNE ROCHESTER
*Methodist Children's Hospital*

YVONNE VERA
*Northside Independent School District*

BELINDA BUSTOS FLORES
*University of Texas at San Antonio*

## Introduction

Assessing bicultural-bilingual learners (BBLs) is a complex process requiring an understanding that BBLs' language development is distinct from monolingual learners. Flores et al. (in press) contend that as critical pedagogues, bilingual teachers must be linguistically and culturally efficacious in their instructional practices, as well as in their assessment approaches. Assessment also requires bilingual educators to have the capacity to distinguish language differences from disorders. Approaching this chapter from this transdisciplinary lens based on our expertise allowed us to consider the knowledge and skills bilingual educators must possess to make appropriate referral and pedagogical decisions.

Speech-Language Pathologists (SLPs) are often asked to assess BBLs because teachers note difficulties understanding the BBLs' speech production and/or observe that some may have difficulty being understood when engaging with peers. Other referrals are based on observations of BBLs' capacity to learn or cognitively engage. While some of these referrals do indeed result in identifying a language communication disorder needing clinical intervention, there are referrals that simply reflect BBLs' typical language development. We contend that inequitable educational opportunities for BBLs occur with the over- or under-representation of speech-language referrals. Sánchez et al. (2013) suggest that a multidimensional approach must be employed when assessing BBLs. Given the critical importance of preparing bilingual educators with a strong theoretical and research grounding of language differences versus language disorders, in this chapter, we will provide an overview of key factors to consider when determining the appropriateness of language referrals.

## *Theoretical Framework*

In order to ensure that we are operating from a common framework and to reduce misinterpretation, we must define common terms that are shared in the educational context which are distinct when examined from a clinical lens. For example, when defining levels of language functioning, terminology such as the words "poor" and "within normal limits" as well as typical (when referring to age-appropriate development) and "atypical" (when referring to delayed development) are utilized as appropriate descriptors, even though these terms are often associated with a deficit perspective when viewed from an educational lens. These terms are very common in a clinical/medical setting because of the relationship between the provider, payor and recipient of services. Private and public insurance companies will not cover services unless diagnosed to be medically necessary as defined by their framework, which can change based on government regulation. Deficits and areas of need must be clearly identified to have access to treatment. Thus, school-based SLPs use the same vocabulary and operate from the same framework as other medical professionals. Additionally, the preparation of SLPs is not currently delineated based on the setting (i.e., educational or medical). SLPs are equally qualified to enter either setting. While a medical model is used for identification of communication and language disorders, SLPs' approaches to treatment encompass an asset-based perspective in which the learner's cultural and linguistic capital is used to support their zone of proximal development (Vygotsky et al., 1971).

## Language Development versus Communication Disorder

When assessing BBLs, it is important to consider all languages spoken in order to ensure that language differences and language disorders are distinguished. Language differences are reflective of typical language development, whereas language disorders include deviations for typical language development patterns (Prezas & Jo, 2017). Importantly, educators and SLPs vary on their approaches as to how language is assessed. For example, bilingual educators often assess BBLs for proficiency with tools such as the Woodcock-Muñoz Language Battery-Revised (Woodcock et al., 2005), the English Language Proficiency Assessment for the 21$^{st}$ century (2015) and other norm-reference tools to assess all four language domains. As Huang and Flores (2018) noted,

> The results of these assessments are used to determine placement in ESL services and reclassification of ESL students. The results are also used to measure ELL students' progress in English language development, and for designing professional development and formative assessments (p. 2).

The focus on language assessment is to measure the attainment of proficiency across language domains. The results of these normed or criterion-referenced assessments are also used to determine grade level placements.

In contrast, SLPs examine language functionality and competence via a myriad of formal and informal assessment methods to evaluate language in the areas of content (semantics), form (grammar, syntax, morphology) and use (pragmatics) at a much deeper level than what language proficiency evaluations measure. Additionally, the SLP delves into the causative factors of dysfunction (areas of difficulty/concern) and how to therapeutically habilitate or remediate areas of identified need. Not all SLPs feel prepared or competent to work with English Learners (Roseberry-McKibbin & Eicholtz, 1994), yet 35% of students in SLPs' caseloads come from culturally linguistically diverse (CLD) populations (Guiberson & Atkins, 2012). SLPs who have been specifically prepared to work with bilingual populations are less biased in assessment processes and feel competent (Roseberry-McKibbin et al., 2005; Kimble, 2013) as compared to their monolingual peers (Prezas & Jo, 2017).

Regardless of the field, it is important that bilingual educators and SLPs understand language development and proficiency. Identifying the characteristics of language development makes it possible to determine if a BBL is experiencing a typical process in language development or a language disorder.

## Characteristics Bicultural-Bilingual Learners

Over the years, different views on bilingualism have been explored in research literature. Bloomfield (1933) described bilingualism as full native-like fluency in two languages. Grosjean (1989) referred to bilingualism as the ability to use different languages to communicate across different contexts. The American Speech-Language-Hearing Association ([ASHA], 2020b) refers to bilingualism as the ability to use more than one language to communicate.

The Speech Pathology field views language(s) as developing along a continuum. Two types are recognized: simultaneous bilinguals and sequential bilinguals. Simultaneous bilinguals are those individuals that acquired two languages at the same time since birth. Sequential bilinguals are individuals who learn a second language (L2) after learning a first language (L1). According to Kohnert (2010) and Bedore and Peña (2008), more children develop L1 from birth at home and acquire L2 later, usually upon entering school. In the US, BBLs are often sequential rather than simultaneous bilinguals. We briefly provide an overview of simultaneous and sequential bilingualism in the subsequent section.

**Simultaneous Bilingualism.** Bilingual children's acquisition of early language milestones (i.e., first words, two-word utterances, and vocabulary development) are comparable to their monolingual counterparts (Kohnet, 2010; Pettitio et al., 2001; Yip, 2013). Despite these findings, there continues to be a debate as to whether simultaneous bilingual children have one or two language systems. The Unitary Language System hypothesizes that bilingual children have a singular language system (Volterra & Taeschner, 1978). However, Grosjean (1989) cautioned that a holistic view of bilingualism using monolingual standards should not be used to assess bilinguals. Genesee (1989) suggested the Dual Language Hypothesis in which two separate language systems are developed in bilingual children since the onset of language acquisition. Similarly, De Houwer (1990) proposed the Separate Development Hypothesis in which he suggests that bilingual children develop two separate and independent language systems.

Other studies further postulated that simultaneous bilinguals' dual language systems assist them with distinguishing between languages and early speech (sound) perception. For example, Bosh and Sebastian-Galles (2001) reported that simultaneous bilingual Spanish-Catalan infants have the ability to discriminate speech of two phonetically similar languages. Similarly, another study found that 10–12 month old French-English bilinguals had the capacity to differentiate language specific phonetic stimuli (Burns et al., 2007; Sundara et al., 2008).

While these studies have demonstrated that bilinguals possess two distinct language systems, given the evidence of cross-linguistic transfer, there is a need for further exploration. As compared to Spanish monolingual counterparts, Paradis and Navarro (2003) observed that simultaneous English-Spanish bilinguals were less likely to use null subjects when speaking as compared to Spanish monolingual peers. The researchers contend that this evidence, along with other syntactic patterns, supports cross-linguistic transfer from English. Additional studies can assist in further understanding the notion of two separate language systems and the cross-linguistic transfers that occur among simultaneous bilinguals.

**Sequential Bilingualism.** Sequential bilingualism, or successive bilingualism, occurs when children or adults acquire a second language after developing their first language. Second language acquisition can occur at any point in an individual's lifetime. Therefore, sequential language acquisition is a distinct process from simultaneous language development; hence, it is important to understand these differences.

External factors (e.g., age, acculturation or schooling history) can mediate the sequential language acquisition patterns. Thus, prototypical language development patterns are not found among sequential language learners. For example, Jacobson and Cairns (2008) noted that adult sequential bilinguals use overregularization of irregular past tense verb forms such as *catched* instead of *caught* (Jacobson & Cairns, 2008). Fabiano-Smith and Barlow (2010) suggested that phonological skills vary among sequential bilingual children. In their study, sequential bilinguals acquired and had the ability to only correctly produce strident (/s/, /z/, and /ʃ/) sounds in their L1.

Studies have also investigated the syntactic and semantic skills of sequential bilinguals. In comparison to monolingual children, Kohner et al. (2010) observed that there was a weaker correlation between the vocabulary and grammatical skills of sequential bilinguals. Bedore and Peña (2008) documented that demand placed on different linguistic elements across languages can affect sequential language development. Further, Fiestas and Peña (2004) found that bilingual children engaged in a retelling narrative task produced more initiating events in Spanish and more story consequences in English.

**Multilingualism.** While our focus is on BBLs and the majority of U.S. research has explored bilinguals, it is also important to examine the language development of multilingual learners. Multilinguals, similar to BBLs, may learn their first language, L2, and L3 simultaneously or sequentially; if learners acquire languages simultaneously, then this is considered an example of bilingual first language [2L1] development (Miesel, 2001).

Multilingual development, according to Kecskes and Papp (2000), tends to be affected by the similarities and differences of the target languages and cultures. They reported that if languages and cultures being learned are significantly distinct in their structures and functional features then the development will be slower compared to languages and cultures whose characteristics are similar. Baker (2006) cited Leopold's work (1939–1949) on bilinguals who demonstrated a *shifting balance*, or a change in competence, based on situations and level of exposure to different languages. In a similar study of multilingualism, Quay (2001) found that change in exposure as well as incentive for using different languages directly affects multilingual language development. Whether the learner is bilingual or multilingual, it is important to consider if any delays or errors are a result of language development, cross-linguistic transfer, or are indeed a language disorder.

## *Bilingualism in Speech and Language Disorders*

Views on bilingualism have changed over the past decade from an idea of bilingualism creating a burden to a more positive view of bilingualism (Grosjean & Li, 2013). Thus, research advocates for the maintenance of bilingual language development (Genesee et al., 2004). This holds true for individuals with and without speech and language disorders.

Importantly, BBLs with speech and language disorders follow the same acquisition patterns as their monolingual counterparts with disorders. Paradis et al. (2003) observed that bilingual children with specific language disorders demonstrated the same level of accuracy in morphological markers as their monolingual peers with the same diagnosis. Further, sequential bilinguals with a speech and language diagnosis demonstrate similar semantic skills as compared to their monolingual counterparts (Sheng et al., 2012). Monolingual and bilingual children with language disorders have demonstrated a similar length of utterance and vocabulary skills (Bird et al., 2005). Noteworthy, bilingual infants may take longer processing speech as compared to monolingual peers due to higher language demands; however, Mattock et al. (2010) noted that "experience with abundant phonetic variability is a precursor to the metalinguistic advantages seen in bilingual preschoolers" (p. 241).

In summary, whether a bilingual learner has acquired the L2 simultaneously or sequentially, there are similarities and differences when compared to monolingual peers. Noteworthy, similar patterns are observed when comparing BBLs with language disorders to their monolingual counterparts with similar diagnosis. These observations of BBLs' typical and atypical language development support the need for bilingual educators to understand and differentiate between language development and language disorders.

## Understanding Language Development and Proficiency

### Language Development Stages

Krashen (1981, 1982) proposed that typically developing sequential BBLs undergo various stages in acquiring the second language. He suggested that BBLs acquiring a second language initially experience a silent period in which there is comprehension, yet limited expressive production. Some BBLs also demonstrate cultural influences that correlate with the silent period that reflect cultural norms, such as 'it is best to be seen not heard.' If learners are not provided language opportunities to continue development in both languages, then language loss occurs in L1. Two phenomena observed in bilingual children are the use of cross-linguistic transfer and code-switching in which the syntax and semantics from one language are incorporated into the other language.

In contrast, simultaneous bilinguals do not follow Krashen's stages of silent period and language loss. However, researchers have observed language transfer and code-switching in simultaneous bilinguals. Infants and toddlers learning more than one language are able to develop two separate linguistic systems allowing them to distinguish language-specific perceptions (Burns et al., 2007; Byers-Heinlein & Lew-Williams, 2013). Although simultaneous bilinguals develop two separate interaction systems, an interchange between the languages occurs. Yip and Matthews (2007) noted that cross-linguistic interactions, including transfer of word order and phonetic structures, are observed among simultaneous bilinguals. Similarly, Fabiano-Smith and Barlow (2010) observed BBLs' cross-linguistic transfer of phonological skills and use of their bilingual language inventories. Code-switching is typically observed among young simultaneous bilinguals (Pearson, 2008). Young children developing more than one language mix words and phrases of one language into another, manipulating languages, and following language specific constraints and rules (Paradis et al., 2003). Code-switching in a rule-governed way is a metalinguistic skill that BBLs possess.

### Language Proficiency

In contrast to language stages, Cummins (1979) proposed the notions of Basic Interpersonal Communication Skills (BICS) and Cognitive Academic

Language Proficiency (CALP) for examining the development of bilinguals' language proficiency. BICS is the conversational, social language in the L2, which is acquired quickly by BBLs who are exposed to and interact with native speakers. CALP represents the academic language, which is often decontextualized, that is required to be successful in the school environment. A two-year period of immersion in the target language may result in the development of social language (Cummins, 1979). On the other hand, it may take between five and seven years for a bilingual learner to acquire academic language that is on the level of native speakers. Cummins further extended his notions of BICS and CALP by considering the Language Interdependence Hypothesis. Rather than considering BICS and CALP as two distinct processes, these occur in conjunction with each other. For example, when a child produces the word "mama," there is a cognitive association between the primary caregiver and the word. As children continue to make more cognitive connections to concepts in their environment, they first generalize the concept. For example, all four-legged animals become doggies or kitties. With increased exposure to concepts and vocabulary, children begin to categorize; "doggies" become horses, cows, etc. These types of cognitive associations are prototypical of all children. Also, it is important to note that children's receptive (e.g., listening, comprehending) language is different from their expressive (e.g., spoken, written) language. Often, bilingual learners may understand more than they can express (see Byers-Heinlein & Lew-Williams, 2013).

These two primary theories provide a general overview of BBLs' language development and proficiency. We must consider that all children's development occurs over time and while there are language milestones, language development and proficiency is influenced by a variety of factors, especially opportunities to engage in language-rich environments. In the subsequent section, we explore the commonalities observed between typical developing BBLs with learners with language disorders.

## *Commonalities between BBLs versus Learners with Language Disorder*

When differentiating between speech-language differences and disorders, it is vital that educators and SLPs consider commonalities to ensure that individuals are not over- or under-identified. We have compiled a list from various references (Ortiz & Maldonado-Colon, 1986; Roseberry-McKibbin, 2008; Willig & Greenberg, 1986) of common characteristics that are often observed in bilingual language learners (typical) and individuals who present with a language disorder (atypical):

- speaks infrequently
- uses gestures
- speaks in single words or phrases
- doesn't volunteer information
- comments inappropriately
- poor recall
- poor syntax/grammar
- poor comprehension
- poor vocabulary
- difficulty sequencing ideas
- difficulty sequencing events
- unable to tell or retell stories
- confuses similar sounding words
- poor pronunciation

## Identification of Language Disorder

The similar characteristics of typically developing BBLs with atypically developing counterparts make the assessment process challenging. When assessing BBLs, SLPs must: (a) evaluate both languages and determine if the disorder is present in one or both languages; (b) individually and holistically analyze the difficulty in each language with respect to the learner's articulation and components of language; (c) compare the learner's language and cognitive abilities to same-age, typical and atypical monolingual and bilingual peers; and (d) design appropriate intervention plans in one or both languages to address language and cognitive skills (ASHA, 2020b; Beyers-Heinlein & Lew-Williams, 2013; Kohnert, 2010). Bilingual educators must provide language-rich experiences in both languages while also encouraging the families' and caregivers' daily cultural and linguistic practices (Mattock et al., 2010). Further, as Prezas and Jo (2017) recommended, language learning opportunities should be culturally and linguistically responsive and efficacious, including peer interactions, playing with language and multimodal experiences.

Professionals who comprehend typical second language development can better distinguish atypical development and correctly identify children who exhibit a disorder. Moreover, if an educator is having difficulty discerning whether a learner is presenting with a language disorder, Prezas and Jo (2017) suggested the following (Table 5-1):

*Table 5-1.* Some Initial Considerations for Suspected Language Disorder

1. Whether parent(s)/caregiver(s) have concerns
2. Languages spoken by the student/dialects
3. Language use (both at school and at home)
4. Proficiency in both languages
5. Whether the concern is present in both languages
6. Age of child
7. Age of U.S. public school exposure/enrollment
8. School Program (e.g., Dual-Language, English Immersion).

Prezas and Jo (2017, p. 10).

Drawing from the research on language development, it is clear that "bilinguals are not two monolinguals in one person" (Grosjean, 1989, p. 4). Additionally, it is well understood that languages, especially those using nonalphabetic writing systems, have distinct patterns of acquisition. It is important to consider the intersectionality of language, culture and cognition that influences language development.

### *Intersectionality of Culture and Language in Assessing Bicultural-Bilingual Learners*

Culture is interrelated with language and cognitive development. In today's multicultural, dynamic nation, educators are challenged with developing culturally responsive educational and instructional programs that effectively serve BBLs. According to Bilinguistics (2020a), "Effectively accounting for the influence of culture enables us to distinguish between the children who are simply making the errors that are normal when learning a second language and the children who have speech and language disorders" (1st paragraph).

Professionals working with BBLs must acknowledge differences and initially develop cultural competence in order to determine best practices. Betancourt et al. (2003) defined cultural competence as

> understanding the importance of social and cultural influences on patients' health, beliefs, and behaviors, and how these factors interact at multiple levels of the healthcare delivery system, and finally, devising interventions that take these issues into account to ensure effective healthcare delivery to diverse patient populations. (p. 294)

Beyond cultural competence, Flores et al. (2018) posited that professionals must be culturally efficacious; that is, they exhibit both competence and confidence in addressing the needs of BBLs. Having a deep understanding of how different groups interpret and make sense of the world will assist professionals in differentiating second language learning from speech and language disorders. Thus, it is imperative that we recognize and understand the diverse social and cultural backgrounds of BBLs during the assessment process.

**Family's Acculturation and Education Level.** In addition to language, a vital part of assessing any student for a potential speech/language disorder is the gathering of family and health information. Moreover, when assessing BBLs, the culture and education level of the family must be taken into consideration.

Robinson-Zañartu (1996) stated that "world view and belief systems, acculturation stress, school-home discontinuity, learning styles, and communication patterns, are useful reference points from which to develop more culturally compatible evaluation approaches" (p. 373). When discussing Native American students, Havighurst (1978) reported that at the time, 66% of teachers did not understand or appreciate cultural differences between them and their Native American students. Presently, we still find educators who are not prepared to work with culturally and linguistically diverse populations, especially bilingual populations (Flores et al., 2018).

Therefore, similar to other bilingual educators, when SLPs serve culturally diverse students, they must learn about the culture of the individuals they serve (Delgado-Gaitan, 1991). We concur that the "Assessment of language skills should be culturally relevant and functional and involve the collaborative efforts of families/caregivers, classroom teachers, SLPs, special educators, and other professionals as needed" (ASHA, 2017, 1$^{st}$ paragraph under Comprehensive Assessment). Further, SLPs must be knowledgeable and aware of these differences in order to appropriately assess and provide effective therapy. To prevent the diagnosis of a language difference as a language disorder, SLPs must conduct valid screenings, assessments and interventions. Consideration must also be given to providing the family with information on normal speech development of BBLs and home strategies/activities (Commins, 1992; Kayser, 1998; Lieberman, 1989; Lynch & Hanson, 1998). As professionals serving bilingual populations, we must work together to ensure educational equity and access. Hence, in the next section, we present the process of assessment and diagnosis.

## Speech and Language Disorder Assessment Process and Tools

To obtain a comprehensive assessment of the language skills and needs of the bilingual/multilingual learner, researchers concur that all languages of exposure should be evaluated (Peña & Bedore, 2011; Yavas & Goldstein, 1998).

When assessing bilingual/multilingual populations, it is important to note that standardized assessments may not reflect valid results (Laing & Kamhi, 2003; Bedore & Peña, 2008).

While this is not an extensive review of the literature on assessment, based on our experience as SLPs and bilingual educators, we concur with Sánchez et al.'s (2013) recommendations. Clearly, all diagnostic decisions should be based on a comprehensive battery of formal and informal measures that consider all languages of exposure. As mentioned in the initial sections of this chapter, there is an over-identification of BBLs for special education services. In the United States, there are increasing concerns regarding over- and under-identification of BBLs with disabilities (Zacarin, 2011a). Over-identification is typically reflective of a lack of educator preparation, teacher preparedness and familiarity with working with bicultural-bilingual populations, while under-identification is reflective of fears that school personnel are making referrals too quickly and not allowing sufficient time for English language learning. This phenomenon appears to suggest that there is a disconnect between research and practice. This continued occurrence calls for further research on the education, preparation and practices of professionals that work with and diagnose bilingual/multilingual learners.

IDEA mandates that highly qualified personnel obtain data-based documentation conducted at reasonable intervals (Texas Speech-Language Hearing Association, [TSHA], 2009). Quality data ensures that suspected disorders are not a result of lack of instruction. Researchers, therefore, have advocated for other comprehensive means in addition to standardized and criterion-referenced tests when assessing children's language skills. According to ASHA (2020a)

> Clinical approaches—such as interview style, assessment tools, and therapeutic techniques—that are appropriate for one individual may not be appropriate for another. It is important to recognize that the unique influence of an individual's cultural and linguistic background may change over time and according to circumstance (e.g., interactions in the workplace, with authority figures, within a social context), necessitating adjustments in clinical approaches. (5th paragraph)

When assessing bicultural-bilingual populations, professionals must consider the diverse cultural norms including verbal and non-verbal, gestures, and silence across different groups that affect the language behaviors that learners demonstrate. In the subsequent section, we highlight tools to be used alongside prototypical assessment techniques when determining language disorders in bilingual populations: Ethnographic Interviewing, Response to Intervention (RTI), PLUSS Model, Dynamic Assessment and Language Sampling.

**Ethnographic Interviewing.** Given the intersectionality of language, culture and cognition, ASHA (2020a) encourages the use of ethnographic interviewing as part of the speech and language assessment. As opposed to asking questions from a checklist, this technique allows for the gathering of educational and background information from family/caregiver, student and teacher. Ethnographic interviewing employs "open-ended questions, restatement, and summarizing for clarification" (ASHA, 2020a, Ethnographic Interviewing Section, paragraph 1). The ethnographic technique assists in the validation of the assessment findings. We recommend this technique also be utilized by classroom educators.

**RTI Process.** RTI is a three-tier model/support system designed to help educators identify children who are struggling and prevent long-term academic failure. Instruction is intensified systemically and targeted towards each child's needs. According to TSHA (2009), the Tiers of RTI include:

Tier 1: Core Instruction
Tier 2: Targeted Group Intervention
Tier 3: Intensive Individualized Intervention (p. 1, column 2).

While valuable information is gathered during the RTI process, Zacarin (2011b) cautioned that the RTI process may not address the distinct needs of BBLs. Zacarin recommended that the school curriculum attend to language development and differences, provide appropriate cultural and linguistic pedagogy and tools and incorporate an understanding of various cultural backgrounds of BBLs. Essentially, as is delineated by the U.S. Office of Special Education Program (2020), the school environment should be providing opportunities for learning language and academic success.

Linan-Thompson et al. (2006) contended that it is crucial to recognize that the needs of BBLs differ slightly from monolingual peers in order to make sure they receive the appropriate instructional support in a timely manner. Richards-Tutor et al. (2016) identified five key recommendations to consider for BBLs during academic instruction:

1. Provide students the opportunity to develop academic oral language skills while simultaneously teaching literacy and other content areas
2. Teach vocabulary across content areas
3. Provide instruction and/or instructional support in the primary language as needed
4. Provide appropriate interventions for English learners who need support beyond Tier 1 instruction
5. Implement culturally responsive instruction (p. 3).

We accept Castro-Villarreal et al.'s (2015) assertion that there is a need for more professional development specifically targeting bicultural-bilingual populations to ensure that the RTI process is being used appropriately.

**PLUSS Model.** Evidence-based practices for teaching BBLs in an RTI framework is included in the PLUSS model, which is a conceptual framework based on a synthesis of the research identifying what supports successful learning for BBLs. Sandford et al. (2012) identified the following components:

- **P:** Pre-teach critical vocabulary
- **L:** Language modeling and opportunities for using academic language
- **U:** Use visuals and graphic organizers
- **S:** Systematic and explicit instruction in reading components and strategies
- **S:** Strategic use of native language (p. 61).

PLUSS is an instructional planning and lesson delivery tool that bridges research with practice. It was developed in response to difficulties that educators experience in identifying and implementing research-based instruction and intervention for BBLs within an RTI framework. PLUSS is unique in that its components can be implemented in instruction and intervention across all RTI tiers, and specifically in tiers designed to provide secondary and tertiary support (Sanford et al., 2012). In the case of bilingual teachers, RTI is a form of dynamic assessment as discussed in the subsequent section that can be used to inform data-driven instruction.

**Dynamic Assessment.** Grounded in Peña et al.'s (2014) extensive research, dynamic assessment is considered an essential tool in assessing BBLs. According to ASHA (2020c), "dynamic assessment is a method of conducting a language assessment which seeks to identify the skills that an individual child possesses as well as their learning potential" (Dynamic Assessment Section, 1st paragraph). It emphasizes the learning process and accounts for the amount and nature of examiner investment.

Likewise, Kapantzoglou et al. (2012) suggested using dynamic assessment or a pretest-teach-posttest approach. This approach allows SLPs to distinguish the cognitive capacity or learning abilities needed to acquire language and communication skills. It also allows the identification of language and communication disorders that may need further intervention. In the pretest phase, a testing format of the concept to be taught is created and the SLP probes linguistic concepts with which the student has difficulty via formal and/or informal measures. Then a baseline level for comparison during the post-test phase is obtained. In the teaching phase, strategies and techniques for learning concepts are provided. In the post-test phase, a testing format of the concept taught is re-introduced to determine if there was improvement. When a child's response to this mediated learning experience is examined, results can have direct implications for intervention and help distinguish between a language difference and a language disorder, especially for children from bicultural-bilingual backgrounds. Children who are able to make significant changes in short term intervention sessions likely do not have an underlying language learning difficulty and are merely experiencing a language difference. Children who are unable to make changes are more likely to have an underlying language disorder. In the case of teachers, they can embed the results into their curriculum. Bilinguistics (2020b) suggested that dynamic assessment along with storytelling provides valuable information regarding the learner's language repertoire. Classroom teachers can also use dynamic assessment (see Melick, 2017).

**Language Samples.** Bedore et al. (2010) suggested the use of language samples when evaluating bilingual children. Further, they recommended that "When evaluating the language abilities of bilingual children, it is important to account for their distributed language knowledge" (p. 499). Collecting language samples for three to five minutes or in intervals when BBLs are interacting with their peers can provide a wealth of data and useful metrics for the identification of language disorders. Language samples allow for the measurement of length of utterance, semantic inventories, syntax accuracy, phonological abilities and pragmatic skills (Bedore et al., 2010). These language samples can be used in planning instructional activities to assist the language and communication development needs of all learners.

## Conclusion

As previously stated, the number of BBLs over-/under-identified in special education continues to grow. To address the disconnect between research and practice as well as to ensure that we as professionals meet the language needs of BBLs, our intent is for bicultural-bilingual teachers to have a deeper understanding of the language and communication development continuum of typical bilingual children as compared to atypical bilingual children. While bilingual classroom educators and SLPs have distinct functions, they each play a key role in supporting BBLs' language development. Due to the need for continued education, preparation and practices to meet the needs of the growing U.S. bilingual/multilingual population, we recommend that bilingual education teacher preparation as well as professional development for bilingual educators attend to critical examination of the differences between BBL language development versus language disorders. A fundamental indicator that bilingual educators need to know is that BBLs who present with language disorders will demonstrate difficulty in both languages. Early childhood bilingual classroom teachers play a crucial role in supporting learners' language development and identifying the potential need for further evaluation (Prezas & Jo, 2017). All bilingual educators must demonstrate language awareness in which they focus on language acquisition as well as the form and function of language in their practices (Lindahl & Henderson, 2019). We suggest that this heightened understanding will ensure that bilingual children are appropriately identified and that language development opportunities are provided to assist children's cognitive, language and communication development.

## *References*

American Speech Hearing Association (2017). *Comprehensive assessment.* Retrieved from https://www.asha.org/PRPSpecificTopic.aspx?folderid=8589935327&section=Resources

American Speech Hearing Association (2020a). *Assessment tools, techniques, and data sources.* Retrieved from https://www.asha.org/Practice-Portal/Clinical-Topics/Late-Language-Emergence/Assessment-Tools-Techniques-and-Data-Sources/

American Speech Hearing Association (2020b). *Bilingual service delivery.* Retrieved from https://www.asha.org/PRPSpecificTopic.aspx?folderid=8589935225&section=Key_Issues#Second-Language_Acquisitionw.urbancollaborative.org/files/tampa_presentation_shorter.pdf

American Speech Hearing Association (2020c). *Dynamic assessment.* Retrieved from https://www.asha.org/practice/multicultural/issues/Dynamic-Assessment/

Baker, C. (2006). *Foundations of bilingual education and bilingualism* (4th ed.). Multilingual Matters.

Bedore, L. M., & Peña, E. D. (2008). Assessment of bilingual children for identification of language disorder: Current findings and implications for practice. *International Journal of Bilingual Education and Bilingualism, 11,* 1.

Bedore, L. M., Peña, E. D., Gillam, R. B., & Ho, T. H. (2010). Language sample measure and language ability in Spanish-English bilingual kindergarteners. *Journal of Communication Disorders, 43,* 498–510.

Betancourt, J. R., Green, A. R., Carrillo, J. E., & Ananeh-Firempong, O. (2003). Defining cultural competence: A practical framework for addressing racial/ethnic disparities in health and health care. *Public Health Reports, 118,* 293–302.

Bilinguistics (2020a). *Cultural values: Cultural differences in speech therapy.* Retrieved from https://bilinguistics.com/cultural-values/

Bilinguistics (2020b). *Why understanding cultural parameters is important to SLPs.* Retrieved from https://bilinguistics.com/cultural-parameters/

Bird, E. K., Cleave, P., Trudeau, N., Thordardottir, E., Stutton, A., & Thorpe, A. (2005). The language abilities of bilingual children with down syndrome. *American Journal of Speech-Language Pathology, 14*(3), 187–199.

Bloomfield, L. (1933). *Language.* Holt.

Bosh, L., & Sebastian-Galles, N. (2001). Evidence of early language discrimination abilities in infants from bilingual environments. *Infancy, 2,* 29–49.

Burns, T. C., Yoshida, K. A., Hill, K., & Werker, J. (2007). The development of phonetic representation in bilingual and monolingual infants. *Applied Psycholinguistics, 28,* 455–474.

Byers-Heinlein, K., & Lew-Williams, C. (2013). Bilingualism in the early years: What the science says. *LEARNing landscapes, 7*(1), 95–112.

Castro-Villarreal, F., Villarreal, V., & Sullivan, J. R. (2015). Special education policy and response to intervention: Identifying promises and pitfalls to advance social justice for diverse students. *Contemporary School Psychology, 20*(1), 10–20.

Commins, N. L. (1992). Parents and public schools: The experiences of four Mexican immigrant families. *Equity and Choice, 8,* 40–45.

Cummins, J. (1979). Linguistic interdependence and the educational development of bilingual children. *Review of Educational Research, 49*(2), 222–251.

De Houwer, A. (1990). *The acquisition of two languages from birth: A case study.* Cambridge University Press.

Delgado-Gaitan, C. (1991). Involving parents in the schools: A process of empowerment. *American Journal of Education, 100,* 20–16.

Fabiano-Smith, L., & Barlow, J. A. (2010). Interaction in bilingual phonological acquisition: Evidence from phonetic inventories. *International Journal of Bilingual Education and Bilingualism, 13*(1), 81–97.

Fiestas, C. E., & Peña, E. D. (2004). Narrative discourse in bilingual children: Language and task effects. *Language, Speech, and Hearing Services in Schools, 35,* 155–168.

Flores, B. B., Abundis, A., García, C. T., & Santillan, L. (in press). ReFraming our work: Critical bicultural-bilingual pedagogues.

Flores, B. B., Claeys, L. C., & Gist, C. (2018). *Culturally efficacious teacher preparation and pedagogies for social justice.* Lexington.

Genesee, F. (1989). Early bilingual development: One language or two? *Journal of Child Language, 16,* 161–179.

Genesee, F., Paradis, J., & Crago, M. (2004). *Dual language development and disorders.* Brokes.

Grosjean, F. (1989). Neurolinguists, beware! The bilingual is not two monolinguals in one person. *Brain and Language, 36,* 3–15.

Grosjean, F., & Li, P. (2013). *The psycholinguistics of bilingualism.* Wiley-Blackwell.

Guiberson, M. M., & Atkins, J. (2012). Speech-language pathologists' preparation, practices, and perspectives on serving culturally and linguistically diverse children.

*Communication Disorders Quarterly, 33*(3),169–180. https://doi.org/10.1177/ 1525740110384132

Havighurst, R. J. (1978). *The education of American Indian children and youth* (Summary report and recommendations: National Study of American Indians Education, Series No. 4, No. 6). University of Minnesota.

Huang, B. H., & Flores, B. B. (2018). English language proficiency Assessment for the 21st century (ELPA 21). *Language Assessment Quarterly*, 1–10. https://doi.org/ 10.1080/15434303

Jacobson, P. F., & Cairns, H. S. (2008). Considering linguistic input in a bilingual situation: Implications for acquisition. *Language, Speech, and Hearing Services in Schools*, 352–364.

Kapantzoglou, M., Restrepo, M. A., & Thompson, M. S. (2012). Dynamic assessment of word learning skills: Identifying language impairment in bilingual children. *Language, Speech, and Hearing Services in Schools, 43*, 81–96.

Kayser, H. (1998). *Assessment and intervention resource for Hispanic children*. Singular.

Kecskes, I., & Papp, T. (2000). *Foreign language and mother tongue*. Lawrence Erlbaum Associates.

Kimble, C. (2013). Speech-language pathologists' comfort levels in English language learner service delivery. *Communication Disorders Quarterly, 35*, 21–27.

Kohnert, K. (2010). Bilingual children with primary language disorder: Issues, evidence and implications for clinical actions. *Journal of Communication Disorders, 43*, 456–473.

Kohnert, K., Kan, P. F., & Conboy, B. T. (2010). Lexical and grammatical associations in sequential bilingual preschoolers. *Journal of Speech, Language, and Hearing Research, 53*, 684–698.

Krashen, S. (1981). Second language acquisition. *Second Language Learning, 3*(7), 19–39.

Krashen, S. (1982). *Principles and practice in second language acquisition*. Pergamon Press, Inc.

Laing, S., & Kamhi, A. (2003). Alternative assessment of language and literacy in culturally and linguistically diverse populations. *Language, Speech, and Hearing Services in Schools, 34*, 44–55.

Lieberman, A. F. (1989). What is culturally sensitive intervention? *Early Child Development and Care, 50*, 197–204.

Linan-Thompson, S., Vaughn, S., Prater, K., & Cirino, P. (2006). The response to intervention of English language learners at risk for reading problems. *Journal of Learning Disabilities, 39*(5), 390–398.

Lindahl, K. M., & Henderson, K. I. (2019). The intersection of language awareness and ideology among in-service teachers of emerging bilinguals. *Journal of Immersion and Content-Based Language Education, 7*(1), 61–87

Lynch, E. W., & Hanson, M. J. (1998). *Developing cross-cultural competence* (2nd ed.). Paul H. Brookes.

Mattock, K., Polka, L., Rvachew, S., & Krehm, M. (2010). The first steps in word learning are easier when the shoes fit: Comparing monolingual and bilingual infants. *Developmental Science, 13*(1), 229–243. https://doi.org/10.1111/j.1467-7687.2009.00891.x.

Meisel, I. M. (2001). The simultaneous acquisition of two first languages. *Trends in Bilingual Acquisition, 1*, 11. https://doi.org/10.1515/ZFSW.2009.002

Melick, N. (2017). *The SLP's guide to dynamic assessment for culturally and linguistically diverse (CLD) children.* Retrieved from https://www.uwo.ca/fhs/lwm/teaching/dld2_2017_18/Melick_DynamicAx.pdf

Ortiz, A. A., & Maldonado-Colon, A. (1986). Reducing inappropriate referral of language minority students in special education. In A. C. Willig & H. F. Greenberg (Eds.), *Bilingualism and learning disabilities* (pp. 37–52). American Library.

Paradis, J., Crago, M., Genesee, F., & Rice, M. (2003). French-English bilingual children with SLI: How they compare with their monolingual peers. *Journal of Speech, Language, and Hearing Research, 46*, 113–127.

Paradis, J., & Navarro, S. (2003). Subject realization and cross-linguistic interference in the bilingual acquisition of Spanish and English: What is the role of the input? *Journal of Child Language, 30*, 371–393.

Pearson, B. Z. (2008). *Raising a bilingual child.* Random House.

Pena, E. D., & Bedore, L. M. (2011). It takes two: Improving assessment accuracy in bilingual children. *The ASHA Leader.*

Peña, E. D., Gillam, R. B., & Bedore, L. M. (2014). Dynamic assessment accurately identifies language disorder in ELLs. *Journal of Speech, Language, Hearing Research. 57,* 2208–2220.

Petitto, L., Katerelos, M., Levy, B., Gauna, K., Te′treault, K., & Ferraro, V. (2001). Bilingual signed and spoken language acquisition from birth: Implications for the mechanisms underlying early bilingual language acquisition. *Journal of Child Language, 28,* 453–496.

Prezas, R. F., & Jo, A. A. (2017). Differentiating language difference and language disorder: Information for teachers working with English language learners in the schools. *Journal of Human Services: Training, Research, and Practice, 2*(1), article 2. Retrieved from https://scholarworks.sfasu.edu/cgi/viewcontent.cgi?article=1033&context=jhstrp

Quay, S. (2001). Managing linguistic boundaries in early trilingual development. In J. Cenoz & F. Genesee (Eds.), *Trends in bilingual acquisition.* John Benjamins.

Richards-Tutor, C., Aceves, T., & Reese, L. (2016). Evidence-based practices for English learners (Document No. IC-18). Retrieved from University of Florida, Collaboration for Effective Educator, Development, Accountability, and Reform Center website http://ceedar.education.ufl.edu/tools/innovation-configurations/

Robison-Zañatu, C. (1996). Serving Native American children and families, considering cultural variables. *Language, Speech and Hearing Services in Schools, 27*(4), 373–384.

Roseberry-McKibbin, C. (2008). *Multicultural students with special language needs* (3rd ed.). Academic Communication Associates, Inc.

Roseberry-McKibbin, C. A., Brice, A., & O'Hanlon, L. (2005). Serving English language learners in public school settings: A national survey. *Language, Speech, and Hearing Services in Schools, 36*, 48–61.

Roseberry-McKibbin C. A., & Eicholtz, G. E. (1994). Serving limited English proficient children in schools: A national survey. *Language, Speech, and Hearing Services in Schools, 25*, 156–164.

Sánchez, S. V., Rodríguez, B., Soto-Huerta, M. E., Castro-Villarreal, F., Guerra, N., & Flores, B. B. (2013). A case for multidimensional bilingual assessment. *Language Assessment Quarterly, 10*(3), 160–177. https://doi.org/1080/15434303.2013.769544

Sanford, A. K., Brown, J., & Turner, M. (2012). Enhancing instruction for English learners in response to intervention systems: The PLUSS Model. *Multiple Voices For Ethnically Diverse Exceptional Learners, 13*(1), 56–70.

Sheng, L., Pena, E. D., Bedore, L. M., & Fiestas, C. E. (2012). Semantic deficits in Spanish-English bilingual children with language impairment. *Journal of Speech, Language, and Hearing Research, 55*, 1–15.

Sundara, M., Polka, L., & Molnar, M. (2008). Development of coronal stop perception: Bilingual infants keep pace with their monolingual peers. *Cognition, 108*, 232–242.

Texas Speech-Language Hearing Association (2009). *RTI and SLP services*. Retrieved from https://www.txsha.org/professional_resources

U.S. Office of Special Education Programs (2020). *Response to intervention and learning disability eligibility*. Retrieved from https://www.txasp.org/assets/evaluation%20of%20learning%20disability%20eligibility.pdf

Volterra, V., & Taeschner, T. (1978). The acquisition and development of language by bilingual children. *Journal of Child Language, 5*, 311–326.

Vygotsky, L. S., Hanfmann, E., Vakar, G., & Kozulin, A. (1971). *Thought and language*. MIT Press.

Willig, A. C., & Greenburg, H. F. (Eds.). (1986). *Bilingualism and learning disabilities*. American Library.

Woodcock, R. W., Muñoz-Sandoval, A. F., Ruef, M. L., & Alvarado, C. G. (2005). *Woodcock-Munoz Language Survey-Revised*. Riverside Publishing.

Yavas, M., & Goldstein, B. (1998). Phonological assessment and treatment of bilingual speakers. *American Journal of Speech-Language Pathology, 7*, 49–59.

Yip, V. (2013). Simultaneous language acquisition. In F. Grosjean & P. Li (Eds.), *The psycholinguistics of bilingualism* (pp. 119–144). Wiley-Blackwell.

Yip, V., & Matthews, S. (2007). Relative clauses in Cantonese-English bilingual children: Typological challenges and processing motivations. *Studies in Second Language Acquisition, 29*(2), 277–300.

Zacarin, D. (2011a). *The over-under-identification of ELLs in special education*. Retrieved from https://www.colorincolorado.org/article/over-and-under-identification-ells-special-education

Zacarin, D. (2011b). *Using RTI effectively with English language learners*. Retrieved from https://www.colorincolorado.org/article/rti-and-english-language-learners

# *Developing Bilingual/Dual Language Educators' Assessment Practices*

# 6. Understanding Assessment and Evaluation When Preparing Bilingual Teacher Candidates

MARGARITA MACHADO-CASAS
*San Diego State University*

KATHERINE ESPINOZA
*Texas A&M University, San Antonio*

## Introduction

Understanding the systematic structures in place to assess bilingual students in Spanish is one of the areas bilingual teacher candidates desperately need. Most teachers lack the proper preparation, expertise and previous experience with assessments used in schools today. Their understanding of how Spanish language proficiency assessments are used in schools to place, monitor and exit bilingual students is an area where universities with bilingual education programs must invest time in order to prepare their bilingual teacher candidates to enter the field. In this chapter, we will offer suggestions for bilingual preservice teacher preparation programs to implement courses dedicated to the assessment of bilingual learners' Spanish language assessments. Throughout their reflection, the bilingual teacher candidates tap into their own linguistic abilities to express themselves in both English and Spanish.[1] Bilingual preservice teacher preparation programs must understand the importance of implementing courses that address assessment instruments and strategies used in local, state and national systems for culturally and linguistically diverse students and it must be emphasized. In addition, this chapter will focus on the development of successful assessments for culturally and linguistically diverse students that can be used in classrooms to align with best practices.

## Cultural Validity Framework

Cultural validity in assessment is used as a framework as it serves as a lens to understand how cultural background plays a factor in the ways students and teachers interpret assessments (Basterra, Trumball, & Solano-Flores, 2011). This framework provides a lens to explore the assessment needs to better understand and address the needs of culturally and linguistically diverse students. Exploring such needs is crucial as assessment continues to play a central role in the educational system of the United States. Researchers, policy makers and educators must continue to consider the hegemonic implications that result from assessment systems that continue to hinder the academic success of students who do not match the status-quo: students whose backgrounds reflect White middle class. Further, a cultural validity framework "introduces the construct of cultural validity as an organizing principle for addressing the issues entailed in ensuring the fair and valid assessment of students from ethno-linguistic minority backgrounds" (Basterra et al., 2011).

## Conceptualizing Cultural Validity in Assessment

When accounting for culturally and linguistically diverse students, one must begin by accounting for the roles that language and culture play in assessment (Cole, 1999). Darling-Hammond (1997) first identified the usefulness of cultural validity in assessment as a means for approaching and creating a conceptual framework that would serve the needs of culturally and linguistically diverse (CLD) students in an era of continued globalization. Solano-Flores (2011) introduces the concept of assessments and tests as representations of cultural artifacts. These cultural artifacts result as part of our educational system in the US, which places a grave amount of importance on instructional accountability to ensure that students are making adequate progress in school. These societal mandates are oftentimes imposed by individuals in power who do not understand the challenges faced by CLD students. One must begin to understand how assessment in and of itself is a cultural practice and consider the ways in which cultural validity has been defined in research and practice by drawing connections between cultural validity and making it into a fair assessment practice for CLD students. Therefore, Solano-Flores and Nelson-Barber (2001) provided the following definition of cultural validity:

> The effectiveness with which [...] assessment addresses the socio-cultural influences that shape student thinking and the ways in which students make sense of [...] items and respond to them. These socio-cultural influences include the sets of values, beliefs, experiences, communication patterns, teaching and learning

styles, and epistemologies inherent in the students' cultural backgrounds, and the socio-economic conditions prevailing the cultural groups. (p. 555)

As such, this definition provides us with the necessary tools to better understand and investigate the complexities surrounding assessment and CLD students. A cultural validity framework provides a space for addressing the validity and effectiveness of sociocultural influences on assessments. Solano-Flores and Nelson-Barber contended that "Although we agree with this view, we contend that current approaches to assessing cultural minorities do not enable assessment developers to identify with accuracy what in an assessment prevents students from a given cultural group from demonstrating their competence" (p. 555). Therefore, we must take on different approaches to addressing challenges and gaps currently present in the assessment of CLD students.

## How Language Impacts Assessment

One of the major implications for CLD students in assessment is addressing the issues that are associated with language. CLD students are labeled as English Learners (ELS) and along with this they automatically become subjected to linguistic biases found in tests and assessments. Linguistic bias in assessment has been defined as any type of bias or hindrances on speakers of other languages, bilingual speakers, which results in an imprecise assessment of CLD students who are not proficient in English. Such biases can manifest themselves throughout different aspects of testing and assessment both in overt and covert ways including testing materials and in the administration of the test. In terms of testing materials, these may not be sensitive to the needs of CLD students.

Linguistic bias can be pervasively found in assessment materials especially because standardized tests are typically designed to meet the needs of English dominant students. Depending on how assessments were constructed they may contain information that CLD students cannot decipher such as analogies and other questions with vocabulary that is not commonly used or have yet to be exposed to.

The ways in which tests are administered can also pose a myriad of obstacles for CLD students. For example, limitations on time can cause a hindrance to completion of a test if a student has not mastered English. Research has proven that it takes ELs between five to seven years to adequately develop their academic use of English. However, testing systems in the US begin to evaluate students based on their ability to function in English as early as kindergarten. Time restrictions prove to be one of the major issues related to how language differences impact testing for CLD students. Harry and Klinger (2006) attribute issues related to language differences encountered by minority students as a pervasive problem that is attributed to the overrepresentation of language minority students in special education.

## Considerations

Although we agree with this view, we contend that current approaches to assessing cultural minorities do not enable assessment developers to identify with accuracy what in an assessment prevents students from a given cultural group from demonstrating their competencies.

Ultimately the objectives of bilingual education programs across the U.S. are to cultivate students' academic achievement, bilingualism, biliteracy and sociocultural competence, which includes "identity development, cross-cultural competence, and multicultural appreciation" (Howard, Lindholm-Leary, Rogers, Olague, Medina, Kennedy, Sugarman, & Christian, 2018, p. 3). These additive approaches are ideologies that must be instilled in bilingual teacher educator preparation programs. However, currently, a scant number of research studies focus on the need for developing such programs (Trent & Artiles, 1998).

## **Review of Relevant Literature**

In considering the assessment of bilingual and immigrant students, we must consider the impact their national background plays in their acculturation of schooling practices in the U.S. As such, bilingual and immigrant students are simultaneously situated in international, national and local communities. This diverse background requires that they develop an awareness of globalization and nationalism (Gibson & Koyama, 2011). Suarez-Orozco (2001) defined globalization as a process of economic, social, and cultural change that decouples geopolitical boundaries "from powerful market forces" via "unprecedented new patterns of large-scale immigration" (p. 348).

In their article "Sustaining the Sociopolitical Spirit of Bilingual Education," Maldonado and Machado-Casas discussed a similar instance about bilingual students that may be more proficient in one of their languages but higher in content. It may be that one English learner may be very high- functioning in their first language which indicates that what they need to develop is their language abilities in English versus the other student that may also be scoring very low in their native language, which goes to the point that just focusing on the language abilities in English may be inappropriate

(Maldonado & Machado-Casas, 2019). This shows that bilingual students' needs have to be considered in all aspects of assessments and current policies should reflect the needs of multicultural populations.

As educators, it is our responsibility to provide the students with a curriculum that is socioculturally appropriate. The teacher should consider the sociocultural background of every student. Not all students have the same access to resources. Some students within the bilingual program may have parents that have had access to higher education (Maldonado & Machado- Casas, 2019). In school, educators must make learning meaningful for students who are typically marginalized by traditional notions of schooling by capitalizing on ways of connecting their home and school lives. Families that are economically disadvantaged work hard but may not have the experiences necessary in education that will allow their kids to see a future beyond high school.

Maldonado, Mosqueda, Bravo and Solis (2020) suggested providing a professional development model for assessing and teaching mathematics to bilingual students. They find that oftentimes there is inequality, especially in assessment and teaching mathematics, which tends to put bilingual students at a disadvantage (Maldonado et al., 2020). Their study undertakes a research design involving workshops where they used formative assessments to help educators achieve equity. Importantly, they examine the four different domains in their efforts of developing formative assessment; that is conceptual understanding (understanding of mathematical concepts), procedural fluency (ability to carry out procedures accurately), mathematics vocabulary and writing conventions. They recommended the use of explicit mathematical concepts for emergent bilingual students to build their English language fluency, arguing that teachers can leverage formative assessments to enhance equity in the learning of emergent bilinguals.

## *Methodology*

This chapter draws from data from a bilingual preservice teacher preparation program at a Hispanic Serving Institution (HSI) in South Texas. The bilingual teacher candidates are required to take an assessment course during the semester before student teaching as part of their formation courses with a duration of 16 weeks. Drawing from narrative research methods (Merriam, 1998), the following data sources were collected for analysis: student responses, assessment analysis and student Spanish assessment projects. We analyzed data that examined how bilingual teacher candidates at the HSI related theory and knowledge as the basis for bilingual and bicultural education programs.

## Study Participants

There was a total of 24 participants who identified as Latinx, all of them were in their junior year of their teacher preparation program. Of the 24, 20 were female and 4 were male. Twenty-one were also first-generation college students. Along with their assessment course, the cohort also took an additional three courses together: bilingual reading methods, bilingual science methods and bilingual social studies methods. In addition to their course work they were also required to complete a field internship experience twice a week for a total of 15 hours in a bilingual EC-6 classroom setting. During the field internships in the bilingual courses, the teacher candidates had to complete several assignments that were aligned to the assessment course.

## Course Objectives and Assignments

The course was divided into two principal functions; the first part of the course was intended to familiarize students with the complex issues found in schools of linguistically and culturally diverse populations and with the connection on assessment practices (current and historical). State guides regarding language programs, essential elements and academic assessments for students who are learning English (ELLs) were covered in addition to an overview of bilingual education in Texas. The course was designed for bilingual teacher candidates to interact with the materials and topics of the course; therefore, small collaborative groups, discussions about readings and other activities were to be carried out for homework and class sessions.

The other part of the course offered practice in the administration and interpretation of standardized assessments that are used in public schools that have students who are linguistically and culturally diverse. Theories about basic measurements were studied during sessions and practices. Teacher candidates examined the instruments used to assess the oral and language proficiency of bilingual students and students who are learning a second language. The course attempts to cover a wide range of factors that affect students and teachers in bilingual and bicultural classrooms. Class assignments are as follows:

1. This assignment is designed for you to align the ways in which assessments have interacted in your life. What was your first experience with assessment, what is your first recollection of the term assessment? How do you feel about giving or taking assessments? What is the role

of assessments in your life as a teacher? What is your overall fear, if any? What are your overall thoughts about assessment? And what are some doubts that you may have? What do you want to learn about assessment?

2. **Academic Assessments Review**
   By pairs, you will review and evaluate a standardized academic test from the library's test collection, or assessment exams available at the office. To present in the fourth class—You will:
   1. Read the manual and get to know the exam.
   2. Give the exam to each other (one will give the test, the second will take the test, then together you will take notes).
   3. Come up with a list of pros and cons of the exams for working with English language learners. These should include aspects in the form of content of the test, procedures, implementation and scoring.
   4. What are some considerations that you would take into account when giving this test to an English language learner—student?
   5. Note your thoughts about the exam and any questions you or your classmates may have.
   6. In class, each pair will present the information acquired on a poster including the information collected. Also, have a page with the same information to provide to each of your classmates. Bring the test just for your classmates to see. Please be careful with copyrights on all these materials.

3. **Language (ORAL) Assessments Review**
   In trios, you will review and evaluate one of the following standardized language proficiency (oral, reading & writing) assessments for one grade level: Woodcock-Muñoz, LAS Links, or IPT. The review and evaluation will be the Spanish versions of the test. To present in the fifth class.
   1. Read the manual and get to know the exam.
   2. Give the exam to the classmate (one will give the test, the second will take the test, and the third will watch and take notes).
   3. Come up with a list of pros and cons of the exams for working with English language learners. These should include observations in the form of content of the test, procedures, implementation and scoring.
   4. What are some considerations that you would take into account when giving this test to a student—an English language learner?
   5. Note your thoughts about the exam and any questions you or your classmates may have.

6. In class, each pair will present the information collected in a poster. Also, have a page with the same information to provide to each of your classmates. Bring the test just for your classmates to see. Please be careful with copyrights on all these materials.

4. **Guided Reading Assessment**
Guided reading is one of the current approaches for reading in many school districts around the area. Although the method or programs may vary, the focus of guided reading is, as its name indicates, to guide the students through the process of developing literacy skills (e.g. listening, speaking, reading, comprehension). During the class, we will briefly review this approach. The assignment will consist of performing a guided reading practice assessment and a running record with a student (your case study student) at your assigned school.

5. **Teacher-made Assessment**
Based on a lesson plan from one of your block classes, you will create formative and summative evaluations. Detailed guidelines will be provided in class. Also, a template will be provided that outlines all requirements.

6. **Assessments to Case Study Participant**
You will work with one child and you will give that child **two academic assessments (science & mathematics)**. For this assignment, you will evaluate and submit your report on findings based on the readings and your observations about the child's academic and language skills and abilities.

7. **Written Reflections**
**Reflection question #1:** How did this assignment help you develop a better understanding of your future teaching? Be specific. Give examples.
**Reflection question #2:** How could you use results from standardized and alternative assessments to better inform your lesson planning, resources gathered and curriculum evaluation? In addition, how would you use test results to better inform parents of their child's academic achievement?

Further, we will provide a greater understanding of how bilingual teacher candidates define terminology commonly used to interpret standardized test results. Thus, in an effort to promote bilingual preservice preparation programs that supply their students with knowledge necessary to review and critique Spanish language proficiency tests. From our data analysis, we plan to present relevant information regarding course objectives, theory and assignments bilingual teacher candidates should be exposed to in their preservice preparation programs.

## Research Findings

Three main themes emerged from the data collection: (a) The role of biliteracy in understanding the implications of assessment in bilingual setting, (b) assessing language and the language of assessment in bilingual classrooms and (c) beyond the punitive assessment approach to draw connections between pedagogy and practice/building sociocultural competence. To demonstrate a full scope of these findings in this chapter, we describe the themes and provide examples from teacher candidates' written reflections on the various assessments they used.

### The Role of Biliteracy in Understanding the Implications of Assessment in Bilingual Settings

The foundational work of Pérez and Torres-Guzman (2002) address the dichotomy bilingual, bicultural and biliterate children are exposed to by *Learning in Two Worlds* (English and Spanish). They address notions on how teachers must carefully design instruction which is conducive to a learning environment that allows children to engage in literacy practices that are in both languages. Bilingual teacher candidates are tasked with these same responsibilities, through their self-reflections we view how they grapple with these complexities of teaching biliteracy and assessment in Figure 6-1.

Jocelyn's example demonstrates how she engaged in the process of self-reflection by questioning herself. She expresses feelings of self-doubt and fears for teaching because of not understanding the concepts of assessment and testing. After taking a preservice teacher preparation course that focused specifically on the needs for testing and assessing bilingual students, Jocelyn describes her experience as an "aha" moment. Similarly, Clara during the same semester described her encounter with the assessment course as a moment of *"abierto los ojos"* (eye opening) opportunity where she became better acquainted with the process of assessment in schools. Clara reveals that as a result of taking this course she now feels more confident in her ability to assess bilingual students because she understands the process of biliteracy. She reflects on learning the continua of biliteracy framework (Hornberger, 2003). This teaching model offers a framework for grounding biliteracy development including research, teaching and language planning in linguistically diverse settings (Hornberger, 2003). After acquainting herself with what this framework entails, Clara states

*Figure 6-1.* Bilingual Teacher Candidate Reflections on Biliteracy and Assessment

| | |
|---|---|
| Jocelyn | "Before starting this class I was so scared. To be honest, evaluation is what scares me the most about teaching. I used to ask myself, 'how do I know?' What do I look for aside from a test score, especially when working with bilingual kids? Taking this class and this assignment led me to understand that to understand assessment for bilingual kids, I had to learn how they learn. That was the first aha moment for me." |
| Clara | "Esta clase me ha abierto los ojos y la verdad me siento más segura. Ya entiendo y sé que lo que están pasando mis estudiantes es parte del "continuum of biliteracy." En otras palabras es un proceso el cual ya entendido se puede derivar a donde esta el estudiante con los exámenes. En realidad son una herramienta para ayudar a verificar lo que vemos con nuestros estudiantes. Ya no tengo miedo." |
| Mercedes | "Nunca se me va a olvidar cuando nuestra profesora nos [dijo] hoy va[n] a conocer la base de lo que necesitan para entender cómo evaluar a estudiantes bilingües. Y comenzó...nos habló de proceso de biliteracidad, de los "stages" o facetas que pasan los estudiantes y nos dio ejemplos. Ese día la clase fue lo mejor! La siguiente clase nos trajo resultados de exámenes y nos dijo ok, hoy van a aprender como ver un examen como una herramienta. Y utilizando lo que aprendimos del proceso de biliteracidad comenzamos a determinar en qué nivel estaba cada estudiante y qué estrategias funcionan para ese estudiante. Nos dijo, 'to know the biliteracy process is the first step towards assessment, and evaluation in a bilingual classroom.' Luego cuando trabajamos en el "Case study" pues fue difícil pero poco a poco comenzamos a conectar la biliteracidad con la evaluación. Al final... me siento cómoda, y confiada de que tengo más que la base para apoyar a mis estudiantes." |

that she will draw on this new knowledge as a tool moving forward for working with bilingual students and that she is no longer afraid. Similarly, Mercedes also describes how in the course she recalls learning about the different stages of biliteracy development. Mercedes describes how she used what she learned about the stages to biliteracy development with carrying out her case study project and connecting biliteracy with assessment and evaluation of bilingual students. Again, similar to her peers Mercedes describes how initially she was apprehensive and did not feel she knew enough to carry out the project, but after understanding the role of biliteracy more clearly, she was successful.

## *Assessing Language and the Language of Assessment in Bilingual Classrooms*

As future bilingual teachers, bilingual teacher candidates must learn and understand the roles language plays in assessing bilingual, bicultural and biliterate students. Specifically, bilingual teacher candidates must expand notions of language and recognize language variations opportunities for expanding academic linguistic repertoire and knowledge (Figure 6-2). Bilingual teacher preparation requires equipping teacher candidates with the ability to assess using all linguistic domains (i.e. listening, speaking, reading and writing) in both English in Spanish is critical to their success as bilingual educators.

*Figure 6-2.* Bilingual Teacher Candidate Reflections on Languages and Assessment

| | |
|---|---|
| Linda | "To take a class entitled, 'Assessment and evaluation in Bilingual Classrooms' in SPANISH is amazing! Prior to being in this program I was enrolled in another university in a bilingual program. Most of it was in English and assessment was not a class option to those in the teacher credential program. Having classes in Spanish makes a difference and it helps us better understand what our students go through but also what it is like to look at assessment in Spanish. Using our language and our culture as the key and assessments as the tool. You can't turn the tool without the key." |
| Marta | "When I started this class I thought … Seriously? We don't need to learn this in Spanish … only English. Most schools use English anyways to assess students. Then our professor showed us several items and asked in Spanish …. '*Como se llaman estos artículos?*' … *Y todos comenzamos a escribir como le llamábamos a cada artículo.* We had a pen, bus, and a notebook. We came up with over six different names for each item. The professor explained that the pictures we were looking at were from a test called the 'Woodcock Muñoz.' A test used to determine student placement in and eligibility for various programs including dual language programs. Then it became clear to me that language has a direct effect on student success in tests. Just saying one thing differently, maybe because you call a laundromat a "Washateria" (what they are called in many Latino areas in the city because there is a huge chain called washateria) rather than "lavandería" (what the test counts as correct). So what counts? If their point is for students to know the content … and why should washateria be marked wrong? And there lies the moral dilemma for many bilingual teachers. Do we accept what the book says or do we use culturally and linguistically appropriate terms that the kids give us? Really this blew my mind." |
| Valeria | "*Somos futuras maestras bilingües y poder asesorar a nuestros estudiantes en español y en inglés es basico. Después de hacer el case study, y ver la diferencia en mi estudiante en los resultados en inglés y español me di cuenta de la diferencia. Si ocupo los examenes en inglés mi estudiante estaria super bajo. Pero en español salio super alto. Ahí me di cuenta que no podemos solamente ocupar un examen en un idioma para determinar lo que saben. Tiene que ser en dos idiomas y más de una vez.*" |

All three of the examples above demonstrate the influential role a course on assessment instruments and strategies used in local, state and national systems for linguistically diverse students has on preservice teacher formation. In addition, these courses focus on the development of successful assessment practices for linguistically diverse students that can be used in bilingual classrooms by examining the role of languages. Linda specifically reveals how at a prior institution she was not afforded this opportunity, and she realizes the important impact this specific course has had on her and her future. She brings to light that for bilingual teacher candidates exposure and practice in assessment in both languages is critical to their progress. Marta's experience reveals the misconception that many bilingual teacher candidates have that they will only be assessing their students in English. She reflects on a powerful experience in the course where her professor exposed her to an assessment instrument that is used nationally to determine placement for bilingual Spanish speaking students. Participating in this activity allowed Marta to understand how subjective and complex the role of language in assessment is. For example, she says "we came up with over six different names for each item." Going through this experience herself will now allow her to be more sensitive to her students in the future, she has now been equipped with the tools for understanding how language tests operate in an idiosyncratic way. Valeria's example shows us how bilingual teacher candidates must also be aware of the process of learning languages and the impact this has on assessment. She shares, *"Ahí me di cuenta que no podemos solamente ocupar un examen en un idioma para determinar lo que saben"* [That's when I learned that we can not simply use one test in one language to determine what they know]. Unfortunately, when teachers do not acknowledge the process of second language acquisition, bilingual students are oftentimes misidentified and are seen as lacking in ability when compared to their English dominant peers. Linda, Marta and Valeria emphasize the importance of equipping bilingual teacher candidates with effective practices for screening and assessment, in the areas of language in schools.

## *Beyond the Punitive Assessment Approach: Drawing Connections between Pedagogy and Practice/Building Sociocultural Competence*

Teacher candidates oftentimes relate assessment with their own experiences with testing and evaluation. More often than not, these encounters are reflective of a punitive assessment approach that they have been subjected to in their own K-12 schooling (Figure 6-3). Preservice teacher preparation programs must teach their bilingual teacher candidates how to draw connections between pedagogy and practice. This, in order to build the capacity for teacher candidates to build their sociocultural competence in order to move beyond the punitive assessment approach.

*Figure 6-3.* Bilingual Teacher Candidate Reflections on Sociocultural Competence and Assessment

| | |
|---|---|
| Isleny | "I learned to look at the whole child when doing assessment. To look at his/her surroundings, the community. What languages he/she is exposed to. We had to do a community project. We went to the areas around the school where we were placed and asked community members about language, identity of the community and what they believed about bilingual education. That was the most eye-opening experience. I learned that although some communities say they are bilingual, sometimes they 'act' or portray something else. That is also part of who students see their language, culture and identity". |
| Ana | "Using different ways of evaluating the student is important. We did a community project. I went out to the community and I learned that everything outside of the school was all in Spanish! People value language and culture. And the school is struggling to maintain their bilingual program. The bilingual education kids are being called 'Spanish kids' and I see how they are not so welcomed. The school is contradicting what the community is telling the kids. I took this and added ways for students to connect with their language but also their culture. Having these different ways of assessment is important. We should use their culture to reward them not to punish them." |
| Rachel | "Being exposed to different ways of evaluating our students is important. I feel that it gave me confidence to know that it is not always about a test that 'punishes.' *No se trata solo de castigo pero de crecer y mejorar. El poder decirle a un niño o a un papá los niveles de su hijo en dos idiomas es importante. No solo ocupamos el inglés pero también el español para determinar. Además, poder tener diferentes evaluaciones como herramientas. No solo un examen pero también de la comunidad, lenguaje, matemáticas, escritura, en dos idiomas, le ofrece al padre otra vista de su hijo. Y para mi como maestra me dice en realidad dónde está mi estudiante. Asi, asesoramos, ajustar el currículo, individualizados, y actuamos para mejorar. Al estudiante le dice--- ok puedes mejorar aca pero aca vas bien. Y así celebramos los éxitos y mejoramos las áreas de necesidades. Pero siempre sin castigar. La escuela nunca debería de castigar!"* |

Isleny recalls a community based project she had to complete in her assessment course. Here she reflects on the impact she had with going out into the students' community to explain their ideologies regarding "language, identity of the community and what they believed about bilingual education."

Through this experience, Isleny learned about how the surrounding community of a school can impact the language practices adopted by individuals who live there. Ana also connects to this by sharing a similar experience with her community project. Through this experience, she learns that much of the surrounding community of the school greatly adopts the use of Spanish. She shares, "*I went out into the community and I learned that everything outside of the school was all in Spanish! People value language and culture.*" This alternative assessment project required her to view the disconnects between the school and the community. In her example, we see how Spanish speaking students are placed and even named in demeaning ways, which contradicts how Spanish is viewed in the community. Rachel then took this alternative assessment assignment as an opportunity to allow students to connect with their Spanish language in a positive manner for assessment purposes. She reconceptualizes her interpretation of assessment by saying "Being exposed to different ways of evaluating our students is important. I feel that it gave me confidence to know that it is not always about a test that 'punishes.'"

## *Implications: Weaving in Teacher Candidates' Voice on Assessment*

Implications from this study suggest moving beyond the assessment culture of fear and equipping bilingual teacher candidates with transformational lenses. Throughout their reflection, several teacher candidates discussed their apprehensions with assessment related to fear of the unknown. After taking this foundational course on assessment and evaluation of bilingual students they no longer feel that way. One said, "*Ya no tengo miedo. Ya se que cuando hable con mis estudiantes de los exámenes no lo haré con miedo. Pero con mucha confianza.*" Now that she understands what assessment and evaluation entails she will no longer approach conversations about tests in a way of fear, but with confidence, because she now understands the reasoning and process behind assessment. Teacher candidates also reported learning that assessments are not indicative of a student's ultimate capabilities, one shared, "*Porque se que aunque [son] importante, no determina quien son ni qué saben. Solo es una imagen de un momento y nosotros podemos tomar toda la foto con otras maneras de asesorarlos.*" She views formative assessment as more of a snapshot of where students are academically at a specific time, realizing that there are different ways of assessing students in order to gain a clear picture of their capabilities.

The bilingual teacher candidates also relate their feelings of fear for not knowing what to do to help students. One bilingual student teacher candidate wrote, *"Tenía mucho miedo de no saber cómo tomar los resultados de los exámenes y hacer los cambios necesarios para ayudar a mi estudiante. Siento que de eso se trata. Pero después de esta clase y de leer resultados de exámenes y diferentes evaluaciones, y especialmente del 'case study' se que no tendre problema."* Teacher candidates are able to better understand the purposes of assessment and how results should be used to drive instruction. Bilingual teacher candidates also reveal that they now realize that assessments are tools to help them understand what they should focus instruction on. They share, *"En esta clase aprendí a ver un examen por lo que es ... una herramienta. A enseñarle a mis estudiantes lo mismo---nos ayuda a ver como van y cómo mejoran. Cambie mi pedagogía basado en lo que veo, aprendí a leer resultados de exámenes, pero lo más importante que aprendí es a no tenerle miedo a los 'high stakes test.' It is high stakes if we see it that way. I can control my classroom and how my students see it. So for us, these exams will show how brilliant they are!"* They are able to connect pedagogy to assessment as a result of their assessment course.

Ultimately, the bilingual teacher candidates left the class with an understanding of how crucial it is to have a foundational course in the preparation program that delves into topics related to the assessment and evaluation of bilingual students. Another bilingual teacher candidates wrote, *"Todos los programas de education deberían de tener una clase como esta y quitarnos el miedo que nos has puesto desde siempre! Desde que tomamos exámenes cuando estábamos en la escuela hasta el SAT, y los exámenes para ser maestras. Debemos de parar el ciclo de miedo como dice mi profesora."*

## Conclusions

This chapter focused on the processes of theoretical assessment of learning, motivation and examination of evaluation and measurement procedures in bilingual and bicultural environments for bililiterate students. Our research findings focused on and explained the role of biliteracy in understanding the implications of assessment in bilingual settings for assessing language and the language of assessment in bilingual classrooms Our findings also show the importance of moving assessment beyond the punitive assessment approach to drawing connections between pedagogy and practice/building sociocultural competence. Finally, our findings call for preparing and engaging bilingual teacher candidates to move beyond the assessment culture of fear and to equipping bilingual teacher candidates with transformational lenses and tools for assessment. To demonstrate a full scope of these findings in this chapter, we described the themes and provided examples from bilingual teacher candidates' written reflections on the various assessments they used. We examined both formal and informal Spanish assessments of language proficiency and learning for instructional purposes. Particularly, we discussed the importance of bilingual preservice teacher preparation programs exposing their students to topics and studies on the forms of the appropriate use of Spanish standardized tests in minority language populations in their bilingual programs as well as the implications for future bilingual teacher candidates.

## Note

1 We weave together the use of Spanish and English as this is the most accurate representation of the participants' linguistic repertoire depending on content. We choose to translate at certain times in order to provide clarification on discussions only when we feel necessary. Thus, coinciding with Anzaldúa's (1987) definition of linguistic identity, "Ethnic identity is twin skin to linguistic identity—I am my language. Until I can take pride in my language I cannot take pride in myself" (p. 81).

## References

Anzaldúa, G. (1987). *Borderlands/a frontera: The New Mestiza*. San Francisco: Aunt Lute Books.

Cole, C. (1999). Effects of a parent-implemented intervention on the academic readiness skills of five Puerto Rican Kindergarten students in an urban school. *School Psychology Review, 28*(3), 439–447.

Darling-Hammond, L. (1997). *The right to learn: A blueprint for creating schools that work. The Jossey-Bass education series*. Jossey-Bass, Inc., Publishers, 350 Sansome Street, San Francisco, CA 94104.

Del Rosario Basterra, M., Trumbull, E., & Solano-Flores, G. (Eds.). (2011). *Cultural validity in assessment: Addressing linguistic and cultural diversity*. Routledge.

Gibson, M., & Koyama, J. (2011). Immigrants and education. In B. Levinson & M. Pollock (Eds.), *A Blackwell companion to anthropology of education*. Walden, MA: Wiley Blackwell.

Harry, B. & Klingner, J., (2006). *Why are so many minority students in special education?: Understanding race and disability in schools*. New York: Teachers College Press, Columbia University.

Hornberger, N. H. (Ed.). (2003). *Continua of biliteracy: An ecological framework for educational policy, research, and practice in multilingual settings* (Vol. 41). Multilingual Matters.

Howard, E. R., Lindholm-Leary, D., Rogers, D., Olague, N., Medina, J., Kennedy, B., Sugarman, J., & Christian, D. (2018). *Guiding principles for dual language education* (3rd ed.). Washington, DC: Center for Applied Linguistics.

Maldonado, S. I., & Machado-Casas, M. (2019). Sustaining the sociopolitical spirit of bilingual education: Assessment practices and evaluative policies for students minoritized by national background and english-language proficiency. In *Handbook of Research on Assessment Practices and Pedagogical Models for Immigrant Students* (pp. 1–17). IGI Global.

Maldonado, S., Mosqueda, E., Bravo, M., Solis, J. (2020). Assessing and teaching biliteracy in mathematics: A professional development model. *Multilingual Educator*, 36–45. https://www.gocabe.org/wp-content/uploads/2020/07/Online-Version-ME-2020-v2.pdf

Pérez, B., & Torres-Guzmán, M. E. (2002). *Learning in two worlds: An integrated Spanish/English biliteracy approach* (3rd ed.). Boston: Allyn & Bacon.

Solano-Flores, G., & Nelson-Barber, S. (2001). On the cultural validity of science assessments. *Journal of Research in Science Teaching: The Official Journal of the National Association for Research in Science Teaching*, 38(5), 553–573.

Suarez-Orozco, M. (2001). Globalization, immigration, and education: The research agenda. *Harvard Educational Review*, 71(3), 345–365.

Trent, S. C., & Artiles, A. J. (1998). Multicultural teacher education in special and bilingual education exploring multiple measurement strategies to assess teacher learning. *Remedial and Special Education*, 19(1), 2–6.

# 7. Uncovering Surprises: Teacher Candidates Learning to Assess Biliteracy in Argumentative Writing

LESLIE C. BANES
*California State University, Sacramento*

## Purpose

A common thread across the Common Core Standards and Next Generation Science Standards in all grades and content areas is the requirement for students to construct arguments using evidence to support their claims. In addition to measuring students' content knowledge, high-stakes assessments now purport to measure students' *communication* of their content knowledge in discipline-specific writing tasks (SBAC, 2016) and teachers must learn to support students' argumentative writing skills across the curriculum, including in subjects that traditionally have not included much writing. However, recent surveys suggest classroom teachers seldom engage students in argumentative writing, especially in math and science (Banilower et al., 2013; Kiuhara, Graham, & Hawken, 2009), due, in part, to lack of clarity around what this writing should include (Casa et al., 2016; Kosko, 2016). This creates an area of inquiry ripe for preservice teachers to collaborate, compare and connect across grades and content areas.

To assess writing in ways that guide instruction and support learning, teachers must first grapple with what counts as effective argumentative writing in each grade and content area. In addition, the growing number of teachers in dual language contexts must grapple with how to capture what students know and can do in two languages (Lindholm-Leary, 2012). This participatory design project explored the impact of engaging 19 preservice teachers (PSTs) in collaboratively designing rubrics as a tool for formative assessment and professional reflection through a process that included (a) looking through a holistic biliteracy lens (Escamilla, 2000) (b) exploring a new genre and (c) analyzing students' writing using teacher-developed rubrics.

Bilingual education researchers call for tools and protocols that display English and Spanish writing together as part of an assessment process (Escamilla, Butvilofsky, & Hopewell, 2017), as well as for teachers to develop concrete strategies to identify, honor and more equitably assess the diverse linguistic repertoires present in emergent bilinguals' writing (Lewis & Zisselsberger, 2016). This study responds to these calls. Building on the Literacy Squared research that used a rubric to analyze *narrative* writing in English and Spanish side by side (Escamilla et al., 2014), PSTs and I explored how a biliteracy framework could be implemented to analyze argumentative writing across grades and content areas. The following research question guided the study: *How does co-designing and implementing a biliteracy rubric impact preservice teachers' reflections on their students' argumentative writing?*

## *A Holistic Biliteracy View of Writing*

This work is grounded in the notion that language suffuses learning and communication in all content areas (Cole, 1998). "Looking through a holistic biliteracy lens" includes recognizing that bilinguals are not simply two monolinguals in one (Grosjean, 1989). Contradicting the myth of "balanced bilingualism," research points to bilingual individuals developing proficiency in each language in different ways and to different degrees (Grosjean, 2010; Reyes & Moll, 2008). Because language development depends on experiences and learning opportunities in each language, students undergoing normal bilingual development may not perform as well as monolingual speakers of each language at all times or in all domains (Paradis, Genesee, & Crago, 2011). Moreover, bilingual literacy development is a flexible, dynamic process which includes bidirectional transfer of knowledge and skills between languages (Reyes & Costanzo, 2002).

Thus, when bilingual students are assessed in only one language, only a portion of what they know is accounted for, and their knowledge and skills may appear limited (Escamilla, 2000). This is especially problematic given that bilingual students are over-represented in special education (Abedi, 2006) and lower-track classes (Thompson, 2015). The ability to fairly and accurately assess bilingual students is an equity issue and is essential to ensuring students receive high quality education and equal opportunity to learn (e.g. Espinosa & Garcia, 2012).

Unfortunately, in English-medium classrooms, students are often assessed only in English. Even in dual language programs with the expressed goal of developing bilingualism and biliteracy, students are often only assessed in English, and when they are assessed in their other language, it is usually done as separate from their English assessment (Boyle et al., 2015). This is what Cummins (2007) refers to as the "two solitudes" approach to bilingualism, in which English is taught and assessed as though students were monolingual in English, and Spanish is taught and assessed as though students were monolingual in Spanish. This assessment approach will always lead to an incomplete picture of what students know and can do and offers teachers little information that could guide their instruction in both languages (Lindholm-Leary, 2012).

Countering the two solitudes approach to bilingual assessment, a holistic view of bilingualism posits that "the totality of what bilinguals know and can do is distributed across languages" (Soltero-González, Escamilla, & Hopewell, 2010). This includes a positive view of translanguaging or language crossing in writing, not as "mistakes" or "errors" as they are sometimes positioned (Soltero-González, Escamilla, & Hopewell, 2010), but as "bilingual writing strategies" representing students' dynamic and flexible progression along the continua of biliteracy (Hornberger, 2004).

## *Argumentative Writing as a Genre*

Language is used differently in different contexts and for different purposes (Halliday, 1985; Swales, 1990), and genres develop in response to situations that writers encounter repeatedly (Devitt, 1993, p. 676). Martin (1992) defines genre as a "staged, goal-oriented, social process" (p. 505), while for Swales (1990), the criterial feature that turns a collection of communicative events into a genre is a shared set of "communicative purposes" (p. 46). Thus, it is the goal or the communicative purpose which is central to both creating and classifying a genre, shaping its structure and content (Martin, 1992; Swales, 1990).

Linguistics research traditions have much to offer studies of school writing. In particular, genre analysis can help us develop a better understanding of school-based genres, offering a way of looking at what students have to do linguistically, and allowing teachers to make the patterns of particular genres transparent for their students (e.g. Cope & Kalantzis, 1993; Gebhard & Harman, 2011; Schleppegrell & Oliveira, 2006). This is crucial given that expectations for academic writing genres often contain "hidden rules" governing what information should be included and how to include it (Lea & Street, 1998).

## Argument: A Fuzzy Genre

Due to the emphasis on argumentation in the Common Core Standards, several recent studies focus on argumentation as a subset of writing in math, science, language arts, and history classrooms (e.g. De La Paz et al., 2012; Herrenkohl & Cornelius, 2013; Newell, Bloome, Kim, & Goff, 2019; Kosko & Zimmerman, 2019). Much of this work draws on Toulmin's model of argumentation (1958/2003), which includes the following elements:

> Claim: statement or proposition the writer seeks to establish as truth
> Data/evidence: information that supports or justifies the claim (facts, reasons)
> Warrant: explanation of why or how the data support the claim
> Backing: a rationale appealing to a socially recognized rule, definition, or theorem
> Rebuttal: evidence that negates a counterclaim

However, as with all genres, some blurring and overlap exist between these elements and the features that distinguish arguments from other related written genres such as "explanations" and "opinions." This is because genres are not bounded and static, but dynamic and fuzzy (Chandler, 2000). In fact, some genre theorists describe genres in terms of "family resemblances" among texts (Wittgenstein, 1978/2010).

Hence, those who research written and oral discourse in classrooms often disagree on labels and descriptions of each genre. In mathematics for example, some stipulate that to qualify as an "explanation," the text must include an argument or justification, not simply a description of the procedure used to solve (e.g. Yackel, 1992; Kazemi & Stipek, 2001). Others, such as Casa et al. (2016) contrast "procedural explanations" describing the problem-solving process with "conceptual explanations" that include justifications of why those procedures were used, while Bicknell (1999) uses the term "justification" to refer to writing that includes an argument. Cirillo and colleagues (2015) discuss conceptions and consequences of what we call argumentation, justification, and proof, suggesting a need to clarify terms to improve learning opportunities and engagement in these practices. These overlapping genres and terms may confound students and teachers seeking to better understand features of argumentative writing.

## Hidden Rules of Academic Discourse

Clark (2005) argues that a genre approach to teaching school-based writing assignments can foster teachers' awareness of the "unexpressed expectations" of the writing tasks they assign (p. 1). Similarly, Lea and Street (1998) discuss the hidden rules of writing assignments that govern what can be said and how it needs to be said, offering the example of a student who thought he/she had written an effective argument for a history class, only to have it deemed by a tutor to "lack structure" and "have no argument." Authors suggest the student understood linkages in his/her argument to be implied or obvious, while the tutor did not recognize any attempts at constructing a cohesive argument. When students attempt to work out the hidden rules of writing assignments, they feel teachers have unspoken requirements, and their questions about the expectations are often exacerbated instead of resolved as they progress through school (Lillis, 2001).

## Socio-disciplinary Norms of Argumentation

Drawing on Yackel's and Cobb's (1996) notion of "socio-mathematical norms," I posit that what constitutes a "good" argument in each discipline is value-laden and related to socio-disciplinary norms, including teachers' beliefs about the content. For the current study, it was therefore imperative that the design process was infused with inquiry and discussion to uncover the socio-disciplinary beliefs PSTs held in relation to their developing understanding of the argument genre in their selected content areas. For example, one PST initially believed written words should be valued over visual representations in mathematical arguments. After reading about bilingual students' mathematical communication (Moschkovich, 2007) and examining her own students' writing, she came to believe that writing and visual representations were equally valid means of communication. The process used to support PSTs in exploring features of argumentative writing is described further in the following section.

## Methods & Data Sources

Nineteen PSTs participated in this project, all of which were earning a bilingual authorization which would qualify them to teach in dual language bilingual classrooms and/or offer instruction in their credentialed content areas in Spanish. This project was conducted in a course on bilingual teaching methodology and classroom inquiry in a post-baccalaureate teacher credential program in an urban area of California. The course was a requirement for earning a bilingual authorization and a prerequisite inquiry course for the Master of Arts (MA) students would complete the following year. Of the 19 PSTs, 12 were multiple-subject candidates who were student-teaching in dual language elementary or middle school classrooms at the time of the study.

The particular model of dual language instruction varied across school sites, with two schools following a school-wide 90–10 model (one K-6 and one K-8th grade), and three others offering a dual language track within the school, all K-6, 80–20 models. The remaining seven PSTs were earning a single-subject credential in various subjects (3 social science, 2 science, 1 English, 1 math). Single subject PSTs all had year-long student teaching placements in high school classrooms with English-as-the-language-of-instruction and conducted a shorter placement (3–10 weeks) in a bilingual context, which was either a small pull-out group instructed in Spanish or in a dual language middle school classroom in which content was delivered in Spanish.

The author and instructor of the course is a former bilingual elementary and middle school teacher, proficient in English and Spanish, and was also serving as university supervisor for 10 of the students in the course, and thus had intimate knowledge of the contexts in which they conducted their student teaching. At the time of the study, the author had been teaching the inquiry course series for preservice and MA candidates for four years.

## *Student Writing Samples*

PSTs collected argumentative writing samples in English and Spanish from their students, providing students with similar, though not identical, prompts in both languages. The goal of the writing prompts was to elicit argumentative writing in which students make a claim and support it with evidence. PSTs' approach to designing prompts was to find a prompt related to the content currently being covered in their student teaching classroom, often using one from the adopted curricula, or adapting one found online. PSTs then translated and modified the prompt in the other language so as to cover similar content, but avoid having students write the exact same argument in each language. For example, in a dual language middle school science unit on the environment, PSTs provided students with a writing prompt in Spanish asking whether people should use plastic bags or reusable bags, and a prompt in English asking whether people should use tap water or bottled water. For both prompts, students were provided articles in the appropriate language that included research and facts they could cite to support their arguments.

In elementary and middle school dual language classrooms, writing samples were collected in both languages from the whole class, even in programs that have language separation policies. In programs where the focal content is taught only in one language (e.g., science is taught only in Spanish), some students found it strange that they were asked to write in the other language.

In English-medium high school classrooms, writing samples were collected in both languages only from students who were bilingual in English and Spanish (3–10 students). These included students who had attended dual language elementary and/or middle schools, students who recently immigrated to the US and had received academic instruction in Spanish in their home countries, as well as students who learned Spanish primarily at home and had received little to no formal academic instruction in Spanish. PSTs were asked to keep the classroom context, students' linguistic backgrounds, and opportunities to learn in mind throughout the project.

## *Engaging PSTs in a Collaborative Rubric Design Process*

PSTs worked together, supported by the instructor, to design their own rubrics. The purpose for this was twofold. First, there were few available rubrics at the time that adequately captured the specific features of disciplinary argumentative writing and even fewer that were capable of capturing students' developing biliteracy skills. Second, I theorized the process of designing a rubric would create an authentic need for PSTs to articulate their understanding of "effective" writing an argumentative genre expectations that could foster improvements in assessment and instructional practices.

The collaborative rubric design process included both deductive and inductive approaches. PSTs began deductively by exploring the research literature, content standards and their own assumptions regarding the most important and valued features of argumentation in each discipline. They also searched for existing published argumentative writing rubrics to mine for ideas they could include. These resources shaped their understandings of the genre and offered them a starting point with rubric dimensions that reflected the features they hoped to see in their own students' writing.

For inductive design methods, PSTs looked to their actual students' writing to inform their rubric design. They categorized students' writing samples as high, medium, or low for each task, in each language (DiRanna et al., 2008). To build rich descriptions of each level, PSTs worked in content area or similar grade-level groups and discussed how they decided to categorize samples, described similarities and differences, and selected the "strongest" responses for each task to identify the features that make them effective arguments. This was challenging work, and PSTs argued in depth about the reasons for their categorization decisions, forcing them to more clearly articulate their conceptualization of what counts as a strong argument. Typical discussion among PSTs included the following dialogue, "Okay, but *why* is that one the best? What does it do that the others don't? If we can't explain for ourselves what makes it strong, how are we going to teach our students to do this kind of writing?"

To evaluate bilingual learners' competencies, PSTs and I aimed to capture discipline-specific practices, linguistic resources used to communicate ideas and modes of expression other than language (e.g. drawings, symbols) (Moschkovich, 2007). PSTs pilot tested and revised their rubrics to increase clarity and reliability. Two project-developed rubrics are included as examples in the appendices.

## Analyzing Students' Bilingual Writing

PSTs used the rubrics they designed to quantitatively analyze their students' writing in both languages. In addition, they conducted a qualitative analysis of the translanguaging present in students' writing, following a process we adapted from Soltero-González, Escamilla, and Hopewell (2012). The goal of this qualitative analysis was to identify the "linguistic hypotheses and strategies children are utilizing as they develop bilingual writing competencies" (p. 77) and focuses attention on cross-language analysis at four levels: sentence, word, spelling/phonics and punctuation. PSTs recorded their observations of students' bilingual writing strategies in a three-column chart (Figure 7-1). For this project, PSTs did not specifically focus on bilingual strategies at the discourse level, as in Soltero-González and colleagues' study, because we felt the nature of the genre- and content-specific argumentation rubrics already captured the rhetorical moves students made in each language to convince the audience of the veracity of their claims. When a student produced a strong claim in both languages, this was evident in their rubric scores.

PSTs focused their analyses on whole class patterns and deep reflection on three selected focal students. They then used information gleaned from their quantitative and qualitative analysis to design learning opportunities intended to clarify the genre expectations and support students' bilingual writing development. PSTs' written reflections on their students' bilingual writing were collected before and after they engaged in the rubric-design process, and notes from class discussions in the university course were recorded as PSTs collaboratively analyzed their students' work and developed their rubrics. In their final analytic reflections, students were asked to report two or more claims supported by evidence from their data and to explain the instructional implications of their findings. They could elect to write their claims using evidence from either their rubrics or from the qualitative analysis of bilingual writing strategies. A brief description of this process is

# Learning to Assess Biliteracy

provided as an appendix, which may be used or adapted by teacher educators or instructional coaches to engage teachers in designing and using their own biliteracy rubrics.

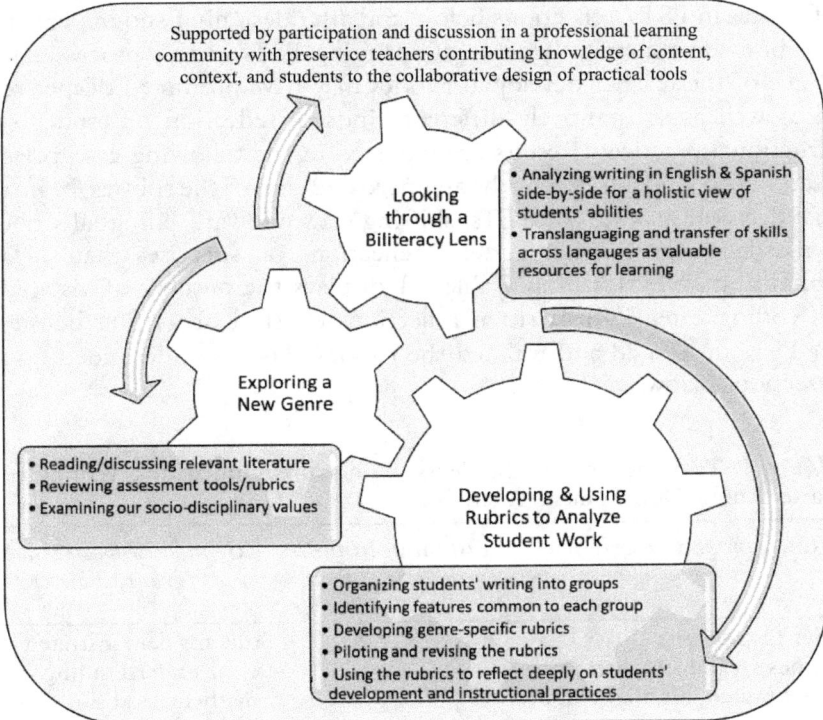

*Figure 7-1.* PSTs' Reflections on Students' Bilingual Argumentative Writing before and after Rubric Development/Analysis.

## Thematic Analysis

To code PSTs' reflections, I used Marshall's and Rossman's (1999) stages in thematic analysis: (1) organize the data, (2) generate categories or themes, (3) code the data, (4) test emergent understandings of the data, (5) search for alternative explanations of the data and (6) write-up the data analysis. I used repeated readings of class discussion notes and PSTs' written reflections to uncover salient themes. I then categorized teachers' pre- and post- reflections on their students' writing into broad themes and noted key differences between PSTs' pre- and post- reflections, highlighting the language used to describe students' performance and abilities.

## Results

Differences in PSTs' reflections before and after designing and implementing the rubrics demonstrate benefits of engaging PSTs in this process. Design and use of the teacher-developed rubrics may have prompted deeper reflection as well as substantively different kinds of reflection on students and instructional practices. Results are reported in the following categories: (1) reflections on students' strengths and needs, (2) use of the rubrics for instructional decision-making, (3) PSTs' shifting stance toward bilingual strategies or cross-language transfer and (4) reflections on surprises that surfaced, highlighting PSTs' learning. Table 7-1 displays the number of instances of each coding category in written reflections on student writing before and after PSTs developed and utilized the rubrics. These are expanded upon in the sections below.

*Table 7-1.* PSTs' Reflections on Students' Bilingual Argumentative Writing before and after Rubric Development/Analysis

| Category and Description | Instances Pre-Rubric | Instances Post-Rubric | Condensed Data Sample (grade, subject) |
|---|---|---|---|
| **Student Strengths** Identifies area of strength that can be valued, highlighted, or built upon | 20 | 34 | Students demonstrated clear understanding of the mathematical situation in the word problem (3rd, math) |
| **Student Needs** Identifies area in which students need further support | 27 | 16 | They need to write more supportive statements (1st, language arts) |
| **Instructional Implications** Identifies specific instructional practices that would support students' bilingual writing development and/or content-area argumentation | 15 | 27 | I plan to model and support with writing stronger conclusions (7th/8th, science) |
| **Cross-linguistic Transfer** Reflection on bilingual strategies such as code-switching, lexical borrowing, bidirectional transfer | 6 | 12 | (see stance below) |

*Learning to Assess Biliteracy*

*Table 7-1. Continued*

| Category and Description | Instances Pre-Rubric | Instances Post-Rubric | Condensed Data Sample (grade, subject) |
|---|---|---|---|
| **Corrective Stance** Indicates a need to edit or correct the cross-linguistic transfer; may interpret as student 'being confused.' | 3 | 3 | Some direct translation. It doesn't really make sense in Spanish (3rd, math) |
| **Neutral Stance** PST simply notes cross-linguistic transfer was observed | 2 | 1 | Noticed students used some spelling rules of English to write in Spanish (9th, math) |
| **Positive Stance** Indicates understanding of benefits of cross-language transfer and as a normal part of biliteracy development. | 1 | 8 | Student is able to map sounds to letters in Spanish and is applying that skill when writing in English (1st, language arts) |
| **Surprises** Articulates previously unknown insights about students (markers: "now I realize, I was surprised ... ") | 5 | 16 | I was surprised that [student] wrote a stronger argument in English even though he is an English learner (5th, language arts) |

## Using the Rubric to Identify Student Strengths

Although PSTs were asked to reflect on their students' strengths and needs in both their pre- and post- rubric reflections, the pre-rubric reflections tended to focus on student needs, with fewer reflections on student strengths. In contrast, post-rubric reflections included twice as many reflections on student strengths as needs, shifting the balance and suggesting PSTs were better able to identify student strengths after developing and using the rubrics. One PST reported, "the different dimensions of the rubric allowed me to see my students' strengths in different aspects of [scientific] communication, and their use of resources beyond written words. This gives me information about my students I can build on." Thus, the specificity of the rubrics and the ability to look at several different features of writing at once may have supported her in developing more asset-based reflections on her students' argumentative writing.

Further, PSTs drew on the metalanguage embedded in their rubrics, which described specific features of a strong argument (claim, data/evidence, warrants), to more precisely articulate what students did well and where they could strengthen their responses. Although this metalanguage was nearly non-existent in pre-rubric reflections, it surfaced repeatedly in PSTs' post-rubric reflections. In pre-rubric reflections, PSTs' comments were general, reflecting uncertainty around what features were worthy of attention (e.g. "He wrote a lot more on this one."). After using the rubric, however, the same PST reflected, "He made his *warrant* more *explicit*, so it's clear how his *evidence* supports the *claim* he's trying to make" using language from the rubric (italicized) to identify precisely what the student did well. Engaging in this process may have positioned PSTs to be able to look more carefully at their students' writing to notice what students are already doing well and to develop asset-based interpretations of their students' writing.

## *Instructional Decision Making*

PSTs had nearly twice as many ideas for supporting their students' writing in post-rubric reflections as in pre-rubric reflections. PSTs expanded on the ideas they mentioned in pre-rubric reflections (e.g. "I need to offer more practice and examples"), by adding specificity that reflected their growing understanding of the argument genre and what makes it unique in each content area. One teacher noted, "I can model for them the thought process behind using visual representations that *connect* to their written explanations in mathematics." Moreover, PSTs suggested the rubric helped them see students needed experience with a wider variety of argumentative writing prompts "so they can see how different kinds of evidence work best for different goals" and to "help them practice writing different kinds of claims."

One teacher reported how she would build on her current practices: "I need to start going into using complete sentences, visuals, math terminology, and supporting claims to make it more clear what I expect." To support language demands she would give students sentence frames and have students discuss ideas before writing, "I'm going to have them test out their arguments by sharing them with their first-grade reading buddies. This will give them an audience to write to. They'll see that they need to more fully explain their ideas so they make sense to their audience." Another teacher discussed the use of mentor texts to offer models of strong argument writing in history and how evidence can be built up by making inferences from primary sources: "Historians are like detectives, using evidence to fill in the gaps in what they know." Many PSTs discussed establishing authentic audiences for writing, which textbook prompts often lack, and using the rubrics for self-assessment, in English and Spanish, to help students understand genre expectations.

Finally, PSTs used the process of looking at students' writing in both languages side by side to better understand their students' ideas, fueling ideas for language instruction that meets the particular needs of bilingual learners. One PST reported, One of our students gave a literal translation of her English thinking into Spanish. When we first read it in Spanish it didn't make sense, but when we read it through an English lens we understood what she was trying to communicate. For example, in Spanish she wrote, "Si, solo lo que los centímetros y las pulgadas son iguales no significa que son lo mismo." The English literal translation would read, "Yes, only what centimeters and inches are equal does not mean they are the same." This shows that she is using literal translation, perhaps because she is still learning the differences between syntax in English and Spanish. This is important to know because now we see that she was able to communicate an important idea and we can explicitly address the differences in syntax with her in instruction (3rd grade, math).

This PST highlights how the process of analyzing students' English and Spanish simultaneously allowed a deeper understanding of her students' ideas to surface, demonstrating value for her developing bilingual communicative competence and guiding instruction to support biliteracy with a bilingual bridge lesson that uses contrastive analysis to compare and discuss the features of each language (Beeman & Urow, 2013).

## Shifting Views of Bilingual Writing Strategies

The qualitative analysis table prompted PSTs to reflect carefully on students' use of bilingual writing strategies and supported them with labels and categories to name what they observed. In their pre- reflections, teachers identified only 6 instances of cross-linguistic transfer, while in the post-rubric reflections they identified 12. Though only about half of PSTs chose to include evidence from the qualitative analysis chart in their final reflections, it is clear that those who did hold a more positive stance towards cross-linguistic transfer after engaging in analysis/discussion than they indicated in their pre- reflections.

In pre- reflections, PST's initial observations of their students' writing indicated mostly corrective (3 instances) and neutral (2 instances) stances towards cross-linguistic transfer, with only one PST indicating a positive stance. However, in post- reflections, the majority of reports of cross-linguistic transfer (8/12 instances) indicated a positive stance. For example, one PST noted, "I now see that using Spanish words or sentence structures in their English arguments, or vice versa, isn't necessarily a bad thing. This student used resources from both languages to provide historically accurate evidence for her claim and even commented on the credibility of the source document" (11th grade, history). This PST reflected a positive stance of bilingual writing strategies in favor of students using their full linguistic repertoire to communicate important content understandings.

In the following example, another PST reflected on his first-grade students' cross-linguistic transfer at the spelling/phonics level.

> It is stated that "students often combined spelling conventions from each language to approximate a single word" (Soltero-González 2012, pg. 79). This can be found in [student A's] writing, "because dey sew gen drgs." In this example, the th sound is substituted for the Spanish d sound, in the word they. Another example of using d, to substitute the th sound, is found in [student B's] writing. She wrote the following; "Picas bel meicambrgrs." In this example the d was written backward. The work "bel" in this sentence could be an attempt to spell they or the. This would indicate that the student intended to write "because they make burgers." This observation indicates that students are using knowledge of the Spanish language to help them spell in English (1st grade, language arts).

This PST demonstrated a positive stance towards bilingual writing strategies, describing his understanding of how students draw on their skills from one language to support their communication of ideas in the other.

Soltero-González and colleagues (2012) report that even experienced bilingual teachers can overlook observable bilingual strategies in students' writing, especially those that involve syntactic or phonetic transfers. Thus, it is likely that students' writing may have included more translanguaging and bilingual writing strategies than these PSTs recognized. Importantly, these PSTs were able to identify more bilingual writing strategies and were more reflective in their discussion of what these strategies mean in regard to students' understanding and biliteracy development after engaging in the rubric development and analysis process. Though the qualitative table of bilingual writing strategies was not content specific and not developed by the PSTs themselves, it fueled analysis and discussion as an important part of our process for assessing students' writing through a holistic biliteracy lens (Soltero-González, Escamilla, & Hopewell, 2102).

## *Uncovering Surprises*

PSTs reported several students constructed thoughtful and thorough arguments in their supposedly "weaker" language, exceeding expectations and blurring the boundaries between Spanish-dominant and English-dominant students. For example, one PST reflected on a native Spanish-speaking student who "typically struggles with reading and writing in English," "I was really shocked to see how he could explain and supported his ideas as well in English as Spanish. That was a surprise." Similarly, another PST reflected on her class as a whole, noting, "I was surprised by the amount of students that performed better in Spanish because students gravitate towards English vastly more [when speaking in class]. I did not expect to see as many students perform better in Spanish" (7/8th grade, science).

Finally, another PST reflected, "The rubric helped me see what I didn't know, and sometimes what I thought turned out to be wrong." As PSTs learn to notice students' strengths and needs in content-specific writing genres, they may see that students develop writing skills differently in each language and at different rates (Escamilla, 2000). The surprises PSTs encountered stood in contrast to what they thought their students were capable of in each language. This has the potential to shift PSTs' view of their students as either English- or Spanish-dominant to positioning them all as "bilingual learners" undergoing the fluid process of developing two languages (Soltero-González et al., 2012) and highlights the importance of evaluating content-area writing in both languages for a more complete view of students' abilities.

## *Conclusions*

The contribution of this study is two-fold. First, the teacher-developed biliteracy rubrics have been found useful by both preservice and in-service teachers in other classrooms and may help counter the current assessment regime that has embedded writing into content assessments without considering implications for bilingual students. Second, I posit the shifts in PSTs' thinking documented in this study resulted, in part, from engaging in the collaborative design process. When teachers are supported in thinking about what it means to develop as a bilingual writer and to construct a discipline-specific argument, they may also begin to rethink their instruction and their beliefs about their students.

In this study, PSTs in both English-medium and dual language classrooms demonstrated shifts toward more positive views of cross-language transfer. This is especially important given that the climate of high-stakes testing (often only in English) can lead teachers to adopt deficit views of students with imperfect English. Teachers often see their role as that of "corrector" of their students' language rather than understanding cross-language transfer as a normal part of biliteracy development representing a communicative resource on which to build (Hornberger, 2004). Tools and processes that support teachers to understand and capture their students' communicative competence in two languages, such as those described here, may help teachers move away from narrow views of academic language to broader, more holistic views of their students' growing capabilities.

PSTs in this study negotiated which features of argumentation were most important to include in their rubrics and what weight to assign each feature. Aligning tools with teachers' developing values in this way ensures the design of useful and sustainable tools for classroom practice (Penuel et al., 2007). Teachers and teacher educators may find the process outlined here and the teacher-developed rubrics helpful as they grapple with what it means to engage in argumentative writing in bilingual classrooms. However, our project-developed rubrics have not gone through a rigorous content and construct validation process. The purpose of developing the rubrics was to offer opportunities for PSTs to engage deeply in reflection and discussion of their own and their students' understanding of the argumentative writing genre and biliteracy development. PSTs and I suggest anyone wishing to use the rubrics we included in this chapter should do so with the understanding that their own values and expectations for students may differ and that the rubrics are not designed to align with every argumentative writing task.

Following Moschkovich (2007), we note that it is not possible to decipher whether written work reflects a students' conceptual understanding, language proficiency or a combination of both. We add to this mix students' understanding of genre expectations. In addition to content and bilingual writing development, the rubrics helped beginning teachers capture what their students understood about the expectations of written arguments as a genre, and how those understandings may differ from their own, grappling with issues like, "do you need to explain something that seems obvious?" or "do you need to provide evidence for a counterclaim?" We suggest teachers and students together may need to unpack the features of an effective argument, what it does and includes, and what language may be used to best communicate it to others. In this way, both teachers and students can begin to expose the "hidden rules" of argumentative writing.

## *References*

Abedi, J. (2006). Psychometric issues in ELL assessment and special education eligibility. *Teachers College Record, 108*(11), 2282–2303.

Banilower, E. R., Smith, P. S., Weiss, I. R., Malzahn, K. A., Campbell, K. M., & Weis, A. M. (2013). *Report of the 2012 National Survey of Science and Mathematics Education*. Horizon Research, Inc.(NJ1).

Beeman, K., & Urow, C. (2013). *Teaching for biliteracy*. Philadelphia, PA: CASLON.

Bicknell, B. (1999). The writing of explanations and justifications in mathematics: Differences and dilemmas. In *Making the difference: Proceedings of the 22nd annual conference of the Mathematics Education Research Group of Australasia Incorporated* (pp. 75–83).

Boyle, A., August, D., Tabaku, L., Cole, S., & Simpson-Baird, A. (2015). *Dual language education programs: Current state policies and practices.* Washington, DC: American Institutes for Research.

Casa, T. M., Firmender, J. M., Cahill, J., Cardetti, F., Choppin, J. M., Cohen, J., ... Zawodniak, R. (2016). *Types of and purposes for elementary mathematical writing: Task force recommendations.* Retrieved from http://mathwriting.education.uconn.edu

Chandler, D. (2000). The problem of definition. *An introduction to genre theory.* Retrieved July 28, 2016, from http://www.aber.ac.uk/media/Documents/intgenre/intgenre1.html

Cirillo, M., Kosko, K., Newton, J., Staples, M., Weber, K., Bieda, K., ... & Hummer, J. (2015). Conceptions and consequences of what we call argumentation, justification, and proof. In *Proceedings of the 37th annual meeting of the North American Chapter of the Psychology of Mathematics Education* (pp. 1343–1351).

Clark, I. (2005). A genre approach to writing assignments. In *Composition forum* (Vol. 14, No. 2, p. n2). Association of Teachers of Advanced Composition.

Cole, M. (1998). *Cultural psychology: A once and future discipline.* Harvard University Press.

Cope, B., & Kalantzis, M. (1993). The power of literacy and the literacy of power. In B. Cope, & M. Kalantzis (Eds.), *The Powers of Literacy: A Genre Approach to Teaching Writing* Routledge. http://10.4324/9780203149812-12

Cummins, J. (2007). Rethinking monolingual instructional strategies in multilingual classrooms. *The Canadian Journal of Applied Linguistics, 10,* 221–240.

De La Paz, S., Ferretti, R., Wissinger, D., Yee, L., & MacArthur, C. (2012). Adolescents' disciplinary use of evidence, argumentative strategies, and organizational structure in writing about historical controversies. *Written Communication, 29*(4), 412–454.

Devitt, A. J. (1993). Generalizing about genre: New conceptions of an old concept. *College Composition and Communication, 44*(4), 573–586.

DiRanna, K., Osmundson, E., Topps, J., Barakos, L., Gearhart, M., Cerwin, K.... & Strang, C. (2008). *Assessment-centered teaching.* Thousand Oaks, CA: Corwin Press.

Escamilla, K. (2000). *Bilingual means two: Assessment issues, early literacy and two language children.* In Research in literacy for limited English proficient students, 10028. Washington, DC: National Clearinghouse for Bilingual Education.

Escamilla, K., Butvilofsky, S., & Hopewell, S. (2017). What gets lost when English-only writing assessment is used to assess writing proficiency in Spanish-English emerging bilingual learners?. *International Multilingual Research Journal, 12*(4), 221–236.

Escamilla, K., Hopewell, S., Butvilofsky, S., Sparrow, W., Soltero-González, L., Ruiz-Figueroa, O., & Escamilla, M. (2014). *Biliteracy from the start: Literacy squared in action.* Philadelphia, PA: Caslon Publishing.

Espinosa, L. M., & Garcia, E. (2012). *Developmental assessment of young dual language learners with a focus on kindergarten entry assessments: Implications for state policies, Working Paper 1.* Center for Early Care and Education Research–Dual Language Learners (CECER-DLL). Chapel Hill, NC: University of North Carolina, Frank Porter Graham Child Development Institute.

Gebhard, M., & Harman, R. (2011). Reconsidering genre theory in K-12 schools: A response to school reforms in the United States. *Journal of Second Language Writing, 20*(1), 45–55.

Grosjean, F. (1989). Neurolinguists, beware! The bilingual is not two monolinguals in one person. *Brain and Language, 36*(1), 3–15.

Grosjean, F. (2010). *Bilingual: Life and reality.* Harvard University Press.

Halliday, M. A. (1985). *An introduction to functional linguistics* (p. 94). London: Edward Arnold.

Herrenkohl, L. R., & Cornelius, L. (2013). Investigating elementary students' scientific and historical argumentation. *Journal of the Learning Sciences, 22*(3), 413–461.

Hornberger, N. H. (2004). The continua of biliteracy and the bilingual educator: Educational linguistics in practice. *International Journal of Bilingual Education and Bilingualism, 7*(2–3), 155–171.

Kazemi, E., & Stipek, D. (2001). Promoting conceptual thinking in four upper-elementary mathematics classrooms. *The Elementary School Journal, 102*(1), 59–80.

Kiuhara, S. A., Graham, S., & Hawken, L. S. (2009). Teaching writing to high school students: A national survey. *Journal of Educational Psychology, 101*(1), 136.

Kosko, K. W. (2016). Writing in mathematics: A survey of K-12 teachers' reported frequency in the classroom. *School Science and Mathematics, 116*(5), 276–285.

Kosko, K. W., & Zimmerman, B. S. (2019). Emergence of argument in children's mathematical writing. *Journal of Early Childhood Literacy, 19*(1), 82–106. https://doi.org/10.1177/1468798417712065

Lea, M. R., & Street, B. V. (1998). Student writing in higher education: An academic literacies approach. *Studies in Higher Education, 23*(2), 157–172.

Lewis, M. A., & Zisselsberger, M. (2016). "But there's gotta be a strength": Toward the equitable assessment of the writing of emerging bilinguals. In *Teaching English language arts to English language learners* (pp. 147–169). London: Palgrave Macmillan.

Lillis, T. M. (2001). *Student writing: Access, regulation, desire.* UK: Routledge.

Lindholm-Leary, K. (2012). Success and challenges in dual language education. *Theory into Practice, 51*(4), 256–262.

Marshall, C., & Rossman, G. B. (1999). *Designing qualitative research.* Thousand Oaks, CA: Sage Publications.

Martin, J. (1992). Genre and literacy-modeling context in educational linguistics. *Annual Review of Applied Linguistics.* Retrieved from http://journals.cambridge.org/article_S0267190500002440

Moschkovich, J. N. (2007). Beyond words to mathematical content: Assessing English learners in the mathematics classroom. *Assessing mathematical proficiency, 53,* 345–352.

Newell, G. E., Bloome, D., Kim, M. Y., & Goff, B. (2019). Shifting epistemologies during instructional conversations about "good" argumentative writing in a high school English language arts classroom. *Reading and Writing, 32*(6), 1359–1382.

Paradis, J., Genesee, F., & Crago, M. B. (2011). *Dual language development and disorders: A handbook on bilingualism and second language learning.* Brookes Publishing Company. PO Box 10624, Baltimore, MD 21285.

Penuel, W. R., Roschelle, J., & Shechtman, N. (2007). Designing formative assessment software with teachers: An analysis of the co-design process. *Research and Practice in Technology Enhanced Learning, 2*(01), 51–74.

Reyes, M. D. L. L., & Costanzo, L. (2002). On the threshold of biliteracy: A first grader's personal journey. In L. D. Soto (Ed.), *Making a difference in the lives of bilingual/bicultural children* (pp. 145–156). New York, NY: Peter Lang.

Reyes, I., & Moll, L. C. (2008). Bilingual and biliterate practices at home and school. In B. Spolsky & F. Hult (Eds.), *The handbook of educational linguistics* (pp. 147–160). Malden, MA: Blackwell.

Schleppegrell, M., & de Oliveira, L. C. (2006). An integrated language and content approach for history teachers. *Journal of English for academic purposes, 5*(4), 254–268.

Smarter Balanced Assessment Consortium (2016). *Mathematics summative assessment blueprint.* Retrieved from http://www.smarterbalanced.org/assessments/development/

Soltero-González, L., Escamilla, K., & Hopewell, S. (2010). A bilingual perspective on writing assessment: Implications for teachers of emerging bilingual writers. In G. Li & P. Edwards (Eds.), *Best Practices in ELL Instruction* (pp. 222–244). New York: Guilford Press.

Soltero-González, L., Escamilla, K., & Hopewell, S. (2012). Changing teachers' perceptions about the writing abilities of emerging bilingual students: Towards a holistic bilingual perspective on writing assessment. *International Journal of Bilingual Education and Bilingualism, 15*(1), 71–94.

Swales, J. (1990). *Genre analysis: English in academic and research settings.* Cambridge University Press.

Thompson, K. D. (2015). What blocks the gate? Exploring current and former English learners' math course-taking in secondary school. Paper presented at the annual conference of the American Educational Research Association, Chicago, IL.

Toulmin, S. E. (1958/2003). *The uses of argument* (Vol. 70). Cambridge: Cambridge University Press.

Wittgenstein, L. (1978/2010). *Philosophical investigations.* (Translated by GE Anscombe). Oxford: Blackwell.

Yackel, E. (1992). *The evolution of second grade children's understanding of what constitutes an explanation in a mathematics class.* Paper presented at the Seventh International Congress of Mathematics Education, Quebec City.

Yackel, E., & Cobb, P. (1996). Sociomathematical norms, argumentation, and autonomy in mathematics. *Journal for Research in Mathematics Education, 27*(4), 458–477.

# 8. A Classroom Observation Tool for Assessing Mathematics in Two Languages

Marco A. Bravo
*Santa Clara University*

Eduardo Mosqueda
*University of California Santa Cruz*

Jorge L. Solís
*University of Texas at San Antonio*

Although there are few research studies on math instruction in dual language programs, there is ample evidence that Emergent Bilingual Learners (EBLs) are not performing to their potential in this discipline. Trends in the National Assessment of Educational Progress (NAEP) illustrate a continued disparity between students designated as English Language Learners and native English speakers in terms of math achievement (NAEP, 2017). For more than a decade, on average a statistically significant gap of 25 points has existed between these two student groups. Other research on the achievement gap suggests that forms of tracking students based on students' native languages may be a significant explanatory factor (Mosqueda & Maldonado, 2013). Still, others have found that the structure of assessments and their validity do not allow EBLs to fully demonstrate their understandings (Martiniello, 2008; Solano-Flores & Chía, 2017).

These results are further problematized with the implementation of the Common Core State Standards (CCSS, 2010) in several states (e.g., California, Arizona) and the pronounced attentiveness to the role of language in teaching and learning mathematics that are now a part of the instructional goals of teachers (Lee, Quinn & Valdés, 2013). With the renewed focus of language across content areas, teachers must develop new forms of instructing EBLs across content areas that account for not just conceptual development but bilingual development as well.

To assist teachers to further develop the knowledge, skills and dispositions that are necessary to work with EBLs, we developed the Mathematics and Language, Literacy Integration (MALLI) project.[1] The goals of MALLI are to bring to bear seasoned teachers, parents and math methods instructors' knowledge to prepare the next generation of bilingual teachers. The project draws from the literature that has shown promise to assist EBLs acquire language in and across content areas (Llosa, Lee, Jiang, Haas, O'Connor, Van Booven, & Kieffer, 2016; Musanti & Celedón-Pattichis, 2013; Zavala, 2017) and share these practices with pre-service teachers, cooperating teachers, and parents. Vocabulary, literacy and discourse practices that are germane to the mathematic discipline are integrated into the pre-service teacher education program. The research project developed an observation instrument to capture pre-service teacher's enactment of instructional practices that utilized language and literacy as tools for mathematics learning and bilingual development. In this chapter, we chronicle the development of this instrument that we refer to as the Mathematics Classroom Observation Protocol (M-COP). The M-COP was modeled after the Science-Classroom Observation Protocol (SCOP) (Cervetti, Kulikowich, and Bravo (2015). Before we describe the development and piloting of this instrument, we describe the MALLI project to offer a context for this instrument and what we intend for it to capture.

## *MALLI*

The MALLI project addresses the shortage of bilingual teachers in California and Texas (Arroyo-Romano, 2016; Carver-Thomas & Darling-Hammond, 2017; Kennedy, 2018). The main goals of the MALLI project involve supporting the learning of new bilingual teachers by providing models of effective pedagogy that support math learning and language development.

The research that we are conducting is guided by the following Theory of Change (Figure 8-1):

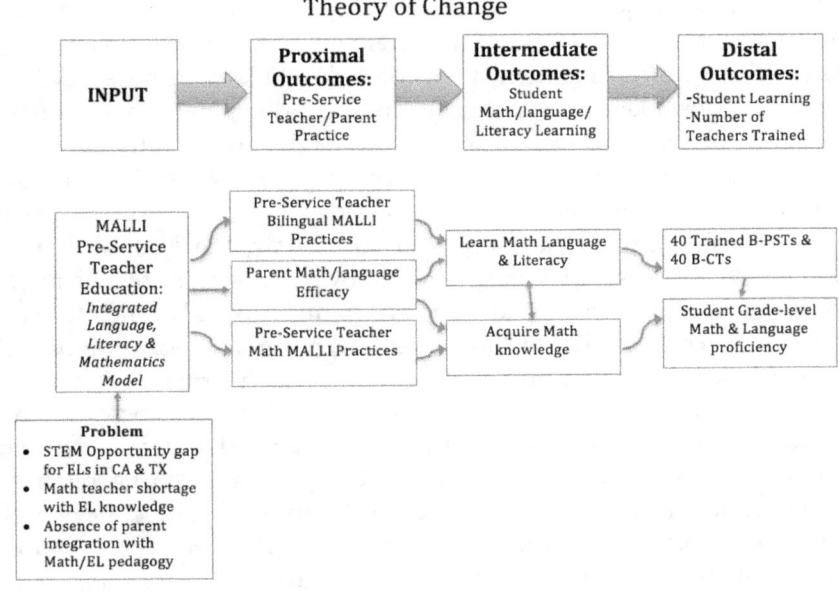

*Figure 8-1.* MALLI Theory of Change

To support the bilingual pre-service teachers, the MALLI project also involves bilingual master teachers (experienced teachers that host bilingual pre-service teachers in their classroom) and bilingual parents of the children that pre-service teachers work with at their student teaching placement. Both groups receive professional development opportunities in the MALLI practices in order to support the pre-service teacher in implementing instruction that develops content while students also sharpen their bilingual skills.

There are three MALLI teaching practices: (1) Mathematical Discourse, (2) Mathematics Vocabulary and; (3) Mathematics Bi/literacy. *Mathematical Discourse* refers to the structure of written or oral explanations and arguments that take place within the mathematics discipline (Rumsey & Langrall, 2016) as well as the evidence that is suggested to be leveraged to support explanations and arguments in mathematics (Knudsen, Stevens, Lara-Meloy, Kim & Shectman, 2018). Moschkovich (1999) states that this form of talking and writing is different than merely using particular math vocabulary. Rather, mathematics discourse means talking and acting "to prove or explain statements." Additionally, allowances for translanguaging practices are promoted, as EBLs pose a wide array of linguistic tools that they can bring to bear to solve problems (Garcia & Wei, 2014).

The MALLI project addresses *Mathematics Vocabulary* by drawing attention to the nature of vocabulary and strategies that can be applied to give access to these words in mathematics. Math vocabulary includes words that are rare and most likely to be encountered in the discipline. These words are commonly referred to as technical tier 3 words due to the infrequency with which they appear in everyday contexts (Beck, McKeown & Kucan, 2002). Math vocabulary often is present in collocation form (e.g., Distributive Property, surface area), that if not read collectively, can lead EBLs to the wrong meaning. These issues are addressed by providing pre-service teachers with instructional models to address these linguistic pitfalls which take place across languages. Strategies include attention to cognate relationships which can provide access to the meaning of unfamiliar math terms.

*Mathematics Literacy/Biliteracy* practices include the types of reading and writing that are part of the mathematics discipline. Pre-service teachers are provided with models for teaching writing during math time that can include such practices as written explanations that describe how they solved a math problem, writing math word problems for others, and constructing tables and diagrams to explain their mathematical thinking. Similar instructional models are offered regarding reading math texts that include reading strategies (e.g., changing rate of reading, utilizing their native language) and how to make sense of diagrams, tables and charts, which require explicit instructional attention (Mosqueda, Bravo, Solís, Maldonado & De La Rosa, 2016).

While this study is preparing pre-service teachers to teach integrated math, language and literacy in Spanish, pre-service teachers are regularly given examples to help elicit the full linguistic repertoire that is afforded to EBLs (García & Wei, 2014). This is especially the case when asking students to construct oral explanations and arguments or writing about their procedures to solve math problems. Saliency for particular words, phrases and experiences drive what pre-service teachers elicit from students when teaching mathematics. Moreover, the goal of MALLI is also to promote instructional strategies that are not didactic or follow the typical interaction in classrooms where a teacher *Initiates*, a student *Responds*, and the teacher again takes a turn to *Evaluate*. This IRE-model (Mehan, 1979), is not very conducive for bilingual and biliteracy development and hence we promote more interaction and opportunities for student-to-student talk where students take more turns in talking than does the teacher. The MCOP instrument is structured to capture these practices and how they are enacted. A description of this instrument is presented below with exemplars that we have captured thus far in our observations of pre-service teachers after participating in the MALLI project.

## M-COP

The MALLI classroom observation protocol is designed to document the array of practices employed by mathematics teachers at the elementary level with a special focus on literacy and language development activities in Spanish as math is taught. The tool was developed to capture instruction taking place in bilingual education programs. This includes the wide array of bilingual programs (e.g., Early-Exit Bilingual Programs, Two-way Bilingual Programs) where two languages are used for instruction.

This observation protocol includes three parts. The first involves capturing information about the classroom setting. This is followed by the observer taking ethnographic notes of the instruction taking place. Observers take ethnographic notes for seven-minute chunks of instruction and then identify which codes (MALLI Practices) were noticed during the seven-minutes of instruction. This pattern is repeated for the duration of the observation which usually takes between 30 and 45 minutes. The last part of the observation scheme is an Implementation Questionnaire—a series of questions and activities that ask the observer to reflect back on what was observed and document implementation of language learner adaptations.

### Part 1: Pre-Observation Data Gathering

This section of the observation scheme gathers information about the classroom setting, including grade level, teacher code, date, start time and number of learners in the class. Observers are asked to gather additional information from the pre-service teacher, including a lesson plan and the number of English Learners and Spanish Learners in the classroom. The observer checks in with the pre-service teacher before the observation to ask if the lesson will be in English-only, Spanish-only or flexible language use. The number of adults in the room is also gathered including documenting if the adult is a teacher, teaching aid, parent, other pre-service teacher or other adult.

The observer gathers physical environment data of the classroom. The observer notes what technology is available in the classroom, the environmental print on the walls and in what language that print is written in and classroom library. The observer draws a sketch of the arrangement of tables and desks as well. This portion of the M-COP is attempting to capture the general linguistic ethos of the classroom. Here we recognize the classroom as a dynamic, complex and socially constructed space (Candela, Rockwell, & Coll, 2004), yet a context that requires professional vision (i.e., relevance of seating arrangements, student roles, materials, use of technology, etc.) in order to contextualize the focal classroom events and activities (Sherin, 2014).

## Part 2: Narrative Notes and Coding

*Narrative Notes.* To capture the instructional practices of pre-service teachers, particularly the attention to language and literacy development as they taught mathematics, observers write narrative notes of the instruction taking place. The shorthand description of pre-service teacher activity and student response captures not only what students and pre-service teachers are doing, but the language of instruction, use of technology, grouping structures, the use of vocabulary, literacy involved in the task as well as any discourse activities. These narrative notes take place over a seven-minute span. Below we provide a short example of these narrative notes by drawing from an observation of a bilingual teacher candidate (Ms. Betty) placed in a 1st grade classroom teaching a full math lesson for the first time (Figure 8-2).

*Figure 8-2.* Sample Narrative Notes

| Time | Notes |
| --- | --- |
| 0 | T asks—"what's a strategy?". Calls on Ariel |
| | Ariel. Alby, Haley, Junior all respond to the same question; science, math, using things in diff ways |
| | T writes "strategy" on the board and then asks again for more ss definitions |
| 2:30 | T says "talk with partner". Question "what strategies are used for addition" while T writes the definition on the board |
| 3:13 | "Eyes on me". T stops partner talk and asks Ss to share with class |
| | S1 offers "counting" |
| | T asks for an example |
| | S1 then writes the example on a paper poster under "strategy example" |
| | T then asks Emilia do it with fingers too and others |
| | T asks then for another strategy |
| | Abby says "doubles" |
| | T asks Abby to "show us" |
| | Abby writes on the poster |
| | T asks for another |
| | Haley offer skip count |
| | T says "ok show us" |
| | Haley goes up and writes it on poster |
| | T repeats strategy |
| | T ok another one |
| | S "number patterns". T number four writes number patterns |
| 7:10 | S explains |

In this case, Ms. Betty's lesson lasted more than 65 minutes which means that a narrative excerpt like the one in Figure 8-2 was repeated approximately nine times covering the entire observation using the MCOP instrument. Moreover, the narrative notes were used as an additional reference to identify and support the MCOP codes that were found present in the instruction.

*Codes.* After each seven-minutes of coding, the observer then turns to the codes for three minutes of coding. The coding scheme is made up of five levels: (1) Languages; (2) Major Instructional Focus; (3) Instructional Activities; (4) Teacher Interactions and; (5) Student Response.

*Language.* Each seven-minute segment of instruction is given a *Language* code that can be Spanish (S), English (E), or Translanguaging (T). As can be expected a code of (S) or (E) means the pre-service teacher provides the majority of instruction in either Spanish or English. Yet, if the pre-service teacher provides instruction across languages flexibly and/or allows/promotes this from students (e.g., allow for google translate, discussion allowed in either or both languages), then the *Translanguaging* code (T) is utilized.

*Major Instructional Focus* captures what the main goal was for students during the seven-minutes of instruction. This included whether students were involved in doing a math activity, including watching the teacher demonstrate an example math problem (D), reading (R) about mathematics, including making sense of data tables, writing (W) about math concepts, procedures or reasoning, listening (L) to the teacher or other students about a math activity, talking (T) about data or how to solve a math problem. There is a code in the instrument to capture non-relevant activities (e.g., interruption to the class, pre-service teacher taking attendance) (O).

The transcript above in Figure 8-2, received the code (T), given the major focus for students was talking and discussing the math task.

*Instructional Activities.* The Instructional Activities domain contains four major sets of codes, including (1) math instruction; (2) Vocabulary; (3) Literacy; (4) Discourse. Each of these domains contain sub-domains and each sub-domain is further detailed by what the teacher was doing (*Teacher Interaction*) and what the *Student Response* was, both of these level 4 and 5 codes will be explained below, as they pertain to the *Instructional Activities* code. The codes pertaining to the math instruction domain are presented below in Table 8-1.

*Table 8-1.* Math Instruction

| Math Concepts | MC | Focus is on concepts. Teacher or students are introducing, composing, or reviewing math concepts. This may include:<br>• writing key concepts about math<br>• teacher expands a student's response in a conceptual way |
|---|---|---|
| Math Procedural | MP | Focus is on helping students complete procedural task or skill development (e.g., multiplication table). |
| Math Procedural & Conceptual Connected | MCP | Focus is on making connections between procedural knowledge and conceptual development (***MC supersedes MP***). |
| Math Models | MM | Focus is on using models to illustrate math concepts.<br>• Models include diagrams, physical replicas, mathematical representations, analogies, and computer simulations. |
| Analyzing or sharing data | AD | Focus is on making sense of or sharing data. Students may be:<br>• Organizing data, e.g., transforming data into a data table.<br>• Making sense of their data<br>• Making claims about their data or drawing conclusions<br>Use this code when the teacher is discussing or modeling these activities, as well as when the students are engaged in them. |

These codes help capture what the instructional focus was for the math lesson. Whether the pre-service teacher focused on developing a math concept or build students' computational knowledge (Math Procedural), we code MCP if the teacher makes a connection between the MC and MP code. The instrument also captures whether the teacher is utilizing models to make math concepts clearer or the use of data and how to draw conclusions from a data set.

The vocabulary domain contains two subdomains. Table 8-2 below describes these two sub-scales.

## Table 8-2. Vocabulary

| | | |
|---|---|---|
| **Vocabulary Concepts** | VC | Focus is on word meanings. Students/teachers are engaged in discussing/ working on word meanings; students are recording words and definitions or synonyms; the teacher is previewing, introducing, or reinforcing word meanings; or the teacher is defining words in context. |
| **Vocabulary Strategy** | VS | This may include discussions of cognates. A focus on word analysis, such as strategies for using morphology to discern the meanings of words. |

Codes VC and VS refer to whether the vocabulary instruction was focused on getting at the meaning of a particular math concept or helping students build a strategy to make sense of unfamiliar math vocabulary. Note that within these constructs, language of instruction is fluid and the instrument is set to capture nuances of language use, whether English, Spanish, or both.

For example, in the following exchange we see how the language in use can shift sometimes momentarily, other times more extensively, and usually strategically. The segment scored covering this stretch of the lesson would be coded as *translanguaging* given that the teacher manages both languages in the lesson (García & Kleyn, 2016). The example draws from an observation of a bilingual teacher candidate teaching a math lesson on addition in a dual language Kinder classroom. The bilingual teacher candidate (BTC) asks the class, while holding up a six-inch die, "¿Quién me puede decir qué es esto?" ((who can tell me what this is?)). Here several students make observations of the large die held by the BTC. Tony promptly responds first to the BTC's Spanish-constructed question with the response of "a die" in English (line 5). The BTC responds strategically by repeating his response in English and then asking for a response in Spanish (line 6).

## Excerpt 1

| | | |
|---|---|---|
| 5 | Tony | A die |
| 6 | BTC | A die, ¿*en español*? ((a die, in Spanish?)) |
| 7 | Stu2 | *Un cubo* ((a cube)) |

After several exchanges in Spanish and specially no one yet identifying the name of "die" or "dice" in Spanish, the BTC asks again in Spanish "*¿Quién sabe cómo se llama en español?*" ((who knows what it's called in Spanish?)) (line 18). But here again we see another student (Lupe) shifting to English to address the question with her response of "it's a die" like Tony previously. Lupe had previously revoiced a student observation with "*y tiene círculos*" ((and it has circles)) in Spanish (line 16) as well.

**Excerpt 2**

| 16 | Lupe | *Y tiene círculos* ((and it has circles)) |
| 17 | BTC | *Tiene círculos* ((it has circles)) |
| 18 | | *¿Quién sabe cómo se llama en español?* ((who knows what its called in Spanish?) |
| 19 | Stu4 | *Un cubo* ((a cube)) |
| 20 | BTC | *¿Un cubo? Sí, muy bien* ((a cube, yes very good)) |
| 21 | | *¿Quién los ha visto? Levanten la mano* ((who has seen it? Raise your hand)) |
| 22 | | *Sí*, Lupe ((Yes, Lupe)) |
| 23 | Lupe | It's a die |

By noting how these language shifts are managed, expanded on, or restricted throughout a lesson, we can learn more about the language goals of each lesson, schoolwide dual language policies, and more broadly, how these decisions reflect broader language ideologies.

The *Literacy* domain consists of five sub-scales, focused on reading, writing and language development. Table 8-3 below further defines the type of literacy that we coded for during the observations.

*Table 8-3.* Literacy

| | | |
|---|---|---|
| **Reading** | R | Activity involves reading various math texts (e.g., ruler, diagrams, book, chart, graph, worksheet, poster, traffic signs). |
| | | Students may also be searching for information to answer questions, to support their Math activity, or to write or present. |
| **Reading Instruction/ Discussion** | RI | Focus is on instruction or discussion about math texts (diagrams, graphs, ruler, table). This may include: |
| | | • Students are learning about text structures or features of math text or genres of math text. |
| **Writing** | W | Focus is on writing math texts (e.g., word problem, table, graph, diagram), including writing organization or instruction on important elements of math compositions. (showing work with numbers not W) |
| **Writing Instructions** | WI | Focus is on instruction or discussion about writing math texts (diagrams, graphs, ruler, table, converting units). This may include: |
| | | • Students are learning about how to construct text math texts in appropriate genre. |
| **Language Development** | LD | Focus is on language development (e.g., metaphors, idioms, subject/verb agreement). |

The *Literacy* domain specifically captures literacy that is germane to the mathematics discipline. That is, we code for reading and writing of math texts such as reading diagrams, word problems and reading a protractor for example. We noted that there were examples of teachers attending to accompanying literacy features such as those related to pronunciation of key terms and concepts (language development), classification of concepts (i.e., pictographs as a type of graph), and reading visual representations commonly found in the math texts. We see literacy supports provided by the teacher in Excerpt 3. In the example below, the BTC is teaching a 1st grade class focused on reading mathematical information represented in different types of graphs. She begins the lesson by announcing to the class that the lesson was going to be related to graphs and asks students, "*¿Qué tipos de gráficas hemos aprendido?*" ((What types of graphs have we learned about?)). The BTC guides the discussion by noting precisely her interest in "types of graphs" and not merely graphs (line 8). This led to students identifying both bar graphs and pictographs as related to the topic of graphs (lines 9–11). Moreover, the BTC provides language development support by helping students repeatedly hear and pronounce the word "*pictografía*" ((pictograph)). Student clearly have difficulty articulating this word (Lines 11,13), and the teacher picks up on it.

**Excerpt 3: Language and Literacy Support**

| 8 | BTC | *¿Sí, pero qué tipo de gráficas hemos visto?* <br> ((Yes, but what type of graphs have we seen?)) |
|---|---|---|
| 9 | Stu2 | *Estamos viendo graficas de barra* <br> ((We are seeing bar graphs)) |
| 10 | BTC | *Graficas de barra* <br> ((bar graphs)) |
| 11 | Stu3 | *Picto, Pictografia, no sabia como pronunciarlo* <br> ((Picto, pictograph, I didn't know how to say it)) |
| 12 | BTC | *Hemos aprendido sobre gráficas de barra y pictografía* <br> ((We have learned about bar graphs and pictographs)) |
| 13 | Stu4 | *Y también picto—* <br> ((and also picto)) |
| 14 | BTC | *¿Se acuerdan que es pictografía?* <br> ((Do you remember what is a pictograph?)) |
| 15 | Stu5 | *Sí, cuando tiene fotos* <br> ((Yes when it has pictures)) |
| 16 | BTC | *Cuando tiene símbolos de fotos* <br> ((when it has symbols of pictures)) |

Of note as well is that the teacher reinforces academic terminology while augmenting students' contributions through reformulation of their definitions (Line 15–16). Our task as observers using the MCOP instrument was therefore to notice these overlapping literacy events and code the segments accordingly.

Moreover, in the case of literacy, we can observe and collect a range of mathematical representations created by students to demonstrate how a particular lesson evolved and support specific math practices. Figure 8-3 is an example of how a 1st grade bilingual lesson resulted in the production of different forms of writing following the model of 4 squares or "el modelo de 4 cuadros" to solve a word problem.

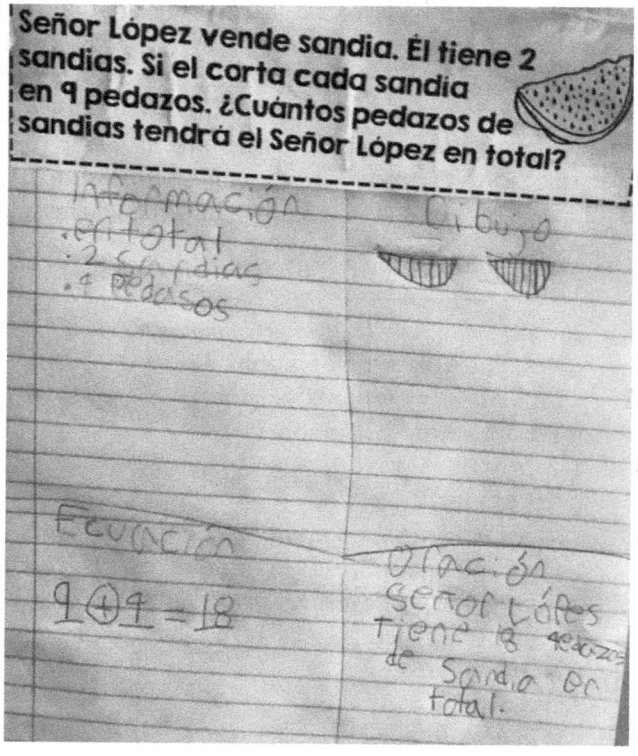

Figure 8-3. Writing Math

*Math Discourse* consists of five sub-scales that include whether the focus of instruction was making explanations about math activities, arguing for a position with respect to the math activity, the structure of the math talk activity, posing questions about math (e.g., Why do these numbers repeat?; Which words tell us to subtract?), and if prior knowledge is elicited. Table 8-4 below describe the codes.

*Table 8-4.* Math Discourse

| | | |
|---|---|---|
| Explanations/ Use of Evidence | EE | Focus is on the construction of math explanations supported by evidence (showing work of how to solve the problem in either orally, visual, or written form). |
| Math Argumentation | MA | Focus is on discovering new math ideas through convincing or being convinced that a math claim is valid (claim, evidence, reasoning-connecting evidence to claim--do you agree . . .). |
| Math Talk | MT | Focus is on structured talk about mathematics (concept; math careers; procedures; discourse of math). These structures can include Think-Pair-Share, Fish Bowl, Discourse Circle, elbow partner. |
| Questions About Math | QM | Focus is on posing questions about math. |
| Eliciting Prior Math Knowledge | PK | Different forms of mathematical contextualization that elicit students to share prior knowledge (outside of school) about math related ideas or topics. |

Below we provide a prototypical example of how math discourse is constrained. The example illustrates how a teacher structures an activity that allows students to share and explain their solutions. In the example below (Excerpt 4), a Kindergarten class is grappling with learning how to add two, three and four-digit numbers. A student (Beto) offers a solution to 1,000 plus 1,000 as equaling 1,002 (lines 24–26). The teacher (Ms.C) questions his solution (line 27) and then goes on to suggest they can solve it together (line 29).

## Excerpt 4: Missed Math Discourse Opportunity

| 22 | Beto  | Miss Cortez |
|----|-------|-------------|
| 23 | Ms.C  | Beto |
| 24 | Beto  | A thousand and a thousand |
| 25 | Ms.C  | Uh-uh |
| 26 | Beto  | It's a thousand-two |
| 27 | Ms.C  | A thousand plus a thousand is one-thousand-two? |
| 28 | Beto  | Yeah |
| 29 | Ms.C  | *Tal vez lo podemos resolver ahorita* ((perhaps we can solve it here now)) |
| 30 | Beto  | Yeah |
| 31 | Ms.C  | Okay |

This exchange exemplifies the rush to solve problems sometimes without engaging in reflective and explanatory math conversations with children. The missed opportunity occurs in Line 27 and Line 29 where instead of questioning Beto's solution or solving the problem, the teacher could have asked Beto to explain and/or describe how he solved the problem (MCOP codes EE, MA).

However, math lessons may contain activities that do promote a range of math discourse practices and with the MCOP, we can capture specific math discourse instances such as the lesson highlighted in Excerpt 5. The lesson begins with Ms. Lopez asking her 3rd grade bilingual students to pick-up their math notebooks. The lesson objectives are posted on the screen and read collectively. In addition to being able to multiply two-digit numbers, the lesson objectives include writing a mathematical solution in a complete sentence and being able to use previously identified math strategies and reasoning to solve a problem. The student read each objective in Spanish as most of the lesson was conducted in Spanish including this last part of the lesson objectives: *"[yo] puedo compartir mis estrategias con mis compañeros y describir mi razonamiento a la clase usando mi propia hoja de ancla "*/((I can share my strategies with my classmates and describe my reasoning to the class using my own anchor sheet)).

Ms. Lopez first checked with students if they knew what an "hoja de ancla" ((poster paper)) meant and then also checked with students if they knew the meaning of "auditorio" ((auditorium)) while showing them a picture of a lecture-style auditorium. Ms. Lopez then read a word problem together with the students projected on the screen asking students to find how many people can sit in a university auditorium with 14 rows and 38 seats in each row. She created eight groups of three students each assigned with one large, white blank piece of poster paper. Each student group then worked for approximately 25 minutes on solving the problem by including selecting a specific strategy for solving the word problem (MCOP codes MT, EE). Excerpt 5 describes part of the ensuing activity where each student group was asked to go to the front of the class, present their poster paper solution and express their reasoning for their solution.

**Excerpt 5: Promoting Student Math Talk and Reasoning**

| 85 | Ms.L | *Bueno para empezar, ¿ qué estrategia usaron?* ((well to begin, what strategy did you (group) use?)) |
| 86 | Chuy | *...area* ((area)) |
| 87 | Ms.L | *¿Y como resolvieron eso?* ((And how do you solve that?)) |
| 88 | Chuy | *Hicimos 14 por 10 que es 140 y lugo los hicimos dos mas veces* ((we did 14 by 10 which is 140 and then we did that two more times)) |
| 89 | | *Y despues hicimos 8 por 14 que es 112* ((And then we did 8 by 14 which is 112)) |
| 90 | | *Entonces despues hicimos 140 mas 140* ((Then after we did 140 plus 140)) |
| 91 | | *140 mas 112 que es igual a 532* ((140 plus 112 which is the same as 532)) |
| 92 | Ms.L | *Muy bien* ((Very good)) |
| 93 | | *¿Y quien me puede leer la oración completa?* ((And who can read for me the complete sentence?)) |
| 94 | Maria | *532 estudiantes pueden sentar en el adentro del auditorio* ((532 student can sit inside the auditorium)) |
| 95 | Ms.L | *Muy bien* ((Very good)) |
| 96 | | *¿Y algo se les hizo difícil al principio o cambiaron su estrategia?* ((And at the start was anything difficult or did you change your strategy?)) |
| 97 | Marta | ((looks at the poster)) |

This example highlights both repeated attempts by the teacher to augment, deepen and extend student math discourse through the use of explanatory prompts (Lines 87) as well as how a lesson can be structured, as in small groupwork, to enable greater student-to-student math talk and interaction (MCOP codes MT).

*Level 4. Teacher Interaction.* Each code referenced above correlates with a level 4 code that looks to capture the manner in which the preservice teacher is enacting the MALLI practices. We code if the teacher is telling or giving information (T), modeling (M) an activity, coaching or scaffolding (C) a task, listening (L) to students engage in an activity, reading aloud (RA) to students, engaging in a question and answer (QA) with students in an IRE sequence, having a discussion (D) with students that allows for more student to student interaction, eliciting prior knowledge (PK) or other (O) non-instructional activity.

*Level 5. Student Interaction.* For each level 4 code that the preservice teacher utilizes to engage students in the MALLI practices, we code the student response. We code if the student is reading (R), orally responding (OR), involved in discussion with the teacher (D), engaged with a student to student conversation (CV), observing a model (OB), listening to another student or to the teacher, manipulating objects (M), visually representing (VR) such as drawings, diagram or tables, writing (W) responses to math tasks, and other (O) non-instructional task.

## *Validation and Reliability*

The observation protocol was developed through a thorough review of the research literature regarding mathematics instruction (Hiebert & Carpenter, 1992; Rittle-Johnson, Siegler, & Alibali, 2001), bilingual education (Gándara, 2015; Jong, 2009), and content and language integration (Cervetti, Barber, Dorph, Pearson, & Goldschmidt, 2012; Lee, Quinn, & Valdés, 2013). This review helped us build our constructs of integration and the pedagogy necessary in working in dual language classroom settings. The instrument was then shared with five experts in the fields of mathematics, language, and teacher learning. This helped us further refine the constructs.

Six observers took part in a two-day training of the instrument. The training included an overview of the M-COP and four rounds of scoring using the coding scheme and a video of math instruction. These initial scoring sessions were followed by detailed discussions of observer scores and evidence to support those codes from their narrative notes. We conducted Interrater Reliability (IRR) checks and calculated IRR as percentage of absolute agreement to the main author of the instrument and differences in codes were discussed. By the eighth round of scoring we achieved an IRR score of 74%. These IRR checks are taking place after 1/3 of observations are collected to revisit the instrument and ensure the codes are being applied appropriately.

## *Discussion*

The MALLI Project goals discussed in this chapter attempt to support novice teachers and their EBL students in acquiring a powerful voice for explaining their mathematical thinking using sophisticated academic language, discuss and solve critical problems in mathematics, construct and extract meaning from mathematical texts, and accomplish these goals cross-linguistically, with the expectation that students' foundational knowledge in Spanish will transfer to English (and vice versa) (Cummins, 1991). Further, one of the deliverables of the MALLI project is an observational tool that can help capture, evaluate and provide guidance for teachers in the models of instruction that can best support EBLs' dual role of acquiring content while sharpening their biliteracy/bilingual skills.

The various dimensions of the M-COP offer a model for capturing classroom instruction, particularly instruction that is taking place across languages and within a content that is often thought of as being 'language-free'. If EBLs are to develop academic biliteracies, attention to language development across content areas will be necessary, as it is in content areas texts where the disciplinary language is made available. The M-COP is a valid and reliable instrument to capture these practices, which in turn can be utilized to evaluate bilingual programs, as well as provide guidance as to the focus of professional learning opportunities that can be made available to bilingual teachers. In our current work, we utilize these observation data to augment the bilingual teacher education program courses. We feed these data to the math methods instructors that work with our bilingual teachers so that they may emphasize (or de-emphasize) particular foci of the course that deals with the integration of mathematics and language. We have found that in order to get a consistent pattern of interaction, at least 30 minutes of instruction need to be observed. This would provide three segments of coding, a sufficient amount to decipher the instructional supports provided to emergent bilinguals. The evaluation of practice with the M-COP should be administered at least three times in order to see progression, but can also be administered as a pre/post observation in order to gauge growth in pedagogy.

This tool does not come without limitations. Learning the various codes to the point of reaching IRR was a challenge for the group of bilingual faculty and bilingual graduate students that are involved in the MALLI project.

The training that was needed was substantial and continues during data collection. With so many codes to keep in mind, conducting live scoring every seven minutes is an intense process. Also, the instrument attempts to capture multiple types of interaction and possible instructional activities that can take place during math instruction in bilingual settings, for which we may have not accounted for all. For example, it is clear that bilingual classrooms also house students with special needs (Baca & Cervantes, 2004) and the instructional supports a teacher might provide a special needs bilingual student may look different than the codes we present.

## *Conclusion*

The MCOP was developed to evaluate the efficacy of the MALLI project. The M-COP is a valid and reliable instrument. It has been tested and provided critical information about the academic biliteracy instruction that bilingual preservice teachers employ when teaching mathematics. For our research purposes, it captured fidelity of implementation of the MALLI practices. Pedagogically, it has helped identify preservice teachers' areas for growth and provided guidance to help focus future professional learning opportunities.

The MCOP results presented in this paper have important implications for policymakers, researchers and practitioners interested in improving teaching practices that maximize the linguistic knowledge and skills of bilingual students. The MALLI project recognizes that schools face persistent accountability pressures to demonstrate impact in dual language programs, we therefore draw from scholarship that advances a closer alignment between teaching and assessment practices and a holistic bilingual orientation to instruct and assess EBLs (García & DeNicolo, 2016; Soltero-González, Escamilla, & Hopewell, 2012). In terms of gauging EBLs mathematical learning, the MALLI project acknowledges that any assessment of content knowledge also is also an assessment of language. Moreover, to understand the mutual influence and development of two languages requires that both languages be examined together. Our project aims to demonstrate how the M-COP observation tool can support the development of mathematical biliteracy in dual language programs. While math instruction in Spanish is common in dual language programs, our aim is to contribute to pedagogical improvements that promote equity for EBLs by having a positive impact on students' mathematical achievement in dual language contexts. The next steps for this work are to continue to add new codes to the instrument in order to capture the wide range of practices utilized to maximize biliteracy and mathematical knowledge and skills.

## Note

1 Research reported in this publication was supported by the US Department of Education, Office of English Language Acquisition, National Professional Development (NPD) grant (2016–2021), The Mathematics and Language, Literacy Integration (MALLI) project (Grant # T365Z170070). The research content is solely the responsibility of the authors and does not necessarily represent the official views of the US Department of Education.

## References

Arroyo-Romano, J. E. (2016). Bilingual education candidates' challenges meeting the Spanish language/bilingual certification exam and the impact on teacher shortages in the state of Texas, USA. *Journal of Latinos and Education*, 15(4), 275–286.

Baca, L. M., & Cervantes, S. (2004). *Bilingual special education interface*. Upper Saddle River, NJ: Pearson Education.

Beck, I., McKeown, M., & Kucan, L. (2002). Bringing words to life. New York: Guilford Press.

Bravo, M., Mosqueda, E., Solís, J. L., & Stoddart, T. (2014). Possibilities and limits of integrating science and diversity education in preservice elementary teacher preparation. *Journal of Science Teacher Education*, 25(5), 601–619.

Candela, A., Rockwell, E., & Coll, C. (2004). What in the world happens in classrooms? Qualitative classroom research. *European Educational Research Journal*, 3(3), 692–713.

Carver-Thomas, D., & Darling-Hammond, L. (2017). *Addressing California's growing teacher shortage*. Palo Alto, CA: Learning Policy Institute.

Cervetti, G., Barber, J. Dorph, R. Pearson, P. D., & Goldschmidt, P. (2012). The impact of an integrated approach to science and literacy in elementary school classrooms. *Journal of Research in Science Teaching*, 49(5), 631–658.

Cervetti, G. N., Kulikowich, J. M., & Bravo, M. A. (2015). The effects of educative curriculum materials on teachers' use of instructional strategies for english language learners in science and on student learning. *Contemporary Educational Psychology*, 40, 86–98.

Cummins, J. (1991). Interdependence of first- and second-language proficiency in bilingual children. In E. Bialystok (Ed.), *Language processing in bilingual children* (pp. 70–89). Cambridge, England: Cambridge University Press.

Gándara, P. (2015). Rethinking bilingual instruction. *Educational Leadership*, 72, 60–64.

García, G. E., & DeNicolo, C. P. (2016). Improving the language and literacy assessment of emergent bilinguals. In L. Helman (Ed.), *Literacy Development with English Learners: Research-Based Instruction in Grades K-6* (2 ed., pp. 78-108). Guilford Press.

García, O., & Kleyn, T. (2016). Translanguaging theory in education. In *Translanguaging with multilingual students* (pp. 23–47). Routledge.

García, O., & Wei, L. (2014). Translanguaging and education. In *Translanguaging: Language, bilingualism and education* (pp. 63–77). London: Palgrave Macmillan.

Hiebert, J., & Carpenter, T. P. (1992). Learning and teaching with understanding. In D. A. Grouws (Ed.), *Handbook of research on mathematics teaching and learning* (pp. 65–97). New York, NY: Macmillan.

Jong, E. D., & Howard, E. (2009). Integration in two-way immersion education: Equalising linguistic benefits for all students. *International Journal of Bilingual Education and Bilingualism, 12*(1), 81–99.

Kennedy, B. (2018). The bilingual teacher shortage in one Texas school district: Practitioner perspectives. *Journal of Latinos and Education, 19*(4), 338–354, DOI: 10.1080/15348431.2018.1526688

Knudsen, J., Stevens, H. S., Lara-Meloy, T., Kim H. J., & Shechtman, N. (2018). *Mathematical Argumentation in Middle School: The what, why, and how*. Thousand Oaks, CA: Corwin Mathematics.

Lee, O., Quinn, H., & Valdés, G. (2013). Science and language for English language learners in relation to next generation science standards and with implications for common core state standards for English language arts and mathematics. *Educational Researcher, 43*, 223–233.

Llosa, L., Lee, O., Jiang, F., Haas, A., O'Connor, C., Van Booven, C. D., & Kieffer, M. J. (2016). Impact of a large-scale science intervention focused on English language learners. *American Educational Research Journal, 53*, 395–424.

Martiniello, M. (2008). Language and the performance of English language learners in math word problems. *Harvard Educational Review, 78*, 333–368.

Mehan, H. (1979). *Learning lessons: Social organization in the classroom*. Cambridge, MA: Harvard University Press.

Moschkovich, J. (1999). Supporting the participation of English language learners in mathematical discussions. *For the learning of mathematics, 19*(1), 11–19.

Mosqueda, E., Bravo, M. A., Solis, J. L., Maldonado, S. I., & De La Rosa, J. (2016). Preparing middle school students for the transition to high school mathematics: Assessing Latinas/os' mathematical understanding, academic language and English language proficiency. *The Bilingual Review/La Revista Bilingüe,1*(1), 1–20.

Mosqueda, E. & Maldonado, S. I. (2013). The effects of English language proficiency and curricular pathways: Latina/os' mathematics achievement in secondary schools. *Equity & Excellence in Education 46*(2), 202–219.

Musanti, S. I., & Celedón-Pattichis, S. (2013). Promising pedagogical practices for emergent bilinguals in kindergarten: Towards a mathematics discourse community. Journal of Multilingual Education Research, 4, Article 4. https://fordham.bepress.com/jmer/vol4/iss1/4/

National Assessment of Educational Progress (2017). *2017 Mathematics and reading assessment reports*. Retrieved January 15, 2018 from http://www.nationsreportcard.gov/reading_math_g12_2013/#/

National Governors Association Center for Best Practices & Council of Chief State School Officers (2010). *Common core state standards for mathematics.* Washington, DC.

Rittle-Johnson, B., Siegler, R. S., & Alibali, M. W. (2001). Developing conceptual understanding and procedural skill in mathematics: An iterative process. *Journal of Educational Psychology, 93*(2), 346.

Rumsey, C., & Langrall, C.W. (2016). Promoting mathematical argumentation: These evidence-based instructional strategies can lead to deeper mathematical conversations in upper elementary school classrooms. *Teaching Children Mathematics, 22*(7), 413–419.

Sherin, M. G. (2014). Developing a professional vision of classroom events. In *Beyond classical pedagogy* (pp. 89–108). Routledge.

Solano-Flores, G., & Chía, M. (2017). Validation of score meaning in multiple language versions of tests. In K. Ercikan & J. Pellegrino (Eds.), Validation of score meaning in the next generation of assessments: The use of response processes (pp. 127-137). New York: Routledge.

Soltero-González, L., Escamilla, K., & Hopewell, S. (2012): Changing teachers' perceptions about the writing abilities of emerging bilingual students: Towards a holistic bilingual perspective on writing assessment. *International Journal of Bilingual Education and Bilingualism, 15*(1), 71–94

Zavala, M. R. (2017). Bilingual pre-service teachers grapples with academic and social roles of language in mathematics discussions. *Issues in Teacher Education, 26*(2), 49–66.

# 9. *Evaluating Teacher Attitudes towards Bilingualism and Best Science Teaching Practices for Bilingual Learners*

TIBERIO GARZA
*University of Nevada, Las Vegas*

MARGARITA HUERTA
*University of Nevada, Las Vegas*

JULIE K. JACKSON
*Texas State University*

Evaluating bilingual education programs requires careful attention to the data sources, assessments and analysis methods used to evaluate programs. Often, evaluations require specialized and innovative instruments to capture data which can help contextualize larger findings and lead to practical implications. In this book chapter, we present results of a study using an instrument created to assess teachers' attitudes regarding the role of language—including bilingualism—in the content areas, specifically science. In doing so, our aim is to provide educators and policymakers with a tool for evaluating teachers' attitudes towards teaching English learners (ELs) or bilingual learners in science as a way to inform future professional development training.

### *Terminology Background*

In this chapter, we use the terms "EL(s)" and "bilingual learners" interchangeably. Though it is possible ELs may be multilingual, as opposed to bilingual, the terms EL and bilingual serve as a form of language baseline in the United States setting. That is, the terms assume a student has a repertoire of *at least* two languages and is at some stage of development in developing one or both languages. Hence, some researchers prefer the term "emergent bilingual"—but even this term is problematic if an individual is not developing two languages in their context. In the United States, students in bilingual programs are assumed to be developing two languages at school; but if developing only one language (i.e., English) they are likely in an English as a Second Language (ESL) program or a content-area classroom not providing bilingual education.

The latter is often the case in science education past elementary school or in settings focused on English-only and is inclusive of students in all kinds of settings across the United States—which is why, the term "EL" is often used in science education research and in teacher preparation research in states where bilingual education may not exist. Here, we wish to further note that the term English Language Learner (ELL) is often used in research as well and is aligned with the term EL, so the term ELL may be used when we discuss previous literature when using direct quotations. Regardless, EL or bilingual learners should receive equitable access to learning (Equal Educational Opportunities Act of 1974), which is why it is critical to evaluate the extent to which professional development is assisting teachers to work effectively with EL or bilingual learners, regardless of context.

## *Science Education Background*

Science education is important because it provides students with foundational knowledge to deal with our increasingly technological societies (International Council for Science [ICSU], 2001). Science education should also be accessible to all students (NGSS Lead States, 2013), including the 4.5 million English Leaners (ELs) enrolled in U.S. public schools (McFarland et al., 2017). However, ELs, or students who are in the process of learning English as a second or other language, often struggle on measures of science achievement, scoring below average on national test scores (McFarland et al., 2017).

Research informs how ELs or bilingual learners benefit from instruction in which teachers effectively integrate academic language and science content in the classroom (e.g., Lara-Alecio, Tong, Irby, Guerrero, Huerta, & Fan, 2012; Llosa et al., 2016; Maerten-Rivera, Ahn, Lanier, Diaz, & Lee, 2016). For example, studies in science education with ELs or bilingual learners have integrated direct vocabulary and reading and writing instruction (Lara-Alecio et al., 2012) via student booklets and teacher guides that include activities, strategies and native language supports (e.g., Llosa et al., 2016; Maerten-Rivera et al., 2016).

While conceptual and practical resources exist to guide science-literacy integrated instruction (e.g., Douglas, 2006; Rupp Fulwiler, 2011; Saul, 2004), teachers still need effective and on-going quality professional development to implement integrated language and science instruction effectively (Lee, Lewis, Adamson, Maerten-Rivera, & Secada, 2008; Santau, Secada, Maerten-Rivera, & Lee, 2010). On-going, quality professional development includes teacher attention to their attitudes about their students' linguistic diversity and their attitudes regarding what they are being asked to implement in the classroom. The instrument proposed and illustrated in this chapter can help professional development leaders understand where their educator- participants are and adjust emphasis on different parts of the professional development appropriately. These adjustments could lead to higher quality professional development based on participants' needs. The instrument can also serve as a pre and post comparison to evaluate the effectiveness of professional development in impacting teacher attitudes towards working with ELs in science, assisting with the quality of similar future professional development planning, implementation and revision.

## *Framework*

Effective teacher practice is related to teacher attitudes and beliefs about their students (Borg, 2003; Fang, 1996; Farell & Kun, 2008; Pajares, 1992; Pettit, 2011b). Teacher beliefs about their ELs or bilingual learners can affect what the students learn, their overall learning and academic achievement and what teachers consider effective practice for this group of students (e.g., Mantero & McViccker, 2006; Peregoy & Boyle, 1997; Shim, 2014). Critically, teachers without proper training can exhibit misinformed beliefs about ELs or bilingual learners and bilingualism. For example, teachers may believe it is not their responsibility to modify coursework or use the native home language as an asset/support to learning in the classroom (e.g., Karathanos, 2009; Reeves, 2006; Song & Samimy, 2015).

Effective professional development can promote asset-based views about linguistic diversity and how to work with ELs or bilingual learners effectively in content-areas. For example, in science education studies, teacher beliefs (Hart & Lee, 2003) and their practices (Lee, 2004) have been noted to positively change as a result of professional development interventions. The term attitudes and beliefs are terms often used interchangeably (Flores & Smith, 2009; Pajares, 1992). It is helpful to think about attitudes as an overarching construct made up of belief statements. That is, beliefs can be statements beginning with "I believe ... "; while attitudes are clusters of belief statements (Pajares, 1992; For a more detailed discussion of this construct definition: Huerta, Garza, Jackson, & Murukutla (2019)).

## Literature Review

In what follows we synthesize previous research on teacher attitudes towards ELs or bilingual learners in content-area learning, including science, and what variables seem to influence teacher attitudes towards ELs or bilingual learners.

### *Attitudinal Focus*

**Linguistic diversity.** Researchers who have measured teacher attitudes with respect to content-area pedagogy for ELs have done so with two main foci. The first, is a focus on teacher *attitudes towards linguistic diversity* (e.g., Byrnes & Kiger, 1994; Flores & Smith, 2009; Youngs & Youngs, 2001). For example, Byrnes and Kiger (1994) asked K-12 regular classroom teachers questions regarding whether they thought English should be the official language of the United States or to what extent ELs should quickly be transitioned to learning English at the expense of losing their home language. Similarly, Youngs and Youngs (2001) asked middle school classroom teachers questions regarding how much they would like or dislike having ELs in their classroom.

**Language in practice.** The second, is a focus on teacher *attitudes towards language in practice* (e.g., Huerta et al., 2019; Polat & Mahalingappa, 2013; Song & Samimy, 2015). For example, Polat and Mahalingappa (2013) asked in-service teachers questions regarding their attitudes toward modifying coursework for ELs. Song and Samimy (2015) asked in-service teachers questions regarding attitudes towards the positive or negative interplay of the home language with the target language (i.e., English) in the classroom. In science education, Hart and Lee (2003) qualitatively asked elementary teachers about what they believed the role of literacy was in science education. Huerta et al. (2019) quantitatively asked similar questions in an attempt to gauge in-service K-12 teacher attitudes towards literacy integration in the science classroom.

### *Study Findings*

In what follows we discuss the study findings with respect to both *linguistic diversity* and *language in practice*. In our analysis of the literature, we group the findings by the following variables: Demographic, contextual and educational.

**Demographic variables.** Researchers have explored teacher attitudes with respect to gender, bilingualism and race with findings noting the importance of considering other variables at play in the analysis. For example, female teachers have been noted to have more positive attitudes regarding language in practice as well as in terms of linguistic diversity than male teachers (Pettit, 2011a; Polat & Mahalingappa, 2013). However, gender differences seem to disappear when other variables are accounted for such as teachers' exposure to diverse students (Polat & Mahalingappa, 2013). Similarly, race has also been found to be related to more positive attitudes towards linguistic diversity (Flores & Smith, 2009), with non-significant results occurring when other factors such as diversity training were present in the analysis. However, researchers have found teachers who report being bilingual have overall more positive attitudes towards linguistic diversity (Flores & Smith, 2009; Huerta et al., 2019; Rader-Brown & Howley, 2014).

**Contextual variables.** Exposure to diverse populations, grade levels taught (elementary vs. secondary) and experience working with ELs or bilingual learners have been found to relate to teacher attitudes. For example, teachers exposed to diverse populations seem to have more positive attitudes towards linguistic diversity and language in practice (Byrnes, Kiger, & Manning, 1997; Polat & Mahalingappa, 2013; Youngs & Youngs, 2001). Teachers working with elementary school students, overall, have more positive attitudes towards linguistic diversity (Huerta et al., 2019; Karakathanos, 2009); though some past research has found no differences between elementary and secondary teachers' attitudes towards linguistic diversity (Byrnes, Kiger, & Manning, 1997).

**Educational variables.** Last, teacher attitudes toward linguistic diversity and language practice have been significantly related to educational variables, though with varying evidence. For example, teachers' attainment of a graduate degree (Byrnes, Kiger, & Manning, 1997), experiences with multicultural language learning courses (Flores & Smith, 2009), formal training in a second language (Byrnes, Kiger, & Manning, 1997) and experience abroad (Youngs & Youngs, 2001) were significantly related to teacher attitudes (i.e., more positive attitudes with these variables) in *individual* studies. However, professional and formal training to work with ELs or bilingual learners has been significantly related to teacher attitudes *across several* studies (i.e., professional training = more positive attitudes: e.g., Huerta et al., 2019; Pettit, 2011a; Polat & Mahalingappa, 2013).

## *Purpose*

We aim to provide educators and policymakers with an instrument for evaluating EL/bilingual professional development in science in terms of teacher attitudes. The instrument could be used to gauge teacher attitudes and help plan a professional development training. The instrument could also be used to measure pre and post gains of teacher attitudes after a professional development series of training. In our presentation of this instrument, we provide an instrument model and show how the instrument was used to measure science teacher attitudes towards ELs or bilingual learners. Last, we discuss practical implications for educators and policymakers.

Our motivation is driven by our joint backgrounds in assessment and evaluation, bilingual education, and science education. The first author is currently the Associate Director of the Center of Research, Evaluation, and Assessment at the University of Nevada, Las Vegas where he focuses on providing culturally-relevant evaluation to grant-funded and contracted projects in the university and community. The second author is currently an Associate Professor of EL education at the University of Nevada, Las Vegas researching the integration of literacy and science for bilingual learners. The third author is currently an Associate Professor of science education at Texas State University focusing on professional development assisting science teachers to effectively integrate science and literacy to promote all students' learning, including bilingual students.

## *Method*

**Instrument.** A version of the instrument, the *Attitudes Towards Teaching Science to Bilingual Learners* (ATTS-BL), is presented at the end of the book for replication use in bilingual settings. In addition, the appendix explains how to use, administer and interpret scores from the ATTS-BL. We created the original instrument using Qualtrics, an online platform; however, the questions can be recreated and integrated into any platform. For the attitudinal scales discussed below, we included which items would need to be reverse-coded for analysis. In this way, higher sum values for each participants' scores are associated with more positive attitudes while lower sum values are associated with more negative attitudes (See: Descriptive attitudinal measures below).

**Demographic questions.** The ATTS-BL includes demographic questions and two attitudinal scales. Demographic questions are based on both practical/standard information usually collected (e.g., age, teaching role) and the reviewed literature (e.g., exposure to diversity, bilingualism and professional development). These questions included: participants' age, gender, race, educational level, role working with students, grade levels taught, contact with ELs or bilingual learners and diverse populations, language, and professional training.

**Attitudinal Scales.** The ATTS-BL also includes two attitudinal scales. The first attitudinal scale measures teachers' *Attitudes Towards Linguistic Diversity* (adapted from Byrnes & Kiger, 1994), here re-labeled *Attitudes Towards Bilingualism* (Cronbach's alpha = .812). We slightly adapted the scale wording to our context. For example, phrases such as "detrimental to the learning" were replaced with "inhibits the learning." We also changed terms such as "linguistic minority" and "non-limited English proficient students" to "English learner" to fit our context of general science educators who may or may not have been working in bilingual settings. The ATTS-BL presented in this chapter includes a further adaptation replacing the term "English Learner" with "Bilingual Learner"; the wording can be adapted depending on the context of where the instrument is going to be used.

Here, we wish to note that even small changes to the rating scales such as changing *Bilingual Learner* to *English Learner* could potentially change the way in which respondents answer questions and impact the validity and reliability of the scales. However, we anticipate that the users would use the terminology most appropriate and familiar to the respondents in their context. The demographic questions can be changed without concern for impacting the validity or reliability of the instrument because they are not measuring constructs (e.g., attitudinal constructs). Still, we recommend two important considerations if adapting the instrument attitudinal scales. First, adaptation should be small/slight (e.g., changing terminology to fit the context) and not major (e.g., eliminating half the questions of a scale) to maintain the reliability and validity of the original instrument. Second, if larger adaptations are made for research purposes (and even smaller adaptations in different contexts), we recommend the researchers re-run reliability and validity measures. Last, we caution both practitioners and researchers to interpret their results with the context in which the instrument is used. The findings can be generalized to the population being evaluated, but the findings cannot and should not be generalized beyond the context(s) in which it is used (unless the instrument is used with a randomized, national sample).

The second attitudinal scale measures teachers' *Attitudes Towards Research-Based Practices for Teaching Academic Content and Language for ELs in Science* (Huerta et al., 2019), here re-labeled *Attitudes Towards Best Science Teaching Practices for Bilingual Learners* (Cronbach's alpha = .825). We created this scale for our study. We used both general evidence-based research and science-specific research to create the items in the instrument. General evidence-based practices for teaching academic content and literacy to ELs or bilingual learners has been summarized by *What Works Clearinghouse* (U.S. Department of Education, 2014):

1. Teach a set of academic vocabulary words intensively across several days using a variety of instructional activities.
2. Integrate oral and written English language instruction into content-area teaching.
3. Provide regular, structured opportunities to develop written language skills.
4. Provide small-group instructional intervention to students struggling in areas of literacy and English language development.

Specific science-based research includes elements from above in addition to the importance of using students' native language and culture in the classroom (Janzen, 2008; Lee, 2004; Quinn, Lee, & Valdés, 2013). In addition to the strong reliability measure noted above, principal component analysis (PCA) demonstrated strong content validity for the scale (For those interested in the PCA analysis and results see: Huerta et al. (2019)). Again, adaptations to this scale should adhere to the cautions and recommendations noted above in the discussion following our description of the first scale.

## *Sample*

In order to demonstrate the use of the ATTS-BL, we analyzed data collected using the instrument in a process approved by our university's institutional review board (Huerta et al., 2019). The process included soliciting participants who attended professional development workshops in the Southwestern United States from November 2017 to May 2018. The workshops were aimed at training educators to integrate language and science into their practice. The participants were asked to complete a survey (i.e., the instrument). In the end, our sample included 553 participants who completed the survey and were working directly with children in the classroom (we eliminated a small percentage who indicated they were administrators or university instructors for this analysis because we wanted to analyze results from participants working with children day-to-day). Table 9-1 presents data on the characteristics of our sample which is important for contextualizing the data.

*Table 9-1.* Sample Characteristics

| Variables | Statistics |
|---|---|
| **Demographic** | |
| Age | Range of 18–70 ($M = 40.46$; $SD = 9.94$) |
| Gender | 93.5% women |
| Race | 67.3% White; 23.1% Hispanic; 4.4% Black; 2.0% Asian; 0.4% American Indian; 2.5% other |
| Teaching Roles | 86.1% practicing teachers; 13.9% instructional coaches |
| Language | 82.5% only English; 16.5% bilingual |
| **Contextual** | |
| Worked with ELs or bilingual learners | 95.1% have worked with ELs or bilingual learners |
| Contact with diverse populations | 95.1% reported frequent contact with diverse populations |
| Grade levels taught | 75.9% worked in PK-5$^{th}$ grade (Elementary) |
| **Educational** | |
| College Degree | 57.5% Bachelor's degree; 40.7% Master's degree; 1.8% Doctoral degree |
| Have an ESL/TESOL/Bilingual Endorsement or Certificate | 64.1% yes; 35.9% no |
| Professional Development (PD) to work with ELs or bilingual learners | 90.1% reported having received PD to work with ELs or bilingual learners |
| Professional Development (PD) to work with ELs or bilingual learners | 41.6% reported having received PD to work with ELs or bilingual learners in science |

## *Analysis*

Using the data collected, we sought to analyze the extent to which teacher variables of interest predicted teachers' *Attitudes Towards Best Science Teaching Practices for Bilingual Learners*. Given the relationship between teachers' exposure to diversity and specific EL/bilingual training most frequently noted in the literature, we hypothesize that teachers' *Attitudes Towards Bilingualism* would be a significant predictor of teachers' *Attitudes Towards Best Science Teaching Practices for Bilingual Learners*. Knowing this information could help us know to what extent professional development related to ELs or bilingual learners in science needs to also attend to teachers' attitudes about bilingualism.

To test our hypothesis, we first made sure our data met all relevant assumptions related to multicollinearity, outliers, normality, linearity, homoscedasticity and independence of residuals (Tabachnick & Fidell, 2013). We also dummy coded variables such as language to include English-only or bilingual and grade level to include elementary or secondary. We then ran two multiple regression models in which we entered variables simultaneously into each model. In the first model, we used teacher variables as predictors. We included variables related to race, language, education, grade levels and professional development based on previous literature. Because our sample included such a high percentage of females (93.5%), participants who had worked with ELs or bilingual learners (95.1%) and had contact with diverse populations (95.1%) and professional development to work with ELs or bilingual learners (90.1%), we excluded these variables from the regression analysis. Future studies with more diverse samples would do well to explore these variables. In the second model, we introduced *Attitudes Toward Bilingualism* to analyze how well the variables predict *Attitudes Towards Best Science Teaching Practices for Bilingual Learners*. In doing this, we were able to see what role all these variables played in predicting teachers' attitudes towards best practices in the science classroom for bilingual learners within our sample.

## *Results*

**Descriptive attitudinal measures.** How many sample scores fall below or above the mean of an instruments' scale is the theoretical midpoint. This measure is calculated to better understand how "high" or "low" participants' scores are. For the two 13 item scales provided, the range of scores is 13 (lowest = more negative attitude) to 65 (highest = more positive attitude). The theoretical midpoint, then, is 39 (65–13 = 52; 52/2 = 26; 13+26). Educators using this scale can then calculate the sum score of their participants and see if the total falls above or below this midpoint of 39. In our sample, participants' mean scores for *Attitudes Toward Bilingualism* was 48.26 (SD = 8.46) and their mean score for *Attitudes Towards Best Science Teaching Practices for Bilingual Learners* was 50.58 (SD = 7.36). Therefore, both measures were above the midpoint, meaning their attitudes were generally positive.

**Regression Analysis.** The results of the two regression models are presented in Table 9-2.

*Table 9-2.* Standardized beta coefficients for predictors of *Attitudes Towards Best Science Teaching Practices for Bilingual Learners* among a sample of science educators, according to two regression models

| Predictors | Model 1 Adjusted $R^2 = .127$ | | Model 2 Adjusted $R^2 = .254$ | |
| --- | --- | --- | --- | --- |
| | $\beta$ | $p$ | $\beta$ | $p$ |
| Race | .000 | .995 | -.040 | .359 |
| Bilingual | .161 | .001** | .103 | .020* |
| Education | .124 | .002** | .084 | .026* |
| Grade Level | .169 | .0001*** | .105 | .008** |
| EL/Bilingual Endorsement or Certificate | .118 | .005** | .080 | .042* |
| PD for ELs or Bilingual Learners in Science | .159 | .0001*** | .126 | .001** |
| *Attitudes Toward Bilingualism* | | | .382 | .0001*** |

* $p < .05$.
** $p < .01$.
*** $p < .001$.

As can be noted in Table 9-2, Model 1 explained 12.7% of the variance in *Attitudes Towards Best Science Teaching Practices for Bilingual Learners* (Adjusted $R^2 = .127$, $F (6, 546) = 14.192$, $p < .0001$: Cohen's $f^2 = .145$—small effect). Grade level (whether the participants taught elementary or secondary) made the largest contribution to the model ($\beta = .169$, $p < .0001$). Language (whether the participants were bilingual or not; $\beta = .161$, $p < .001$) and Professional Development for ELs or Bilingual Learners in Science (whether the participants had received this type of professional development; $\beta = .159$, $p < .0001$) also made large contributions to the model. All the predictors, except race contributed significantly to Model 1.

Model 2 explained 25.8% of the variance in *Attitudes Towards Best Science Teaching Practices for Bilingual Learners* (Adjusted $R^2 = .254$, $F (7, 546) = 27.549$, $p < .0001$: Cohen's $f^2 = .340$—medium effect). Of the independent variables, *Attitudes Towards Bilingualism* made the largest unique contribution to the model ($\beta = .382$, $p < .0001$) followed by professional development to work with ELs or bilingual learners in science ($\beta = .126$, $p < .001$). Again, race did not make a significant contribution to the model.

## Discussion

In this chapter, we have presented readers with an example of using the ATTS-BL to evaluate teachers' attitudes regarding bilingualism (*Attitudes Towards Bilingualism*) as well as their attitudes about working with bilingual students in the science classroom (*Attitudes Towards Best Science Teaching Practices for Bilingual Learners*). In what follows we discuss the findings of the study example and discuss practical implications for educators and policymakers.

### *Study Findings*

**Demographics.** Our study participants were composed of science educators attending professional development training on integrating language and science in the classroom. Demographic results indicated the participants were primarily college-educated, White, English-speaking-only women in their 40's working in elementary grades, having frequent contact with diverse populations and having received professional development to work with ELs or bilingual learners. Notably, less than half of the participants reported receiving professional development to work with ELs or bilingual learners in science and a little over half reported having an ESL/TESOL/Bilingual endorsement or certificate.

**Attitudes.** Our participants' *Attitudes Towards Bilingualism* and *Attitudes Towards Best Science Teaching Practices for Bilingual Learners* were both over the theoretical mean of our scales. However, regression analysis indicated variables based in the literature made significant contributions to their *Attitudes Towards Best Science Teaching Practices for Bilingual Learners*. In Model 1, all the variables explored made significant contributions to the model except for race. This finding is in alignment to previous studies which found race to be non-significant in light of other variables including teacher training to work with diverse learners (Flores & Smith, 2009). The largest contributors to our model included grade level taught (elementary vs. secondary), language (English-only or bilingual) and received professional development to work with ELs in science (yes or no). Descriptive analysis indicated elementary teachers, bilinguals and teachers who had received professional development to work with ELs in science demonstrated more positive *Attitudes Towards Best Science Teaching Practices for Bilingual Learners*. These findings align with previous literature noting the significance of variables such as grade level (Huerta et al., 2019; Karakathanos, 2009), bilingualism (Flores & Smith, 2009; Huerta et al., 2019; Rader-Brown & Howley, 2014) and professional development (Huerta et al., 2019; Pettit, 2011a; Polat

& Mahalingappa, 2013; Song & Samimy, 2015) on teachers' overall attitudes towards working with ELs or bilingual learners in the content-areas.

In Model 2, *Attitudes Towards Bilingualism* made the largest unique contribution toward teachers *Attitudes Towards Best Science Teaching Practices for Bilingual Learners*. Whether participants had received professional development for ELs or bilingual learners in science made the second largest unique contribution to the model. This finding aligns with previous work noting the importance of targeted professional development for teachers working with diverse learners in content-areas (Huerta et al., 2019).

## *Implications for Educators and Policymakers*

Given the findings, three things are clear (a) race is not a predictor of teacher attitudes in light of teacher training (b) language, training, and grade levels are important variables to accountant for teacher attitudes and (c) teacher attitudes towards language is an important construct impacting teachers' attitudes towards practice with ELs or bilingual learners in the science classroom. Though we did not analyze gender within the regression because the majority of the participants were female, previous studies have found race and gender to not be significant in light of teachers' exposure to diversity and/or training to work with diverse students (Flores & Smith, 2009; Polat & Mahalingappa, 2013). In this sense, it seems promising that variables that cannot or are not easily changed such as race and gender can become non-significant in terms of attitudes in light of education and training. On the other hand, variables such as language and training, which can be changed (i.e., teachers could, for example, receive language training in addition to professional development), are significant in terms of attitudes. Such findings should lead educators and policymakers to consider the importance of both language and professional development training (especially target professional development towards specific content-areas) for teachers working with ELs or bilingual learners.

With regard to grade-levels taught, research seems to indicate that elementary teachers generally have more positive *Attitudes Towards Bilingualism* (Huerta et al., 2019; Karakathanos, 2009). Educators and policymakers would do well, then, to understand teachers' initial attitudes towards both language and best teaching practices in content-areas for ELs or bilingual learners.

For example, before a professional development, the ATTS-BL could be used to measure a group of elementary or high school teachers' overall attitudes. Educators and policymakers can then use the information to make decisions regarding how much they need to teach about language, best teaching practices integrating language and content, or both.

At the same time, the findings indicate that teachers' *Attitudes Towards Bilingualism* is a large contributor towards a model predicting how teachers view evidence-based practices impacting EL/bilingual learners in the science classroom. This finding implies that teacher education (e.g., professional development and other forms of education) would do well to focus on targeting teacher's attitudes towards linguistic diversity in the context of education and working with EL or bilingual learners.

As previously discussed (See: "Science Education Background") the ATTS-BL can be used to help gauge teacher attitudes regarding teaching science to bilingual learners. Both educators themselves or educational trainers (i.e. educational administrators or university faculty implementing professional development) can use the instrument to evaluate the quality of bilingual education programs in school districts. We also anticipate the instrument could be used in higher education settings as both an evaluative and instructional tool for teacher educators. Both scales have undergone face and content validity with samples of pre and in-service teachers (Byrnes & Kiger, 1994; Huerta et al., 2019).

## *Concluding Remarks*

In summary, we recommend that educators and policymakers use tools such as the one presented here to help make targeted and informed decisions to aid effective training of teachers of ELs or bilingual learners in their specific contexts. To date, the ATTS-BL has been used with a sample of teachers working in a variety of settings ranging from ESL (only English with support) classrooms to bilingual education (including dual language programs). The instrument, then, appears to be flexible in addressing ranges of bilingual education programs. We also recommend educators and policymakers take the results of the study presented in the context of past research findings as a foundation for professional development for teachers working with ELs or bilingual learners in science and beyond. Namely, language and evidence-based content training are critical in affecting teachers' attitudes about working effectively with our population of ELs or bilingual learners.

## *References*

Borg, S. (2003). Teacher cognition in language teaching: A review of research on what language teachers think, know, believe, and do. *Language Teaching, 36*(2), 81–109. https://doi.org/10.1017/S0261444803001903

Byrnes, D. A., & Kiger, G. (1994). Language attitudes of teachers scale (LATS). *Educational and Psychological Measurement, 54*(1), 227–231. https://doi.org/10.1177/0013164494054001029

Byrnes, D. A., Kiger, G., & Manning, M. L. (1997). Teachers' attitudes about language diversity. *Teaching and Teacher Education, 13*(6), 637–644. doi.org/10.1016/S0742-051X(97)80006-6

Douglas, R., Klentschy, M. P., Worth, K., & Binder, W. (Eds.) (2006). *Linking science and literacy in the K-8 classroom*. U.S.A.: NSTA.

Equal Education Opportunities Act (1974). 20 USC Sec. 1701–1758.

Fang, Z. (1996). A review of research on teacher beliefs and practices. *Educational Research, 38*(1), 47–65. https://doi.org/10.1080/0013188960380104

Farrell, T. S. C., & Kun, S. T. K. (2008). Language policy, language teachers' beliefs, and classroom practices. *Applied Linguistics, 29*(3), 381–403. https://doi.org/10.1093/applin/amm050

Flores, B. B., & Smith, H. L. (2009). Teachers' characteristics and attitudinal beliefs about linguistic and cultural diversity. *Bilingual Research Journal, 31*(1–2), 323–358. https://doi.org/10.1080/15235880802640789

Fulwiler, B. R. (2011). *Writing in science in action: Strategies, tools, and classroom video*. Portsmouth, NH: Heinemann.

Hart, J. E., & Lee, O. (2003). Teacher professional development to improve the science and literacy achievement of English language learners. *Bilingual Research Journal, 27*(3), 475–501. https://doi.org/10.1080/15235882.2003.10162604

Huerta, M., Garza, T., Jackson, J. K., & Murukutla, M. (2019). Science teachers' attitudes towards English learners. *Teaching and Teacher Education, 77*, 1–9. https://doi.org/10.1016/j.tate.2018.09.007

International Council for Science [ICSU] (2011). *Report of the ICSU Ad-hoc review panel on science education*. Paris, France : International Council for Science.

Janzen, J. (2008). Teaching English language learners in the content areas. *Review of Educational Research, 78*(4), 1010–1038. https://doi.org/10.3102/0034654308325580

Karathanos, K. (2009). Exploring US mainstream teachers' perspective on use of the native language in instruction with English language learner students. *International Journal of Bilingual Education and Bilingualism, 12*(6), 615–633. https://doi.org/10.1080/13670050802372760

Lara-Alecio, R., Tong, F., Irby, B. J., Guerrero, C., Huerta, M., & Fan, Y. (2012). The effect of an instructional intervention on middle school learners' science and English reading achievement. *Journal of Research in Science Teaching, 49*(8), 987–1011. https://doi.org/10.1002/tea.21031

Lee, O. (2004). Teacher change in beliefs and practices in science and literacy instruction with English language learners. *Journal of Research in Science Teaching, 41*(1), 65–93. https://doi.org/10.1002/tea.10125

Lee, O., Lewis, S., Adamson, K., Maerten-Rivera, J., & Secada, W. G. (2008). Urban elementary school teachers' knowledge and practices in teaching science to English language learners. *Science Education, 92*(4), 733–758. https://doi.org/10.1002/sce.20255

Llosa, L., Lee, O., Jian, F., Haas, A., O'Connor, C., Van Booven, C. D., & Kieffer, M. J. (2016). Impact of a large-scale science intervention focused on English language learners. *American Educational Research Journal, 53*(2), 395–424. https://doi.org/10.3102/0002831216637348

Maerten-Rivera, J., Ahn, S., Lanier, K., Diaz, J., & Lee, O. (2016). Effect of a multiyear intervention on science achievement of all students including English language learners. *The Elementary School Journal, 116*(4), 600–624. https://doi.org/10.1086/686250

Mantero, M., & McVicker, P. (2006). The impact of experience and coursework: Perceptions of second language learners in the mainstream classroom. *Radical Pedagogy, 8*(1). https://radicalpedagogy.icaap.org/content/issue8_1/mantero.html

McFarland, J., Hussar, B., de Brey, C., Snyder, T., Wang, X., Wilkinson-Flicker, S., Gebrekristos, S., Zhang, J., Rathbun, A., Barmer, A., Bullock Mann, F., and Hinz, S. (2017). The Condition of Education 2017 (NCES 2017-144). U.S. Department of Education. Washington, DC: National Center for Education Statistics. https://nces.ed.gov/pubsearch/pubsinfo.asp?pubid=2017144.

NGSS Lead States (2013). *Next generation science standards: For states, by states.* Washington, DC: Achieve, Inc. on behalf of the twenty-six states and partners that collaborated on the NGSS.

Pajares, M. F. (1992). Teachers' beliefs and educational research: Cleaning up a messy construct. *Review of Educational Research, 62*(3), 307–332. https://doi.org/10.3102/00346543062003307

Peregoy, S. F., & Boyle, O. F. (1997). *Reading, writing, and learning in ESL* (2nd ed.). New York, NY: Longman.

Pettit, S. K. (2011a). Factors influencing middle school mathematics teachers' beliefs about ELLs in mainstream classrooms. *Issues in the Undergraduate Mathematics Preparation of School Teachers: The Journal, 5*. www.k-12prep.math.ttu.edu

Pettit, S. K. (2011b). Teachers' beliefs about English language learners in mainstream classrooms: A Review of the literature. *International Multilingual Research Journal, 5*(2), 123–147. https://doi.org/10.1080/19313152.2011.594357

Polat, N., & Mahalingappa, L. (2013). Pre- and in-service teachers' beliefs about ELLs in content area classes: A case for inclusion, responsibility, and instructional support. *Teaching Education, 24*(1), 58–83. https://doi.org/10.1080/10476210.2012.713930

Quinn, H., Lee, O., & Valdés, G. (2013). *Language demands and opportunities in relation to next generation science standards for English-language learners: What teachers need to know.* White paper written for Understanding Language. Available: http://ell.stanford.edu/publication/language-demands-and-opportunities-relation-next-generation-science-standards-ells

Rader-Brown, L., & Howley, A. (2014). Predictors of the instructional strategies that elementary school teachers use with English language learners. *Teachers College Record, 116*(5), 1–34.

Reeves, J. R. (2006). Secondary teacher attitudes toward including English-language learners in mainstream classrooms. *The Journal of Educational Research, 99*(3), 131–143. https://doi.org/10.3200/JOER.99.3.131-143

Santau, A. O., Secada, W., Maerten-Rivera, J., Cone, N., & Lee, O. (2010). US urban elementary teachers' knowledge and practices in teaching science to English language learners: Results from the first year of a professional development intervention. *International Journal of Science Education, 32*(1), 2007–2032. https://doi.org/10.1080/09500690903280588

Saul, W. (Ed.). (2004). *Crossing boarders in literacy and science instruction: Perspectives on theory and practice.* Newark, DE: International Reading Association.

Shim, J. M. (2014). A Bourdieuian analysis: Teachers' beliefs about English language learners' academic challenges. *International Journal of Multicultural Education, 16*(1), 40–55. https://doi.org/10.18251/ijme.v16i1.783

Song, S. Y., & Samimy, K. (2015). The beliefs of secondary content teachers of English language learners regarding language learning and teaching. *International Journal of TESOL and Learning, 4*(1), 3–19.

Tabachnick, B. G., & Fidell, L. S. (2013). *Using multivariate statistics* (6th ed.). Upper Saddle, NJ: Pearson Education, Inc.

U.S. Department of Education, Institute of Education Sciences, National Center for Education and Regional Assistance (2014). *What works clearinghouse: Teaching academic content and literacy to English learners in elementary and middle school* (NCEE 2014-4012). Retrieved from https://ies.ed.gov/ncee/wwc/Docs/PracticeGuide/english_learners_pg_040114.pdf

Youngs, C. S., & Youngs, G. A. (2001). Predictors of mainstream teachers' attitudes toward ESL students. *TESOL Quarterly, 35*(1), 97–120. https://doi.org/10.2307/3587861

## 10. How Institutions of Higher Education Prepare Bilingual Teachers' Understanding, Developing and Use of Diversity-Differentiated Assessments

XOCHITL ARCHEY
*California State University, San Marcos*

### Introduction

Educators who enter the field of K-12 public education must be capable of not only administering externally-produced assessments, but also possessing the epistemic capability to internally produce assessments that meet students' instructional needs. Moreover, teacher competence in assessment infrastructure, that is the creation of-, delivery of-, and progress monitoring of- assessments to make data-driven instructional decisions, should consider the integration of student-diversity in language proficiency, ability and culture. Institutions of Higher Education (IHEs) play an integral role in preparing teachers to assess all learners (Chen, 2005). Often seen in practice and research is an unbalanced focus on either assessment or diversity as if the intersectionality of these teaching components did not manifest as a common entity in teaching and learning environments. Consequently, teachers enter the workforce feeling unprepared to differentiate assessments, and conversely instruction (Tigelaar & Beljaard, 2013), leaving school site administration with the responsibility to prepare teachers onsite.

This chapter emerges with several purposes in mind: (a) to reveal the inherit dysfunction of policy on diversity-differentiated assessment, (b) to highlight the urgency for diversity-differentiated assessment practices across teacher preparation levels, most specifically in BILA programs and (c) to share some notable coursework on differentiating assessments with others attempting to bring this principle into their educational frameworks.

## *Bilingual Education as the Promise*

Three decades ago, Cazden and Snow (1990) called the bilingual education approach "a simple label for a complex phenomenon" (p. 9). A complex concept, indeed, as bilingual education re-conceptualizes instruction by connecting teaching and learning to learners' lived experiences. Bilingual programs represent transformative educational programming in that they are hypothesized to enrich educational opportunities for all students by leveraging ability, linguistic and cultural statuses (Baca & Cervantes, 1998; Cummins, 2000). The bilingual setting is not a traditional system of education and therefore its assessments should not be encompassing of traditional uniform practices. Traditional assessments are passive and routinely ignore the needs and strengths of students, specifically of diverse students. Within bilingual settings, student-diversity often has a greater role than in English-only programs (Cartledge & Kourea, 2008). At minimum, these programs ensure access as required under the Civil Rights Act and the Equal Educational Opportunities Act. At maximum benefit, they purport authentic interpretations of equity and access in where student-diversity is a valued trait and assessment practices are carried out within that vision.

There is a long overdue urgency to re-conceptualize, self-produce and effectively deliver diversity-differentiated assessments. Given that ability, linguistic, and cultural diversity are evermore present in bilingual education, many researchers argue for the development of new assessment approaches (Howard, Lindholm-Leary, Rogers, Olague, Media, Kennedy, Sugarman, & Christian, 2018). Accordingly, for those bilingual classrooms wanting to shift the assessment paradigm, it is worthy to remember that the global trend towards the promotion of bilingual education, garnished awareness of language rights, and state-level sentiment (e.g. the Multilingual Education Act of 2016) are opportunities to embrace diversity-differentiated assessments today. New policy calls for an increased need to build bilingual teacher capacity. Presently, bilingual authorizing institutions in California include the University of California (UC) system, private universities, local education agencies, examination sites and California State Universities (CSU). Since 2007, UCs and CSUs have recommended 4,383 BILA teachers. CSUs alone have recommended 3,512 BILA teachers (Uy, 2018). IHEs have a grand role and responsibility in preparing bilingual teachers.

## IHEs as the Preparatory Workforce

The large body of literature on the deeply rooted biases of uniform tests corroborates that "an adequate assessment system that takes into consideration the needs of bilingual students must address students' academic and linguistic development" (Sánchez & Brisk, 2004, p. 196). Presently, schools continue to struggle with employing assessments beyond those that are standard- or criterion-normed (Bland & Gareis, 2018; Ghaicha, 2016; Sanchez & Brisk, 2004). Accountability pressures induce much of this struggle. DeLuca and Lam (2014) found that pre-service teachers conducted assessments most prominently "to satisfy external audiences other than the teacher or the student" (p. 13). Yet, the goal of any assessment should always be to enhance students' education journeys, not to attest to test performance.

Today across education fields, and evermore present in bilingual settings, the ability, linguistic and cultural diversity of students is at the core of conducting instruction and assessment, but not all teachers emerge from their preparation programs ready to differentiate. Teachers who are able to more successfully interpret, develop and use diversity-differentiated assessments are those who had some measure of preparation in their credential program (Impara, Divine, Bruce, Liverman, & Gay, 1991; Plake & Impara, 1997). Across the California State Universities, pre-service teachers reported high percentages of perceived levels of competence (96–98% adequately to very well prepared) in the many components involving diversity-differentiated assessment (California State University Educator Quality (EdQ), 2017–2018). Keep in mind that the data is representative of a perceived level of competence. This leaves unanswered questions about what actually happens when teachers step into diverse classrooms (DeLuca & Klinger, 2010). DeLuca and Lam (2014) suggest that although some pre-service teachers "are able to establish meaningful linkages between their learning about assessment and their learning about student diversity, these linkages were not deeply articulated nor were they extended through examples or significant implications on their future teaching practice" (p. 17). It is during the preparation phase that authentic practices that engage pre-service teachers with real students and real student data, per se, will yield better odds for praxis.

If teachers are to hold their K-12 students accountable for lessons learned, and we are to hold our pre-service teachers accountable for their learnings, then we need to uphold the content with instruction that empowers them as developing teachers to effectively navigate curricular policy and negotiate assessments (Jackson & Boutte, 2018). This means that teacher preparation programs across credentials and authorizations share responsibility in engaging teachers in planning, developing, and implementing the use of linguistically and culturally responsive differentiation strategies for assessment (Bilingual Authorization Program Standards, California Commission on Teacher Credentialing (CCTC), 2017; California Commission on Teaching Credentialing (CCTC), Teaching Performance Expectations, 2016).

Given this, IHEs should commit to integrating instruction, activities, and assignments around the teaching of diversity-differentiated assessment. Although most teacher preparation programs and more specifically BILA programs have course components addressing ability, language and culture in assessment education, this does not ascertain the effective and consistent exposure of such methods (DeLuca & Klinger, 2010).

## *The Intersection of Classroom Diversity and Assessment*

Regardless of how assessment and diversity are sequenced—whether diversity is the precursor to differentiating assessments or whether assessment is positioned as the vehicle to understanding diversity—both are unequivocally woven into today's educational climate. A typical classroom is full of diverse students across the linguistic, ability and cultural spectrum. To understand the immense diversity that exits, a quick walk into any classroom will reveal not only student diversity, but also the disproportionality of student to teacher makeup.

In the 2017–2018 reporting year, the California State University system reported a 54.3% Hispanic student population to a 20.9% Hispanic teacher workforce. The underlying concerns with teacher-student mismatches range from perpetuation of stereotypes to poor academic achievement (Correa, Hudson, & Hayes, 2004; Patton, Williams, Floyd, & Cobb, 2003; Shim & Shur, 2018; Tyler & Smith, 2000). In studies with low percentages of teacher diversity, African American students, in comparison to their White counterparts, received more negative interactions and less scaffolding (Casteel, 1998). Conversely, culturally and linguistically diverse teachers were able to, more effectively, recognize and address students' complex learning diversity (Patton, Williams, Floyd, & Cobb, 2003). On the linguistic diversity front, the California Department of Education reported 1.27 million emergent bilinguals (EBs) in the 2017–2018 reporting period and 1.196 million during the 2018–2019 reporting period. More surprisingly is the Emergent Bilingual student to teacher ratio. From 2007 to 2018, the California Department of Education awarded bilingual authorizations to a total of 9,036 teachers (across languages: Armenian, Cantonese, Chinese, French, Hmong, Japanese, Khmer, Korean, Mandarin, Portuguese, Spanish, Vietnamese) (Uy, 2018).

Assuming that all the bilingually authorized teachers since 2007 are still teaching, the ratio of EBs to a qualified language teacher would be 130 students to 1 teacher.

Today's research reflects a viable path for attending to the teacher-student mismatch, regardless of culture or language. Teacher preparation programs have an opportunity to change the disparity (Correa, Hudson, & Hayes, 2004; Jackson & Boutte, 2018) by providing spaces in where pre-service teachers are pushed to critically challenge their "own socialization and its impact on their attitudes and behaviors in shaping the classroom," including but not limited to diversity and assessment (Ford, Stuart, & Vakil, 2004, p. 58).

Unfortunately, diversity is often undermined in assessments—often assessments are not inclusive of students' funds of knowledge and not responsive to differences. Much of it is dependent on the ability to thoroughly and thoughtfully examine core goals free of social, economic, cultural, ability and linguistic discrimination. Not surprisingly, assessments become situations that can limit students' educational experiences (Freire, 1970). As we move from the old paradigm of instruction and traditional assessment to a new paradigm of reformed curriculum, constructivist learning and classroom assessment, diversity-differentiated assessments house an implicit directive that can potentially narrow the assessment/diversity gap (Shepard, 2000).

## *Diversity-Differentiated Assessment as Entry Points for Every Student*

Differentiated instruction for many educators is a household concept, but diversity-differentiated assessments does not fare with the same familiarity as its counterpart (Noman & Kaur, 2014). If differentiated instruction is to be carried out as regular practice within our schools, diversity-differentiated assessments need to form part of the teaching and learning conversations across education levels, including IHEs (Ghaicha, 2016).

What constitutes a good assessment is a highly debated topic. Determining appropriateness is considering the purpose, context and users. Take, for instance, all the purposes that educational assessments serve; from informing district, state, and national policy, curricula and programs, to making decisions *about* students, such as managing instruction, program placement, and classification of students (Nitko, 2016). There is no doubt that assessment is a central component to education, but how often is student language, culture and ability used to make authentic decisions? Here, diversity-differentiated assessment is envisioned as a student-rooted cycle of addressing instructional content and students' lived experiences. It is positioned as the key to making decisions *about* instruction in not only discovering what students know and are able to do, but also intended to improve learning through the constant gathering of information to plan and modify instruction *with* students' language, culture and ability as integral to the process. In this regard, assessments that shadow curriculum should match student- performance to student ability and language proficiency level.

In part, diversity-differentiated assessments offer the opportunity to treat continuous assessment as part of instruction in that they are measures related to real situations and/problems, they collect multiple indicators of learning, and alike differentiated instruction, provide a range of entry points to ensure that all students have the opportunity to meet or progress to meeting established learning goals. Where it differs significantly from other types of formative assessments is in the added and highly important step of using students' funds of knowledge to inform the assessment. Funds of knowledge are collections of knowledge and expertise based on cultural practices that are part of families' inner culture, work experience or their daily routines that are essential for household or individual functioning and well-being (Moll, Amanti, Neff, Gonzalez, 1992). Funds of knowledge tell us what students know and are capable of doing and for that reason are used in effective assessment. In this perspective, assessment is a dance—an interactive process that engages both teacher and student, where the teachers invest in discovering students' funds of knowledge, where students have opportunities to show their learnings, and where ongoing assessments are directed towards individual levels of student culture, language and ability (CAST, 2011). If teachers capitalize on these as catalysts for learning, such type of assessment can have great potential in accelerating learning for all learners.

Diversity-differentiated assessment is not lowering expectations for students. It is, rather, a strategic approach that creates opportunities for every student to meet the same rigorous standards in different ways. In this way, it illustrates a clearer picture of student learning and boosts students' abilities by showing what they have learned and where they need to go. Because language learning greatly depends on the development of communication skills with meaningful contexts and engaging content, the opportunity to have more than one opportunity to ascertain performance is valuable. This aspect is particularly important in the preparation of bilingual teachers because language learners will experience complex non-linear trajectories in their language acquisition and so making judgments about progress in language using diversity-differentiated assessments is a much more authentic approach to monitoring and planning for language proficiency.

In the end, diversity-differentiated assessment can take many forms (projects, simulations, writings), but most importantly it is accompanied by a realization that students—humans—have different ways of knowing. Because of this, the process must address essential learning goals, a range of possible levels that promote a viable path for growth (e.g. rubric), encompass language, culture and ability as determinants that inform assessment development and instructional planning, assessment of learning developed through authentic tasks and provide multiple ways in which students display learnings (Chapman & King, 2012; Moon, Callahan, Brighton, & Tomlinson, 2002; Oberg, 2010; Wiggins, 1990). This is assessment for learning.

## Learnings

Given that California State Universities (CSUs), to date, have recommended more bilingual teachers than any other public agency (Uy, 2018), the information gathered here is comprised of course-catalog descriptions and syllabi (2017–2019 academic years) from BILA program courses across the top five recommending CSUs. The learnings, in part, elucidate BILA programs' efforts in addressing assessment for diverse classrooms in bilingual settings.

To encapsulate these efforts the three-tiered framework for learning and assessment provides the theoretical underpinnings (Fostaty Young, 2005) for the different stages of teaching and learning about diversity-differentiated assessments. Figure 10-1 delivers a snapshot of course syllabi assignments that integrate diversity-differentiated processes within each tier, respectively.

**Understanding the idea tier.** In this tier, instructors provide explicit instruction on fundamental principles—these are often the "building blocks" of diversity and assessment learning. During this initial phase, faculty engage bilingual teachers in exploration of K-12 students' identities and/or their own identities (e.g. culture, language, ability). Through reflective activities, bilingual teachers forge relationships between their ideologies and their practice. Assignments vary from reflections to actual data collection. These opportunities provide the very first insights on funds of knowledge and their role in the teaching and learning cycle. In practice, I have also borrowed the use of student questionnaires for exploring funds of knowledge. These questionnaires are guided by instructors, but developed by bilingual teachers as ways of getting to know their K-12 students. Some creative questions and prompts that have yielded great insight are: what does a typical day at home look for you? Please draw how you see yourself. These preliminary tasks help bilingual teachers design assessments and lessons around real-life situations. Through this, teachers make connections as they begin to apply their knowledge, dispositions and

| UNDERSTAND  | DEVELOP  | USE  |
|---|---|---|
| The fundamentals of new learning. | Webs of information tied together between material and learners' real-world experience/other acquired knowledge. | The ability to think deeply and use learning to generalize across disciplines and in novel ways. |
| **Dialectical Journals:** Teachers identify key quotes from the readings and write brief reflections that connect back to implications for classroom practice. **Ideology Statements:** Articulation of positionality/ideology on biliteracy. **My Culture & Identity:** Personal histories via photographs and narration, including a cultural bag activity representing dimensions of culture. **Observations**: Analysis of lessons during fieldwork, specifically to analyze curriculum, instruction, and assessment. **Community Scans:** Community profiles, including sociocultural characteristics of a school community. **Community Footprint:** Investigation through school site visits, interviews, observations, websites, classrooms, program brochures. **Emergent Bilingual Interview:** Interview of an EB, including a student profile (e.g. description of language development, student work) and recommendations based on the information. **Student Language Profiles:** Profiles of students' language capacities via language surveys, writing samples, ELPAC data. Data are used to plan lessons. **Formative Assessments:** Instructor embedded modeling of formative assessments to ascertain understanding of course readings. | **Literacy Lesson Plans:** Practice planning Spanish reading and writing instruction with either developed or selected formal and informal assessments. **Mini-Thematic Unit Plans / Presentation Rubrics:** Design lessons with appropriate objectives, including assessments for content and language objectives. **Content Area Unit Plan with Lessons:** A biliteracy unit plan that integrates the CCSS and ELD/SLD Standards, with attention to the provision of support for language learners and struggling readers. | **Diagnostic Assessments:** Instructor embeds modeling within course. Bilingual teachers take a diagnostic series of Spanish-language competence assessments. Instructor uses formative assessment results to guide the differentiation of instructional activities. **Case Studies:** Conduct a case study of one student to identify and address literacy needs and strengths using a battery of assessments. **Differentiated Lesson Plans:** Lessons based on student needs stem from case studies. **Primary Language / Spanish Lesson Plan:** Lessons with standards, objectives, and assessment based on students' level of competencies that include all diverse students. |

*Figure 10-1.* Course Syllabi Assignments that Integrated Diversity-Differentiated Processes

skills. Another fundamental piece to this tier is the introduction of concepts (e.g. funds of knowledge and differentiation), definitions (e.g. formative v. summative assessments) and facts (e.g. research on diversity-differentiated assessment). A creative way to introduce this concept is to model it. A modeling activity has instructors, themselves, embed formative assessments to ascertain comprehension of various course topics. In this case, a recommendation would be to not stop at formative assessment, but rather introduce the concept of diversity-differentiated assessments as a step beyond formative assessments. At this level, the goal is for bilingual teachers to understand- and for instructors to explicitly introduce the elements of diversity-differentiated assessments.

**Developing the connections tier.** In this tier, webs of information are tied together between material and learners' real-world experience/other acquired knowledge. Assignments in this tier represent development. Examples include lesson plans and unit plans that are directly linked to who K-12 students are. These elements should be crafted with the intention to include diverse learners. Intentionality, within this scope, means that the need to include diverse learners is made clear by proposing specific guidelines on how differentiated instruction *and* assessment are used to create access plans. This means assessments are created as informed by, yes, the standards, but also students' abilities, language levels and cultural funds of knowledge. A recommendation is to have bilingual teachers annotate the lesson plans. These annotations are easily done by creating margin comment boxes at every point during the lesson. It is assumed that during the development of the lesson, bilingual teachers were intentional about assessing diverse learners. The margin comments should note their rationales on how assessment informed that decision or how the assessment will inform student learning. Highly recommended is facilitating diversity-differentiated assessments through the development of rubrics. Whether rubrics are used in the beginning of planning or through/across lessons, they are an incomparable approach to effectively gauge and guide learning. Serving a dual purpose, rubrics can be used by instructors as a way to model diversity-differentiated assessment to assess bilingual teachers throughout course assignments or specific topics. Of importance, instructors modeling diversity-differentiated assessments through their own practice are encouraged to be explicit as some bilingual teachers may be unaware that this modeling is serving an important purpose. As teachers begin to recognize components of diversity-differentiated assessment through their personal or professional experiences (e.g. fieldwork), instructors should encourage them to make the links to application.

**Using the extensions tier.** In this tier, teachers are to engage in application—the praxis component of being able to use knowledge and experiences about diversity and assessment while addressing the implications diversity has on assessment measures. Some notable examples from the data are initiatives where teachers assess their own language levels and the instructor uses the results to differentiate instructional activities based on the development of "advanced" and "superior" levels of competence. Other examples are assignments where teachers use actual student work samples, cultural information and language and ability data to plan instruction. For these instances, I propose to not only use assessments to dictate instruction, but also use multidimensional student data to inform the development and use of assessments. A simple, but impactful example of an instructor-modeled diversity-differentiated assessment with the use of a rubric comes from an assignment titled social justice and equity plan. In this course assignment, teachers choose an issue at their clinical practice sites; they name it, reframe it, and act on their proposed plans. The process looks something like this: the school site's culture largely informs the teacher candidate's identification of an issue, next, each teacher develops a plan, and throughout, the instructor and teacher use the rubric to assess. The rubric is used repeatedly for identification of the issue, planning, monitoring progress and checking for completeness. For instance, in this assignment the differentiation occurs in the choice teachers have to select an issue. Each issue is different and varies significantly on involvement of the teacher within the school, the sociopolitical landscape of the area, the surrounding community and the K-12 student population, etc. This very first phase allows them to begin where *they are*, not where the instructor dictates *they are*. Differentiation happens again during the development of the action plan. Each plan is different and varies on bilingual teachers' readiness and capability to implement small or large undertakings. The rubric is used according to where they started; some started in a magical conforming (beginning level), others in naïve reforming (approaching level), and some in critical transforming (meeting level)—the goal is growth. Using assessments such as these allow bilingual teachers, and K-12 students alike, to work with relevance to who they are and where they are in the learning process. In sum, this tier pushes instructors to draw on the skills bilingual teachers possess and, conversely, bilingual teachers are to demonstrate their knowledge in novel ways—novel ways being the ability to differentiate assessment for any student that may enter their classrooms at any given point and with any given characteristics.

Although, conclusions cannot be drawn on whether these assignments have lasting and positive implications on bilingual teachers' actual assessment and students' learning outcomes, they do provide meaningful strategical sequencing for the future of teacher preparation on assessment in diverse classrooms.

## Discussion

As a reminder, it is the collective charge of all individuals with educational stakes to maximize opportunities of access for students. Moreover, diversity-differentiated assessments elevate students' humanity as active and valued members in the learning process because they give us information about how students achieve learning targets, benchmarks and standards in manners consistent with their cultures, languages and abilities. As the demand for qualified bilingual teachers grows, it is important that the preparation of teachers continues to explore this concept of assessment and diversity as constructs that inform each other.

Although most BILA programs have some component of assessment and diversity in their method courses, whether it is teaching how to develop culturally and linguistically responsive learning environments or why to use authentic assessments, these need to be consistently and cohesively taught across courses, especially because the depth (e.g. tiers of understanding, development, and use) cannot all be addressed substantially in a single course; this is the basis of an integrated approach that will yield greater practical application. Lastly, having teachers select assessments created by others is acceptable, however it denies them the opportunity to apply their skills and to see the value of getting to know their students.

Acknowledged herein is the long national history we have for demanding uniform, unwavering assessments to quantify learning. As Moon et al. (2002) point out, "we have failed in working with classroom teachers in developing classroom assessments that provide [] information about student learning" (p. 30). Acknowledged here is also the understanding that because of accountability measures, educators (K-12 teachers and university faculty alike) may resist the idea of significant change, particularly one that forces us to routinely recognize our learners' diversities as instrumental to how we teach and assess. Research exists suggesting that with proper preparation, teachers emerge from programs with skill competency in the creation, delivery and use of diversity-differentiated assessment (Ball & Tyson, 2011; Shepard, Hammerness, Darling-Hammond, & Rust, 2005; Zeichner & Conklin, 2008). To begin, we need to sacrifice the insistence of the one-size-fits-all testing approach in our classrooms and embrace a conviction to foster diversity-differentiated assessment literacy as an integrated entity (DeLuca & Lam, 2014).

## *References*

Baca, L. M., & Cervantes, H. T. (1998). The bilingual special education interface (3rd ed.). Upper Saddle River, NJ: Merrill.

Ball, A. F., & Tyson, C. A. (2011). Preparing teachers for diversity in the twenty-first century. In A. F. Ball & C. A. Tyson (Eds.), *Studying diversity in teacher education* (pp. 399–416). Lanham, MD: Rowman & Littlefied.

Bland, L. M. & Gareis, C. R. (2018). Performance assessments: A review of definitions, quality, characteristics, and outcomes associated with their use in the k-12 schools. *Teacher Educators' Journal, 11*(spring), 52–69.

California Commission on Teacher Credentialing (2016). *California teaching performance expectations.*

California Commission on Teacher Credentialing (2017). *Bilingual authorization program standards.* Retrieved from http://www.ctc.ca.gov/

California Department of Education (2017–2018). *Facts about English learners in California – CalEdFacts.*

California State University (2017–2018). *Completer survey. Educator quality data view.*

Cartledge, G., & Kourea, L. (2008). Culturally responsive classrooms for culturally diverse students with and at risk for disabilities. *Council for Exceptional Children, 74*(3), 351–371.

Casteel, C. A. (1998). Teacher–student interactions and race in integrated classrooms. *The Journal of Educational Research, 92,* 115–120.

Cazden, C. B., & Snow, C. E. (1990). Issues in bilingual education. *Annals of the American Academy of Political and Social Science, 508,* 9–11.

Center for Applied Special Technology (CAST) (2011). *Universal design for learning guidelines, version 2.0.* Retrieved from http://www.udlcenter.org/aboutudl/udlguidelines

Chapman, C. M. & King, R. S. (2012). *Differentiated assessment strategies: One tool doesn't fit all (2012).* Thousand Oaks, CA: Corwin.

Chen, P. (2005). Teacher candidates' assessment literacy. *Academic Exchange Quarterly, 62*(5), 62–66.

Correa, V. I., Hudson, R. F., & Hayes, M. T. (2004). Preparing early childhood special educators to serve culturally and linguistically diverse children and families: Can a multicultural education course make a difference? *Teacher Education and Special Education, 27*(4), 323–341.

Cummins, J. (2000). *Language, power, and pedagogy: Bilingual children in the crossfire.* Buffalo, NY: Multilingual Matters, Ltd.

DeLuca, C., & Klinger, D. A. (2010) Assessment literacy development: Identifying gaps in pre-service teachers' learning. *Assessment in Education: Principles, Policy & Practice, 17*(4), 419–438.

DeLuca, C. & Lam, C. L. (2014). Preparing teachers for assessment within diverse classrooms: An analysis of pre-service teachers' conceptualizations. *Teacher Education Quarterly, 41*(3), 3–24.

Ford, B. A., Stuart, D. H., & Vakil, S. (2004). Culturally responsive teaching in the 21st century inclusive classroom. *The Journal of the International Association of Special Education, 15*(2), 56–62.

Fostaty Young, S. (2005). Teaching, learning, and assessment in higher education: Using ideas, connections, and extensions to improve student learning. *Improving Student Learning Symposium. London, UK, Imperial College, 13*, 105–115.

Freire, P. (1970). *Pedagogy of the oppressed.* New York, NY: Continuum International Publishing Group.

Ghaicha, A. (2016). Theoretical framework for educational assessment: A synoptic review. *Journal of Education and Practice, 7*(4), 212–231.

Howard, E. R., Lindholm-Leary, K. J., Rogers, D., Olague, N., Medina, J., Kennedy, D., Sugarman, J., & Christian, D. (2018). *Guiding principles for dual language education* (3rd ed.). Washington, DC: Center for Applied Linguistics.

Impara, J. C., Divine, K. P., Bruce, F. A., Liverman, M. R., & Gay, A. (1991). Does interpretative test scores information help teachers? *Educational Measurement: Issues and Practice, 10*(4), 16–18.

Jackson, T. O., & Boutte, G. S. (2018). Exploring culturally relevant/responsive pedagogy as praxis in teacher education. *The New Educator, 14*(2), 87–90.

Moll, L. C., Amanti, C., Neff, D., & Gonzalez, N. (1992). Funds of knowledge for teaching: Using a qualitative approach to connect homes and classrooms. *Theory into Practice, 31*(2), 132–141.

Moon, T. R., Callahan, C. M., Brighton, C. M., & Tomlinson, C. A. (2002). *Development of differentiated performance assessment tasks for middle school classrooms* (report). Retrieved from Office of Educational Research and Improvement (ED): https://files.eric.ed.gov/fulltext/ED476371.pdf

Noman, M., & Kaur, A. (2014). Differentiated assessment: A new paradigm in assessment practices for diverse learners. *International Journal of Education and Applied Sciences, 1*, 167–174.

Oberg, C. (2010). Guiding classroom instruction through performance assessment. *Journal of Case Studies in Accreditation and Assessment, 1*, 1–11.

Patton, J. M., Williams, B. T., Floyd, L. O., & Cobb, T. R. (2003). Recruiting and retaining culturally and linguistically diverse teachers in special education: Models for successful personnel preparation. *Teacher Education and Special Education: The Journal of the Teacher Education Division of the Council for Exceptional Children, 26*, 288–303.

Plake, B. S., & Impara, J. C. (1997). Teacher assessment literacy: What do teachers know about assessment? In G. D. Phye (Ed.), *Handbook of classroom assessment* (pp. 55–68). New York: Academic Press.

Sanchez, M. T., & Brisk, M. E. (2004). Teachers' assessment practices and understandings in a bilingual program. *NABE Journal of Research and Practice, 2*(1), 193–213.

Shepard, L. (2000). The role of assessment in a learning culture. *Educational Researcher, 29*(7), 4–14.

Shepard, L., Hammerness, K., Darling-Hammond, L., & Rust, F. (2005). Assessment. In L. Darling-Hammond & J. Bransford (Eds.), *Preparing teachers for a changing world: What teachers should learn and be able to do* (pp. 275–326). San Francisco: Jossey-Bass.

Shim, J. M., & Shur, A. M. (2018). Learning from ELL's perspectives: Mismatch between ELL, and teacher perspectives on ELL learning experiences. *English Language Teaching, 11*(1), 21–32.

Tigelaar, D. E. H., & Beljaard, D. (2013). Special issue: Formative assessment and teacher professional learning. *Teachers and Teaching: Theory and Practice, 19*(2), 109–114.

Tyler, N. C., & Smith, D. D. (2000). Welcome to the TESE special issue: Preparation of culturally and linguistically diverse special teachers. *Teacher Education and Special Education, 23* (4), 261–263.

Uy, F. L. (2018, November). *Educator Preparation and Public School Programs (EP&PSP): Bilingual authorization convening*. Presented at The California State University (CSU) Office of the Chancellor, Long Beach, CA.

Wiggins, G. (1990). *The case for authentic assessment*. Office of Educational Research and Improvement, U.S. Department of Education.

Zeichner, K. M., & Conklin, H. G. (2008). Teacher education programs as sites for teacher preparation. In M. Cochran-Smith, S. Freiman-Nemser, D. J. McIntyre, & K. E. Demers (Eds.), *Handbook of research on teacher education: Enduring questions in changing contexts* (3rd ed., pp. 269–289). New York: Routledge.

*Measuring Bilingualism, Biliteracy and Sociocultural Competence*

## 11. Assessing Emergent Bilingual Learners' Mathematical Biliteracy: Authentic Mathematics Writing Assessment System

EDUARDO MOSQUEDA
*University of California Santa Cruz*

MARCO A. BRAVO
*Santa Clara University*

JORGE L. SOLÍS
*University of Texas at San Antonio*

SAÚL I. MALDONADO
*San Diego State University*

### Introduction

The implementation of the Common Core State Standards (CCSS) in several states as well as the explicit attention to the role of language in teaching and learning mathematics (Lee, Quinn & Valdés, 2013) has increased language demands in the classroom, which can hamper a teachers' ability to provide linguistic support for Emergent Bilingual Learners (EBLs). For example, the CCSS expects students to use mathematical evidence to construct viable arguments, to demonstrate conceptual understanding and to critique their peers' reasoning (Lee et al., 2013). The CCSS' increased content and language demands raises important considerations regarding the implementation of educational practices that promote students' access to advanced mathematics content as well as the integration of pedagogical practices that promote the concurrent learning of English, academic content and the language and literacy specific to mathematics (Aguirre & Bunch, 2012; van Lier & Walqui,

2012; Wong Fillmore, 2007). Teachers with EBLs in their classrooms need to take into account the language and literacy demands of their curriculum (e.g., reading, writing, speaking and listening comprehension) for students to meaningfully participate and benefit from mathematical instructional activities being taught in English.

As bilingual teacher educators, researchers and professional development leaders, in this chapter we propose a bilingual approach to teaching and assessing mathematical understanding and reasoning. Our goal was to leverage EBLs' native language to both promote students' simultaneous development of literacy as well as mathematics concepts, which we refer to as mathematical biliteracy. Our proposed approach will also help teachers identify instructional strategies to support the development of EBLs' mathematical language and reasoning. Our study examined assessments of adolescent EBLs' open-ended responses in Spanish to mathematical writing prompts in English using a Spanish-language rubric created by researchers. The administration guidelines for the assessment rubric encouraged students to write their response in English as much as possible but to use Spanish if necessary (See Appendix). Building on our prior research using language and content focused rubrics to assess EBLs' mathematical understanding, academic language and language proficiency (Mosqueda, Bravo, Solís, Maldonado, & De La Rosa, 2016; Maldonado, Mosqueda, Bravo, & Solís, 2020), in this chapter we present findings from our examination of EBLs' mathematical reasoning and computation as well as language conventions and mathematical vocabulary in Spanish. Our objective in creating and using a Spanish-language version of the rubric to assess EBLs' mathematical writing responses was to provide teachers with a bilingual tool to collect, analyze and use progress measures of mathematics achievement, and, at the same time, of biliteracy and language acquisition. As statewide academic assessments aligned with CCSS include more open-response items in end-of-year tests, issues of validity and reliability are raised resulting from the process of testing EBLs exclusively in English (Solano-Flores, 2016). Our study contributes a bilingual approach to assess emergent bilingual students' mathematical understanding in Spanish to counteract the perpetuation and exacerbation of linguistic disadvantages for EBLs' in measures of mathematics achievement.

## *Conceptual Framework*

Recent developments in the use of open-response assessments to gauge multiple dimensions of students' understanding have the potential to support the development of English-language skills in content area courses such as mathematics for EBLs (Martinello, 2008; Téllez & Mosqueda, 2015). Specifically, the formative assessment process can allow educators to account for language development in EBLs as well as measure conceptual understanding of mathematics in English or Spanish. Heritage (2010) defines formative assessment as data collection to help teachers understand what students are learning as instruction is taking place rather than at the end of a curricular unit. Teachers collecting formative assessment data can use evidence of EBLs' understanding to adapt and improve instructional approaches to more adequately support students' learning goals (Ruiz-Primo, Furtak, Ayala, Yin, & Shavelson, 2010; Solano-Flores, 2006). Formative assessment can provide an effective means for measuring multiple student learning goals, including: (a) identifying weaknesses and strengths, (b) helping students guide their own learning, (c) providing students guidance for revisions and evaluations of their own work and (d) fostering a sense of autonomy for learning (Cizek, 2010). We developed the Authentic Mathematics Writing Assessment System (AMWAS) as a formative assessment tool for middle school mathematics teachers' to analyze how bilingual students use writing to communicate their mathematical understanding (Duran, 2008; Martinello, 2008; Téllez & Mosqueda, 2015).

## *Teaching and Learning in Mathematics Classrooms*

Teaching and learning in mathematics classrooms that serve EBLs results in both opportunities and challenges, yet limited research has been conducted examining these contexts (Janzen, 2008). The contextualized nature of mathematics teaching and learning (e.g., visual representations of concepts, the presence of manipulatives) provides some of the needed language supports for EBLs to fully engage in mathematics lessons (Aguirre & Bunch, 2012; van Lier & Walqui, 2012; Wong Fillmore, 2007). However, the presence of abstract mathematical concepts, mathematical symbols and notations, and unfamiliar ways of using academic language for mathematical reasoning (Echevarria, Richards-Tutor, Chinn, & Ratleff, 2011; Wong Fillmore, 2007) present issues for EBLs that teachers need to address. Several studies have shown promise when language features receive explicit instructional attention while promoting authentic disciplinary practices (Duran, 2008; Martinello, 2008; Snow, Lawrence, & White, 2009; Téllez & Mosqueda, 2015). For instance, instruction that includes attention to literacy functions, as proposed by CCSS, extends far beyond merely addressing challenges EBLs may face with academic vocabulary in the content areas. van Lier and Walqui (2012) argue that "academic understandings and skills are permeated by language, both in terms of understanding concepts and accepted subject-specific procedures, and in terms of processes of learning to understand, to share, to consolidate, and to present" (p. 1). Therefore, beyond the need for language supports to understand mathematical content, EBLs also require language support to make sense of relationships between concepts, as well as to articulate explanations and arguments in writing. Ryve (2011) evaluated 108 mathematical literacy focused studies and found that the majority of research attention on understanding and promoting mathematical discourse practices has focused on oral language functions (78%), and under-examined written texts (7%). Therefore, our study of EBLs' mathematical discourse in writing has the potential to provide significant educational insights.

In mathematics, as well as in science, professional development (PD) opportunities for teachers to emphasize language and literacy have been associated with improvements in student achievement. Lee, Maerten-Rivera, Penfield, LeRoy, and Secada (2008) provided PD to elementary teachers for building on EBLs' native language as a resource to access abstract science and mathematics concepts. Results from the impact of PD participation showed that EBLs in the treatment group improved their achievement scores on a statewide mathematics assessment, relative to a comparison group of students. Avalos and Secada (2019) provided PD to sixth-grade teachers focused on research-based strategies to foster EBLs' engagement and participation in classroom discourse that emphasized developing students' mathematics register and improving mathematical content understanding. Specifically, results demonstrated the effect of instructional strategies in urban classrooms that focused on the use of semiotics, such as language, symbols, and visual representations during teaching that provided relevant mathematical meaning-making opportunities to prepare EBLs to communally engage in problem-solving discussions.

Celedón-Pattichis (2008) examined how a bilingual teacher in an urban middle school used students' language and culture to support mathematical discourse. In this classroom case study, the observed teacher used two languages (English and Spanish) to develop students' mathematics register by building on everyday language in English and providing students with connections to vocabulary development in a context that was specific to mathematics. The findings showed that the teacher's emphasis on mathematical language helped students expand their register of mathematical terms, and the language scaffolding practices (e.g., emphasizing cognates) helped students transfer mathematical meanings from Spanish to English (Celedón-Pattichis, 2008). Building on prior research of PD for teachers serving EBLs (Avalos & Secada, 2019; Celedón-Pattichis, 2008; Lee et al., 2008), our study examines the relationship between formative assessment approaches in mathematics and EBLs' mathematical understanding in writing responses.

## *Prioritizing Bilingual Formative Assessment*

The Standards for Educational and Psychological Testing remind us that every assessment of content area knowledge is also an assessment of language (AERA, APA, & NCME, 1999). Research on assessing EBLs has examined the linguistic and cultural sources of measurement error on summative assessments, providing a useful set of criteria to improve the effectiveness of formative assessment for EBLs (Duran, 2008; Llosa, 2011; Solano-Flores, 2006). For example, language-based psychometric limitations arise when assessing EBLs, including construct-irrelevant variance, or errors in measurement of subject-matter understanding due to EBLs' levels of English-language proficiency (Abedi, 2004; Duran, 2008). In addition, an examination of EBL students' responses on the Massachusetts state exam showed how bias resulting from unnecessary syntactic and lexical complexity in test items created difficulties for EBLs' sense-making of mathematical concepts and contributed to the underperformance of EBLs (Martiniello, 2008). Abedi and Lord (2001) made linguistic modifications to items from the mathematics subtest of the National Assessment of Educational Progress (NAEP) and administered the assessment to EBLs. By reducing the linguistic complexity of the items (e.g., changing passive to active voice) without compromising the mathematical content, EBLs reported a preference for the modified items during interviews and also demonstrated higher assessment scores. As the language demands of mathematics teaching and learning increase in classrooms and schools as emphasized by CCSS, EBLs will benefit from teachers participating in professional development that supports the implementation of bilingual formative assessment systems.

Guided by a conceptual framework of formative assessment and the research literature on EBLs and mathematics teaching and learning, our study examined the design and implementation of a bilingual rubric for open-response writing prompts in a mathematics assessment process that simultaneously measured students' content understanding and language acquisition.

## *Setting and Participants*

The Authentic Mathematics Writing Assessment System (AMWAS) is a tool to help middle school mathematics teachers integrate both mathematical language and content development in their teaching through an iterative formative assessment process. The project and study took place during a summer program at a charter school in northern California. Students designated as English learners by the state comprised 96% of the school population and 95% of all students were eligible for free/reduced-price meals in the National School Lunch Program (DataQuest, 2016). The summer program was designed to prepare 118 incoming ninth grade students, with English-language and socioeconomic backgrounds representative of the schools' composition, for their mathematics courses in high school and students had access to an in-class tutor, after-school tutoring and field trips to local universities. Students participated in preparatory mathematics courses taught by eight teachers. Although the school had a one-way transitional program in place, the presence of bilingual mathematics teachers facilitated opportunities for bilingual instruction. Teachers' experience ranged between 5 and 25 years, and three teachers self-reported as Spanish/English bilinguals. As bilingual Spanish/English teacher educators, we designed and implemented a professional development (PD) program with three workshops to support mathematics teachers in the CCSS integration of language and literacy in mathematics instruction. Workshops included presentations of recent research findings, collective viewing and discussion of mathematics instruction and the co-construction of lessons using the instructional practices presented and discussed during workshops. Teachers and researchers co-created AMWAS as an iterative formative assessment process to assess both how bilingual students' used writing to communicate their mathematical thinking as well as the influence of the PD model on mathematics teachers' instructional practices and students' progress on mathematical understanding and language acquisition. The PD model involved: (a) administration, scoring and analysis of AMWAS writing prompts; (b) customized workshops with opportunities to continuously calibrate scoring of AMWAS data; and (c) individualized coaching sessions that included co-designing lessons, classroom observations and post-instruction conversation.

## *Authentic Mathematics Writing Assessment System*

We co-created a formative assessment process with teachers to simultaneously assess students' mathematical understanding and language understanding in open-ended writing prompts that addressed language and literacy functions as expected by CCSS. All students completed three formative assessments. Prior to the first administration, teachers participated in a workshop where the AMWAS administration guidelines and rubric aligned to mathematics and English-language development standards were reviewed. The specific themes for each session were decided collectively between the PD coaches and the participating teachers. Additionally, the teachers and PD coaches collectively discussed, aligned and coordinated the use of key vocabulary from each lesson then translated the focal terms (e.g., slope/*pendiente*, rate/*taza*, savings account/*cuenta de ahorros*, representing/*representando*) and included discipline-specific as well as process-oriented vocabulary used in academic settings in the planning, teaching and assessment of each lesson. The collaborative nature of the PD sessions and the prioritization of students' needs for learning mathematics concepts and connecting their understanding to their home or community experiences, mirrored Díaz and Flores (2001) notion of teachers as sociocultural and sociohistorical mediators. Diaz and Flores (2001) posited that teachers facilitate the link between student's home and school experiences, and thus viewed the teacher's role as that of a "Sociocultural [and] sociohistorical mediator of important formal and informal knowledge about the culture and society in which children develop" (pg. 33). The AMWAS writing assessment prompts also attempted to reflect students' home and school experiences.

The first assessment presented a plot graphic of "John's Saving Account Balance for the Year" with the y-axis representing the dollars quantity in the savings account ($0–2000) and the x-axis representing the number of months (1–12). The graphic was introduced as follows:

> *Directions*: Write *at least* a paragraph that explains the graph below to someone that is unfamiliar with the graph. Make sure you use complete sentences and correct punctuation. Use mathematics vocabulary in your response and also explain the math involved in interpreting the graph.

The second assessment presented a plot graphic of "Saúl's Wireless Phone Plan" with the y-axis representing dollars ($0–$60) and the x-axis representing the number of minutes used (0–80). This assessment integrated suggestions from teachers to modify the context of the problem from a savings account to a wireless phone plan and the addition of the description of the base price and per minute charge. The third and final assessment was introduced as follows:

> *Directions*: In the box above, represent the following information in equation form: divide a number by 5 and add 4 to the result. The answer is 9. Solve the equation. In the space below, write *at least* a paragraph explaining to someone the steps you took to solve the equation. Use mathematics vocabulary in your response.

Formative assessments were administered every three weeks of the summer program. After collecting assessments from teachers, researchers independently scored a randomized set of 10 samples using the AMWAS rubric and reached inter-rater reliability percentages of 89%. Although AMWAS administration guidelines encouraged students to write their response in English as much as possible but to use Spanish if necessary, students selected to write their responses in either English or Spanish. Prior to administering AMWAS, we had developed a rubric in English; however, based on student responses, we needed to translate the rubric to Spanish.

*Spanish-language AMWAS Rubric.* The Rúbrica de Escritura Matemática assesses students' Spanish-language formative assessments across four domains: *Razonamiento Matemático* (Mathematical Reasoning), *Computación Matemática* (Mathematics Computation), *Vocabulario Matemático* (Mathematics Vocabulary), *y Convenciones de Escritura* (Writing Conventions). The rubric scale represents four levels (Table 11-1). A score of three signals reaching mathematics and writing standards; a score of four illustrates "above grade-level expectations;" a score of two captures a "below grade-level expectation" response; and a score of one is given to responses that do not address all aspects of the mathematics writing assessment. Below, we describe the range of scores for each of the domains.

*Razonamiento Matemático.* Mathematics reasoning encapsulates two dimensions that include: (a) the logic and organization used to solve the mathematics problem and (b) an understanding of the underlying mathematical concept, such as the appropriate order of operations, mathematical theorems, formulas or postulates leveraged to solve the problem. CCSS refers to this domain as conceptual understanding. A response score of four, as "above grade-level," would demonstrate well-organized reasoning and clear logic that explicitly includes well-developed explanations and justifications using theorems, formulas and postulates. A response score of three, as "grade-level," would demonstrate appropriate reasoning and logical explanations and justifications that are correct but may not be clear or well-organized. A response score of two, as "below grade-level," would demonstrate an explanation or justification of concepts or operations that demonstrate logical reasoning, although potentially incorrect. Considering this domain is designed to capture mathematical reasoning, collected data offers teachers information regarding which concepts and operations students believe are appropriate. A response that does not demonstrate reasoning is scored a one.

*Computación Matemática.* Mathematics computation captures students' ability to carry out mathematical procedures, such as adding polynomials, dividing exponents or multiplying fractions. CCSS refers to this domain as procedural fluency. A response score of four, as "above grade-level," would

*Table 11-1. Rúbrica de Escritura Matemática (REM)*

Rúbrica de Escritura Matemática (REM)

| PUNTUA-CIÓN | RAZONAMIENTO MATEMÁTICOS | COMPUTACIÓN MATEMÁTICOS | VOCABULARIO MATEMÁTICO | CONVENCIONES |
|---|---|---|---|---|
| 4 | • El razonamiento muestra una lógica clara y bien organizada para explicar y justificar la solución.<br>• El razonamiento muestra la comprensión de los conceptos matemáticos, operaciones y relaciones con teoremas, fórmulas o postulados. | • Los procedimientos matemáticos (suma, resta, multiplicación y división) se realizan de manera precisa y eficiente.<br>• Las estrategias de resolución de problemas usan conceptos y procedimientos apropiadamente | • Utiliza varias palabras de nivel 3 (por ejemplo, vértices, propiedad asociativa) y nivel 2 (por ejemplo, dígito, cociente, variable) con precisión y precisión para describir el razonamiento y el cálculo. | • Puntuación y sangría apropiadas utilizadas en toda la respuesta<br>• No hay problemas de ortografía o gramática en respuesta<br>• Las palabras de transición como primero, a continuación, como resultado de, etc. se usan cuando sea apropiado para organizar la respuesta y hace que las ideas sean claras y fáciles de entender |
| 3 | • El razonamiento muestra lógica para explicar y justificar la solución.<br>• El razonamiento muestra la comprensión de los conceptos matemáticos y las operaciones para resolver problemas | • Los procedimientos matemáticos (suma, resta, multiplicación y división) se llevan a cabo con precisión.<br>• Las estrategias de resolución de problemas utilizan conceptos y procedimientos de manera apropiada. | • Utiliza una palabra de nivel 3 (por ejemplo, vértices, propiedad asociativa) y de nivel 2 (por ejemplo, dígito, cociente, variable) con precisión y precisión para describir el razonamiento y el cálculo. | • Mínimo (1–2) problemas de puntuación o sangría que no impidan la comprensión<br>• Mínimo (1–2) problemas de ortografía o gramática que no impidan la comprensión<br>• Las palabras de transición se utilizan para organizar ideas, pero más palabras de transición mejorarán la claridad |

*Continued*

Table 11-1. Continued

Rúbrica de Escritura Matemática (REM)

| PUNTUACIÓN | RAZONAMIENTO MATEMÁTICOS | COMPUTACIÓN MATEMÁTICOS | VOCABULARIO MATEMÁTICO | CONVENCIONES |
|---|---|---|---|---|
| 2 | • El razonamiento muestra parcialmente cierta lógica para explicar o justificar la solución. U<br>• El razonamiento muestra la comprensión de conceptos matemáticos u operaciones para resolver problemas | • Los procedimientos matemáticos pueden ser inexactos.<br>• Las estrategias de resolución de problemas utilizan conceptos y procedimientos que no son apropiados. | • Utiliza palabras de nivel 3 (por ejemplo, vértices, propiedad asociativa) o de nivel 2 (por ejemplo, dígito, cociente, variable) para describir el razonamiento y el cálculo<br>Puede usar palabras incorrectamente | • Algunos (3-5) problemas de puntuación y / o sangría que pueden impedir la comprensión<br>• Algunos (3-5) problemas de ortografía y / o gramática que pueden impedir la comprensión<br>• Utiliza 1 palabra de transición cuando se pueden utilizar palabras de transición adicionales |
| 1 | • Ningún razonamiento incluido no explica la solución.<br>• El razonamiento no muestra comprensión de los conceptos matemáticos u operaciones para resolver problema | • No se incluye ningún cálculo, O, en su mayoría, se incluye un cálculo irrelevante. | • Usa vocabulario cotidiano en lugar de vocabulario matemático. | • Muchos (6+) problemas de puntuación y / o sangría que impiden la comprensión.<br>• Muchos (6+) problemas de ortografía y / o gramática que impiden la comprensión<br>• No son utilizadas las palabras de transición y estas palabras habrían hecho las ideas más fáciles de entender |

demonstrate use of precise mathematical procedures to solve the problem accurately as well as efficiently. An example of algorithmic efficiency is multiplying by 0.5 rather than dividing by 2. A response score of three, as "grade-level," would demonstrate appropriate computations that may be correct, but not the most efficient. A response score of two, "below grade-level," would demonstrate appropriate procedures to solve the problem with inaccurate algorithmic computations. A response that does not demonstrate computations or uses inappropriate computational procedures is scored a one.

*Vocabulario Matemático.* Mathematics vocabulary captures students' use and quantity of discipline-specific vocabulary, referred to as tier 3 in the rubric, as well as process-oriented vocabulary used in academic settings, referred to as tier 2 in the rubric. A response score of four, "above grade-level," would include both tier 3 and tier 2 words and use these words accurately and with precision. Using these words accurately refers to recognizing for example that while the word *integer* and *number* share some meaning, the word *integer* refers to only whole numbers, including zero. Hence, referring to a fraction as a number would not be using this term accurately. Similarly, using mathematics vocabulary with precision refers to using the mathematical term instead of an everyday equivalent. For example, using the vocabulary "product" instead of "answer" to the solution of a problem that includes a multiplication procedure. A response score of three, "grade-level," would include use of at least one tier 3 and one tier 2 vocabulary in their response. A response score of two, "below grade-level," would include either one tier 2 or tier 3 word, and may inaccurately use this word. A response that does not include any tier 2 or tier 3 vocabulary is scored a one.

*Convenciones de Escritura.* Writing conventions captures students' use of: (a) punctuation, indentation, (b) spelling, grammar and (c) use of transitional words. A response score of four, "above grade-level," would be free of punctuation, indentation, grammar and spelling errors and would use transitional words to communicate ideas clearly. A response score of three, "grade-level," would demonstrate minimal errors in punctuation, indentation, grammar and spelling and would be missing transitional words that would improve the clarity of the ideas being communicated. A response score of two, "below grade-level," would demonstrate three-to-five errors in punctuation, indentation, spelling and grammar category that impede the reader's comprehension and would include only one transitional word. A response with significant errors (i.e., 6 or more) in punctuation, indentation, grammar and spelling that compromise the reader's comprehension and that also does not include any transitional words is scored a one.

## *Professional Development Model for Emergent Bilingual Learners*

Prior to developing and implementing the AMWAS formative assessment process, we met with the eight mathematics teachers to learn what they believed would be useful professional development (PD) topics for teaching EBLs. Teachers reported vocabulary, students' motivation and explanations of students' thinking in mathematics as areas of interest. We conducted three customized PD workshops during the summer program that presented research findings on teachers' areas of interest and integrated opportunities to calibrate scoring of AMWAS data and discuss how formative assessment trends could inform instructional decisions.

The first workshop presented research findings about community cultural wealth (Yosso, 2005), and teachers were also provided with a resource repository of readings about Latinx mathematicians to provide access to authentic literacy sources that could also influence students' motivation. Readings included the biography of José M. Hernández, a bilingual, Mexican-American, astronaut from California who was a seasonal farmworker growing-up. Hernández would visit the school and meet with students the following academic year, after being contacted by administrators. The second workshop presented research findings about academic vocabulary and literacy and teachers were provided with daily journal exercises that would promote explanations of students' thinking in mathematics, as expected by CCSS. Teachers encouraged students to respond to daily prompts such as: "Solve the problem written on the board and then write an explanation that describes how you solved the problem." Some teachers permitted students to participate in peer-editing prior to submitting their writing responses.

The third workshop presented research findings about disciplinary discourse as well as integrated and designated English-language development and teachers were provided with suggested daily language acquisition exercises and mathematics discourse routines to create authentic learning situations for students' development of oral and compositional language. Teachers were asked to write mathematics word problems on the board with various punctuation, indentation, grammar, vocabulary use and spelling errors. We asked teachers to encourage students to: (a) rewrite word problems without language convention errors, (b) solve the word problem, and (c) explain how they solved the problem to a partner, the teacher, or the entire class. Language acquisition exercises contextualized in mathematics problems provided teachers insights regarding the distinction between integrated and designated English-language development. Mathematics discourse routines provided students with access to explicit models for identifying language convention errors as well as talking about mathematical processes for solving problems.

*Coaching Sessions.* After every PD workshop, teachers and researchers worked in pairs to discuss the formative assessment trends and co-design lessons that would concurrently develop students' mathematical reasoning, computation and vocabulary as well as language conventions. Teacher and researcher pairs co-identified complementary mathematical and language learning objectives as well as appropriate instructional activities to simultaneously develop students' mathematical understanding and language acquisition. Researchers conducted classroom observations of co-designed lessons and shared narrative notes with teachers. Teacher and researcher pairs participated in post-instruction conversations to co-identify areas of interest to inform future instruction. We designed and implemented the PD model for EBLs and the AMWAS formative assessment process to contribute a bilingual approach to assess emergent bilingual students' mathematical understanding in Spanish.

## *Results*

We analyzed the AMWAS formative assessment process using both quantitative and qualitative measures. We analyzed the results of the first assessment (N = 99) and the results from the third assessment (N = 118) to evaluate bilingual students' mathematical understanding and language acquisition during the summer program. Aggregated results show a positive change from pre- (first assessment) to post- (third assessment) on the *Razonamiento Matemático* and the *Convenciones de Escritura* dimensions (Table 11-2). Results from the *Computación Matemática* and the *Vocabulario Matemático* dimensions remained constant.

*Table 11-2.* Mean Pre- and Post-Scores by Domain

| Domain | Pre | Post |
| --- | --- | --- |
| Mathematics Reasoning | 2.41 (N = 99) | 2.59 (N = 118) |
| Mathematics Computation | 2.27 (N = 99) | 2.28 (N = 118) |
| Mathematics Vocabulary | 2.46 (N = 99) | 2.42 (N = 118) |
| Writing Conventions | 2.33 (N = 99) | 2.40 (N = 118) |

On average, two trends existed in formative assessment data: (a) students demonstrated grade-level results on *Razonamiento Matemático* but below grade-level results on *Convenciones de Escritura*, and (b) students demonstrated grade-level results on *Convenciones de Escritura* but below grade-level results on *Razonamiento Matemático*. The administration guidelines of the assessment encouraged students to write their responses in English as much as possible but to use Spanish, if necessary. AMWAS was designed for a bilingual learning content where students are encouraged to use their full linguistic repertoire (García, 2009). We anticipated students' responses to communicate mathematical understanding in English with some Spanish; however, students' responses were written completely in either English or Spanish. Teachers and researchers discussed instructional implications based on formative assessment trends during both PD workshops as well as coaching sessions. We co-identified potential opportunities in upcoming lessons to bolster EBLs' mathematics reasoning, computation, vocabulary as well as writing conventions. We provide two samples of student responses written in Spanish to illustrate numerous instructional possibilities and limitations associated with bilingual formative assessment results, PD workshops and coaching sessions. We assessed the open-ended student responses using the Spanish-language AMWAS Rubric. Students' names are pseudonyms.

*Paco.* Paco's response to the second assessment illustrates the trend of grade-level results on *Razonamiento Matemático* but below grade-level results on *Convenciones de Escritura*. Paco's assessment was scored 3 for *Razonamiento Matemático*, 3 for *Computación Matemática*, 1 for *Vocabulario Matemático*, and 1 for *Convenciones de Escritura* (Figure 11-1). Paco demonstrated the grade-level mathematical understanding by responding to the plot graphic:

> "*a el le cobran 30 dolares llame o no llame si el se pasa por tiempo como se puede mirar en la grafica el se pasa por una hora y le cobran $.50 centavos por cada minuto que se pasa en la grafica se mira que le cobraron $60 30 dolares por un mes que es lo que tine que pagar y otros $30 dolares que se paso de tiempo.*"

Paco's response translates to, "He is charged $30 whether he uses it or not, but as you can see in the graph he goes over by one hour and they charge him $.50 per minute that he goes over on the graph. You can see on the graph that they charge $60, $30 for one month [of service], which is what has to be paid and another $30 that he went over on time." Paco's response includes specific terms that describe units and actual increases in dollar amounts per month. This level of description is a feature of the academic register of mathematics that is often not present in EBLs' responses. Similarly, the presence of actual units, dollars, also signals a level of precision in the development of the mathematics register that would not be evident in a response that mentions "money" as the unit. Additionally, Paco's response signals the unit of time (month), which can serve as an anchor from which to build understanding by ensuring to include a complete reference of the units involved in the problem. Paco reads the graph correctly and is able to identify the reasons why there is an intercept and an increase to the wireless phone plan. Paco's response mentions *"le cobran 30 dolares llame o no llame . . ."* or "he is charged $30 whether he uses it or not . . ." which accurately describes the y-intercept. Paco is also able to correctly identify the slope or constant rate of change represented on the graph, *"se pasa por una hora y le cobran $.50 centavos por cada minuto que se pasa en la grafica,"* which translates to "he goes over by one hour and they charge him $.50 per minute that he goes over on the graph." Paco's description of the slope reflects a level of understanding that is a step above what is represented on the graph. Based on the units used on the graph in the problem, the rate of change is for every 10 minutes used there is a charge of $5; however, Paco correctly simplified the rate of change to every minute used there is a charge of $.50.

While Paco's written response reflects "grade-level" mathematical reasoning and computation of linear functions, his response also reflects "below grade-level" mathematical vocabulary to communicate the mathematical reasoning and computation of the graph-based problem. A rating of "below grade-level" for mathematical vocabulary would include either one tier 2 or one tier 3 word and response that does not include any tier 2 or tier 3 vocabulary is scored a one. In this formative assessment, tier 3 words would include algebraic terminology (e.g., x-axis, slope, linear function) and tier 2 words would include mathematics process terms (e.g., calculate, increase). Paco's response does not use either algebraic terminology or mathematics process terms (the word graph was duplicated from the prompt's directions). After presenting Paco's response at a PD workshop to advocate for more writing and oral explanation opportunities, we recommended teachers explicitly structure tier 2 and tier 3 words in daily journal exercises and mathematics discourse routines. Specifically, we suggested strategies using culturally-relevant mathematics problems that included the words slope and rate, as well as their respective Spanish translations, *pendiente*, and *taza* in sustained reading, writing, listening and speaking opportunities with partners as well as in whole-class discussions.

Paco's response also reflects "below grade-level" language conventions. Paco did not address the directions of composing at least one paragraph, instead Paco wrote one long passage that does not include any indentation or punctuation marks, such as commas or periods. Moreover, Paco's response does not demonstrate appropriate spelling in Spanish, such as accentuation for the words: *dólares* and *gráfica*. Paco's response also does not include any transitional words and the significant errors in punctuation and spelling compromise the reader's comprehension. Importantly, Paco's response exemplifies that although mathematical vocabulary and language conventions are "below grade-level," the assessment communicates "grade-level" mathematical reasoning and computation of linear functions. Paco's response demonstrates the concurrent expectation of EBLs to develop: (a) mathematical reasoning and computation, (b) fluency and literacy of mathematical vocabulary, as well as (c) using language conventions to explaining their mathematical thinking orally and in writing. In the PD workshops, we referenced Paco's response to recommended mathematics teachers explicitly use integrated and designated language acquisition exercises in daily journal exercises and mathematics discourse routines.

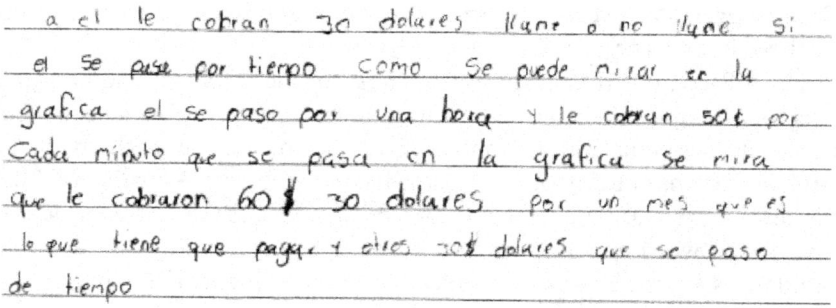

*Figure 11-1.* Paco's Response to Second Formative Assessment

***Josi.*** Josi's response to the third assessment illustrates the trend of below grade-level results on three dimensions. Josi's assessment was scored 2 for *Razonamiento Matemático,* 2 for *Computación Matemática,* 3 for *Vocabulario Matemático,* and 2 for *Convenciones de Escritura* (Figure 11-2). Josi's response did not demonstrate understanding of the underlying mathematical concept or precise mathematical procedures to solve the problem accurately and efficiently:

> "*primero se divide por el numero que es y luego se saca el resultado. despues se le agrega al numero positivo para poder sacar el resultado de la ecuacion.*"

Josi's response translates to, "First it is divided by the number that is [given] and then the result is gotten. After that the positive number is added to be able to get the result from the equation." In the answer box, Josi computed two operations including dividing 25 by 5 and then adding 4–5 to equal 9. She then concludes by writing out an equation with $x$ divided by 5 plus 4 equaling 9. Josi's response demonstrates comprehension of the order of operations when solving for x in an algebraic equation. Josie's response describes division by the number (or $x$) as the first step, to be followed by a solution, and complemented by adding a positive number. While Josi's response reflects some procedural understanding including comprehension of the order of operations in an equation (e.g., parenthesis, exponents, multiplication and division from left to right, addition and subtraction), but understanding of the underlying mathematical concepts of the equation is not communicated. Logical explanations about the components of an equation, their relationship, the manipulation of variables, or the importance of balancing expressions to solve an equation would have demonstrated grade-level mathematical reasoning. Additionally, Josi's computations are accurate but the selected procedures are not efficient. While Josi's response solves for $x$ correctly, subtracting 4 from both sides in the initial equation and dividing by 5 on both sides to maintain equivalent expressions are necessary algorithmic procedures that are required to demonstrate grade-level mathematics computation.

Josi's response also reflects "grade-level" mathematical vocabulary as well as "below grade-level" language conventions. Josi's response includes both tier 2 mathematics process vocabulary as well as tier 3 word algebraic terminology: (a) ecuacion, (b) numero, (c) resultado, (d) divide, (e) numero positivo and (f) agregar. Importantly, Josi's response exemplifies the linguistic dexterity of bilingual students. Drawing on both cognates and non-cognates (e.g., agrega/add) in mathematical vocabulary, we referenced Josi's response at a PD workshop of how tier 2 and tier 3 words could serve as markers of mathematical biliteracy. Josi's response also demonstrates mathematical biliteracy in the use of a generic third person. Selecting the impersonal, third-person, indexical of *"se"* in Spanish as in *"primero se divide"*/ "first it is divided" emphasizes the action, not the person carrying out the operation, and shows how equations are meant to be interpreted by anyone.

Finally, Josi's response reflects "below grade-level" language conventions. Josi did not address the directions of composing at least one paragraph, instead Josi wrote two sentences without appropriate capitalization and indentation. Additionally, Josi's response does not demonstrate appropriate spelling in Spanish, such as accentuation for the words: *ecuación, número* and *después*. Josi's response includes three transitional words that improve the clarity of the ideas communicated and contribute to not compromising the comprehension of the written and graphic response: *primero* (first), *luego* (then), and *después* (afterward).

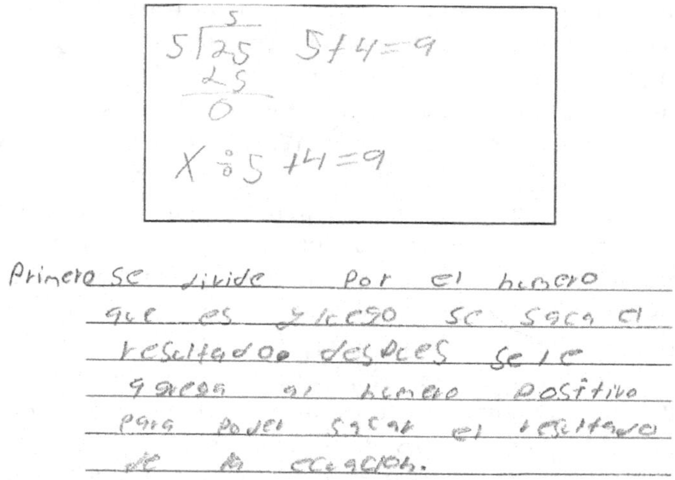

```
    5
5 ⟌ 2̄5̄    5+4=9
   25
    0

X ÷ 5 +4 = 9
```

Primero se divide por el humero
que es y luego se saca el
resultado despues se le
quema al humero positivo
para poder sacar el resultado
de la ecuación.

*Figure 11-2.* Josi's Response to Third Formative Assessment

## Conclusion

Our study has important implications for policymakers, researchers and practitioners interested in improving instructional approaches and assessment processes for bilingual students. We learned from this study that content area assessment models applied to EBLs must be linguistically flexible to better capture EBLs' mathematical understandings. Allowing students to respond to the writing prompt in the language of their choice provided insights into student mathematical understandings that would not have been possible if students had been directed to respond in their non-dominant language, which was English for most of our secondary school EBLs.

The written responses in Spanish by *Paco* and *Josi* we analyzed in this chapter revealed that both students had foundational mathematics knowledge. Paco's response provided teachers with an example of a student able to descriptively explain the slope or constant rate of change of a function without using the Spanish term for rate. Josi's response provided teachers with an example of a student able to use higher tier academic vocabulary terms, solve problems correctly, but required support in communicating mathematical reasoning and computation. Paco and Josi's responses in Spanish highlighted mathematical understanding and areas for growth that would have been overlooked in a non-bilingual context. Thus, the writing prompts about solving two-step equations that were applied to contextualized linear functions allowed us to gauge EBLs' potential to develop mathematical literacy. We also found that assessment models must also capture EBLs' language development, and the AMWAS did just that for the teachers in our study. Results from the bilingual AMWAS formative assessment process allowed teachers to quickly pivot their instruction to meet the specific needs of EBLs in their classrooms. Moreover, mathematics teachers in the summer program expressed having particular areas of expertise as well as acknowledging areas for improvement in their teaching. This dynamic is important to note because EBLs, like *Paco* and *Josi,* benefitted most from lessons where their Spanish skills were leveraged in the service of mathematical reasoning. While this study took place in a charter public school setting, we believe that the collaborative and iterative nature of the AMWAS process can be utilized in traditional public school contexts (non-charter) as well as during the regular school calendar year. Ultimately, we found that teachers using the bilingual formative assessment AMWAS, as an instructional compass, illustrates a potential approach for leveraging EBLs' linguistic repertoire in the service of developing mathematical biliteracy.

## References

Abedi, J. (2004). The No Child Left Behind Act and English language learners: Assessment and accountability issues. *Educational Researcher, 33*(1), 4–14.

Abedi, J., & Lord, C. (2001). The language factor in mathematics tests. *Applied Measurement in Education, 14,* 219–234.

Aguirre, J. M., & Bunch, G. C. (2012). What's language got to do with it?: Identifying language demands in mathematics instruction for English Language Learners. In S. Celedon-Pattichis & N. G. Ramirez (Eds.), *Beyond good teaching: Advancing mathematics education for ELLs* (pp. 183–194). Reston, VA: National Council of Teachers of Mathematics.

American Educational Research Association, American Psychological Association, & National Council on Measurement in Education (1999). *Standards for educational and psychological testing.* Washington, DC: American Psychological Association.

Avalos M. A., & Secada W. G. (2019). Linguistically responsive teaching to Foster ELL engagement, reasoning, and participation in a mathematics discourse community. In L. de Oliveira, K. Obenchain, R. Kenney, A. Oliveira (Eds.), *Teaching the content areas to English language learners in secondary schools.* English Language Education (Vol. 17). Cham: Springer.

Celedón-Pattichis, S. (2008). "What does that mean?": Drawing on Latino and Latina students' language and culture to make mathematical meaning. In M. W. Ellis (Ed.), *Mathematics for every student: Responding to diversity, grades 6–8* (pp. 59–73). Reston, VA: National Council of Teachers of Mathematics.

Cizek, G. J. (2010). An introduction to formative assessment. In H. Andrade & G. Cizek (Eds.), *Handbook of formative assessment*. New York: Routledge.

Diaz, E., & Flores, B. (2001). Teacher as sociocultural, sociohistorical mediator: Teaching to the potential. In M. D. Reyes & J. J. Halcón (Eds.), *The best for our children: Critical perspectives on literacy for Latino students* (pp. 29–47). New York: Teachers College Press.

Data Quest (2016). *2014–15 enrollment by English language acquisition status and grade*. Sacramento: California Department of Education.

Durán, R. P. (2008). Assessing English language learners' achievement. *Review of Research in Education, 32*(1), 292.

Echevarria, J., Richards-Tutor, C., Chinn, V. P., & Ratleff, A. R. (2011). Did they get it? The role of fidelity in teaching English learners. *Journal of Adolescent & Adult Literacy, 54*, 425–234.

García, O. (2009). Emergent bilinguals and TESOL: What's in a name?. *Tesol Quarterly, 43*(2), 322–326.

Heritage, M. (2010). Formative assessment and next-generation assessment systems: Are we losing an opportunity? *Council of Chief State School Officers*. National Center for Research on Evaluation, Standards, and Student Testing (CRESST) and the Council of Chief State School Officers (CCSSO). CCSSO: Washington, D.C.

Janzen, J. (2008). Teaching English language learners in the content areas. *Review of Educational Research, 78*(4), 1010–1038.

Lee, O., Maerten-Rivera, J., Penfield, R. D., LeRoy, K., & Secada, W. G. (2008). Science achievement of ELLs in urban elementary schools: Results of a first-year professional development intervention. *Journal of Research in Science Teaching, 45*(1), 31–52.

Lee, O., Quinn, H., & Valdés, G. (2013). Science and language for English language learners in relation to Next Generation Science Standards and with implications for Common Core State Standards for English language arts and mathematics. *Educational Researcher, 43*, 223–233.

Llosa, L. (2011). Standards-based classroom assessment of English proficiency: A review of issues, current developments, and future directions for research. *Language Testing, 28*(3), 367–382.

Maldonado, S. I., Mosqueda, E., Bravo, M. A., & Solís, J. L. (2020). Assessing and teaching biliteracy in mathematics: A professional development model. *The Multilingual Educator*, 36–39.

Martiniello, M. (2008). Language and the performance of English language learners in math word problems. *Harvard Educational Review, 78*(2), 333–368.

Mosqueda, E., Bravo, M. A., Solís, J. L., Maldonado, S. I., & De La Rosa, J. (2016). Preparing middle school students for the transition to high school mathematics: Assessing

Latinas/os' mathematical understanding, academic language and English language proficiency. *The Bilingual Review/La Revista Bilingüe,1*(1), 1–20.

Ruiz-Primo, M. A., Furtak, E. M., Ayala, C., Yin, Y., & Shavelson, R. J. (2010). Formative assessment, motivation, and science learning. In H. Andrade & G. Cizek (Eds.), *Handbook of formative assessment*. New York: Routledge.

Ryve, A. (2011). Discourse research in mathematics education: A critical evaluation of 108 journal articles. *Journal for Research in Mathematics Education, 42*(2), 167–199.

Snow, C., Lawrence, J., & White, C. (2009). Generating knowledge of academic language among urban middle school students. *Journal of Research on Educational Effectiveness, 2*(4), 325–344.

Solano-Flores, G. (2006). Language, dialect, and register: Sociolinguistics and the estimation of measurement error in the testing of English-language learners. *Teachers College Record, 108*(11), 2354–2379.

Solano-Flores, G. (2016). *Assessing English language learners: Theory and practice*. New York: Routledge.

Téllez, K., & Mosqueda, E. (2015). Developing teachers' knowledge and skills at the intersection of language learners and language assessment. *Review of Research in Education, 39*(1), 87–131.

van Lier, L., & Walqui, A. (2012). *Language and the common core state standards*. Paper presented at the Understanding Language Conference, Stanford, CA. Retrieved from https://ell.stanford.edu/sites/default/files/pdf/academic-papers/04-Van%20Lier%20Walqui%20Language%20and%20CCSS%20FINAL.pdf

Wong Fillmore, L. (2007). English learners and mathematical learning: Language issues to consider. *Assessing Mathematical Proficiency, 53*, 333–344.

Yosso, T. J. (2005). Whose culture has capital? A CRT discussion of community cultural wealth. *Race, Ethnicity, and Education, 8*(1), 69–91.

## 12. Learning about My Students: Examination of Cultural Asset-Based Assessments in Dual Language Education

ANA M. HERNÁNDEZ
*School of Education, California State University San Marcos*

ANNETTE M. DAOUD
*School of Education, California State University San Marcos*

### Introduction and Purpose

Given the growing number of dual language education (DLE) programs in the USA today, it is important to examine teachers' biases towards primary and second language instruction as a means of ensuring equitable practices and differentiated lessons that are driven by assessments and accountability of state standards. Developing linguistically and culturally appropriate assessment tools allow DLE teachers to collect, analyze and monitor student progress, as well as examine and reflect on their own practices to challenge unjust and often unintended approaches that result in inequitable outcomes and bias implementation (Alfaro & Hernández, 2016), particularly for Latinx Spanish speakers. This fundamental notion of equity and social justice ascertains that the ideological clarity and instructional practices of teachers are congruent with the goals of DLE (Alfaro, Durán, Hunt, & Aragón, 2015; Bartolomé, 2008) and denounce deficit-oriented use of assessments. Bilingual teachers, who continually engage in formative assessments to guide their instruction, develop lessons with an approach to differentiation and a critical lens on diversity.

This chapter focuses on "learning about my students" from cultural asset-based assessments in dual language settings where PreK-8th grade teachers examined writing samples from their students through a strength-based approach, rather than a deficit mindset towards language development in Spanish and English. The following sections will describe the processes, artifacts and lessons learned about student performance on formative assessments with the use of grade level rubrics, summary tables and lesson study feedback forms to analyze their own practices and student progress free of bias intentions towards diverse populations.

## *A Framework for Learning about My Students*

The conceptual underpinnings adapted from the notion of valuing diversity and equity in the classroom (Pang, 2018) allow teachers to develop strong trusting and reciprocal relationships with their students through culture-centered assessments. This culturally responsive mindset begins with the concept of "learning about my students" through the examination of student work samples. It fosters a caring, student-centered learning environment that nurtures the language development of students through cultural asset-based assessments that recognize students' strengths and builds on the learning processes needed for individual academic growth.

The premise of cultural deficit stems from educators placing blame on students' lack of achievement or low scores on assessments on children, their families' educational level and how cultures view the role and value of schooling (Gay, 2018; Pang, 2018). In contrast, an asset-based ideology embraces cultural diversity and strengths of all students as a benefit to the school community. This theoretical grounding stems from the ethnographic research on household "funds of knowledge" (Moll, Amanti, Neff, & González, 1992) in which teachers' strategic knowledge of families' social, economic and productive activities transform teaching by bridging the students/family assets into the classroom practices. Therefore, asset-based teaching and assessments focus on students' strengths and build learning around student assets, cultural identities and biliteracy to assist their academic and intellectual development (Moll et al., 1992; Reyes, 2001).

What led us to this asset-based theory of practice in our work with dual language teachers was our participants' own deficit-oriented comments about their students in anonymous pre-surveys and feedback forms collected during our first professional development workshop. This alarming revelation of DLE teachers' perceptions towards their native Spanish speakers' and native English speakers' proficiency in Spanish confirmed that teachers' ideological stance about their students and their expectations of performance intersect in a manner which looks at instruction and assessments through a deficit-oriented lens that lacks culturally appropriate pedagogy. This intersectionality of how perceptions of student underperformance come together in teachers' constructs about their students augments social and linguistic biases—as an impediment to visualize students' strengths; therefore, continuing the manifestation of "blame of failure" on families and children.

## Literature Review

We have designed assessments following our research on teacher education that are explicitly rooted in the tenets of social justice and equity to transform the instruction of bilingual students with original language (no translations) and consideration to students' Latino culture and home language (Cochran-Smith et al., 2009; Darling-Hammond, French, & Garcia-Lopez, 2002; Freeman, Bullock, & Duque, 2005; Solano-Flores, Trumbull, & Nelson-Barber, 2002) as well as promote a critical multicultural education to design appropriate lessons and assessments (Banks, 2003; Gallavan, 2011; Nieto & Bode, 2012; Sleeter & Carmona, 2017). Teachers often engage in practices that seem to be effective in their contexts, but rarely discuss what theories support their work or ideologies to inform their instruction (Alfaro & Hernández, 2016; Cadiero-Kaplan & Rodríguez, 2008). By engaging in critical examination of politics and ideologies that inform practices, teachers begin to understand that they will either maintain the status quo or chose to engage in work that transforms the sociocultural ramifications in school (Bartolomé, 2008; Valenzuela, 2016).

Educational psychologists identify asset-based assessments as: (a) a focus on assets, (b) individual and community level assessment, (c) collaboration skills and (d) self-reflection (Lubbe & Eloff, 2004). The first three areas are congruent with asset-based theories, but the fourth theme is somewhat under-represented in assessments. Currently, research is moving away from the deficit paradigm of assessments (emphasizing student problems) and toward a model that focuses on the counter constructs, strengths, resources and capacities of students that advance an asset-based approach (Lubbe & Eloff, 2004). This approach implies a culture of dynamic assessments including comprehensive social systems that create coherence, collaboration, partnerships, are strength-focused and facilitate a more holistic conceptualization of an individual or group (Rhee, Furlong, Turner, & Harari, 2001).

First, asset-based assessments imply more than the traditional focus on the strengths and weaknesses of a student by emphasizing the mindset of capacities—rather than deficits, particularly for vulnerable populations (Ebersöhn & Eloff, 2006; Pang, 2018; Rhee et al., 2001). According to Ebersöhn and

Eloff (2003), an asset-based approach is therefore an "internally focused" (p. 462) caring strategy that concentrates on agenda building and problem-solving capacities of the learners. It is described as a "bottom-up approach" (p. 462) that is relationship driven, therefore shifting the emphasis from a service perspective to an empowerment standpoint, such that ...

> Relationships need to be built and rebuilt between individuals and institutions through facilitation ... which offers several returns in terms of ownership, shared responsibility, immediacy, relevancy and practicality of solutions, flexibility, mutual support and a caring environment, as well as individual capacity building" (Ebersöhn & Eloff, 2006, p. 462).

Second, it is critical that in dual language education we use both summative and formative assessments that reflect the achievement of all students not only as evidence of growth and effectiveness of program, but in consideration to the current political rhetoric in the USA against immigrant families, status of languages other than English and policies diminishing the students' culture and heritage language (Gottlieb & Nguyen, 2007; Hernández, 2017). Educators need to use multiple measures that are asset-based assessments to provide authentic and holistic evidence of student learning in both languages, guide professional development and improve program outcomes for English learners (Escamilla et al., 2014; Gottlieb & Nguyen, 2007). This includes time and opportunities for teachers to collaboratively discuss, develop responses to data, receive coaching strategies to adjust practices, build skills and knowledge about test-based accountability damaging to English learners by widening the achievement gap (Valdés, Menken, & Castro, 2015). Pressuring educators to teach to the test defies a student-centered learning environment that builds on the language and cultural assets of students and their strengths in the learning processes for academic growth, such as:

> Teachers who lack sufficient knowledge of EL assessment are likely to have their EL students doing work that is either too difficult or too easy and thus inefficient. On the other hand, a teacher who holds expert knowledge and skills with respect to EL assessment will know students' language levels and have them work at their instructional capacity, which results in efficient teaching and learning (Téllez & Mosqueda, 2015, p. 88).

## *Reconceptualizing Instructional Assessments through Professional Development*

We reviewed research to design our professional development to not only focus on using strategies that promote language development and literacy skills, but also address teachers' deficit discourses and assumptions about their students (Molle, 2013; Kolano, Dávila, Lachance, & Coffey, 2013/2014). We also studied research on the benefits of providing teachers ongoing support throughout the academic year, including time to discuss strategies, their students' work and collaborate with colleagues on their pedagogy, as well as their students' achievement (Babinski, Amendum, Knotek, Sánchez, & Malone, 2018; Green, Gonzalez, López-Velásquez, & Howard, 2013; Walker & Edstam, 2013). We asserted that professional development (PD) in dual language education must focus on both pedagogy and an examination of data through performance assessments for continuous monitoring and acceleration of student achievement.

This work stems from our U.S. Department of Education—National Professional Development grant (2016–2021) Project ACCEPT—*Aligning the Common Core for English Learners, Parents and Teachers: A Professional Development Community in Dual Language Education*. The project is in its third year of implementation with four main goals to improve the education of English learners: (1) certify bilingual pre-service teachers; (2) provide an advanced Dual Language Certificate to inservice teachers; (3) provide professional development for inservice educators; and (4) develop parents' knowledge and skills in technology. However, this chapter will only focus on types of asset-based assessments used in the professional development goal.

The Professional Learning Committee (PLC), composed of the project director, evaluator, instructional coaches and site principals, schedules four professional development days for project teachers throughout the year. The goals include building educators' theoretical knowledge, examining critical consciousness, implementing equitable strategies to support English learners in DLE programs, collecting data through action research, and sharing outcomes with peers through continuous online forum discussions and face-to-face meetings. The examination of critical consciousness draws from the Ideology, Pedagogy, Access and Equity (IPAE) Framework (Alfaro & Hernández, 2016) (see Figure 12-1) in which *ideological clarity* requires that teachers' individual justifications be continually compared and contrasted with those propagated by the dominant society (Bartolomé, 2008. Second, a teacher's *pedagogical clarity* stems from an asset-based perspective centered on the funds of knowledge students bring to the classroom (Moll et al., 1992) free of bias and stereotypes. Third, teachers know how to provide *access* to content by differentiating instruction and assessments for all students. And *equity* is at the core of how teachers define and position the sociolinguistic and sociocultural goals for dual language education. It provides the educator lens to exert their ideological clarity for safe democratic spaces, dismantling their biases, and interrogating inequities.

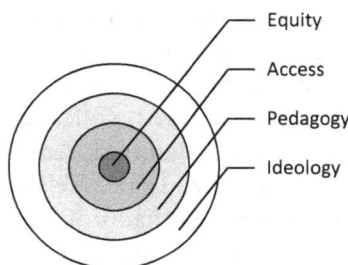

*Figure 12-1.* Dual Language Educator Equity Lens, IPAE Framework (Alfaro & Hernández, 2016)

## *Asset-Based Assessments*

Data collection and analysis include authentic multiple measures in the evaluation of Spanish and English language development (see Table 12-1) across three DLE programs [Transitional Kinder (TK) through 8th grade] in North San Diego County. Transitional kindergarten (TK) is the first year of a two-year kindergarten program that uses a modified kindergarten curriculum that is age and developmentally appropriate. TK curriculum is aligned to the California Preschool Learning Foundations and California Preschool Curriculum Frameworks (California Department of Education, 2019). The lessons and assessments incorporate strategies and activities to examine student work samples through a cultural asset-based methodology. In addition, teachers reflect on the processes to understand language development, status and biases. Triangulation of data through pre/post surveys, reflections, lesson feedback, artifacts and student work samples demonstrate an increase in lesson differentiation by language proficiency levels and attention to students' sociocultural and sociolinguistic development.

We began the PDs by examining the teachers' critical consciousness about the students they serve. This included a pre-survey with questions of their instructional practices and pedagogical stances on the teaching of Spanish and English. We also delved into readings related to social justice curriculum and activities to demystify misconceptions about teaching culturally and linguistically diverse students. We followed with an activity on "Getting to Know my Students" (see Table 12-1) where teachers recreated their seating charts with colored sticky notes and shared charts with grade level groups. Each color represented groups of students identified on district/state assessments as English learners (EL), Redesignated Fluent English Proficient (RFEP) and students with special needs. Teachers discussed strategies on how to group students more equitably for instruction based on their profiles and added other symbols to the sticky notes (e.g., happy faces, stars, hearts) to identify students who seem bored in class, potentially at risk, excelling academically, invisible to others or someone who _____ (teachers could fill in the blank). The charts allowed teachers to notice color clusters of students, a true composite of their classes, and to make sound decisions about access and equity.

*Table 12-1. Asset-Based Assessments Used in Project ACCEPT PD*

| Asset-based Assessment | Purpose | How used in PD | Outcomes |
|---|---|---|---|
| Examination of Teachers' Critical Consciousness | Teachers examined their critical consciousness through readings, discussion and reflections. | To engage teachers in critical discussions of topics, themes, frameworks and instructional activities. | Teachers reflected on deficit myths and created posters on social justice-oriented practices. |
| Getting to Know My Students | Teachers created a seating chart using various colored sticky notes to identify students (e.g., ELs, SPED) needing additional help/attention in their classrooms. | To examine student seating in classroom, proximity to teacher, peers who provide assistance and access to classroom resources. Discuss chart with other teachers. | Teachers made changes to seating charts according to needs of identified students (e.g., grouping students more appropriately for instruction). |
| Spanish Writing Analysis Tool and Rubric | Teachers documented evidence of standards met by students in Spanish writing identifying strengths and then areas of focus in language and content. | To identify strengths in Spanish writing for three focus students in each classroom. Discuss similarities and differences among grade levels and outline patterns across all grade levels. | In grade levels, teachers used results to design next lesson in writing using differentiation of instructional strategies and assessments for their three focus students. |
| Lesson Study Feedback (LSF) Form | Teachers implemented lessons developed in grade level groups. PD colleague(s) observed lesson and completed form together. | To discuss lessons and artifacts from LSF in grade level groups. Teachers complete a grade level summary chart of LSF outcomes and next steps in their lesson planning as grade levels. | LSF forms uploaded to online discussion forum with lesson artifacts, self-reflections, and next steps. Peers provided feedback online and reviewed all work submitted. |

*Table 12-1. Continued*

| Asset-based Assessment | Purpose | How used in PD | Outcomes |
|---|---|---|---|
| Mindset of Generous Eyes: Writing for Growth with EL Students | Teachers learned how to use EL student mentor texts as a strategy for English writing. | To annotate an EL student's English writing sample as a mentor text and to incorporate the mentor text in an ELD lesson. | Teachers implemented lesson using the EL mentor text. Uploaded lessons and artifacts to online peer discussions. |
| Examining English Academic Word Use | Teachers identified misuse of academic words on 1–3 EL or RFEP student papers. Discussed outcomes. | To collect data (pre-test) on misuse of academic words for EL/RFEP papers. Discuss outcomes and most frequent occurrences with grade level and cross-grade level groups. | Teachers developed ELD lesson to address 1–2 common errors from the student papers. Then administer a post-test to compare academic language results. |

## *Spanish Language Development Assessments*

Based on teacher input during the planning year of the grant, the PLC designed the first year of the professional development (AY 2017–18) to concentrate on Spanish language development. The PLC created a series of four workshops with continuous online discussions on documents and artifacts uploaded between sessions.

**Asset-based writing analysis.** During the first workshop, teachers delved deep into the California Spanish language standards [Common Core Español, 2012; Spanish Language Development (SLD) Standards, 2012] and analyzed their student Spanish narrative writing samples through a strength-based approach that allowed them to extract evidence to support claims (see Table 12-2). In grade level teams, teachers developed lessons with data collected from student writing samples to enhance skills and differentiate instruction by proficiency levels.

Findings from the grade level summary tables showed teachers using the same differentiation strategies for ELs, bilinguals and native English speakers. DLE teachers were not differentiating instruction by proficiency levels in Spanish. Data collected through feedback forms, artifacts and surveys demonstrated that teachers mainly used teacher modeling as the main strategy and provided sentence frames for students needing additional help. In upper grades, teachers allowed students to use the internet as a strategy to translate material (e.g., words, sentences) from English to Spanish. Workshop data revealed teachers used limited strategies for differentiation and infrequently used a variety of approaches to build strong Spanish skills. They mainly provided lesson vocabulary through modeling, sentence frames, word banks or use of internet translation.

We concluded the analysis by having teachers create lessons in their grade level groups that aimed at connecting content and language objectives to their activities and outcomes, as well as incorporating differentiation strategies for the students' Spanish language proficiency levels and data collected from student papers. We asked teachers to implement the lessons in their classrooms, upload their lesson plans and resources and respond to two or more of their colleagues online on the project website. The PLC reviewed the online comments, lessons and artifacts to plan the following workshop and collection of student assessments.

*Table 12-2. Asset-based Writing Analysis for Spanish Writing*

| Project ACCEPT Análisis de la escritura | |
|---|---|
| *Grupos: En sus niveles de grados examinen las escrituras de los estudiantes* <br> *Grado: _____ Tipo de escritura: ___opinión ____narrativa _____ informativa* | |
| Documenta el éxito escolar: Tipo de escritura <br> • ¿Cómo han adquirido los estudiantes los estándares del Common Core Español para la escritura? <br> • ¿Cuál es la evidencia (propósito, organización, evidencia y elaboración)? <br> • Nombra 2–3 áreas de enfoque: <br> 1. <br> 2. <br> 3. | Documenta el éxito escolar: El lenguaje <br> • ¿Cómo han adquirido los estudiantes los estándares del lenguaje escrito (Common Core Español) para el nivel del grado? <br> • ¿Cuál es la evidencia (gramática, vocabulario, tipos de oraciones, puntuación, deletreo)? <br> • Nombra 2–3 áreas de enfoque: <br> 1. <br> 2. <br> 3. |
| Próximos pasos para adquirir los estándares y ampliar/mejorar el desarrollo del lenguaje: <br> ¿Qué puedo implementar, modificar o ampliar en mis lecciones para mejorar las metas académicas de los estudiantes? | |
| Diferenciación: Hispanohablantes en programas de doble inmersión <br> ¿Cuáles son los éxitos académicos de los estudiantes hispanohablantes en L1/L2? <br> ¿Cuáles son las áreas de enfoque para el mejoramiento? ¿Cuál es la evidencia? <br> • L1 <br> • L2 | |

*Table 12-2. Continued*

| Project ACCEPT Análisis de la escritura |
|---|
| Grupos: En sus niveles de grados examinen las escrituras de los estudiantes<br>Grado: _____ Tipo de escritura: ___opinión ____narrativa _____ informativa |
| Diferenciación: Angloparlantes en programas de doble inmersión<br>¿Cuáles son los éxitos académicos de los estudiantes hispanohablantes en L1/L2?<br>¿Cuáles son las áreas de enfoque para el mejoramiento? ¿Cuál es la evidencia?<br>• L1<br>• L2<br>Mi Plan de acción para la diferenciación:<br>• ¿Qué pienso sobre los papeles de mis estudiantes?<br>• ¿Cuáles son mis próximos pasos para la diferenciación? |

Because teachers were using limited strategies for differentiation in their instruction, we designed activities for subsequent workshops that allowed teachers to examine their students' work more critically. Teachers engaged in examining their ideological stance and critical consciousness through readings (Valenzuela, 2016) and activities in which they revisited their grade level summary tables (see Table 12-3) to determine bias statements and deficit-oriented scaffolding, including low-level differentiated strategies.

*Table 12-3. Asset-based Grade Level Summary of Writing Analysis, Rubrics and Strategies*

| Project ACCEPT Summary of Results | | | |
|---|---|---|---|
| Grade level _____ Type of Writing _____ | | | |
| Describe what you did ... | Data collected & instrument used | Analysis & results | Next steps |
| Name Spanish Writing Strategies used: | | | |
| Differentiation by linguistic levels: | | | |
| Modifications to grade level rubrics for differentiation: | | | |

Teachers analyzed their students' Spanish informational writing samples and created rubrics to examine the work further in their classrooms. Teachers developed Spanish rubrics for each grade level based on the California

Common Core Español Standards (San Diego County Office of Education, 2012). Table 12-4 provides an example of a 4th grade rubric for Spanish informational writing.

*Table 12-4. Common Core Español Estándar 4.2: Textos informativos y explicativos para examinar un tema y transmitir ideas e información con claridad*

| Nivel 4 – el estándar | Nivel 3 | Nivel 2 | Nivel 1 |
|---|---|---|---|
| Presentan un tema con claridad y agrupan la información en párrafos y secciones; incluyen encabezados, ilustraciones y medios múltiples cuando sean útiles para ayudar a la comprensión. | Presentan un tema con alguna claridad y agrupan la información en párrafos u oraciones y algunas secciones; incluyen algún formato (encabezados), ilustraciones cuando sean útiles para ayudar a la comprensión. | Presentan un tema con poca claridad, quizás la información no está agrupada en párrafos u oraciones; quizás incluyen algún formato (encabezados) o ilustraciones para ayudar a la comprensión. | Presentan un tema limitado sin claridad, sin secciones de oraciones relacionadas; no incluyen formato (encabezados) o ilustraciones para ayudar a la comprensión. |
| Desarrollan el tema con hechos, definiciones, detalles concretos, citas, u otra información y ejemplos relacionados con el tema. | Desarrollan el tema con algunos hechos o definiciones, detalles simples, y citas relacionados con el tema. | Desarrollan el tema con pocos hechos, definiciones, y / o detalles, con o sin citas relacionados con el tema. | Desarrollan el tema limitado con 1–2 hechos, definiciones o detalles (sin citas) acerca del tema. |
| Enlazan ideas dentro de la información, usando palabras y frases (otro, por ejemplo, también, porque . . .). | Enlazan algunas ideas usando palabras o frase. | Enlazan pocas ideas usando palabras (no frases). | No enlazan las ideas. |
| Usan un lenguaje preciso y un vocabulario de dominio específico para informar sobre el tema o explicarlo. | Usan algún lenguaje simple con el voc. de dominio específico para informar sobre el tema o explicarlo. | Usan poco vocabulario de dominio específico para informar o explicar. | No usan vocabulario de dominio específico para informar o explicar. |

*Table 12-4. Continued*

| Nivel 4 – el estándar | Nivel 3 | Nivel 2 | Nivel 1 |
|---|---|---|---|
| Incluyen una conclusión relacionada con la información o explicación presentada. | Incluyen conclusión simple relacionada con la información/ explicación. | Incluyen una oración para concluir la información o explicación. | No incluyen una conclusión al final. |
| **Criterios adicionales** *(el maestro/a puede agregar más elementaos como gramática, estructura de oraciones, deletreo, aquí)* | | | |

**Lesson study of differentiated assessments.** The third workshop began with teachers sharing how they used the rubrics they designed to differentiate assessments for their students and determining a need to develop sentence structures. In response, PLC members provided demonstrations on how to analyze students' writing by using the California Spanish Language Development (SLD) Standards (San Diego County Office of Education, 2012) to show how to expand or condense sentences. Using a *structural input approach* (Lyster, 2007) to writing (a systematic attention to the form and function of language while learning content), the participants elicited simple sentences and transformed them into compound and complex sentences by inserting different types of conjunctions and prepositions. They wrote on sentence strips and then cut out the words individually to manipulate the vocabulary and create sentence variations. Then, teachers looked at their student papers and determined what strengths existed in their written language. Table 12-5 displays the lesson study feedback form used by teachers to implement the strategies in their classrooms. Table 12-6 demonstrates the lesson feedback comments: (1) strategies used, (2) types of differentiation, and (3) lesson impact on the learning of ELs.

# Cultural Asset-Based Assessments in Dual Language 257

*Table 12-5. Asset-based Lesson Study Feedback Form—Spanish Language Development*

Project ACCEPT Professional Development | Lesson Study Feedback Form
School/District _____ Grade Level _____

1. What strategies did you use to continue building and strengthening Spanish writing and language?
2. How did you differentiate instruction for ELs, EOs and/or bilingual students in your classroom?
3. What strategies are you implementing from our Project ACCEPT PDs or readings?
4. Based on the students' participation and outcomes of this lesson … What do you consider your areas of strengths or needs for your next lesson?
5. What is the impact of your lesson on English learner instruction?
6. Other thoughts or comments

*Table 12-6. Teacher Comments on Lesson Study Feedback Form: Reconstructing Sentences in Spanish by Condensing or Expanding*

| Grade | Strategies used | Differentiation | Lesson impact on ELs |
|---|---|---|---|
| TK | I used Input/Output Cycles to engage leaners in semantic processing that allowed them to construct meaning when producing language (Manipular el lenguaje – armar y desarmar). | Students worked as partners at different levels (ELs & EOs). Provided modeling and resources. Choral and echo reading. Gradual release of responsibility. | Learning new vocabulary and manipulating words to make complex sentences. Ability to communicate in their primary language with peers. Building confidence in writing and accomplishing task independently. |
| 1st | Students added details to their sentences. I reviewed simple sentences and taught how to add details with use of conjunctions. I modeled science writing. They practiced with a partner using own sentences. Lastly, they transferred sentences to their science writing books. | I placed my ELs and EOs with high academic Spanish speaking students. My bilingual students were paired with students at grade level to continue developing their language. My high students and bilingual students were models for other students. | Allowed my ELs to have visuals and manipulate words to create sentences, since it's hard for some of them to start a sentence. It also allowed them to build ideas from someone else who is more proficient in the language. |

*Table 12-6. Continued*

| Grade | Strategies used | Differentiation | Lesson impact on ELs |
|---|---|---|---|
| 3rd | We expanded sentences using a sentence pattern chart. We practiced orally and wrote sentences in our composition books. We discussed unique grammatical structures in the language, for example "diminutivos" or "aumentativos." | Paired bilingual/EL students with partner who was able to review sentence structure. Grouped students with several partners to help with spelling and sentence structure. Students needing additional help, worked with me to complete each part of the task step-by-step. | ELs aware of language mechanics and able to collaborate. Students explained functions of verbs, nouns, adjectives and prepositions. Able to explain functions and when partners were missing information. ELs built confidence when writing and speaking. |
| 6th | I used Input/Output Cycles from PD to reconstruct texts. We revised/edited our texts. Part of the lesson included integrating conversations prior to the production of written text. | Strategically partnered students in small teams. Provided resources such as sentence frames, word bank (verbs), images, text, & diagram. I modeled for targeted groups needing help. | Gained oral language development, and vocabulary at all tier levels. Noticed collaboration and teamwork by negotiating for meaning when reconstructing sentences. Improved oral & written sentence structure. Transferred concepts cross-linguistically between Spanish-English. |

Teachers used Table 12-7 to summarize grade level sentence structures through a strengths-based approach and described potential impact on EL instruction. The PLC also invited parents and families participating in digital literacy projects (Project ACCEPT Goal 4) to share their work with the teachers as part of an asset-based professional learning community that involves a comprehensive sociocultural system between school and community that creates coherence, collaboration and partnerships with families of vulnerable populations. It also demonstrated to teachers a focus on community/family assets accessible to their students, which can facilitate a more holistic conceptualization of family skills and strengths unknown or overlooked by educators (Moll et al., 1992; Rhee et al., 2001).

*Table 12-7. Asset-based Grade Level Summary Lesson Study Feedback*

Project ACCEPT Summary of Lesson Study Feedback—Grade level _____

| Strategies Used | Differentiated Instruction | Lesson Strengths | Next steps | Impact of lessons on English learners |
|---|---|---|---|---|
| | | | | |
| | | | | |

Other comments:

## *English Language Development Assessments*

Based on first year teacher post-surveys, the PLC identified English Language Development (ELD) as the overarching topic for Year 2 professional development workshops (AY 2018–19). The PLC collaborated with the San Marcos Writing Project to introduce the notion of using EL students' writings as mentor texts (examples of EL student writings that approximate grade level standards), and provide effective feedback as well as revision strategies for writing growth.

**Mentor texts.** During the first workshop of Year 2, teachers read research articles on teachers and students as writers to give them foundational knowledge for using students' papers as mentor texts. Teachers analyzed their own experiences as writers through an examination of positive and negative early recollections as writers in school and at home. PLC members demonstrated how teachers could annotate their EL students' writing samples as mentor texts—a writing strategy for ELD with the mindset of generous eyes. Teachers selected two of their EL students' writing samples and annotated them with colored sticky notes to model as mentor texts in their classes. After teachers used the mentor texts with their students, they reflected on the experience by discussing these questions on the online forum:

1. How did you use the mentor text to guide your ELD writing instruction?
2. What was the experience like for your EL student(s)?
3. What are your next steps using EL mentor texts as asset-based assessments?
4. What are the areas of need for your focus EL student? And how will you measure growth using mentor texts?

The following reflections are representative of teachers' responses after using their EL students' writing as mentor texts:

> The EL mentor texts were powerful. I was surprised how students rose to the occasion. We worked for a week on sequencing the life cycle of a butterfly, focusing on using descriptive vocabulary and transitional words. After, we brainstormed both opening and concluding sentences. As a game, the students chose an opening sentence and we read their writing, inserting one of them. After we practiced this, the students wrote their independent pieces and most of them used an opening sentence, as well as a concluding sentence. (1st Grade ELD teacher)
>
> My EL students enjoyed the process of analyzing one of their classmate's paragraphs, because it motivated them to do their best in writing. For the student whose paragraph I selected, it was especially meaningful, as it validated his hard work. After this exercise, I have noticed that more students are taking their time in making sure they provide a meaningful commentary and use transitional words/phrases. Using EL mentor texts was a powerful way to improve student writing and to support struggling learners by providing examples to follow. (7th grade English Language Arts teacher)

**Academic word misuse.** The second workshop focused on academic language use and misuse of words for ELs and RFEP students in DLE classrooms. After reading a study on how the use of English academic words determine the effectiveness of text cohesion (Cons, 2012), teachers examined students' writing samples to determine how ELs/RFEPs used academic vocabulary. Teachers individually completed Table 12-8 (Pre-test) by tallying the type of words misused on 2–3 of their class papers (focus students), analyzing academic word misuse with a partner and then discussing patterns across TK-8th grade level teams. Overall results identified *spelling* as the main factor related to word misuse in text cohesion for both ELs and RFEPs. Based on the findings, teachers developed an ELD lesson using the California English Language Development (ELD) Standards (California Department of Education, 2012) to address the type of spelling errors pertinent to their grade level. Also, teachers were asked to select another round of papers for the same EL/RFEP students to conduct a Posttest (see Table 12-8), and then post a discussion about their lessons, artifacts and assessments:

1. What growth did you see in your students' use and misuse of academic words after your lesson?
2. Was there a difference between your Pre- and Posttest results? Explain why or why not.
3. What are your next steps?

*Table 12-8. Structuring Cohesive Texts: Academic Word Misuse* (Adapted from Cons, 2012)

Project ACCEPT Pre-Test/Posttest Individual Class    Grade Level:_____

| Category | English Learner | Reclassified | Pre-Test | Post-Test |
|---|---|---|---|---|
| Orthography | | | | |
| Verb Tense | | | | |
| Derivations | | | | |
| Collocations/Colligations | | | | |
| Plurals | | | | |
| Subject-Verb Agreement | | | | |
| **TOTAL** | | | | |

Results from assessment (Pre-/Post-test) discussion on academic word use demonstrated that teachers in early primary grades (TK-2$^{nd}$ grade) did not document differences between the pre and posttest in terms of improving the consistent use of sight words and spelling. However, they noticed an increase in writing confidence and believed that students needed time to develop knowledge about English—a developmental process. In the upper grades (3$^{rd}$–7$^{th}$), teachers noticed changes in spelling awareness when they focused on types of students' writing errors and developed explicit lessons to target English grammar or spelling rules (e.g., doubling consonants, past tense verbs):

> Results showed an improvement in my students' use of academic words, especially in orthography. I focused on two English Learners (ELD Level 2), a 4$^{th}$ grader and a 5$^{th}$ grader. I discovered that my students were constantly misspelling words that needed double consonants before suffixes like –ing, -est or –ed. For example, they were spelling "swimmer" as "swimer" and "stopped" as "stoped." I remembered that in the article we read in our PD there was a strategy for helping students attain more dominance in English writing: teach more explicit language rules. I went ahead and looked up some resources to help guide my instruction. (4$^{th}$ & 5$^{th}$ grade DLE teacher)
>
> There was a difference between my pre- and posttest results. Students improved in orthography, verb tense, and derivations. In the pre-test, I recorded 6 orthography errors, 8 verb tense errors, and 6 derivation errors. In the posttest, I recorded 3 orthography errors, 3 verb tense errors, and 5 derivation errors. Although students are still making errors in their writing, I am glad to see that the lessons helped them ... Investing the time in developing lessons that target these common errors is necessary, so our students can be successful in communicating. (7$^{th}$ grade DLE teacher)

**Lesson study of academic English language development.** During the third workshop, PLC members guided teachers in an analysis of their students' writing samples by focusing on spelling and vocabulary development. Teachers used spelling inventory guides (Bear, Invernizzi, Templeton, & Johnston, 2015) to analyze their students' writing and identify patterns they could use to design an upcoming lesson. PLC members provided teachers with materials to create a word sort activity to include in a lesson study to be observed by their colleagues. Table 12-9 contains the form teachers used to observe one another, provide lesson reflections and peer feedback and upload to the online discussion board.

*Table 12-9. Asset-based Lesson Study Feedback Form—English Language Development*

| Project ACCEPT Professional Development \| Lesson Study Feedback Form<br>School/District _____ Grade Level _____ |
|---|
| 1. What strategies did you use to continue building and strengthening word knowledge in English?<br>2. How did you differentiate instruction for ELs, EOs and/or bilingual students in your classroom?<br>3. What strategies are you implementing from our Project ACCEPT PDs or readings?<br>4. Based on the students' participation and outcomes of this lesson ... What changes did you notice in your students' academic language use and word knowledge? Did you notice any growth?<br>5. What is the impact of your lesson on English learner instruction?<br>6. Other thoughts or comments |

We began the fourth and culminating workshop by presenting teachers with the following pre-test ELD student writing sample, and discussed the asset-based questions to guide their analysis and responses through a generous mindset approach:

> **Pre-test Writing/Expanding Level English Learner (5th Grade)**
> My opinion is that dogs are better pets than cats. here is a fun fact. dogs are more activ than cats. First, I like dogs because there playfull. For example, You ceold play fetch with them, because there active. For example, You could play in the park with Your dog. anether example is, You could go for a walk with Your dog. Second, You coeld feed dogs. For example, You could order online for the food on website is chicken. For example, The food You buy is a good decent amount of food. another reasen is they have food and water bowls. Third, They keep you safe. For example, if thers an earthquake the dog barks at You when Yar in danger.

1. What are the strengths of this student's writing?
2. Are salient sounds represented or approximated in English?
3. Are most consonant diagraphs and blends spelled correctly or approximated?
4. Are homophones correct or generalized due to second language acquisition?
5. If this were your student, what other asset-based questions would you ask about the writing?

Teachers worked in grade level groups to summarize the lesson study outcomes using the word sort activities (see Table 12-7) and described potential impact on their EL students.

## *Significance to Field*

Due to the growing political and ideological factors that influence education, there is a need to strategically interrupt linguistic biases and advance knowledge of multicultural education to confront the sociopolitical threats impacting DLE. Measures that advance equitable teacher practices provide a working knowledge of their perceptions and student progress. The series of professional development workshops allowed teachers to confront and disrupt the narrative of differential expectations for distinct groups of students.

## *Conclusion*

Workshop activities and online discussions throughout the academic year allowed teachers time to reflect on their pedagogy and denounce deficit-oriented uses of assessments that emphasize students' problems with their writing. By using a "learning about my students" approach to frame the professional development, we guided teachers through a series of activities that brought to light their students' assets. As described in this chapter, we designed instruments for each professional development workshop to help teachers focus on the counter constructs, strengths, languages, resources, cultural aspects and capacities of their students using asset-based assessments, collaborative conversations and an online platform for dialogue. Teachers worked collaboratively in grade-level teams to design and implement lessons with an approach to differentiation and formative assessments to guide instruction and build upon the identified strengths of their students. Our goal was to help teachers foster a critical lens on diversity and equity by understanding the importance of building relationships with their students, collaborating with colleagues and reflecting on their ideology and pedagogy as critically conscious educators.

## *References*

Alfaro, C., Durán, R., Hunt, A., & Aragón, M. J. (2015). Steps toward unifying dual language programs, common core state standards, and critical pedagogy. *Association of Mexican American Educators Open Issue, 8*(2), 17–30.

Alfaro, C., & Hernández, A. M. (2016). Ideology, pedagogy, access, and equity: A critical examination for dual language educators. *Multilingual Educator*, 8–11. California Association for Bilingual Education.

Babinski, L. M., Amendum, S. J., Knotek, S. E., Sánchez, M., & Malone, P. (2018). Improving young English learners' language and literacy skills through teacher professional development: Randomized controlled trial. *American Educational Research Journal, 55*(1), 117–143.

Banks, J. (2003). Teaching literacy for social justice and global literacy. *Language Arts, 81*(1), 18–19.

Bartolomé, L. (2008). *Ideologies in education: Unmasking the trap of teacher neutrality.* New York, NY: Peter Lang.

Bear, D. R, Invernizzi, M., Templeton, S., & Johnston, F. (2015). *Words their way: Words study for phonics, vocabulary and spelling* (6th ed.). England: Pearson.

Cadiero-Kaplan, K. & Rodríguez, J. L. (2008). The preparation of highly qualified teachers of English language learners: Educational responsiveness for unmet needs. *Equity and Excellence in Education, 41*(3), 372–387.

California Department of Education (2012). *California English Language Development Standards, K-12th Grade.* Retrieved from https://www.cde.ca.gov/sp/el/er/documents/eldstndspublication14.pdf

California Department of Education (2019). *Kindergarten in California*. Retrieved from https://www.cde.ca.gov/ci/gs/em/kinderinfo.asp

Cochran-Smith, M., Shakman, K., Jong, C., Terrell, D., Barnatt, J., & McQuillan, P. (2009). Good and Just Teaching: The case for social justice in teacher education. *American Journal of Education, 115*(3), 347–377.

Cons, A. M. (2012). The use and misuse of academic words in writing: Analyzing the writing of secondary English learners and Redesignated learners. *TESOL Journal, 3*(4), 610–638.

Darling-Hammond, L., French, J., & Garcia-Lopez, S. (2002). *Learning to teach for social justice*. New York, NY: Teachers College Press.

Ebersöhn, L., & Eloff, I. (2006). Identifying asset-based trends in sustainable programmes which support vulnerable children. *South African Journal of Education, 26*(3), 4575–472. Retrieved from http://sajournalofeducation.co.za/index.php/saje/article/view/86/48

Escamilla, K., Hopewell, S., Butvilofsky, S., Sparrow, W., Soltero-González, L., Ruiz-Figueroa, O., & Escamilla, M. (2014). *Biliteracy from the start: Literacy squared in action*. Philadelphia: Caslon Publishing.

Freeman, D., Bullock, P., & Duque, G. (2005). Teacher educators' reflections on moments in a secondary teacher education course: Thinking forward by challenging our teaching practices. *Teachers and Teaching: Theory and Practice, 11*(6), 591–602.

Gallavan, N. (2011). *Navigating cultural competence in grades 6–12: A compass for teachers*. Thousand Oaks, CA: Corwin.

Gay, G. (2018). *Culturally responsive teaching: Theory, research and practice* (3rd ed.). New York, NY: Teachers College Press.

Gottlieb, M., & Nguyen, D. (2007). *Assessment and accountability in language education programs: A guide for administrators and teachers*. Philadelphia: Caslon Publishing.

Green, J. D., Gonzalez, E. M., López-Velásquez, A. M., & Howard, E. R. (2013). Hands-on professional development: middle school teachers' experiences with a curriculum intervention research project. *Middle School Journal, 45*(2), 27–32.

Hernández, A. M. (2017). Bilingual against the odds: Examining proposition 227 with bilingual teacher candidates. In E. Barbian, G. Cornell Gonzales, & P. Mejía (Eds.), *Rethinking bilingual education* (pp. 311–320). Milwaukee: Rethinking Schools.

Hernández, A., & Daoud, A. (2014). Cross-cultural equity: Pathway for impoverished and marginalized students in two-way bilingual immersion programs. In M. Mantero, J. Watzke, & P. C. Miller (Eds.), *Readings in language studies (Volume 4): Language and social justice* (pp. 247–268). Grandville, MI: International Society for Language Studies.

Kolano, L.Q., Dávila, L.T., Lachance, J., & Coffey, H. (2013/2014). Multicultural teacher education: Why teachers say it matters in preparing them for English language learners. *The CATESOL Journal, 25*(1), 41–65.

Lubbe, C., & Eloff, I. (2004). Asset-based assessment in educational psychology: Capturing perceptions during a paradigm shift. *The California School Psychologist, 9*(1), 29–38. CA Association of School Psychologists.

Lyster, R. (2007). *Learning and teaching languages through content: A counterbalanced approach.* Philadelphia: John Benjamins.

Moll, L.C., Amanti, C., Neff, D., & González, N. (1992). Funds of knowledge for teaching: Using a qualitative approach to connect home and classrooms. *Theory Into Practice, 31*(2), 132–141. Taylor and Francis, Ltd.

Molle, D. (2013). The pitfalls of focusing on instructional strategies in professional development for teachers of English learners. *Teacher Education Quarterly*, Winter, 101–124.

Nieto, S., & Bode, P. (2012). *Affirming diversity: The sociopolitical context of multicultural education* (6th ed.). Boston, MA: Pearson Education, Inc.

Pang, V. O. (2018). *Diversity and equity in the classroom.* Boston, MA: Cengage Learning.

Reyes, M. L. (2001). Unleashing possibilities: Biliteracy in the primary grades. In M. L. Reyes & J. Halcón (Eds.), *The best for our children: Critical perspectives on literacy for Latino students* (pp. 96–121). New York: Teachers College Press.

Rhee, S., Furlong, M., Turner, J., & Harari, J. (2001). Integrating strength-based perspectives in psychoeducational evaluations. *The California School Psychologist, 6*(1), 5–17. CA Association of School Psychologists.

San Diego County Office of Education (2012). *Common core Español, K-12$^{th}$ grade.* Retrieved from *https://commoncore-espanol.sdcoe.net/CCSS-en-Espanol/SLA-Literacy*

San Diego County Office of Education (2012). *California Spanish language development standards, K-12$^{th}$ grade.* Retrieved from https://commoncore-espanol.sdcoe.net/Portals/commoncore-espanol/Documents/2018_09_18_K-12_SLD_Standards_Translated.pdf?ver=2018-09-18-101554-827

Sleeter, C., & Carmona, J. (2017). *Un-standardizing curriculum: Multicultural teaching in the standards-based classroom* (2nd ed.). New York, NY: Teachers College Press.

Solano-Flores, G., Trumbull, E., & Nelson-Barber, S. (2002). Concurrent development of dual language assessments: An alternative to translating tests for linguistic minorities. *International Journal of Testing, 2*(2), 107–129.

Téllez, K., & Mosqueda, E. (2015). Developing teachers' knowledge and skills at the intersection of English language learners and language assessment. *Review of Research in Education, 39*, 87–121. American Educational Research Association. doi.org/10.3102/0091732X14554552

Valdés, G., Menken, K., & Castro, M. (2015). *Common core bilingual and English language learners: A resource for educators.* Philadelphia: Caslon Publishing.

Valenzuela, A. (2016). *Growing critically conscious teachers: A social justice curriculum for educators of Latino / a Youth.* New York: Teachers College Press.

Walker, C., & Edstam, T. (2013). Staff development while you teach: Collaborating to serve English learners. *TESOL Journal, 42*, 345–359.

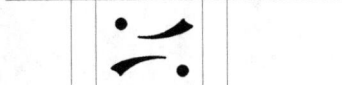

# *Appendices*

# Appendix: List of California's State Standards and Frameworks for Sociocultural Competence Considerations

VERONICA JOHNSON, JANET GABRIELA CARIÑO RAMSAY AND SAÚL I. MALDONADO

*History-Social Science Framework for Public Schools (HSSF)* curricular guidelines for implementing standards in furthering the collective goal of creating, active, engaged and civic-minded students

*California World Languages Standards* primary goal is developing students' global competency and literacy, learning languages and learning cultures is a concurrent process

*Guiding Principles of Dual Language Education (GPDLE)* designed to support dual language programs' learning goals of developing students' bilingualism, biliteracy, grade-level academic achievement and sociocultural competence

*Guiding Principles of Cultural Proficiency (GPCP)* reference tool for educators and administrators preparing teachers to design and implement learning experiences to develop student's sociocultural competence

*Cultural Proficiency Continuum (CPC)* tool for assessing the sociocultural competence of individuals and institutions

*Social Justice Standards (SJS)* framework to design and implement curriculum to address anti-bias, multicultural and social justice learning goals

*Elements of Social Justice Curriculum Design* six curriculum design elements for educators to consider when designing and implementing classroom learning experiences associated with recognition of individual and community strengths, respect of history and characteristics of different persons, relationship between identities and oppression and practicing social action activities

# Appendix: Activities for Evaluating Mathematics Learning in Dual Language Programs

KIP TÉLLEZ

Below are two activities for using the chapter's tool: *List of assessments suitable for evaluating mathematics learning in DLP, including descriptions, benefits and disadvantages of each* (Table 3-1, pp. 77–78).

## Activity 1

As you explore the assessments listed in the chapter's tool (see pages 77–78), think about which assessments would be appropriate for the two, different DLP contexts shared below. Review each of the descriptions and consider which assessments would be the most appropriate for each context. Use the guiding questions below each description to refine your recommendations.

### Escuela Mundial

Escuela Mundial teaches mathematics in Spanish until the 4th grade. In their final year of the program, the students, as fifth graders, transition to mathematics in English. This transition was thought necessary because the middle school where the students all attend did not have a teacher who could teach mathematics in Spanish. However, they recently hired a mathematics teacher who attended secondary school in Mexico City and feels confident in her ability to teach mathematics in Spanish (she holds the state's bilingual authorization/credential). Although the middle school could possibly now offer mathematics in Spanish at the sixth grade, seventh grade mathematics will be in English. The teachers, administrators, and parents want to know the balance of students' mathematics knowledge in both languages, so they can decide if continuing in Spanish mathematics at the sixth grade is a sound idea. The school district is willing to pay for the cost of the assessment.

Guiding Questions:
1. Which test or tests from the tool might be used to make a decision about when to transition from mathematics instruction in Spanish to instruction in English?
2. Which students should be assessed? Just the Escuela Mundial students?
3. Which grade levels should be assessed?
4. How might the school share the data with the school community?
5. What evidence would convince the parents that the school district is making the correct decision?

## *Escuela Dos Alas*

Escuela Dos Alas just adopted a new Spanish mathematics curriculum. Mathematics is taught in Spanish in grades K-3, transitioning to English in grade 4. The teachers and administrators want to know if the new curriculum is teaching the CCSS (Escuela Dos Alas in located in California) sufficiently. Students in the $3^{rd}$–$5^{th}$ grade have taken the Smarter Balanced Assessment (in English only) for the last five years, so the school has some longitudinal data. Because the school and district have no additional funding to purchase additional tests, they must rely on the existing assessments The school also wants to know how much, if any, mathematical content knowledge is lost when students make the transition from Spanish mathematics to English.

Guiding Questions:
1. Which test or tests from the tool might be used to determine if the new curriculum is teaching the CCSS sufficiently? (Recall that no additional funding is available.)
2. Should the school take on the task of developing assessments in Spanish? If so, how can they show that their assessments are valid?
3. Does the curriculum come with summative assessments in Spanish? If so, how might they be used?

## Activity 2

**Finding the best assessment for your program: Using the Mental Measurements Yearbook**

While not well known by many educators, assessment professionals are very familiar with a decades-long effort to catalog and review educational and psychological assessments. Currently known as the Buros Center for Testing, it has been housed at the University of Nebraska since 1938, and has reviewed over 10,000 tests since its inception, which have been published in volumes known as Mental Measurements Yearbook (MMY).

Each assessment is reviewed by two independent reviewers, who are not on the payroll of the publisher or have used the assessment in their research. It is important to note that not all tests are reviewed, but many of the most commonly used educational assessments are included. Of specific interest for DLP educators, the center has published two volumes (thus far) of *Pruebas Publicadas en Español*, a parallel volume to the MMY.

To begin searching, go the search engine for the MMY (https://marketplace.unl.edu/buros/) You'll find several search terms. For the purposes of explanation, type in "Aprenda" and you'll find that a review of the assessment, *Aprenda®: La prueba de logros en español—Segunda edición*. As the site advises, the $15.00 fee buys you the review of the test, not the test itself. Alternatively, most university libraries have a reference copy of the MMY. If you can find a copy of the MMY in print, you will not need to purchase the review online. A quick visit to the online catalog will let you know if your local university library has a copy of the MMY. If you are close to a university library, I would suggest you make a visit and talk to the reference librarian. They are typically very helpful in finding the MMY and helping to find a review of a specific test. With respect to the specific review of the *Aprenda®*, you will find it would be a very useful assessment of mathematics in Spanish and thus a good tool for DLP educators.

Next, try searching using various search of interest to you. Try to find other assessments that would be useful in a DLP context. If you are a teacher working in a school district, you might wish to search for the assessments required by district leadership. Do not be surprised to find that the assessments used in your school or school district are not considered worthy by the experts. I cannot tell you what to do when you find a poor assessment being used in your school, but I do believe that educators have a professional obligation to use valid and reliable assessments to make important instructional decisions. I can also say that most district curriculum leaders do not have a background in tests and measurements and have never heard of the Buros Center or the Mental Measurements Yearbook reviews.

I admit that searching test reviews in the MMY is a bit complicated—and expensive if you have to buy the reviews—but I can say that schools and school districts can spend many thousands of dollars purchasing tests that do not answer the questions they seek. I hope by having the MMY in your DLP evaluation toolkit, you will be the smart teacher or administrator who helps to make a good assessment choice or at least avoid a poor decision.

# *Appendix: Considerations Before Special Education Recommendations for Bilingual Students*

Felicia Castro-Villarreal, Victor Villarreal and Ileana Umaña

When evaluating students for eligibility for special education, it is necessary to consider factors other than those related to a disability that may contribute to their difficulties. These factors must be determined to not be the primary cause of a student's difficulties in order for the student to be found eligible for special education. Not considering these factors can lead to false-positive decisions (i.e., deciding that a child has a disability when the child does not actually have a disability, based on a failure to consider other factors) and/or inappropriate intervention recommendations. For bilingual students, it is particularly important to consider factors related to their instructional history and language proficiency.

Here we present factors that the IEP team should review to determine the extent to which they contribute to a student's difficulties. If these factors do not contribute to a student's difficulties, a special education referral may be appropriate. If these factors do contribute to the student's difficulties, it may be more appropriate to consider additional intervention before considering special education.

General Educational History
o How long has the student been enrolled in schools in the United States?
o For how many years has the student been learning English?

o Does the student have a history of lack of or limited instruction (e.g., not enrolled in school)?
o Instruction in primary language
o Instruction in English
o What is the student's attendance rate?
o Current Year:_____ Previous years:_____
o Have frequent transitions (or other circumstances) impacted the student's school attendance pattern or impacted the student's access to educational opportunities?
o Has the student been provided a targeted intervention to address their area of concern?
o If yes, did they respond similarly to similar peers also provided the intervention?*

Language Proficiency and Instruction

o In what types of classrooms has the student been enrolled (e.g., bilingual education, English as a second language)?
o Did the student learn to read in their primary language?
o Does the student have a history of learning problems their primary language?
o What is the student's language of instruction?
o Current Year:_____ Last Year:_____ Prior Years:_____
o What is the student's estimated proficiency (e.g., CALP) in English?
o Current Year:_____ Previous Assessments:_____
o What is the student's estimated proficiency (e.g., CALP) in their primary language?
o Current Year:_____ Previous assessments:_____
o Is the student's language and academic progress similar to that of other English learners from with similar educational experiences and backgrounds (e.g., similar language history, years learning English)?*

Home Factors

o What is the student's home language exposure?
o Primary Language:_____
o Secondary Language:
o What is the student's preferred language at home?
o Are the student's caregivers able to provide them instructional support in their language of instruction?

- o Does the student have limited access to educational materials at home?
- o If the student has siblings, is the target student's language and academic progress similar to that of siblings?*

*It is helpful to compare the target student to other students with similar backgrounds. If the target student is making less progress as compared to other students with similar backgrounds, it is likely that their difficulties go beyond factors related to their unique cultural and language background and are more likely associated with a disability for which special education services may be necessary.

# *Appendix: Training Sequence for IEP Committee Professional Development*

FELICIA CASTRO-VILLARREAL, VICTOR VILLARREAL AND
ILEANA UMAÑA

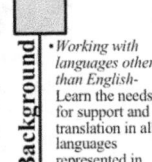

**Student Demographics and Background**
- *Working with languages other than English-* Learn the needs for support and translation in all languages represented in school.
- *Life experiences-* Learn how lived trauma and aculturaltion can affect ability levels and assessment outcomes.
- *Student cultural background-* Learn the norms of each culture group represented in the schools and selecting appropriate assessment tools via examining norm sample.

**Pre-Referral Considerations**
- *Literacy Curriculum-* Examine for responsiveness and overall achievement and success of ELL students.
- *SEL curriculum-* Learn social and emotional needs of students in a cullturally responsive manner.
- *Psycho-Social Developmental Needs of ELLs-* Learn needs of ELL students adujsting to new cultural norms, schooling demands and other stressors.

**Assessment Procedures**
- *Tool selection-* understanding appropriate test selection given training, languages spoken, and referral questions.
- *Asessment of students with unrepresented language-* Understand bias and flaws in assessment for students whose languges are not spoken in the school.
- *Acculturation-* Understanding of how acculturation may affect psychological and academic outcomes.

**Multidisciplinary Teams**
- *Local Cultural Context-* understanding the cultures and language represented in the schools.
- *Data- Based desicion making-* ensure proper use and collection of multiple sources of data, with proper comparision groups.
- *Roles and responsibilities-* creating school/district wide procedures for assessment staff and best course of action for assessments.
- *Learn and understand best practices in team decision making.*

**Working With Families**
- *Trained Interpreters-* Ensure proper use of terminology and confidentiality.
- *Relationship bulding-* Facilitate communication between school team and parents, respecting cultural boundaries and hesitations.
- *Encourage parent participation-* providing training in understanding the evaluation process and meeting procedures.

# Appendix: Critical Points in Collaboration for the Multidisciplinary IEP Committee

FELICIA CASTRO-VILLARREAL, VICTOR VILLARREAL AND
ILEANA UMAÑA

| Improve functioning and decision making of the IEP committee | Involve parents in the IEP process | Communication | Regular & Frequent IEP committee staffings | Final Staffing | Conduct the IEP Admission, Review and Dismissal meeting |
|---|---|---|---|---|---|
| •Systematic, research-based training and PD in collaborative team practices<br>•Intentional diversification of team membership = more equitable services and support for students<br>•Teach and prioritize collaboration and establish equal status relationships among all members<br>•Teach problem solving methods and procedures in team based collaboration | •Parents' sharing of students' home and school experiences is crucial to assessment, eligibility and instructional planning purposes<br>•Always promote inclusion and transparency in the IEP process<br>•Invite parents to trainings on IEP procedures, roles and functions<br>•Aquire parent input through home language surveys & ongoing involvment<br>•Be available for parent support along the process | •Protocols for regular email and shared drive communication and mandatory updates<br>•Protocol for at least 1 or 2 staffings prior to the official IEP meeting<br>•Intentional collaboration and communication to ensure that all questions have been asked, processes have been checked via checklists and forms and assessment and interpretation decisions are *multidisciplinary* and *team-based* | •Procedure to Identify, discuss, and document cases during campus pre-referral/student support/problem solving meetings<br>•Agenda that outlines a problem-solving approach that structures content and fosters effective interpersonal communication skills<br>•Agenda that follows a pre-determined informed process with checkpoints along the way<br>•Develop improved/alternative processes and assessment procedures for ELLs | •Consider additional questions, assessment tools, or data collection procedures<br>•Promote the active and equal participation of well-informed members<br>•Check-in to discuss preliminary findings and results<br>•Discuss findings and results with members to achieve preliminary team consensus<br>•Ensure parent participation and full disclosure after team staffing and prior to official IEP ARD | Conduct the ARD |

# Appendix: Receptive and Expressive Language Pre-Referral Protocol for Bilingual Learners (RELPP-BL)

JANELLE BETH FLORES, KARLA C. GARZA, T. BREANNE ROCHESTER, YVONNE VERA AND BELINDA BUSTOS FLORES

**Purpose:** The RELPP-BL serves to guide bilingual educators in determining if a referral is needed for a bilingual child for who is demonstrating a language delay. RELPP-BL is a tool that can assist in eliminating referrals due to typical bilingual/second language development. The RELPP-BL does not take the place of the district/campus referral process.

**Language Disorders:** According to ASHA (2020), language disorders occur when a person has trouble understanding others (receptive language), or sharing thoughts, ideas, and feelings (expressive language). Language disorders may be spoken or written and may involve the form (phonology, morphology, syntax), content (semantics), and/or use (pragmatics) of language in functional and socially appropriate ways (2nd bullet).

## *Multicultural/linguistic Considerations:*

a. Languages: 20% of American's speak a language other than English. (U.S. Census 2010. Twenty-two percent of U.S. students are bilingual.)
b. Dialects spoken: Be aware of the varieties of dialects within certain languages. (e.g.) Spanish- Caribbean, Mexican, Spanish/Castilian.
c. Gender roles: Some ethnic groups have different roles for boys and girls.

d. Generational Status: Country of birth and how long the student and family have been in the country.
e. Exposure: Education/play groups which provide language opportunities outside the home.

## Decision Graphic

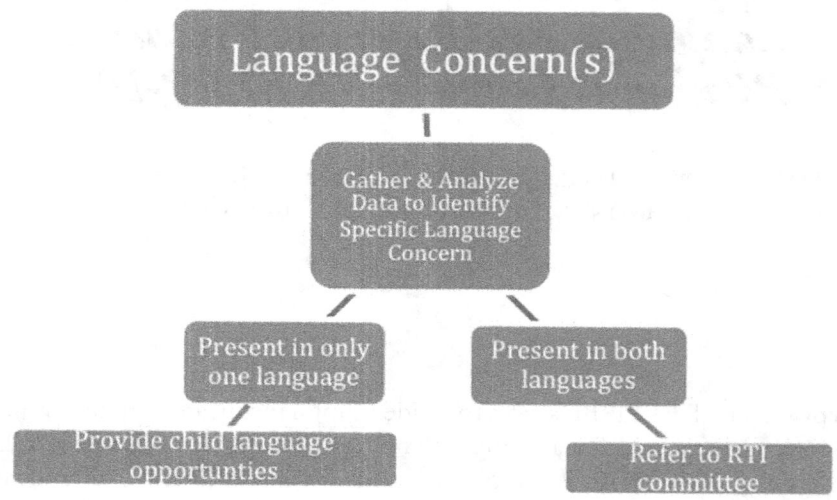

*Receptive and Expressive Language Pre-Referral Protocol for Bilingual Learners (RELPP-BL)\**

Child's Name:_____  Teacher Name: _____
DOB:_____ Gender:____ Grade Level:_____
**Directions:** Please complete the RELPP-BL to the best of your knowledge. Data will need to be gathered from various sources: parents/care-givers, prior teachers, child-observations, and/or student records.

## 1. Complete Ethnographic Interview

   a. Provide parent (caregiver) a brief overview of the ethnographic interview's purpose.
      i. Begin with a positive statement about the child.
      ii. Provide Rationale; for example:
         1. I have concerns about your child's language development and I am gathering information to determine what type of support is needed to help your child
   b. Ask non-intrusive questions (Westby et al., 2003), such as
      i. Begin with a descriptive Questions:
         1. Tell me about how your child communicates his/her needs?
         2. Tell me how your child communicates with others? His peers?
      ii. Friendly open-ended Questions:
         1. What kinds of activities does your child like to do?
         2. What happens if your child cannot communicate with others?
      iii. Means-end Questions:
         1. How does your child feel/act when s/he is not understood?
         2. How do others react to your child's communication difficulties?
      iv. Rationale Questions:
         1. Why do you or a family member think your child has communication issues?
         2. Why do other people think that your child has communication issues?
      v. Inclusion Questions:
         1. Do you think you need support to help your child? How so?
         2. How would you like to see us help your child?

---

\*Complete online: https://tinyurl.com/4kn8djmt

## 2. Language Background

| Parent/Caregiver(s) Language Profile | | | | | | |
|---|---|---|---|---|---|---|
| Relationship to Child | Dominant language | Country of Birth | Languages used in community | Languages used with other adults in home | Languages used with children in home | % of time spent with student per week |
| | | | | | | |
| | | | | | | |
| | | | | | | |
| | | | | | | |

1. **Exposure**

    *Student Language Profile*
    a. What are the languages that the student has been exposed to?
    b. At what age was the student exposed to each and for how long was the exposure?
    c. Where was the student born? How long have they been in the US?
    d. At what age did the student begin babbling?
    e. At what age did the student begin saying single words?
    f. What language(s) did the student use to say single words?
    g. At what age did the student begin combining words?
    h. What language(s) did the student use to combine words?

# Appendices

| What is the student's recent <u>language exposure</u> in the following scenarios? ||||||||| |
|---|---|---|---|---|---|---|---|---|---|
| Check the amount of time for each language in a typical week. ||||||||| Note any special circumstances |
| Language | English |||| Other:_____ |||| |
| | Not at all | Some of the time | Most of the time | All of the time | Not at all | Some of the time | Most of the time | All of the time | |
| Home | | | | | | | | | |
| Daycare/School | | | | | | | | | |
| Grandparents/ Relatives | | | | | | | | | |
| Words of affection | | | | | | | | | |
| TV/radio | | | | | | | | | |
| Friends | | | | | | | | | |
| Other: _____ | | | | | | | | | |

| What is the student's recent <u>language use</u> in the following scenarios? ||||||||| |
|---|---|---|---|---|---|---|---|---|---|
| Check the amount of time for each language in a typical week. ||||||||| Note any special circumstances |
| Language | English |||| Other:_____ |||| |
| | Not at all | Some of the time | Most of the time | All of the time | Not at all | Some of the time | Most of the time | All of the time | |
| Home | | | | | | | | | |
| Daycare/School | | | | | | | | | |
| Grandparents/ Relatives | | | | | | | | | |
| Words of affection | | | | | | | | | |
| TV/radio | | | | | | | | | |
| Friends | | | | | | | | | |
| Other: _____ | | | | | | | | | |

## 3. Educational Background

a. **Check Bilingual or English as Second Language Program and Type**

| Program Model | Type | |
|---|---|---|
| ESL | ☐ Immersion | ☐ Pull-out |
| Transitional BE | ☐ Early-exit | ☐ Late-exit |
| Dual Language | ☐ One-way | ☐ Two-way |
| Other: | ☐ _____ | |

b. **Identify Language Communication**

Languages of classroom instruction: _____
Languages used by the teacher to communicate with student: _____
Languages used by student to respond/communicate with teacher: _____
Languages used by peers to communicate with student: _____
Languages used by student to respond/communicate with peers: _____

c. **Language Checklist (ASHA, 2020b)**

| Check all the milestones that the student exhibits in either/any language: | | | |
|---|---|---|---|
| Grade level | PK/K | 1 | 2 |
| Receptive Language (Listening) | ☐ Follow 1–2 step directions<br>☐ Listen to and understand stories<br>☐ Follow simple conversation | ☐ Remember what was heard<br>☐ Follow 2–3 step directions | ☐ Follow 3–4 step directions<br>☐ Understand direction words (here, there, over, next to, before, later)<br>☐ Answer questions about a grade level story |

*Appendices* | 289

| Check all the milestones that the student exhibits in either/any language: | | | |
|---|---|---|---|
| Grade level | PK/K | 1 | 2 |
| Expressive Language (Speaking) | ☐ Speak clearly enough so that most people understand what he/she says<br>☐ Answer simple yes/no questions<br>☐ Answer "what" questions (i.e. what did you have for lunch today?)<br>☐ Retell a story or talk about something he/she did<br>☐ Take turns talking and keep conversation going<br>☐ Show interest in and start conversations | ☐ Speak clearly so that anyone can understand him/her<br>☐ Answer complex yes/no questions<br>☐ Tell and retell stories that makes sense and in order<br>☐ Use complete sentences to share ideas<br>☐ Use parts of speech and grammar correctly<br>☐ Ask and answer who, what, when, where, and why questions<br>☐ Stay on topic and take turns in a conversation<br>☐ Give directions | ☐ Answer complex yes/no questions<br>☐ Ask and answer who, what, when, where, and why questions<br>☐ Use complex sentences<br>☐ Explain words and ideas<br>☐ Give directions with 3–4 steps<br>☐ Use words to inform, persuade, and entertain<br>☐ Participate, stay on topic, take turns, and keep eye contact in conversations<br>☐ Start and end conversations |

| Check all the milestones that the student exhibits in either/any language: | | | |
|---|---|---|---|
| Grade Level | 3 | 4 | 5 |
| Receptive Language (Listening) | ☐ Pay attention in groups<br>☐ Understand grade level information | ☐ Listen to and understand information presented<br>☐ Form opinions based on information learned<br>☐ Listen for specific reasons (i.e. learn, enjoy, or convince) | ☐ Listen and draw conclusions in different classes |

| Check all the milestones that the student exhibits in either/any language: | | | |
|---|---|---|---|
| Grade Level | 3 | 4 | 5 |
| Expressive Language (Speaking) | ☐ Speak clearly with appropriate voice<br>☐ Ask and answer questions<br>☐ Participates in group conversations and discussions<br>☐ Use vocabulary related to school subjects<br>☐ Stay on topic, use eye contact, and take turns in conversations<br>☐ Summarize a story<br>☐ Explain what he/she learned in school | ☐ Use words correctly in conversation<br>☐ Use language for many reasons, like asking questions, arguing, and joking<br>☐ Understand figurative language<br>☐ Take part in group discussions<br>☐ Give correct directions to others<br>☐ Summarize ideas in his own words<br>☐ Organize information so it is clear | ☐ Make planned presentations appropriate to audience<br>☐ Make eye contact, gestures, and appropriate voice during group presentations<br>☐ Participate in class discussions<br>☐ Summarize main points<br>☐ Report about information from group activities |

a. What are your current areas of language concern?

## 4. *Language Data Gathering Tools*

### a. Language Sample Inventory

A language sample can provide insightful information regarding the child's language usage and understanding.

> 💡 *Tip:* It is helpful to ask parents/guardians for areas of interest (favorite toys, favorite books, favorite games, favorite show, etc.)
> 💡 *Tip:* Engage child in conversation through child-led play
> 💡 *Tip:* Record the interaction
> 💡 *Tip:* Obtain information over various situations (ex: classroom, playground, lunch, art, music, etc.)
>> i. Language Sample Strategies
>>> 1. Wordless Picture Book or Scene- ask prompting questions such as:
>>>    a. What do you see?
>>>    b. What are they doing?
>>>    c. Have the child tell a story about the scene/book

ii. Toys
   1. Use toys to engage in play and encourage language by giving positive praise
   2. Use Apps on electronic devices to elicit language by allowing the child to manipulate
💡 *Tip:* During this time, you can ask the child questions such as: "What has happened?", "What is that?"
iii. Use activities you are already doing within your lesson to obtain information about their language. For example, during a reading group you can use that time to engage the child in a discussion about what is taking place. Prompt the student to:
   a. Point to pictures
   b. Describe pictures in story
   c. Retell story

*b.* **Play-Based Approach**
This approach is usually used to assess a child's current developmental (cognitive, communication, language, socio-emotional, sensorimotor) functioning (Kelly-Vance & Ryalls, 2008). You may use this approach in an unstructured play setting while observing the child. Observe and record the child's language during play.

## *Receptive and Expressive Language Pre-referral Protocol for Bilingual Learners (RELPP-BL) References*

American Speech-Language Hearing Association (2020a). *Speech-language pathologists.* Retrieved from https://www.asha.org/Students/Speech-Language-Pathologists/

American Speech-Language Hearing Association (2020b). *Your child's communication development: Kindergarten through fifth grade.* Retrieved from https://www.asha.org/public/speech/development/communicationdevelopment/

Kelly-Vance, L., & Ryalls, B. O. (2008). Best practices in play assessment and intervention. In A. Thomas & J. Grimes (Eds.), *Best practices in school psychology V* (pp. 549–559). Bethesda, MD: NASP Publications.

Westby, C., Burda, A., & Mehta, Z. (2003). Asking the right questions in the right ways. The ASHA Leader, *8*(8), 4–17.

# Appendix: Process for Engaging Teachers in Collaborative Rubric Design for Biliterate Writing

Leslie C. Banes

Teacher educators, instructional coaches, and professional development leaders can use the process outlined below to guide pre-service and in-service teachers in a collaborative rubric design process. Using this process, teachers use the research literature, their students' work and an examination of their own expectations to better articulate the features of a written genre and design rubrics for formatively assessing students' writing in two languages. Teachers and teacher educators may find the process outlined here and the teacher-developed rubrics helpful as they grapple with what it means to engage in argumentative writing in bilingual classrooms. In this project, teachers explored argumentative writing across grades and content areas, but this process may be adapted for exploring any written genre, especially those that have nebulous expectations or that are frequently misunderstood by students and/or teachers. Examples include a persuasive essay, a research report, or a college admission essay.

## Sample Rubrics

Teachers may find following two rubrics useful for assessing their students' biliterate argumentative writing in elementary math and high school history. More importantly, however, these rubrics may serve as an example of how rubrics for a specific genre can be designed, adapted and revised to fit the needs of the content area, grade level, and writing prompt.

## *Which Features Should We Focus On?*

In this project, student teachers addressed only some of the features of hidden academic genres, those they deemed most important for their content and grade level. We chose to emphasize the features that helped us and students answer the questions, What does my reader need to know? What information should I include? What kinds of data support my argument? and What can make this argument more convincing? Because our selected genre, in this case, was argument, our discussion of genre features focused heavily on evidence and data, and how what counts as effective evidence differs across content areas. A focus on other genres may necessitate emphasizing other salient features of the genre. The goal is to go beyond the surface features of the genre, such as the structure and basic components, to uncover the features that may make the genre unclear or confusing to both students and teachers, and those that differ across content areas.

**Student Perspective:** We recommend keeping the student perspective in mind throughout these activities. Students spend their days in school shifting focus from one content area to another. As students progress through the grades, the expectations of academic writing differ more and more between subjects, with teachers often being unaware that the implicit expectations may differ in the classroom next door.

**Potential Benefits to Teachers:** This inquiry process can support both pre-service and in-service teachers confront their own assumptions of "correct" academic writing and consider how to make the expected features more explicit to strengthen student writing. Articulating the features of a genre offers the group a shared vocabulary to discuss their questions and critiques. Instead of a general feeling that a students' argument isn't as strong or clear as it should be, teachers can specify exactly why it was unclear and discuss meaningful ways to support the student. Learning to look at students' writing through a holistic biliteracy lens, including looking specifically for students' strengths in each language and how they make use of bilingual writing strategies to communicate important ideas, may help teachers move away from narrow views of academic language to broader, more holistic views of their students' growing capabilities.

**Extending Learning Opportunities:** In professional learning programs that are more extensive than the 10 weeks we had for this project, there may be opportunities to take these ideas much further. Teachers may extend the process we outline here by engaging in more inquiry cycles, analyzing more of the features that serve as implicit expectations of the genre, and iteratively designing and trying out classroom activities and discussions with opportunities for students that both clarify the expectations and open possibilities to question, transform and cross between academic genres with the purpose of more fully communicating their ideas to a given audience.

---

### Collaborative Inquiry into Biliterate Argumentative Writing

#### 1. Explore the Research
Selected readings, reflection and discussion addresses the following two areas:
- Bilingual assessment and writing development.
- Genre: what counts as effective argumentation in each content area?

#### 2. Data Collection
- Consider what makes a strong argumentative writing task.
- Design/adapt argument tasks so prompts are similar but not identical in both languages.
- Collect students' argumentative writing in two languages.

#### 3. Rubric Design Methods
Use your student writing samples to collaboratively design a biliteracy rubric specific to your task and content area.
- With your colleagues, sort the writing samples into high, mid and low piles in each language.
- Discuss the specific features you see and justify why you think the writing sample belongs in each pile.
- Create a rubric by articulating levels of the most important features.

#### 4. Data Analysis
- Use the biliteracy rubric to analyze your students' strengths and needs and bilingual writing strategies.
- Focus on whole class trends and go deep in analyzing the writing of three focal students.

#### 5. Findings
Write data-based claims that document what you learned about your students' argumentative writing in both languages.

#### 6. Implications
- Why is this information important? How could it impact your instruction? Your understanding of your students' development?
- Use what you learned to design a lesson or series of lesson for your students. How will you build on their strengths?

| Translanguaging/Bilingual Strategies Assessment Tool |||||
|---|---|---|---|
| **Consider:** How are students using *all* their linguistic resources to state and support claims? ||||
|  | (Spanish ☐ English) | (English ☐ Spanish) | Spanish ☐☐ English (bidirectional) |
| Sentence Level |  |  |  |
| Word Level |  |  |  |
| Phonics/ Spelling Level |  |  |  |
| Punctuation Level |  |  |  |

Inspired by Literacy Squared® Writing Rubric (Soltero-González, Escamilla, & Hopewell, 2012)

### Sample Biliteracy Rubric: 3rd–6th Grade <u>Mathematical</u> Argumentative Writing Justifying a Decision

| Spanish | Content of Argument | English |
|---|---|---|
| 6 | **Clear claim** statement articulating which option they choose and why. Decision is justified with **solid mathematical evidence (data)** that is clearly presented and mathematically correct. Justification connects back to the situation in the word problem. All calculations are shown. Visuals (if included) are clear, labeled, and support the claim. May include more than one reason, solution strategy, or representation. Shows full understanding of mathematical concepts. | 6 |
| 5 | Claim statement and evidence are appropriate, but may be **less precise** or missing a <u>minor</u> component that would strengthen the argument. Computations or visuals (if included) may not be labeled. Connection to the situation in the word problem may be vague. Shows nearly complete understanding of mathematical concepts. | 5 |
| 4 | Claim may need to be inferred. Evidence is **mostly complete**. Computations or visuals (if included) may only be shown for part of the problem, may be more difficult to interpret, or have minor mathematical mistakes. Connection to the situation in the word problem may be missing. Shows partial understanding of mathematical concepts. | 4 |
| 3 | Claim may need to be inferred. Evidence is **weak/incomplete**. Evidence may have mathematical mistakes or calculations may be only shown for <u>one option</u>. Visuals (if included) may be ambiguous or fail to support the students' conclusion. Shows SOME understanding of mathematical concepts. | 3 |

| | | |
|---|---|---|
| 2 | Claim may need to be inferred from visuals/calculations. There is **no viable evidence** to support it. Evidence shown completely misrepresents the problem, has major mathematical mistakes, or is entirely <u>non-mathematical</u>. Shows SOME understanding of mathematical concepts. | 2 |
| 1 | **No discernable claim.** No viable evidence. Shows very limited understanding of mathematical concepts. | 1 |
| 0 | No attempt. | 0 |
| | **Writing/ Vocabulary** | |
| 4 | Student uses complete sentences. Writing includes <u>comparison language</u> to explain which option is better. Visuals (if included) are explained in writing. Precise math terminology (when appropriate) is used correctly. | 4 |
| 3 | Student uses mostly complete sentences. May lack math vocabulary that would make argument more precise, but key ideas are communicated clearly in everyday language. | 3 |
| 2 | Sentences may be incomplete. Verbal explanation may be muddled or ambiguous. | 2 |
| 1 | Only a few words are written (such as labels/units, the word "because"), copied parts of the word problem, OR all writing is in a language other than the prompt. | 1 |
| 0 | No writing. | 0 |
| | **Understanding the Problem** | |
| 2 | Demonstrates clear understanding of the mathematical situation. Student's response corresponds to the information provided in the word problem, interpreted correctly. | 2 |
| 1 | Demonstrates partial understanding of the mathematical situation. Partially correct plan based on the part of the problem understood correctly. | 1 |
| 0 | Complete misunderstanding of the problem, totally inappropriate plan, or no attempt. | 0 |

## Sample Biliteracy Rubric: High School Historical Argumentative Writing

| Spanish | Claim | English |
|---|---|---|
| 5 | Makes a **clear**, well-articulated **claim** that **fully** responds to the prompt. | 5 |
| 4 | Makes an **appropriate** claim that stakes out a position related to the prompt. | 4 |
| 3 | Makes a claim, stakes out a position **vaguely** related to the prompt. | 3 |
| 2 | **References** the **topic** but does not make a clear claim. | 2 |
| 1 | The claim is **off topic** or **non-existent**. | 1 |
| | **Supporting Evidence** | |
| 5 | Includes **strong, convincing and relevant** supporting **evidence**. | 5 |
| 4 | Includes **clear, relevant** supporting **evidence** for the claim. | 4 |
| 3 | Includes supporting **evidence** for the claim. | 3 |
| 2 | Includes **little** supporting **evidence** for the claim. | 2 |
| 1 | There is **no** supporting **evidence** for the claim. | 1 |
| | **Historical Accuracy** | |
| 5 | **Historically accurate** with **insightful, logical** arguments. | 5 |
| 4 | **Historically accurate** with **mostly logical** arguments. | 4 |
| 3 | There may be very **slight historical inaccuracies**. | 3 |
| 2 | There are **historical inaccuracies,** but they do not impede the meaning of the argument. | 2 |
| 1 | There are **historical inaccuracies** that impede the meaning of the argument. | 1 |
| | **Organization** | |
| 5 | The organization maintains a **strong central focus** with each paragraph having strong and clear **topic sentences, supporting details.** | 5 |
| 4 | The organization is supported by a **strong central focus. Transitions** are **mostly appropriate.** | 4 |
| 3 | The organization **supports claim** and purpose. **Transitions** are **mostly appropriate. The sequence** of ideas **could be improved.** | 3 |
| 2 | **Some** signs of **logical organization**. May have abrupt or illogical shifts and ineffective flow of ideas. | 2 |
| 1 | **Unclear organization** or organization plan is inappropriate to the claim. There are no transitions. | 1 |
| | **Grammar and Style** | |
| 5 | The tone is **formal** and **engaging**; there are **minimal** punctuation, grammatical or spelling **mistakes** that do not affect understanding. | 5 |
| 4 | The tone is **formal**; there are **minimal** punctuation, grammatical or spelling **mistakes** that do not affect understanding. | 4 |

| | | |
|---|---|---|
| 3 | The **tone** includes some **informalities**; there are **some** punctuation, grammatical and spelling **mistakes** that do not affect understanding. | 3 |
| 2 | The tone does **not** reflect **academic writing**. There are punctuation, grammatical and spelling **mistakes** that **impede understanding**. | 2 |
| 1 | The tone does **not** reflect **academic writing** (e.g. use of slang). Punctuation, grammatical and spelling mistakes **greatly impede understanding**. | 1 |

# Appendix: MALLI Classroom Observation Protocol

Marco A. Bravo, Eduardo Mosqueda and Jorge L. Solís

## General Information about the Classroom Observations

The MALLI classroom observation protocol is designed to document the array of practices employed by teachers of math at the elementary level with a special focus on literacy development and language development activities in Spanish. This observation protocol includes two parts. The first is a Classroom Observation Scheme designed to describe instruction using narrative and codes during the observation. The second part is an Implementation Questionnaire—a series of questions and activities that ask the observer to reflect back on what was observed and document implementation of language learner adaptations.

### Part I: Classroom Observation Scheme

## Schedule

An observation should be at least 20 minutes in length. Before beginning the observation, observers record general information about the observation and the classroom. During the observation, observers alternate between recording narrative notes about what they observe and categorizing the observations into a set of codes outlined in the Math Instruction Coding Scheme.

Observers record narrative notes for seven minutes at a time. At the end of each seven-minute segment, they take three minutes to (a) count how many students are on task, and (b) begin coding the five-minute segment. Each 60-minute observation allows for the coding of 6 7-minute segments, each followed by 3 minutes of coding.

## *Sample Schedule*

9:00–9:06  Narrative recording
*The observer records a narrative of what is happening in the classroom.*
9:07–9:09  Coding
*The observer takes an on-task count, and records the materials in use by the student.*
9:10–9:16  Narrative recording

9:17–9:19  Students-on-task count and coding
9:20–9:26  Narrative recording
9:27–9:29  Students-on-task count and coding
9:30–9:36  Narrative recording
9:37–9:39  Students-on-task count and coding
9:40–9:46  Narrative recording
9:47–9:49  Students-on-task count and coding
9:50–9:56  Narrative recording
9:57–9:59  Students-on-task count and coding

## *Accurate Time Keeping is Essential*

### *Coding Scheme Overview*

Each seven-minute segment of instruction will be coded at five levels:

**Level 1: Groupings** (What instructional groupings do you see?)
**Level 2: Major Focus** (What is the class mainly doing?)
**Level 3: Instructional Activities** (What were the specific activities?)
**Level 4: Teacher Interactions** (What is the interaction style being used by the classroom teacher during this level 5 event?)
**Level 5: Student Response** (What were the students [expected to be] doing?)

# Appendices

See the Observation Coding Scheme for a list of codes.
## Observation Interface

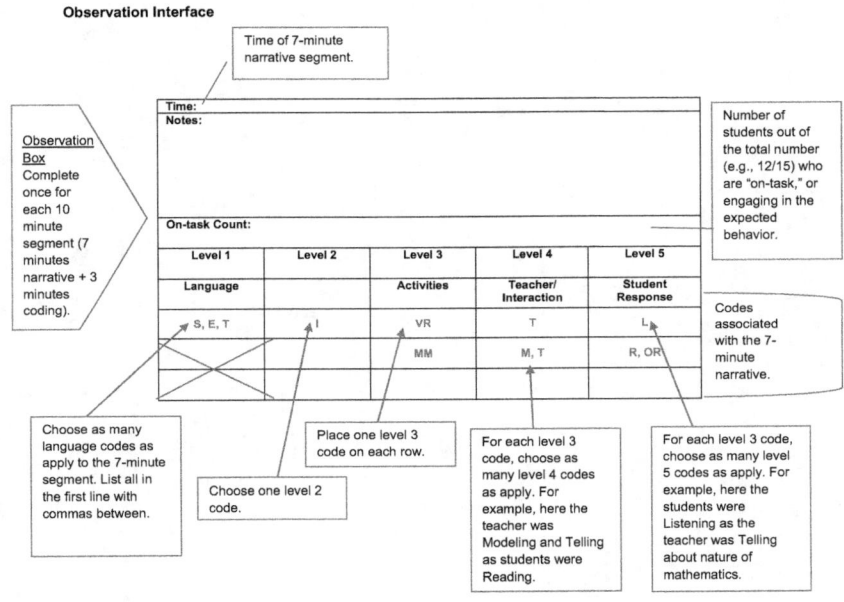

# *Attitudes Towards Teaching Science to Bilingual Learners Instrument (ATTS-BL) Instrument*

TIBERIO GARZA, MARGARITA HUERTA AND JULIE K. JACKSON

What is your age?

18  24  30  36  42  49  55  61  67  73  79

Age

What is your gender?

- o Male
- o Female
- o Prefer not to respond

What do you consider yourself in terms of race/ethnicity?

- o White
- o Black
- o Hispanic
- o Asian
- o American Indian
- o International
- o More than one: please indicate: _____

What is your highest level of education?

- o High School
- o Bachelors
- o Masters
- o Doctorate

What is your current role in working with students?

- o Paraprofessional
- o Practicing Teacher
- o Instructional Coach
- o Administrator
- o Other (Please indicate role):

What grade(s) do you work with? Select all that apply.

- o Pre-K
- o Elementary (K–5th)
- o Middle School (6th–8th)
- o Secondary (9th–12th)

Have you worked with Bilingual students?

- o Yes
- o No

Do you have regular contact with racially/ethnically diverse populations?

- o Yes
- o No

What language(s) do you speak?

- o English only
- o I grew up speaking two or more languages. They are: _____
- o I did not grow up speaking two or more languages, but I consider myself bi/multilingual. My language(s) are: _____

*Appendices*

Do you hold an ESL/ TESOL/ Bilingual Endorsement or Certificate?

o Yes
o No

Have you received professional development training for how to work with Bilingual Learners in general?

o Yes
o No

Have you received professional development training for how to work with Bilingual Learners specifically in science?

o Yes
o No

| **Attitudes Towards Bilingualism** (R = Reverse Code) ||
|---|---|
| Please select how much you agree or disagree with each statement. ||
| To be considered a citizen of my country, one should speak English. (R) | Disagree Strongly (1), Disagree Mildly (2), Neutral (3), Agree Mildly (4), Agree Strongly (5) |
| I would support the government spending additional money to provide better programs for Bilingual Learners. | Disagree Strongly (1), Disagree Mildly (2), Neutral (3), Agree Mildly (4), Agree Strongly (5) |
| Parents of Bilingual Learners should be counseled to speak English with their children whenever possible. (R) | Disagree Strongly (1), Disagree Mildly (2), Neutral (3), Agree Mildly (4), Agree Strongly (5) |
| It is important that people learn a language in addition to English. | Disagree Strongly (1), Disagree Mildly (2), Neutral (3), Agree Mildly (4), Agree Strongly (5) |
| It is unreasonable to expect a regular-classroom teacher to teach a child who does not speak English. (R) | Disagree Strongly (1), Disagree Mildly (2), Neutral (3), Agree Mildly (4), Agree Strongly (5) |
| The rapid learning of English should be a priority for Bilingual Learners, even if it means they lose the ability to speak their native language. (R) | Disagree Strongly (1), Disagree Mildly (2), Neutral (3), Agree Mildly (4), Agree Strongly (5) |

| **Attitudes Towards Bilingualism** (R = Reverse Code) | |
|---|---|
| Please select how much you agree or disagree with each statement. | |
| Local and state/regional governments should require that all government business (including voting) be conducted only in English. (R) | Disagree Strongly (1), Disagree Mildly (2), Neutral (3), Agree Mildly (4), Agree Strongly (5) |
| Having an English Learner in the classroom inhibits the learning of the other students. (R) | Disagree Strongly (1), Disagree Mildly (2) Neutral (3), Agree Mildly (4), Agree Strongly (5) |
| Regular-classroom teachers should be required to receive pre-service or in-service training to be prepared to meet the needs of Bilingual Learners. | Disagree Strongly (1), Disagree Mildly (2), Neutral (3), Agree Mildly (4), Agree Strongly (5) |
| Most Bilingual Learners are not motivated to learn English. (R) | Disagree Strongly (1), Disagree Mildly (2), Neutral (3), Agree Mildly (4), Agree Strongly (5) |
| At school, the learning of English should be a priority for Bilingual Learners and should take precedence over learning subject matter. (R) | Disagree Strongly (1), Disagree Mildly (2), Neutral (3), Agree Mildly (4), Agree Strongly (5) |
| English should be the official language of my country. (R) | Disagree Strongly (1), Disagree Mildly (2), Neutral (3), Agree Mildly (4), Agree Strongly (5) |
| Bilingual Learners often use unjustified claims of discrimination as an excuse for not doing well in school. (R) | Disagree Strongly (1), Disagree Mildly (2), Neutral (3), Agree Mildly (4), Agree Strongly (5) |

Adapted from: Byrnes, D. A., & Kiger, G. (1994). Language attitudes of teachers scale (LATS). *Educational and Psychological Measurement, 54*(1), 227–231. https://doi.org/10.1177/0013164494054001029

| **Attitudes Towards Best Science Teaching Practices for Bilingual Learners** (R = Reverse Code) | |
|---|---|
| Please select the degree to which you believe each question is true. | |
| Questions Pertaining to First Language Use in the Classroom | |
| Does allowing Bilingual Learners to use their first language during instruction help them understand content? | No (1), Not all the time (2), Not sure (3), Yes most of the time (4), Yes all the time (5) |
| Does allowing Bilingual Learners to use their first language during instruction confuse their understanding of content? (R) | No (1), Not all the time (2), Not sure (3), Yes most of the time (4), Yes all the time (5) |

## Attitudes Towards Best Science Teaching Practices for Bilingual Learners
(R = Reverse Code)

Please select the degree to which you believe each question is true.

| | |
|---|---|
| Does allowing Bilingual Learners to use their first language to clarify their understanding of English during instruction help their understanding of the content? | No (1), Not all the time (2), Not sure (3), Yes most of the time (4), Yes all the time (5) |

### Questions Pertaining to Oral Language

| | |
|---|---|
| Does integrating oral language development strategies help Bilingual Learners learn during science instruction? | No (1), Not all the time (2), Not sure (3), Yes most of the time (4), Yes, all the time (5) |
| Is it feasible to incorporate oral language development strategies to help Bilingual Learners during science instruction? | No (1), Not all the time (2), Not sure (3), Yes most of the time (4), Yes all the time (5) |

### Questions Pertaining to Written Language

| | |
|---|---|
| Does providing regular, structured opportunities for Bilingual Learners to develop written language skills help them learn during science instruction? | No (1), Not all the time (2), Not sure (3), Yes most of the time (4), Yes all the time (5) |
| Is it feasible to provide regular, structured opportunities for Bilingual Learners to develop written language skills during science instruction? | No (1), Not all the time (2), Not sure (3), Yes most of the time (4), Yes all the time (5) |

### Questions Pertaining to Vocabulary Words

| | |
|---|---|
| Does teaching a set of vocabulary words intensively across several days help Bilingual Learners learn during science instruction? | No (1), Not all the time (2), Not sure (3), Yes most of the time (4), Yes all the time (5) |
| Is it feasible to incorporate a set of vocabulary words intensively across several days into science instruction? | No (1), Not all the time (2), Not sure (3), Yes most of the time (4), Yes all the time (5) |

### Questions Pertaining to Culture

| | |
|---|---|
| Does incorporating Bilingual Learners' culture and background help them learn during science instruction? | No (1), Not all the time (2), Not sure (3), Yes most of the time (4), Yes all the time (5) |
| Is it feasible to incorporate Bilingual Learners' culture and background into science instruction? | No (1), Not all the time (2), Not sure (3), Yes most of the time (4), Yes all the time (5) |

### Attitudes Towards Best Science Teaching Practices for Bilingual Learners
(R = Reverse Code)

Please select the degree to which you believe each question is true.

#### Questions Pertaining to Small Group Intervention

| | |
|---|---|
| Does providing small group instructional intervention for Bilingual Learners belong in science instruction? | No (1), Not all the time (2), Not sure (3), Yes most of the time (4), Yes all the time (5) |
| Is it feasible to provide small group instructional intervention for Bilingual Learners during science instruction? | No (1), Not all the time (2), Not sure (3), Yes most of the time (4), Yes all the time (5) |

| How to use the Attitudes Towards Teaching Science to Bilingual Learners (ATTS-BL) | |
|---|---|
| Steps | Examples, Guiding Questions, and Parameters for Using the ATTS-BL |
| **Step 1:** Determine your intended users and make any minor wording adjustments for your intended audience. | For example, if you work in a context in which the term "English Learners" is more familiar than "Bilingual Learners", then change the wording throughout the scales to fit your audience.<br>Note: The demographic information can be changed in any way without any threat to the validity or reliability of the instrument. |
| **Step 2:** Decide on how you will distribute the ATTS-BL. | For example, will you use a paper and pencil version? Will you use an electronic platform such as Qualtrics? Will responses be anonymous or not? Will the instrument be used for research? If so, then has Internal Review Board permission been granted? Last, will the ATTS-BL be used as a pre-post measure or as a one-time evaluation of where your audience is in terms of their attitudes? |

# Appendices

| \multicolumn{2}{c}{How to use the Attitudes Towards Teaching Science to Bilingual Learners (ATTS-BL)} | |
|---|---|
| Steps | Examples, Guiding Questions, and Parameters for Using the ATTS-BL |
| **Step 3:** Cite the ATTS-BL | The authors do not require that you email for permission to use the instrument. However, we do ask that if using the ATTS-BL or a modification/adaptation of it, the following reference be cited somewhere on the instrument and on any writing associated with it: <br> Garza, T., Huerta, M., & Jackson, J. K. (2022). Evaluating teacher attitudes towards bilingualism and best science teaching practices for bilingual learners. In M. Machado-Casas, S. I. Maldonado, & B. B. Flores (Eds.), Assessment and evaluation in bilingual education. <br> In addition, the first scale (i.e., *Attitudes Towards Bilingualism*) needs to include the following text underneath the scale as presented in the book chapter: Adapted from: Byrnes, D. A., & Kiger, G. (1994). Language attitudes of teachers scale (LATS). *Educational and Psychological Measurement, 54*(1), 227–231. https://doi.org/10.1177/0013164494054001029 |
| **Step 4:** Distribute the ATTS-BL and analyze the results. | • If using the ATTS-BL for practitioner purposes, then participants scores can be calculated as follows for both scales: <br> o For items with an "(R)", reverse score the item scale so that 1 = 5, 2 = 4, 3 = 3, 4 = 2, and 5 = 1. <br> o Then, total the sum score of the items for each scale individually. <br> o A higher score = a more positive attitude and a lower score = a more negative attitude. Both scales have a theoretical midpoint of 39, so sum scores for each participant can be evaluated to see if they fall above or below the theoretical midpoint. <br> • If using the ATTS-BL for empirical research, we recommend that reliability and validity measures be re-run for new samples (i.e., Cronbach's alpha and factor analysis) and that all data assumptions are met and/or accounted for, for any specific analysis run (e.g., normality). |

# *Diversity-Differentiated Assessments Template*

XOCHITL ARCHEY

This appendix provides a template (matrix) for identifying the teaching of diversity-differentiated assessments across the framework's tiers. Faculty are encouraged to collaborate as they identify assignments that intentionally and explicitly address diversity-differentiated assessments across understanding ideas, developing connections, and using extensions. Where no assignments exist, instructors are encouraged to create ones using the examples (Figure Figure 10-1, p. 214) and discussion above as guidance. This template also assists in planning and visualizing which courses are best suited in addressing the different tiers of teaching about diversity-differentiated assessments. Of note, tier depth should be fostered early in foundational courses and deepened in later courses—the ones listed in the matrix are placeholder examples, adjust accordingly.

| COURSES | UNDERSTAND | DEVELOP | USE |
|---|---|---|---|
| | The fundamentals of new learning. | Webs of information tied together between material and learners' real-world experience/ other acquired knowledge. | The ability to think deeply and use learning to generalize across disciplines and in novel ways. |
| EDUC Course#1 | Title/description of diversity-differentiated assessment assignment#1 | | |
| EDUC Course#2 | Title/description of diversity-differentiated assessment assignment#2 | Title/description of diversity-differentiated assessment assignment#3 | |
| EDUC Course#3 | | Title/description of diversity-differentiated assessment assignment#4 | |
| EDUC Course#4 | | | Title/description of diversity-differentiated assessment assignment#5 |

# *AMWAS Administration Guidelines/Guía de administración de la evaluación AMWAS*

Eduardo Mosqueda, Marco A. Bravo, Jorge L. Solís and Saúl I. Maldonado

*AMWAS Administration Guidelines* **Adolescent Mathematics and Writing Assessment System (AMWAS)**

**Administration.** The AMWAS instrument is designed to assess students' math conceptual understanding and writing skills. The AMWAS assessment gauges students' writing in four domains:

a. Vocabulary use
b. Math conceptual and accuracy
c. Grammar
d. Conventions

Follow the following steps when administering the assessment.

1. Before administering the AMWAS, familiarize yourself with the writing prompt and make copies of the writing prompt. Also, have pencils available for students to use.
2. Before providing students with the writing prompt, explain to students that for the next 30 minutes, they will have time to respond to the writing prompt. Tell students they must do their own work and that it should be quiet during the time of the assessment.
3. Hand out the writing prompt paper and have students write their name and date on the top of the paper.

4. Read the prompt aloud to students *"Write at least a paragraph explaining the graph below to someone that is unfamiliar with the graph. Make sure you use complete sentences and correct punctuation. Use math vocabulary in your response."*
5. Tell students that they should write in English as much as possible, but if they don't know a word in English, they can write it in Spanish.
6. Allow students to read or work on homework if they get done early. Yet, before they are allowed to work on homework or read, have them review their writing before they turn in their final work.
7. Make sure students do their own work and treat the writing assignment as an assessment. Allow students more time if needed. This assessment will be administered three times during the program (Pre, Mid, Post). Results will be shared with teachers to inform instruction.

**Sistema de Evaluación de Matemáticas y Escritura para Adolescentes Adolescent Mathematics and Writing Assessment System (AMWAS)**

**Administración.** El instrumento de evaluación AMWAS está diseñado para evaluar las habilidades de escritura y comprensión conceptual matemática de los estudiantes. La evaluación AMWAS mide la escritura de los estudiantes en 4 dominios:

a. Uso de vocabulario
b. Precisión conceptual matemática
c. Gramática
d. Convenciones

Siga los siguientes pasos cuando administre la evaluación:

1. Antes de administrar la evaluación AMWAS, familiarícese con el tema de la escritura y haga copias del tema de la escritura. Además, tenga lápices disponibles para los estudiantes.
2. Antes de proporcionarles a los estudiantes el tema de la escritura, explíqueles que durante los próximos 30 minutos, tendrán tiempo de responder al tema de la escritura. Dígales a los estudiantes que deben hacer su propio trabajo y que deben estar en silencio durante el tiempo de la evaluación.
3. Entregue el documento del tema de la escritura y haga que los estudiantes escriban su nombre y fecha en la parte superior del papel.
4. Lea el tema en voz alta a los alumnos "Escriba al menos un párrafo que explique la gráfica a continuación a alguien que no esté familiarizado

con la gráfica. Asegúrese de usar oraciones completas y puntuación correcta. Usa vocabulario matemático en tu respuesta".
5. Dígales a los estudiantes que deben escribir en inglés tanto como sea posible, pero si no saben una palabra en inglés, pueden escribirla en español.
6. Permita que los estudiantes lean o trabajen en la tarea si terminan temprano. Sin embargo, antes de que se les permita trabajar en la tarea o leer, pídales que revisen sus escritos antes de entregar su trabajo final.
7. Asegúrese de que los estudiantes hagan su propio trabajo y trate su escrito como una evaluación. Permita a los estudiantes más tiempo si es necesario. Esta evaluación se administrará tres veces durante el programa (antes, mediados, después). Los resultados se compartirán con los maestros para guiar la enseñanza.

# List of Contributors

**Xochitl Archey** is an Assistant Professor at California State University, San Marcos in the School of Education's Multilingual and Multicultural unit. As a former education specialist of Emergent Bilinguals (EBs) with special needs, her scholarship is centrally focused within frameworks of equity and social justice. Her commitment is to advocate for the language and education rights of EBs with special needs and to contribute to the area of teacher preparation through reflective and critical examination of social inequities.

**Leslie C. Banes**, Ph.D., is an Assistant Professor at California State University, Sacramento in the College of Education's Teacher Credential Program. Her work focuses on the intersection between language and mathematics, issues of equity in assessment, bilingual education and teacher learning. She is a former bilingual elementary and middle school teacher, recently served as teacher educator and bilingual coordinator of the University of California, Davis, credential program, and has conducted professional development in the U.S., Spain, and China. She was recently the co-PI of two federally funded projects addressing the needs of emerging bilinguals in content instruction and has recent publications in the *Bilingual Research Journal, Journal of Teacher Education, International Multilingual Research Journal* and *International Journal of Science and Math Education.*

**Marco A. Bravo**, Ph.D., is Professor and Associate Dean of the School of Education and Counseling Psychology at Santa Clara University. Dr. Bravo utilizes mixed methods to research the literacy learning of Emergent Bilinguals in dual language contexts.

**Belinda Bustos Flores**, Ph.D., is Associate Dean of Professional Preparation and Partnerships and Professor of Bicultural-Bilingual Studies. Her publications center on teacher recruitment and development, as well as culturally efficacious pedagogies. Bustos Flores is the founder of the award-winning Academy for Teacher Excellence Research Center at the University of Texas, San Antonio. In 2019, Bustos Flores was the recipient of the AERA Bilingual Education Research SIG Lifetime Achievement Award.

**Janet Gabriela Cariño Ramsay** grew up in Berkeley, California and believes that the most direct link to social change is education. Her determination has led her to become a bilingual Spanish teacher. She prioritizes alternative narratives and adapts mandated curriculum to be more inclusive. Growing up in a multilingual and multicultural home instilled a curiosity in her that led to study cultures different from her own. She cherishes linguistic and cultural diversity and believes that multilingualism can play a positive role in society. She studied Spanish, Portuguese, and Latin American Studies at San Diego State University before returning for her multiple subject bilingual teaching credential and dual language teaching certificate. She currently teaches 50/50 in both English and Spanish at a dual language classroom in the South Bay of San Diego County.

**Felicia Castro-Villarreal** is an Associate Professor in the Department of Educational Psychology at the University of Texas at San Antonio. She holds a Ph.D. in School Psychology from Oklahoma State University and is also a Licensed Specialist in School Psychology. Dr. Castro-Villarreal's research includes evaluation of culturally responsive school psychology practices and examining teacher perspectives and voice as it relates to student mental health, academic and social behavior outcomes. To this end, Dr. Castro-Villarreal has published numerous articles and has presented on culturally responsive school consultation, response to Intervention, and educational policy pertaining to student mental health, academic and social behavior needs. Recently she has extended her research of culturally responsive practice to include issues of social justice and educational equity.

**Annette M. Daoud**, Ph.D., is a Professor of Multicultural and Multilingual Education at California State University, San Marcos. Her research has focused on the sociocultural, sociopolitical and academic experiences of secondary English learners as well as on critical multicultural educational pedagogies for pre-and in-service teachers.

**Katherine Espinoza** is an Assistant Professor in the College of Education and Human Development at *Texas A&M University, San Antonio*. Dr. Espinoza's areas of specialization include: sociocultural approaches to language, biliteracy and identity construction, bilingual education and teacher preparation.

**Janelle Beth Flores**, M.S., CCC-SLP, received a master's degree in communication sciences and disorders from Texas Woman's University in 2005 and a bachelor's degree in Communication Sciences and Disorders in 1999 from the University of Texas at Austin. In addition to her knowledge in Communication Sciences and Disorders, Janelle also received a bachelor's degree in Biology with a concentration in Neuroscience from the University of Texas at San Antonio in 2014. She has worked in the home health, school, and university clinic settings, where she has supervised SLP-Assistants and graduate students. She is currently on the SLP assessment team in Northside ISD. In addition to presentations at Northside ISD to fellow Speech Language Pathologists, she has presented at the University of Texas at San Antonio, as well as the University of Colorado at Boulder. She is interested in continuing to research appropriate assessment and intervention practices with diverse populations, and the effects of utilizing therapy dogs for speech and language therapy.

**Karla C. Garza** is a Ph.D. student in the Culture, Literacy, and Language program at the University of Texas at San Antonio. She earned a master's degree in Communication and Learning Disorders from Our Lady of the Lake University in San Antonio and a bachelor's degree in Communication Disorders from Texas A&M International University in Laredo, TX. Karla is a Bilingual Speech Language Pathologist certified by the American Speech-Language-Hearing Association and licensed by the Texas State Board. Karla has previous experience serving school age children with speech and language impairments and supervising SLP-Assistants. Her research interests include typical/atypical acquisition, bilingualism, and speech and language assessment and intervention for culturally and linguistically diverse populations.

**Tiberio Garza** has a Ph.D. in Educational Psychology with an emphasis in quantitative methods and bilingual education from Texas A&M University. He is currently an Assistant Professor of Educational Psychology and Higher Education at the University of Nevada Las Vegas (UNLV) and Associate Director for UNLV's Center of Research, Evaluation, and Assessment (CREA). His research includes the application of advanced statistical analysis and culturally relevant evaluation research and methods. In his position, he works with community, school and university advocates for the betterment of young students' lives and motivating them to pursue higher education. He is passionate about utilizing evaluation and statistics for helping young people from culturally and linguistically diverse backgrounds become resilient and succeed in their life and educational pursuits.

**Alexandra S. Guilamo** is a leading expert in the effective leadership of dual-language, bilingual and language learner education. As a language learner herself, Alexandra has spent more than twenty years serving a wide range of language learners. She is a former teacher, academic coach, elementary principal and district-level director in highly diverse urban and suburban school districts. This range of experiences offers a unique lens, bringing together a deep knowledge of second-language acquisition, evidence-based practices, and supports tailored to each school's contexts and needs. She is the founder and chief equity and achievement officer at TaJu Educational Solutions, a company dedicated to meeting the needs of language learners while ensuring access and social justice for all students. Alexandra's evidence-based approach to language learner programs has resulted in dramatic improvement for schools across the country. She now works with schools, districts, regional and state leaders in more than forty states across the United States to provide a range of professional development, job-embedded coaching, technical assistance and program evaluation support.

**Ana M. Hernández**, Ed.D., is an Associate Professor of Multicultural and Multilingual Education and Coordinator of the Bilingual Authorization Program at California State University, San Marcos. Her research stems from 32 years of teaching in California public schools as a bilingual/dual language teacher, and examines instructional practices, teacher preparation and cross-cultural equity in dual language education. She currently is the Principal Investigator of Project ACCEPT, a five-year professional development grant funded by the U.S. Department of Education, Office of English Language Acquisition.

**Margarita Huerta** has a Ph.D. in Educational Psychology with an emphasis in bilingual education from Texas A&M University. She is currently an Associate Professor in the College of Education at the University of Nevada, Las Vegas Dr. Huerta has taught culturally and linguistically diverse students ranging from early childhood to adult learners. She is passionate about helping people become life-long learners and enhance their life experiences and opportunities regardless of language, socioeconomic, or cultural backgrounds. Her research includes literacy integration in the science classroom, second language and conceptual development, assessment validity and reliability and higher education paths for culturally and linguistically diverse students.

**Julie K. Jackson** has a Ph.D. in Science Education from the University of Texas at Austin. She is currently an Associate Professor of Science Education at Texas State University in San Marcos, TX. She takes a collaborative approach to teacher and science education and regularly works with stakeholders to improve science education in the P-16 school environment. She has a reputation for promoting inquiry science instruction while simultaneously providing support for reading and writing with special emphasis placed on meeting the needs of English learners and economically disadvantaged students.

**Veronica Johnson** attended the University of California, Riverside and received a B.A. in Liberal Studies with and focus on Education and Spanish, an M.Ed., and a multiple subject credential with a bilingual certification. Her career as an educator began as an AmeriCorp, Read Across America reading tutor in 1999. She has since continued to volunteer at various schools and was a student teacher in a dual language school. In 2003, she began teaching in Lemon Grove where she has been an English and Spanish teacher and has been a leader in multiple roles. Currently, her research is focused on the development of sociocultural competence in educators, how it manifests in their pedagogy, instructional practices, and political stances and its implications on the development of students in dual immersion programs.

**Margarita Machado-Casas** is Professor and Chair of the Dual Language and English Learner Education Department at San Diego State University. She completed her Ph.D. at the University of North Carolina at Chapel Hill and completed the prestigious postdoctoral fellowship at Frank Potter Graham Research Institute at Duke University. Her research interests include immigrant, transnational indigenous and bilingual/multilingual education, and minority agency in the fields of education, literacy, assessment/evaluation and community/family engagement. Dr. Machado-Casas is the editor of several prestigious journals and co-editor of the Critical Studies of Latinxs in the Americas book series with Peter Lang. She is the Co-Chair and creator of the National Bilingual Education Student Organization, the largest bilingual education student organization in the United States. She was proudly born in Bluefields, Nicaragua.

**Saúl I. Maldonado** is Associate Professor at the Department of Dual Language and English Learner Education at San Diego State University. Dr. Maldonado investigates the intersection of language, literacy and K-12 achievement using techniques such as propensity score matching and multi-level modeling on surveys, assessments and observation protocols.

**Eduardo Mosqueda**, Ed.D., is Associate Professor in the Department of Education at the University of California at Santa Cruz. Dr. Mosqueda utilizes quantitative methods to examine mathematics teaching and learning in dual language contexts that leads to student mathematical proficiency and dual language development.

**T. Breanne Rochester**, M.S., CCC-SLP, received a master's degree in speech-language pathology from Texas Tech University Health Science Center in 2011 and a bachelor's degree in English and in Communications from Texas A&M University in College Station in 2007. She has worked in the home health, school and clinic settings with both pediatric and adult clients. While working for Northside ISD from 2011 to 2019, she made contributions to the Bilingual SLP team and SLP Assessment team, supervised three clinical fellows and served as facilitator for the SLP Assessment team. She was also involved on a committee that developed uniform procedures for speech RTI for the district and presented for NISD at several summer institute programs about bilingualism, speech-language evaluation and RTI and presented at TSHA Convention about using literacy activities as a core component of therapy. She is currently venturing into a new setting with Methodist Children's Hospital Pediatric Outpatient Rehab Clinic where she works as a bilingual clinician and feeding therapist.

**Jorge L. Solís** is Associate Professor in the department of Bicultural-Bilingual Studies in the College of Education and Human Development at the University of Texas at San Antonio. Dr. Solís utilizes discourse analysis to study the development of academic literacy with second language learners.

**Kip Téllez** (Ph.D., Claremont Graduate University) is professor and former chair in the Education Department at the University of California at Santa Cruz. His research interests include teacher education, language teaching, and the intersection of the two. He has published in journals such as the Journal of Teacher Education, Teachers and Teacher Education, Bilingual Research Journal, and Review of Research in Education. His book efforts include the edited volume, Latino/as and Mathematics Education: Research on Learning and Teaching in Classrooms and Communities (with Marta Civil and Judit Moschkovich) and the single authored works Teaching English learners: Fostering language and the democratic experience and The Teaching Instinct: Explorations into what makes us human.

**Ileana Umaña** is a doctoral student in School Psychology at Texas A&M University. She obtained her Master's in School Psychology at the University of Texas at San Antonio. She holds a specialist license in school psychology. She has experience as a bilingual specialist in school psychology and as a general education teacher. Her research interest includes culturally and linguistically adopted parent training for children with Autism. She is also interested in cultural considerations in the assessment and identification of children with Autism.

**Yvonne Vera**, M.A., CCC-SLP, received a master's degree in speech-language pathology from Our Lady of the Lake University. She spent 15 years in the medical field working with adults and children in hospital, rehabilitation and private practice settings. She has been a speech-language pathologist with Northside ISD for 12 years and has served as a CFY supervisor and bilingual team facilitator. She currently works as a bilingual assessor on the SLP Assessment team. She has previously presented for NISD during their district speech team meetings and summer institute programs about bilingualism and speech-language evaluation. She has also presented at TSHA on the subject of bilingual speech therapy in an early literacy-based program.

**Victor Villarreal** is an Associate Professor in the Department of Educational Psychology at the University of Texas at San Antonio. He holds a Ph.D. in School Psychology from Texas A&M University and is also a licensed psychologist and specialist in school psychology. Dr. Villarreal's research includes evaluation of how emerging models of school service delivery may better benefit culturally and linguistically diverse students, as well as appropriate ways of adapting typical practice (including education and psychological intervention) for use with diverse individuals. This track covers issues of professional development and training, as well as application in school and community settings. Dr. Villarreal's research also includes an evaluation of the quality of intervention research conducted in school settings, including analysis regarding its utility to practitioners.

# Index

AMWAS. *See* authentic mathematics writing assessment system
*Rúbrica de Escritura Matemática (REM)* 231–232
argumentation
  socio-disciplinary norms 151
  Toulmin's model 150
argumentative writing 149–150
  samples 152–153
ASHA 128, 133, 135–38, 303, 308
attitudes towards teaching science to bilingual learners (ATTS-BL) 13, 194–196, 200–202, 310–311
  Instrument 194–198, 305–311
authentic mathematics writing assessment system (AMWAS) 14, 227–235, 241
  administration guidelines 315–317
  coaching sessions 235
  *Computación Matemática* 230–233
  *Convenciones de Escritura* 233
  *Razonamiento Matemático* 230
  *Vocabulario Matemático* 233

basic interpersonal communication skills (BICS) 111–112
BBLs. *See* bicultural-bilingual learners
BICS. *See* basic interpersonal communication skills
bicultural-bilingual learners (BBLs)
  characteristics 108

dynamic assessment 118–119
  ethnographic interviewing 117
  family's acculturation and education level 115
  language development stages 111
  language disorders 12, 113–114
  language samples 119
  multilingualism 109–110
  RTI Process 117–118
  sequential bilingualism 109
  simultaneous bilingualism 108–109
  speech and language disorders 110–111
bilingual authorization (BILA)
  programs 13–14, 207–208, 210, 213, 217
bilingual education/ dual language
  acquisition theories 46
  assessment principles documents 7
  evaluation criteria 6
  equitable and fair assessment systems 11–12
  evaluation processes 10–11
  guiding principles 26–28
  role of assessment 6–9
bilingual learners (BLs)
  assessments and evaluation needs 1–3, 15–16
  cognitive assessment 90–92
  discriminatory issues 2
  linguistic bias 131–132, 263

mathematical communication 151, 179, 223–224
oral proficiency 134
PK-12 contexts 4
policy and program offerings 45–46
sociocultural appropriateness 133
Spanish language proficiency 129, 224
special education recommendations 275–277
writing effective arguments 12–13
bilingual teacher candidates
additive approaches 132
course objectives and assignments 134–137
cultural validity 130
feelings of fear 142–143
HSI 133
professional development model 133
reflections on biliteracy and assessment 137–138
role of language 131–132, 138–140
sociocultural competence 40–43, 140–142, 269
biliteracy
argumentative writing 149–150
school-based assessment 150–151
writing, holistic view 148–149
Biliterate Writing, Collaborative Rubric Design 293–299
BLs. *See* bilingual learners
BTC. *See* bilingual teacher candidates

CAEP. *See* Council for the Accreditation of Educator Program
California Commission on Teacher Credentialing (CCTC) 210
California State Standards and Frameworks 25, 269
California State Universities (CSUs) 14, 208–209, 213
California World Languages Standards (CWLS) 26, 35, 269
CALP. *See* cognitive academic language proficiency
CBM. *See* curriculum-based measurement
CCSS. *See* Common Core State Standards
CCTC. *See* California Commission on Teacher Credentialing
Center of Research, Evaluation, and Assessment (CREA) 194
CHISPAS. *See* cultural, historical, identity, socio-emotional, pedagogy, action and sustainability
CLD. *See* culturally linguistically diverse students
C-LIM. *See* culture-language interpretive matrix
coding 155–156, 173, 182–183
cognitive ability 90–92
cognitive academic language proficiency (CALP) 89–90
Common Core State Standards (CCSS)
English 224, 272
formative assessment 227
mathematics 70, 167, 223, 228, 230, 234
validity and reliability 224
communication and language disorders, medical model 106
Council for the Accreditation of Educator Program (CAEP) 7–8
CPC. *See* cultural proficiency continuum
CREA. *See* Center of Research, Evaluation, and Assessment
CSUs. *See* California State Universities
cultural, historical, identity, socio-emotional, pedagogy, action and sustainability (CHISPAS) 23, 30–34, 34–36, 39–42
curricular modifications 35
curriculum design elements 28–30
images in student workbooks 36–38
LGBTQ experiences 23, 35
pedagogical responsibility 39–40
reflective process tool 24, 31–34
sociocultural competence 30, 40–43, 140
cultural proficiency continuum (CPC) 27, 269

# Index

culturally linguistically diverse (CLD) students 107, 130–132
culture- language interpretive matrix (C- LIM) 92
curriculum-based measurement (CBM) 93

decolonial approach 3–4, 9, 15
   assessment practices and evaluative processes 1–3
diversity-differentiated assessment
   bilingual education approach 208
   classroom diversity and assessment 210–211
   connections tier 215
   course syllabi assignments 214
   extensions tier 216
   IHEs 209–210
   understanding tier 213
DL. *See* dual language
DLE. *See* dual language education
DLLs. *See* dual language learner
DLLTs. *See* dual language leadership teams
dual language. *See also* dual language education (DLE); dual language leadership teams (DLLTS); dual language learner (DLLs) 46–49
   decision making process 46
   improvement cycle 54–55, 63
   math instruction 69–78
   mission and vision 47–50
dual language education (DLE)
   learning about students approach 263–264
dual language leadership teams (DLLTS) 50–58
   accountability metrics 50–51
   coherent program design 48–49
   comprehensive training to teachers 48
   continuous improvement action planning template 61
   diverse perspectives 46–47
   DL Data Dashboard 62
   DL models 50–52
   hexagon tool for systems planning 59
   macro-level guiding questions 58
   monitoring structures with checkpoints 59–60
   rubric sample 52
   sample annual improvement cycle 55
   stakeholder implications 61
   theory of action protocols 57–58
   three pillars 42, 48, 51–52, 56–57
dual language learners (DLLs) 6, 8–9, 45, 63
   drop- out rates 46
   US demography 45
dynamic assessment and language sampling 116

EBLs. *See* emergent bilingual learners
ELD. *See* English Language Development
Elements of Social Justice Curriculum Design (ESJCD) 28–30
ELLs. *See* English Language Learners
ELs. *See* English Learners
emergent bilingual learners (EBLs) 14–15, 167–168, 223–224
   Common Core State Standards (CCSS) 223
   formative assessment 227
   mathematics assessment 167–170, 224–227, 240–241
   PD workshops 235
   professional development model 234–235
English Language Development
   academic word misuse 260
   asset-based lesson study feedback form 262
   mentor texts 259–260
   San Marcos Writing Project 259
English Language Learners (ELLs)
   academic achievement, assessment 92–93
   cognitive ability evaluations 90–92
   evaluation 88–89
   language proficiency assessment 89–90
   multidisciplinary IEP training 96–99, 271, 289
   pre-test writing 263

roles of IEP committees 87–88, 95
science education 190–191
social-emotional and behavioral functioning assessment 94–95
English as a Second Language (ESL) 190, 200
ESL. *See* English as a Second Language

GPCP. *See* Guiding Principles of Cultural Proficiency
GPDLE. *See* Guiding Principles for Dual Language Education)
Guiding Principles for Dual Language Education (GPDLE) 26–27, 269
Guiding Principles of Cultural Proficiency (GPCP) Framework 27, 269

*History-Social Science Framework for Public Schools (HSSF)* 25, 269

Ideology, Pedagogy, Access and Equity (IPAE) 15, 24, 249–250
IEP. *See* Individualized Education Program
IHEs. *See* Institutions of Higher Education
Individualized Education Program (IEP) 11, 87–88
  challenges and collaborative solutions 95–99
  implications for educators and policymakers 99–100
Institutions of Higher Education (IHEs) 2, 4, 13–14, 207–210
interrater reliability (IRR) 182–183
IPAE. *See* Ideology, Pedagogy, Access and Equity
IRE Sequence 170, 182
IRR. *See* interrater reliability

judgments 3, 212

K-12
  differentiated assessments 210–213
  dual language programs 30, 45, 54
  policymaking 1
  teacher attitudes 192

language other than English (LOTE) 69–71, 74, 82
LOTE. *See* language other than English

MALLI. *See* Mathematics and Language, Literacy Integration
Mathematics and Language, Literacy Integration (MALLI) 168–170
  Classroom Observation Protocol 301–303
  goals 168, 183
  mathematics literacy/biliteracy 170
  mathematics vocabulary 169
  narrative notes and coding 172–173
  pedagogical model 168–169
  pre- observation data gathering 171
  teacher interaction 182
  theory of change 169
mathematics assessments, advantages and disadvantages 76–78
  case studies 78–80
  DLP programs 69–72
  general suggestions to educators 80–83
  mathematics in two languages 72–74
  practical aspects of assessment 74–76
Mathematics Classroom Observation Protocol (M- COP) 13, 168, 171, 173, 178, 180–184
  codes 173
  instructional activities 173–175
  language 173
  literacy domain 176–178
  major instructional focus 173
  math discourse 179–182
  reading aloud 182
  translanguaging 173, 175–176
Mental Measurements Yearbook (MMY) 273–274
MMY. *See* Mental Measurements Yearbook

NABE. *See* National Association Bilingual Education
NAEP. *See* National Assessment of Educational Progress

# Index

National Assessment of Educational Progress (NAEP) 167, 227
National Association Bilingual Education (NABE) 7–8
National Center for Education Statistics 87
National Dual Language Education Teacher Preparation Standards (NDLETPS) 7–8
native English speakers (NES) 79–81
native Spanish speakers (NSS) 78–81
NDLETPS. *See* National Dual Language Education Teacher Preparation Standards
NES. *See* native English speakers
NSS. *See* native Spanish speakers

participatory evaluation 81–82
PCA. *See* principal component analysis
PD. *See* Professional Development
PLC. *See* Professional Learning Committee
PLUSS Model 116, 118
preservice teachers (PSTs)
   analyzing bilingual writing 154–155
   collaborative rubric design 153–154, 157–158
   instructional decision-making 158–159
   pre- and post- reflections 156–157, 159–161
   single subject 152
   student writing samples 152
principal component analysis (PCA) 196
professional development (PD) 54–55, 191–192, 197, 199, 266, 228–229, 234–239, 249–252, 261
Professional Learning Committee (PLC) 249, 252–253, 256, 258–259, 262
Project ACCEPT 249
   Asset-based assessment 15, 250–251
   cultural framework 246–247
   professional development 248–250
   Spanish language development 252–256
PSTs. *See* preservice teachers

redesignated fluent English proficient (RFEPs) 250, 252, 260
RELPP-BL, pre-referral protocol 283–291
REM. *See Rúbrica de Escritura Matemática*
response to intervention (RTI) 116–118
RFEPs. *See* redesignated fluent English proficient
RTI. *See* response to intervention

school performance scores (SPS) 51
science-classroom observation protocol (SCOP) 168
science learning
   ATTS-BL 194–198, 200–202, 305–311
   contextual variables 193
   demographic variables 193
   descriptive attitudinal measures 198–199
   educational variables 193
   language in practice 192
   linguistic diversity 192
   reading and writing instruction 190–191
   terminology 189–190
SCOP. *See* science-classroom observation protocol
SLD. *See* Spanish Language Development
SLOs. *See* student learning outcomes
SLPs. *See* speech-language pathologists
SLTs. *See* student learning targets
social justice 4, 24, 28–29, 35, 39, 48, 216, 245–247, 250–251, 269
Spanish Language Development (SLD) 34, 76, 129, 224, 252–253, 256–257, 266
speech-language pathologists (SLPs) 12, 105–106, 112–113, 115–116, 283–291

SPS. *See* school performance scores
student learning outcomes (SLOs) 63
student learning targets (SLTs) 63

TK. *See* Transitional kindergarten
transitional kindergarten (TK) 250, 257, 260–261
translanguaging 4, 13, 90, 149, 154, 160, 169, 173, 175, 296

UCs. *See* University of California
UDU. *See* understanding, developing, use framework
understanding, developing, use (UDU) framework 14, 213–217
University of California (UCs) 208

visually representing (VR) 182
vocabulary 13, 36, 106, 108–110, 112, 117–118, 131, 133, 168–170, 172–175, 190, 196, 224–226, 229–230, 233–240, 253, 256–258, 260, 262, 290, 294, 297, 309, 315–316
VR. *See* visually representing

workshops 13, 133, 196, 228, 234–238, 252, 254, 259, 263
writing assessment
  bilingual analysis 154–155
  fuzzy genre 150
  hidden rules of academic discourse 150–151
  holistic view 148–149
  student writing samples 14–15, 152–153, 178, 214, 238–240, 246, 252, 254, 259–262, 295
  thematic analysis 155–156

xenophobia 29, 33

www.ingramcontent.com/pod-product-compliance
Lightning Source LLC
Chambersburg PA
CBHW061705300426
44115CB00014B/2572